From Pencil to Pen Tool

From Pencil to Pen Tool

Understanding and Creating the Digital Fashion Image

Jemi Armstrong

American InterContinental University
Santa Monica College

Lorrie Ivas

American InterContinental University
Santa Monica College

Wynn Armstrong

Woodbury University
American InterContinental University

Fairchild Publications, Inc.
New York

Director of Sales and Acquisitions: Dana Berkowitz

Executive Editor: Olga T. Kontzias

Acquisitions Editor: Joseph Miranda

Art Director: Adam B. Bohannon

Production Manager: Ginger Hillman

Senior Development Editor: Amy Zarkos

Production Editor: Elizabeth Marotta

Copy Editor: Vivian Gomez

Text Design: Mary Neal Meador

Cover Design: Adam B. Bohannon

Cover and Text Illustrations by Jemi Armstrong

Library of Congress Catalog Card Number: 2004101107

ISBN-10: 1-56367-364-9

GST R 133004424

Printed in China

TP11

10 9 8 7 6 5 4 3 2

This book is dedicated to Edna Ivas, Ann and Bob Neale,
Phyllis Rossi and Therese Boutet, the Simmonds, Nina Sheffield, and Marv.

Contents

Extended Contents

Preface

From Pencil to Pen Tool: Understanding and Creating the Digital Fashion Image is a book designed for fashion students and industry professionals alike who are curious about the mixed media of fashion illustration and its new partners in artistic communication—Adobe Photoshop and Adobe Illustrator.

To many, the thought of opening a thick computer-software manual and actually having to read it is as daunting as having to tailor a suit without ever having had sewing lessons. Others may have the discipline to read a thick manual but are not stimulated by handbooks that recolor fish or mountain sunsets in the visual how-to exercises. Fashion people want to be stimulated by fashion visuals.

For design students or seasoned professionals, every detail matters—even the color and visual appeal of a book cover. Do people want to have it next to them on the computer/design table? Do people find examples of work they would like to create? We hope the reader will judge this book by its cover and enjoy using it as the guidebook that ventures into the computer world with Adobe Photoshop and Illustrator.

The accompanying CD-ROM includes full-color tutorials, croquis, fabric swatches, and a library of ready-to-use vector construction details. How readers will utilize *From Pencil to Pen Tool* will differ according to varying needs. Is the reader a fashion illustrator who wants to perfect skills through the use of the computer? A fashion designer who does not want to be limited by time? A fashion design professional who desires to improve his or her skills? A fashion marketer who wants to create promotional pieces? Or a fashion

student who is embarking on a fashion career and designs clothing and textiles?

Reading the employment ads in *Women's Wear Daily* or Monster.com is evidence that computer software has changed the fashion industry. Knowledge of Adobe Photoshop and Illustrator today is as important as knowing what a flat, dart, or buttonhole is.

From Pencil to Pen Tool will give readers an understanding of fashion illustration and design. Cleaning up images, duplicating patterns and details, adding backgrounds, or reshaping silhouettes will now take several clicks rather than hours—thanks to newly acquired Photoshop and Illustrator skills. The ability to scan in an already hand-drawn or photographed image and give it a quick change of pattern or color is truly a powerful one. There are also Review Questions, Suggested Practice Projects, and Key Terms included at the end of the chapters where applicable.

Chapter 1 includes an overview of major fashion illustrators of the twentieth century who worked with the traditional mediums of the day. Their artistic styles are important to analyze when students are working to perfect their own skills in fashion illustration. Each illustrator has a signature style. A supplemental timeline of other great fashion illustrators with an abbreviated client list is included as a research tool for further review.

Chapter 2 chronicles the latter twentieth and early twenty-first century's embrace of computer technology, detailing several artistic leaders of fashion's mixed media. Comic books, cartoons, television, and early exposure to computers have a direct influence on the growing importance of the pen and pen tool. A supplemental timeline of the mixed-media fashion illustrators with their client list is included.

Chapter 3 gives an overview of the Who, What, When, Where, and Why of garment design. It is a review of key elements involved in creating anything from a single fashion item to a complete collection. Sources of research for inspiration via high, low, and pop culture are included.

Chapter 4 covers the basics of blocking out and fleshing in the ten-head fashion figure. This step-by-step tutorial includes the female form in a variety of poses. The completed figures are on the CD-ROM, so they can be utilized as templates for garment flats. Male fashion figures are included as well.

Chapter 5 provides a visual reference guide or index of silhouettes and construction details. The construction details are duplicated in the form of a digital library on the CD-ROM.

Chapter 6 translates the "geek speak" and technical slang of the computer world into a basic vocabulary for the drawn and scanned images. File-formatting terminology will be also be reviewed. Raster-based programs and vector-based programs are presented to show each application's visual capacity.

Chapter 7 introduces the reader to Adobe Illustrator and begins the actual journey of practicing on the computer. The desktop environment of toolboxes, menu items, and preference settings in the program will be reviewed in a fashion-friendly way, with the purpose of achieving a basic working knowledge of Illustrator.

Chapter 8 introduces the reader to Adobe Photoshop and the desktop environment of toolboxes, menu items, and preference settings. The fashion designer will have a basic working knowledge of this program and gain the ability to create mood boards and trend boards utilizing scanned images and original illustrations.

Chapter 9 continues working with Photoshop to create textile-pattern designs. Traditional textile-design tools such as watercolors, markers, and pens are being supplemented and often replaced by software such as Photoshop. The reason for this is the speed, accuracy, and lower cost in producing digital images. Digital ren-

dering on fabric allows companies to customize fabric designs and output the result for short-run production. Several Photoshop techniques are described to produce various textile designs.

Chapter 10 introduces Illustrator CS and the desktop environment of toolboxes, menu items, and preference settings for this software. The fashion designer will acquire a basic working knowledge of this program and the ability to create vector illustrations.

Chapter 11 guides the reader toward mastering the Illustrator pen tool. The advantage to having a computer-generated flat, as opposed to a hand-drawn one, is that the designer can easily manipulate, copy, scale, and print out consistent-looking flats. These computer-generated flats can then be used for a variety of purposes in the design and marketing process. The fashion designer will learn to master the pen tool to create computer-generated flats.

Chapter 12 works with both Illustrator and Photoshop to create flats and illustrations. Knowing when to use vector or raster images in creating flats and illustrations is critical to a fashion designer's understanding of computerized design. The fashion designer will learn when to use a vector, raster, or a combination of the two.

Chapter 13 works with Illustrator and Photoshop to create flats. Scanning in technical flats and fabrics, tracing images with the pen tool, filling and fabricating flats and colorways, creating patterns, and importing eps files are explained in this chapter.

Chapter 14 gives an overview of the basic presentation tools users need to communicate their creative skills while seeking positions in the fashion industry. The step-by-step review of analyzing the job market, research preparation for the resume and company interview, formation of a stylish CD-ROM portfolio, e-portfolio, and personal web site are included to clearly lay out the path of matching creativity to the needs of a client or company.

It is clear that *From Pencil to Pen Tool* lives up to its name. This book can be used as a sketching manual for first-time students or by seasoned professionals who are looking to update their technique or as a manual/tutorial for Illustrator and Photoshop. It is, indeed, two books in one!

Acknowledgments

Thanks to all those responsible for our professional and personal happiness, including Joe Conte, Vicki McCarrell, Fereshteh Mobasheri, Cheryl Lyles, Nina Shefield, Dr. Lisa Koenigsberg, Joanne Stillman, Machelle Scott, Marsha Hale, Haven Lin-Kirk, and the late Fr. Edward Hilger for their guidance, motivation, and support through our educational endeavors. Special thanks to our students who remind us every day why we love the fashion industry and the teaching field.

We would also like to thank Olga Kontzias, our executive editor, who made this concept a reality with her unmatched vision of what fashion education could and should be; her support will never be forgotten. To Amy Zarkos, our former development editor and long-distance phone friend, whose patient demeanor got the ball rolling; Adam B. Bohannon, our art director; and Elizabeth Marotta, our production editor, who put it all together!

Thank you also to the following reviewers: Teresa B. Robinson, Middle Tennessee State University; Anita Racine, Cornell University; Elizabeth K. Davic, Kent State University; and Diane Sparks, Colorado State University.

Finally, we would like to thank Ava and Ellie, Blackie and Blu, and Peggy Sue.

—*Jemi Armstrong, Lorrie Ivas, Wynn Armstrong*

1

The Evolution of the Fashion Image

What You Will Learn in Chapter 1

This introductory chapter covers the ebb and flow of fashion illustration as the dominant communication tool in advertising throughout the late nineteenth and twentieth centuries. This tool has changed dramatically at the end of the twentieth century, impacting the industry and the way fashion is presented. Today fashion illustrators and designers work in the digital arena where computers are used as standard artistic tools, just as markers, gouaches, inks, and pastels.

It is interesting to note that the fashion plates of yesteryear (first produced mechanically, then hand-colored) and the technically generated illustrations of today (first hand-sketched, then scanned into the computer for finished artistic manipulation) have the same goal: to document fashion in timely settings to promote the desirability and ultimate sale of the designs. The order of technical assistance may have changed, but the creative skill and ability to incorporate the color, texture, silhouette, and detail on a three-dimensional (3-D) body and translating that result on a two-dimensional (2-D) area have not changed.

Chapter 1 includes an overview of major fashion illustrators of the twentieth century and identifies their preferred media and style. These artists did not have the possibility of crossing creative boundaries with the assistance of a computer's time-saving tools. Illustrators did not explore computer technology until near the end of the nineties. A timeline that includes other important illustrators whose work is not covered in this text is included at the end of this chapter, with an abbreviated summary of their clients and publications.

The scope of each artist in the industry varies; this text covers artists who work for specific designers, reportage, or do editorial art for fashion publications; create commercial print advertisements; or design and illustrate garments for theater or film. By studying the various artists and their styles, students develop and define their own senses of what defines quality illustration and allows them to clearly identify what is irreplaceable: the creativity of the human hand, whether it is holding a brush, pen tool, or mouse.

Introduction

Fashion is communication. Fashion is commerce. It is the blending of form and function with aesthetic purpose. Fashion design is creating a 3-D visual message on the body. Whether they are the great lines of distinctive automobiles moving on the highway or of flowing gowns moving down the red carpet, they all started as sketches—sketches drawn to capture and remember an intricate detail, something different from the expected. The lines of a sketch, whether it is a quick thumbnail or a detailed illustration, formulate the basis of a new idea. Silhouette, detail, texture, and perhaps initial color stem from this pen or pencil sketch. Balance and proportion take shape in the drawing, creating a focal point for emphasis. These elements of design help bring the 2-D creation to life.

Many designers are extremely talented illustrators in their own right. Christian Dior, Bill Blass, Karl Lagerfeld, Isaac Mizrahi, Michael Vollbracht, Manolo Blahnik, Christian Lacroix, and Kareem Iliya, to name a few, have created not only beautiful apparel and accessories but also 2-D illustrations worthy of great appreciation.

The Fashion Illustrator: A Fashion Designer, a Commercial Artist, or a Fine Artist?

The definition of fashion illustrator is as varied as the media they use. Some illustrators translate the creative ideas of fashion designers onto the paper that will be used by the pattern maker. Fashion designers then see their ideas on paper and make adjustments as needed. Next, the first pattern maker begins the construct the actual garment based on the 2-D sketch or illustration. The work of illustrators in this scenario is rarely seen by anyone outside the companies they work for and is either discarded after each season or archived for company records.

Fashion drawings differ from fashion illustrations. Drawings are not labored over. Rather, their objective is to communicate a particular line or detail quickly and stylishly. They act as the shorthand of the creative mind. Illustrations, however, can take on lives of their own.

Fashion illustrations may be used as part of a lineup for a fashion presentation or give journalists a preview of a coming collection. Illustrators attending a runway show act as photographers freeze-framing a model on the runway, capturing the design and how it moves with only their pens as their technical tools. Other fashion illustrations have a more direct commercial purpose. They are commissioned to sell fashions directly to the public via print advertisements. Artists may specialize in fashion illustrations and accept commissions from large and small corporations.

A fashion illustrator's style is as unique as a fingerprint. If an illustrator studied in school, his or her developed style may have been heavily influenced by instructors. Other influential factors may include the illustrator's level of interest in and exposure to art history and his or her immersion in current art movements and popular culture.

Sometimes fashion illustration is meant to evoke a mood as well as document a fashion; the impressionistic style of an artist will fill in the blanks of desire rather than fill in the question of whether there is an invisible zipper or a Velcro closing at the waist. The impressionistic quality of Ruben Alterio (b. 1949), the abstraction of fashion with water-based media and pastels by Mats Gustafson (b. 1951), and linocuts with oils in flattened shadowy forms by François Berthoud (b. 1961) elevate clothing to a higher form, thus elevating a viewer's way of really seeing fashion.

Fashion Illustration: Art or Commerce?

Those who question whether fashion illustration is art or commerce are quick to point out that illustration, unlike painting, always has to perform a particular function—a paid function. The hired illustrator's commercial endeavor of reconciling the tastes of the paying client, art director, or fashion editor with his or her own echo this sentiment. Merely uttering the term **illustrator** seems to imply the adjective **commercial** before it, although few would question whether Leonardo da Vinci (1452–1519), the most prolific technical illustrator of the Renaissance, was truly an artist.

Social and economic forces determine the form and content of illustrations. Because fashion illustrators have the ability to observe and transform what they see into accurate 2-D representations of 3-D objects, they are considered to be technical artists.

This is not meant to suggest that fashion is the only realm put under scrutiny. Andy Warhol (1928–1987), formerly a fashion illustrator, was questioned early in his career for his graphic depiction of commercial entities such as Campbell's soup, Brillo, and other such products. Modern art was defining its place in the twentieth century and was undergoing the same scrutiny as fashion illustration.

Jeffrey Fulvimari, one of the top illustrators today, has humbly defined the role of an illustrator as a supporting one, one where an illustrator performs a service and collaborates with an author, art director, or designer. A commercial artist's next job may be illustrating an ad for iPod or a liquor company although he or she may have just finished an ad campaign for a fashionable cosmetic company or an editorial in *Harper's Bazaar* or *Vogue* magazine.

The late twentieth century saw art auction houses revering the fashion world's art of couture clothing as well as its creation and advertising documentation (design-process sketches of the masters, fashion illustrations, and photography). Tiffany Dubin of Sotheby's created a buzz in the auction world with her efforts to preserve these treasures. Her most notable nod to the importance of fashion illustration and photography was the May 1999 "Pulp Fashion" auction (#7294 "Pulp") where the works of Georges Lepape, Erté, Georges Barbier, Christian Dior, Edith Head, Yves Saint Laurent, Antonio, Ruben Toledo, and others were listed along with fashion photographs, magazines, and archival sketches. Other auction houses have dealt in the sale of costumes and textiles of historical importance, but Tiffany Dubin created a fresh new focus for a new generation ready to begin collecting other artistic extensions of the fashion world.

Fashion Illustration: A Choice for Advertising Presentation

Fashion illustration, rather than photography, is chosen by fashion clients for a reason. In advertising, the goal is to get the target consumer's attention, create desire for the product, and get the consumer to recognize the product and buy it. An advertiser's challenge is to make an ad stand out from the others. Print advertisements in fashion magazines are sandwiched between numerous editorial photographs, sometimes caught in the blur of similar four-color, full-page ad formats that appear one after another. The goal of advertising is to create a unique differential. In other words, when all those four-color, full-page ads showing photographs of Donna Karan, Calvin Klein, Gucci, Nautica, or Estée Lauder fill every page, how can any one ad stand out? The answer is to use another media: fashion illustration.

Prior to the advent of photography as the standard medium used in magazine publication, fashion illustration was the sole route, whether in controlled black-and-white line drawings or colorful renderings of ladies and gentlemen complete with detailed background sets. Photography may have led to the diminished use of illustration in promoting fashions in style publications for several decades, but no garment can be photographed if it isn't created. The pencil or marker is the beginning of the process of creating garments, so fashion drawing never disappeared—it just went behind the scenes while photography took center stage, until the next wave of illustration reappeared at the close of the twentieth century.

A Brief Look into Fashion Illustration's Past

Although commercially based, fashion illustration is truly an art form. Just as cave paintings have stone as their canvas, fashion plates of the eighteenth and nineteenth centuries have high-grade parchment as theirs. The precise details of draped garments worn by Greeks depicted on urns are studied as voraciously as line drawings in *Vogue*. Whether it's depicted on a wall, vase, wood block, or piece of parchment, the ability to illustrate what people wore from head to toe throughout history is part of the process of documenting fashion. The purpose and focus of a fashion plate, a woodcut, an illustration, an etching, a drawing, or a thumbnail sketch is the same.

The birth and advancement of artistic trends in drawing, painting, and illustration are a direct result of the available technology of the day. Painting underwent significant advancement when oil pigment was put in portable aluminum tubes, thus allowing artists to paint outdoors—hence, the birth of Impressionism. Hyperrealism was an artistic response to the advancements of photography, while airbrushing came about through the cultivation of acrylics and dyes in fine arts. Experimentation on various surfaces also opened up many visual avenues. Fashion illustrators are not immune to the culture of the times—past, present, or future. Each art movement they study or experience influences not only their drawings but also their methods of execution. Before gaining an understanding of the technology of the future, it is important to review the

Figure 1.1   A nineteenth-century fashion plate created by Anais Courdoury.

Fashion plates represented the powerful print media of their time. They effectively delivered the desirable fashion of the day in newspapers and magazines to the public. They are now recognized as key to the development of the fashion industry as we know it. Fashion plates showed the buying public not only what they should wear but also how they should wear their hair, how they should do their makeup, and how they should keep their figures. Stylish backdrops, including well-tended gardens or select pieces of furniture, complemented the compositions, setting a tone for the well-dressed and their desirable lifestyles (see Figure 1.1). They were the precursors of the fashion and lifestyle marketing so pervasive today. There is hardly one major designer today who is not involved in home decor and furnishings or lifestyle and recreation products. This concept was documented by the early fashion plates several centuries ago.

The Journal des Dames et des Modes of the early nineteenth century (1797–1839) compiled beautiful fashion plates and became the directory of style. Lucien Vogel, immensely impressed with the journal, launched *La Gazette du Bon Ton* in 1911. He stated that fashion has become an art, so a fashion gazette must also be an art revue. He declared it so with *La Gazette du Bon Ton*, whose subtitle said it all: art, fashion, frivolities.

La Gazette brought together the best graphic artists of the era. Condé Nast later bought the magazine in 1921 and carried on with it until 1925. This peek into that well-lived lifestyle reached indiscriminantly to all who were interested in viewing the latest fashions.

technology that influenced fashion illustration in the past.

Twentieth-century Fashion Illustration

The art of fashion illustration prior to the twentieth century has evolved from the detailed etchings of cave paintings to *Trachtenbücher,* to the German costume chronicles that came about from the sixteenth through eighteenth centuries, to the fashion plates depicting the fine lifestyles of the French and English upper-class societies. They all documented exactly what was worn—drawn from life—prior to the advent of fashion photography.

The original group of artists included Paul Iribe (1883–1935), Georges Lepape (1887–1971), Charles Martin (1884–1934), Georges Barbier (1882–1932), and André Marty (1882–1974).

The birth of the twentieth century encouraged input from the art world in the fashion world. Fashion magazines were on the leading edge of culture and style direction. *Vogue, Harper's Bazaar, Vanity Fair,* and *Delineator* were among those magazines that documented the now often-used term lifestyle merchandising. These publications documented interiors, culture, cuisine, as well as dress. Steven Heller, art director, scholar of visual communication, and coauthor of *Cover Story: The Art of American Magazine Covers 1900–1950,* has stated that the magazine cover is to U.S. twentieth-century history what cave markings were to prehistoric man, what hieroglyphic inscriptions were to the ancient Egyptians, and what painting and sculpture were to fourteenth-century Euopeans: art, communication, and folklore.

The pairing of the art and fashion worlds served to create and predict, rather than just document, what was worn and where it was worn. One of the leaders who encouraged this union of fashion and art was couturier Paul Poiret. Poiret wanted to promote himself and commissioned Paul Iribe in 1908 to document his fashion designs in "Les Robes de Paul Poiret," reproducing them in an album—or in today's vernacular a *look book.* At the end of 1910, Poiret met the young painter Georges Lepape, known for his elegant lines and the amazing colors of his gouaches. He commissioned Lepape in 1911 to document all of his fashion designs in an album entitled *Les Choses de Paul Poiret vues par Lepape.* This relationship led to the link between designers and artists. Illustration not only allows the artist to create and communicate a dress design but also is part of inspiration before a garment is even conceived.

Fabric is the inspiration for many designers. A major textile designer of the time, Raoul Dufy (1877–1953) created some of the most striking aquatic designs with Asian-inspired motifs. Poiret worked with them because they provided a rich canvas on which he could execute his lines. Dufy's intense and vivid colors were evidence of his exposure to a group of painters known as Fauves. This bold handling of intensely vivid colors may have been born from an artist movement, but it was adopted by fashion artists and designers. The textile designs so inspired the couturiers that fabric companies presented their palettes as stylishly as if they were finished garments.

The designers of the haute couture were initially more secretive of their exclusive confections and hesitated to make them public; therefore, they primarily depicted their ready-to-wear versions. Haute couture, a French term meaning *high* or *fine sewing,* is translated as the highest quality of dressmaking, custom-made to the measurements of specific clients and usually one of a kind. Ready-to-wear apparel is not custom-made; rather, it is mass-produced using standardized sizing charts. Soon, however, competition set in with more and more designers who wanted their work to be portrayed on paper for the growing middle class to see and buy. This meant an increase in the need to draw everything from the original

Parisian couture houses, adapting them as ready-to-wear and more affordable garments as the ones sold in the Montgomery Ward and Sears catalogs. The drawn figure was the only way for the public to have access to clothing, until photography changed everything.

The Illusion of Illustration and Reality of Photography

The camera itself was introduced in the 1840s but was actually used more frequently later in the century. The problem with photography was that it captured *reality*. Women's bodies were captured in full-figure sizes. There was no such thing as air-brushing, or now "photoshopping," off extra pounds or folds captured in photographs. Fashion illustration remained more popular than photography for some time because it allowed the pen or brush to be directed by the eye of the beholder—in this case by the illustrator. The body could be changed with the drawing implement.

Editors and art directors felt that painting, drawing, and even collage was a more controllable medium from the standpoint of editorial manipulation. Illustrators could achieve hyperrealistic or stylized effects according to the current trends and beauty ideals of the time, all translated through the pen or brush. This attitude prevailed throughout the 1930s, until the new breed of artist/photographer came on the scene.

The Twentieth-century Timeline of Art Movements and Fashion Illustration

The first half of the twentieth century experienced the birth of many art movements, and fashion was greatly influenced by these, both in actual content as well as the artistic style of translation. Art Nouveau, Art Deco, Cubism, Surrealism, Pop Art, American Punk, and Digital Animation saw their effects on fashion—and fashion illustration.

Commerce also influenced fashion trends. Black-and-white drawings were popular—hence the clean lines of black-and-white clothing—due to the easy and less costly method of printing them in magazines. Certain design lines attributed to each movement such as the Egyptian geometrics in Art Deco, flora and fauna curves of Art Nouveau, or the angular slashings of American Punk translated themselves into the clothing silhouettes, colors, textures, and details of the time. Fashion illustrators would depict these styles on model figures who accurately represented the body dimensions of the time (for example, the flat shapes of arms, legs, and torsos of the Cubists or the exaggerated organic curves of the Surrealists).

It is possible to identify the art movement, and therefore date a drawing, by analyzing fashion illustrations. Influential designers and illustrators of the twentieth century lived and immersed themselves in these movements. Following are some brief descriptions of the major movements embraced by the fashion world.

Art Nouveau

Art Nouveau was the first international design style dating from the 1880s to the mid-1900s (World War I). It was a rebellion against Victorian sensibility and a direct descendant of the Arts and Crafts Movement with its curvilinear and floral abstractions. The Arts and Crafts graphic style was influenced by Gothic manuscript illumination and wall tapestries. Aubrey Beardsley (1872–1898) epitomized Art Nouveau in graphically powerful black and white. Although he was not considered a fashion illustrator, the naturalistic embellishment in his work served as a formal decorative backdrop for his bold and sometimes exaggerated body shapes that had flowing gowns and flowing hair. Magazines and art books grew in popularity due to economical printing methods allowing the Art Nouveau revolution to grow immensely. Poster advertising in the Art Nouveau style played a significant part in spreading the applied arts to a mass audience. The 1960s adopted this linear form but added vivid psychedelic color fills.

Art Deco

Art Deco was inspired by Art Nouveau, the Ballets Russes, and Aztec Indian and North American Indian art. Tutankhamen's tomb discovery in 1922 presented wonderful ornamental inspiration for Art Deco, and it universally affected architecture, furniture, clothing, and graphic arts between the first and second world wars (Figure 1.2). Art Deco was also stylish and appealing to the middle class, so fashions and furnishings of all price points were eagerly embraced. This style regained popularity in the 1980s, where high-tech manipulation sharpened the geometry even further.

Cubism

Cubism defined new silhouettes through flat planes, cylindrical cones, and experimentation that spawned *collage,* a term derived from the French word *coller,* translated as "to stick onto." While Paul Poiret despised Cubism, he appreciated certain aspects of its graphic

Figure 1.2   Illustration by Helen Dryden from *Vogue,* October 15, 1922.

potential that could be incorporated into beautiful fabrics. Magazine covers incorporated Cubist elements, neoclassical, and Art Deco silhouettes as seen in the *Vogue* covers of Eduardo Garcia Benito, also known as Benito (1891–1953), and the artwork of Ernesto Michalles, also known as Thayaht (1893–1959). Artist Sonia Delaunay (1884–1979) and her geometric designs merged Cubist art with fashion. Her primary goal was to graphically represent the geometric pattern; creating wearable apparel was secondary. The unstructured clothing of the 1920s provided the perfect canvas on which she could use color and its contrasting combinations to the fullest extent. Her modernist style of rendering these garments created a new look in fashion illustration as well.

Surrealism

Surrealism came about as a result of spoken and written philosophies. Free thought and imagination allowed people to question and explore the lives of real objects. "Why not?" rather than "Why?" meant that everything from 2-D art to 3-D creations burst with creativity. Artists could question why a shoe should be only for the foot. They further questioned why a shoe could not function as a hat instead. Silhouettes, colors, textures, and details broke all rules of convention, and illustration freely followed. Elsa Schiaparelli, a leading fashion designer and surrealist in her own right, often asked "why not?" in her creative processes and collaboration with the Surrealist artists. The works of Salvador Dalí (1904–1989), Christian Bérard (1902–1949), and Marcel Vertès (1895–1961), among others, really brought art to fashion, still allowing for the fashion public to appreciate the artistry in clothes as well as in the illustrations.

Pop Art

Pop Art was a reflection of the 1960s American youth culture. It was, and is, a union of art, music, and literature and applied itself to newspapers, posters, clothing, jewelry, furniture, and automobiles. Pop Art is seen as a combination of Art Nouveau, East Indian symbology, comic book iconography, and psychedelic motifs—a distinct American style. Cartooning and mural-like silhouettes were the order of the day, with vivid colors and combinations popping out at the viewer. Antonio (1943–1987) led this movement into the high fashion pages of *Vogue* and *Women's Wear Daily* (*WWD*). Today's retro recollection of Pop Art is evident in the merging of cartooning, brand images, and vivid color themes.

Postmodernism

Postmodernism defined a cultural change in the artistic sensibilities of the 1970s and 1980s with a tribute to the clean lines of the Art Deco period but a clear look to the sleek technology of the future. Sharp angles of industrial proportion were balanced by selective and controlled curves. High-tech and avant-garde were the adjectives that best defined the broad-shouldered suits drawn with broad brushstrokes. Antonio once again led the fashion wave in the 1980s with powerfully drawn men and women wearing their power suits. Tony Viramontes (1960–1988) also followed this style with big shoulders, big hair, and big accessories.

Digital Animation

Digital Animation closed the twentieth century and opened the twenty-first by combining 1960s psychedelics with 1970s and 1980s postmodernism in a cartoon image.

Artists blended the 1930s American comic book characters with the Japanese animation of the 1960s to create a futuristic look that still recalled the cartoon images from the past.

The Twentieth-century Illustrators
The best way for artists to explore their creativity with the pen or pen tool is to review the styles of the leaders of the twentieth century. They all had particular personal styles, whether dictated by the climate of the times, their exposure to and comfort with using various medias, or the preferences and restrictions of the clients for whom they worked.

Charles Dana Gibson (1867–1944) was the American illustrator who introduced crisp robustness with the use of the pen. His Gibson Girl personified America's modern woman, adorned in a fitted shirt-waist blouse and full skirt that highlights her S-curve frame. His books [*The Education of Mr. Pipp* (1899), *The American* (1900), and *The Social Ladder* (1902)] represented fashionable, independent women of the twentieth century who had active middle- and upper-middle-class lives. Gibson learned to use a longer stroke, unique to pen-and-ink styles of the time. His work appeared in *Harper's Bazaar, Life, Tid-Bits* (later *Time* magazine), *Collier's*, and many more.

Gordon Conway (1895–1956), a multitalented graphic designer, costume designer, and fashion illustrator began working for *Vogue, Vanity Fair,* and *Harper's Bazaar* around 1915. She, as Charles Dana Gibson before her, was later responsible for portraying the "new woman" image and lifestyle so touted by Condé Nast. Other artists, including

George Petty (1894–1975) and Alberto Vargas (1896–1982), portrayed yet another image of illustrated women—theirs was a more sensual woman who was wearing less clothes but had more personality. These women became "pin-up" icons, striking alluring poses of the time for the sole purpose of men's admiration. They were not walking or playing croquet as the Gibson or Conway females.

Léon Bakst (1866–1924) contributed to the history of fashion through the theater. He was the artistic director of the Ballets Russes (1909). His costume designs for Schéhérazade immensely affected Parisian haute couture and brought together many great artists and designers of the early twentieth century. He led the way in exotic illustration with his form and content.

Paul Iribe (1883–1935) began his career creating cartoons and illustrations for French periodicals. He skyrocketed to fame when he was selected to illustrate the first fashion album for Paul Poiret, entitled "Les Robes de Paul Poiret," in 1908. Afterward, every French publication wanted his fashion illustrations. Furniture, fabric, and wallpaper designs were a natural progression for him since he already had included such beautiful imaginary background settings in each fashion plate.

Iribe's interest in the film industry brought him to America and Cecil B. de Mille. Later he returned to France and the world of illustration, where he worked on books, magazines, and jewelry for Coco Chanel. Iribe's pochoir process, where a monochrome print was hand-colored using a series of

Figure 1.3   Illustration by Paul Iribe from the brochure "Les Robes de Paul Poiret," 1908.

bronze or zinc stencils, allowed the brilliant colors and clean lines to stand out magnificently. The crisp, clean, and balanced line clearly presented the stylish outline of the garments, thus placing the fashion designer's work in the best possible light (see Figure 1.3).

Georges Lepape (1887–1971) began his career as a posterist and advertising artist. Paul Poiret recognized his artistic and selling skills and commissioned him to illustrate *Les Choses de Paul Poiret,* the second Poiret fashion album, thus catapulting him as one of the leaders of Art Deco fashion illustration. His work appeared in *Gazette du Bon Ton, Journal des Dames et des Modes,* and *Modes et Manieres d'Aujourd'hui.*

Figure 1.4   Illustration by Georges Lepape from *Les Robes de Paul Poiret*, February 1911.

Lepape's work was regularly seen in *Vogue, Harper's Bazaar, Femina, House and Garden, L'Illustration, Lu,* and *Vu* from 1920 through 1950. Just as many of his contemporaries, he created designs for sets and costumes for the Ballets Russes, as seen in his books *Costumes de Theatre, Ballet et Divertissements* (1920), and *L'Oiseau Bleu* (1925–1927). His depictions of furniture, gardens, and theaters in his backdrops created a full-scale stylish world (see Figure 1.4).

Georges Barbier (1882–1932)— with Paul Iribe and Georges Lepape—was one of the top artists of the time to be commissioned by Paul Poiret to illustrate his fashions. Barbier began his artistic career as a set and costume designer for the

Figure 1.5   Illustration by Georges Barbier from *Les Modes de Paul Poiret,* April 1912.

Ballets Russes. His rendering was in the classic Greek style, with elegant and sophisticated ladies, suave men, and beautiful backgrounds. Poster art and textile and wallpaper design were a part of his creative focuses. Besides his works in Art Deco book illustration, now considered masterpieces, Barbier illustrated the creations of the fashion houses of Worth, Poiret, and Lanvin in the *Journal des Dames et des Modes* and the *Gazette de Bon Ton,* among others (see Figure 1.5).

Charles Martin (1884–1934) was a member of the friendly circle of Iribe, Lepape, and Barbier, among others. He most strongly embraced the Cubist style among the Art Deco fashion illustrators and peppered the content of his illustrations with sharp wit. He illustrated for many of the top fashion magazines of the time, including *Le Journal des Dames et des Modes* and *La Gazette du Bon Ton*. Martin did only one cover for *Vogue* in 1925 but frequently contributed satirical social commentary sketches to the magazine until his death.

Late 1920s and 1930s fashion magazines aimed to be on the crest of new and progressive waves of culture and design. The fashion cover was always graphically unique, each competing to print the more avant-garde image and image creator. *Harper's Bazaar* led the way in the previous decade by hiring Erté, the Art Moderne master, for their January 1915 cover, leading to an exclusive ten-year contract signed in 1916 to prevent him from providing any artwork for rival *Vogue*. *Vogue* hired the graphic stylist Eduardo Benito for his masterful Art Deco creations, with his first cover appearing in November 1921.

Eduardo Benito (1891–1961) was one of the fashion illustration leaders of the Art Deco period. His extreme elongation of the figure in the 1920s reflected Cubist paintings and sculptures. His skill in rendering stylish and enviable vignettes of the period attracted the interior design and fashion worlds. Benito's *Vogue* illustrations provided a visual directory of the jazz age. His sharp angles as well as his smooth attenuation created his signature pieces (see Figure 1.6 a and b).

Figure 1.6a   Illustration by Benito from *Vogue,* December 15, 1925.

Figure 1.6b   Illustration by Benito from *Vogue,* October 15, 1926.

Figure 1.7   Illustration by Erté from Henri Bendel, 1918.

name, went to Paris from Russia to join the design studio of Paul Poiret, who greatly influenced his work. Erté designed for the Folies-Bergère and illustrated covers for *Harper's Bazaar* in the 1920s. In 1925 Erté went to Hollywood to design for MGM. Titles he worked on included *Ben Hur, The Mystery,* and *La Bohème*. Later he worked mainly for the stage. Throughout each decade of the twentieth century, Erté enjoyed a resurgence of his varied works of sculpture, jewelry, and fashion illustration until his death in 1990 (see Figure 1.7).

Advertising Arts introduced modern graphic trends and fashions to designers and advertising artists in the 1930s. While not purely a fashion read, it was a main ingredient in the blending of art, fashion, and commerce. Because the Great Depression seeped into every aspect of the public's life, fashion illustration needed to escape the harsh realities of the time. Surrealism was the answer. Throughout this decade, the collaboration of great fashion designers and artists of the time (as occurred previously with the Art Nouveau and Art Deco periods) generated some of the most creative fashion designs as well as fashion illustration's translation of the work to this date.

Erté (1892–1990) saw females as goddesses to such an extreme degree that he will be eternally known as creating the most stylized translations of women and fashion. Often referred to as the father of Art Deco, he was the twentieth century's fashion illustrator, costume designer, graphic designer, jewelry designer, and set designer. The modern styles of the 1920s and 1930s were credited to him. Romain de Tirtoff, Erté's given

Marcel Vertès (1895–1961) recorded not only the clothing but also the social lives of the Parisian beau monde with his dreamlike watercolor images for *Vogue*. He also designed sets and costumes for films in Hollywood, including *The Mikado, The Thief of Baghdad, Tonight and Every Night,* and *Moulin Rouge*. His illustrations for Elsa Schiaparelli's perfumes are classics, as well as his lively fashion illustrations depicting people

Figure 1.8   Illustration by Marcel Vertès from *Vogue*, March 15, 1936.

experiencing life in their clothes (see Figure 1.8).

Christian Bérard (1902–1949), like Erté, Vertès, and Jean Cocteau, was multitalented. He painted; designed sets, costumes, and textile prints; and did fashion illustration. He worked for *Vogue* from 1935 to 1949 and designed for many of Jean Cocteau's plays. Bérard's style can be described as romantic expressionism because of his recognizable spidery lines.

Figure 1.9 Illustration by Eric from *Vogue,* October 1, 1948.

Jean Cocteau (1889–1963) wore many hats in the art, entertainment, and fashion worlds. Painting, printmaking, and filmmaking added to his design work for theater, textiles, and accessories. Fashion illustration came as a result of Cocteau's creative eye and his exploration of every aspect of the design process. His relationships with the fashion icons of the time—Chanel and Schiaparelli—allowed him to design fabrics, jewelry, and embroidery.

Surrealism's message was communicated loud and clear, with fashion designers and artists sharing the mindset of unbridled imagination infused in the function of clothing. Salvador Dalí (1904–1989) illustrated with such a unique photorealistic style that even his fashion illustrations provoked fresh curiosity in their execution as well as subject matter. He often collaborated with Schiaparelli in fabric and accessory design.

After World War II, fashion became more democratic, so maintaining the mystique and high glamour rested on the shoulders of the couturier. *Vogue* and *Harper's Bazaar* also relied more on photography to communicate the designers' new creations after the austerity of the past. Carl Erickson (1891–1958), known as Eric, maintained his presence, however, in the world of illustration. He drew from life and had an eye for the minute details of the feminine form. His first illustrations for *Vogue* in 1916 brought Paris high fashion to the pages until the mid-1950s (see Figure 1.9). René Bouché (1906–1963) possessed a style that was a rich amalgam of painting, drawing, and portraiture skills. His work was seen in *Vogue* during the 1940s, 1950s, and 1960s. His illustrations portrayed

Figure 1.10   Illustration by René Bouché from *Vogue*, March 1, 1947.

society with wit and attitude, although he never sacrificed attention to the details of the clothes (see Figure 1.10).

René Gruau (1909–2004), born Renato Zasvagli, epitomized the glamour and style of the fashion world in the 1940s and 1950s. He showed promise for drawing when he was a teenager and moved to Paris when he was in his twenties. Gruau began to work for fashion magazines, including French *Vogue*,

Figure 1.11   Illustration by René Gruau from *Vogue*, September 15, 1949.

century. His style was favored by Givenchy and Balenciaga as well. His style spoke of a strong fashion sense and evoked an elegant advertising message (see Figure 1.11).

When the realism of photography triumphed over fashion drawing at the end of the 1950s, pop music, film, and television triumphed over the traditional art movements, with the exception of Op Art—the last direct expression of an art movement.

Joe Eula (1925–2004) possessed a graphic style that employed movement and fine art with graceful watercolors and pencils. Just as photographer Richard Avedon was known to embrace complete movement in his fashion work, Eula always caught a model in midmovement in his illustrations. He began his career in the 1950s with fashion and social reportage illustration with Eugenia Sheppard in the *Herald Tribune* and later with Ernestine Carter in the London *Sunday Times*. Newspapers kept illustration alive.

Marie Claire, Femina, Elle, and *Harper's Bazaar.* His brushstrokes mirrored effects of classical Japanese drawings as well as Toulouse-Lautrec's Parisian nightlife. The marketing image of Christian Dior's Miss Dior perfume and cosmetics was created through Gruau's vision. He designed posters for the Lido, Moulin Rouge, Roland Petit's ballet "Phantom of the Opera," and Fellini's *Dolce Vita.* Gruau's ink lines defined the shape of fashion while the deep blocks of color, often with Gruau's signature red and black, sealed his place as one of the last grand illustrators of the twentieth

The 1960s found Eula following in the footsteps of Erté, Bérard, and Cocteau with his involvement in set and costume design for the New York City Ballet. He won a Tony for *Private Lives* in 1968. Studio 54, a pop-culture symbol in Manhattan, can claim its logo is one of Eula's creations. In the 1970s he collaborated with Halston as creative director. Chanel, Givenchy, Versace, and Yves Saint Laurent also kept him at the drawing board as well as *Vogue* and *Harper's Bazaar.* He assisted the fashion legend Diana Vreeland in her role as exhibition director of the Costume Institute of the Metropolitan Museum of Art. Models captured in

Figure 1.12   Illustration by Joe Eula from W.

motion were indeed his specialty,
as he could finish a full sketch in
ink or charcoal as a model pivoted
and returned back up the runway
(see Figure 1.12).

The 1960s were the first decade to
really focus on the youth and their

Figure 1.13 Illustration by Mats Guftason.

visions of style. Antonio's wide-eyed baby-doll-like figures in *Women's Wear Daily* and the *New York Times* gave photography a run for its money. Antonio (1942–1987) brought fashion drawing back to the forefront. His mastery of all medias—watercolor, pencil, gouache, and so on—was unmatched. He included surrealistic elements in this work. Antonio worked from life, structuring a set behind each subject as a photographer or cinematographer would. He joined the staff of *Women's Wear Daily* and did freelance assignments for the *New York Times*.

Antonio rendered his early drawings in Conté crayon or brush and ink. His first breakthrough was Pop Art as the defining direction of art, with young liberated models looking like girls from comic strips. By the end of the 1960s, his place in fashion illustration was secure; he had overseas assignments for *Elle* and British *Vogue, Playboy,* the *New York Times* magazine, *Elle,* and *Marie Claire* to name a few.

Antonio's skill energized fashion illustration, a medium that had diminished with the onset of photography. The 1970s were chronicled with high-profile models and socialites as illustration subjects— so different from today's celebrity studio and paparazzi shots. Antonio and illustration were synonymous for three decades.

Andy Warhol (1928–1987) began working as an illustrator for fashion brands as well as *Mademoiselle* and other periodicals. His love of art, fashion, and commerce was evident in his launching of *Interview* magazine in 1969, which became a platform for fashion illustrators from the 1970s to today.

Tony Viromontes (1960–1988) studied fine art and photography in New York before switching to fashion and beauty illustration. He then moved to Paris and Venice, where his striking angular drawing style became the signature of Yves Saint Laurent, Claude Montana, and Valentino. Although there was a classic beauty to his drawings, inspired by Jean Cocteau and Henri Matisse, there was an underlying feel of the 1980s New Wave. He worked with American *Vogue, The Face, Le Monde,* and *Marie Claire,* to name a few. Viromontes began experimenting with drawing over photographs, called "photo-illustration." He would have been a natural with the new computer technology of the 1990s, but his untimely death at 28 years of age ended that possibility.

Mats Guftason (b. 1951) employs beautiful watercolors and brush-strokes in his abstract silhouettes, with suggestions of line and shape working as effectively as a photograph to evoke the desired mood. His work for Yves Saint Laurent, Burberry, H&M, Nike, Tiffany's, and Shiseido attest to his skills (see Figure 1.13).

François Berthoud's (b. 1961) linocuts and woodcuts brought a strong new aesthetic to the usual billowy lines of fashion illustration. His sharp contours and solid angular shapes provide a whole new way of seeing clothes. Berthoud likes engraving fashion plates using such a hard instrument to portray lightness and grace. Berthoud has been the art director of *Vogue Sposa* and has worked with *Vanity Fair, Vogue Bambini,* Italian *Vogue, Visionnaire,* Mondi, Jean Paul Gaultier, Missoni, Moschino, Krizia, Lacroix, Romeo Gigli, Prada, and Vivienne Westwood.

Figure 1.14   Illustration by Thierry Perez.

Thierry Perez (b. 1964) is an illustrator, a photographer, and an artist who has explored various arenas in the pursuit of capturing the ideal fashion image. He studied in the early 1980s and was immediately asked to work exclusively with Jean Paul Gaultier until 1991. He has since worked as a freelance illustrator for Italian *Vogue,* French and Italian *Glamour, Elle,* and *Vogue Hommes.* His combination of baroque, erotic extremes in a sort of untouchably cool comic strip attracted more designers, including Azzedine Alaïa, Gianni Versace, and Dolce&Gabbana, who wanted him to translate their work, much as the designers of the early twentieth century wanted to link themselves with popular illustrators (see Figure 1.14).

The 1990s' obsession with cartoons and video games and the overall increase in film animation introduced a new generation to the visual world of animation cel–style drawing; hence, fashion illustration saw a resurgence again, this time with a definite animation/comic book twist. Therefore, comic book artists study fashion so they can develop their characters as fervently as fashion designers track future buying trends.

The ability to combine the capabilities of photography with Photoshop and the linear distinction of Illustrator has brought the art of fashion illustration back to the forefront.

Retail Reinforcement of Fashion Illustration

Neiman Marcus, one of the most prestigious department and specialty stores in the world, reminded their clients about the art of fashion through photography and illustration with their ad campaigns aptly entitled "The Art of Fashion." Ruben Alterio (b. 1949) was one of the featured artists who translated Neiman Marcus's fall and spring collections in his painterly, dream-like manner with oils, turpentine on paper, strong brushstrokes, and obscured faces and hands.

This same sensibility was expressed by Nordstrom specialty stores when they commissioned Ruben Toledo to illustrate their designer collections rather than photograph them on live models (Figure 1.15). Ruben Toledo (b. 1961) has been involved in many innovations in the fashion and art worlds. He is a sculptor as well as an illustrator and renders stylish design commissions for retailers, exhibitions, books, and catalogs. He has sculpted mannequins for Pucci with a surrealistic bent. Toledo's first book, entitled *Style Dictionary,* is an A-to-Z visualization of fashion terms coupled with a compilation of his past works. He has painted murals, portraits, album covers, and editorial art for *Uomo Vogue, Harper's Bazaar, Paper,* and *Interview.* His ability to create beauty and satire is evident in his unmistakable signature, as seen in *The Bombshell Manual of Style* (authored by Laren Stover) and the adventures of the furry fashionista in *Sweetie: From the Gutter to the Runway.*

The Tools of the Trade

It is important to know the list of tools that fashion illustrators had and still have at their disposal to understand the software created to enlarge the possibilities of those tools. With the exception of Thierry Perez, all the fashion illustrators mentioned utilized traditional mediums without the technological advancements. Chapter 2 will explore this inventory of tools, but also the pen tool, drawing tablet, Photoshop, and Illustrator as creative and time-saving options.

Following is a list of some tools used for illustration:

Acrylic—paint containing acrylate resin that creates solid colors and textures

Airbrush—the process of compressed air and paint passed through a narrow chamber. Photoshop creates the same effect.

Crayon—stick of colored wax, chalk, or charcoal

Collage—interesting way of using flat color combined with tactile images, including neat cutout shapes or torn pieces, found objects, and so on

Charcoal—purest form is stick; compressed charcoal is made from ground powder. With changes in how much pressure is applied, the charcoal can create jagged edges of various thicknesses, which happens

Figure 1.15   Illlustration by Ruben Toledo for Nordstrom.

when raster-based images are manipulated in size on the computer screen. Chapter 2 will introduce raster-based images to the artists' vocabularies.

Pastels (chalk or oil)—made from wax or oil mixed with pigment. Pastels come in stocks or pencils and are excellent for textured papers. They mix well with other medias.

Markers—fiber-tip pens that can be used on metal, concrete, and other unusual surfaces with nibs varying in width and shape. Colors may be applied over one another without dissolving into one another, so there is no bleeding.

Watercolor—made from finely ground pigment mixed with gum. Watercolor paint comes in pans, tubes, or bottles. Wet or dry brush techniques allow for unique texture possibilities.

Gouache—opaque watercolor made by mixing pigment with white. Gouache can be easily combined with other materials.

Pen and Ink—whether quills, reed pens, dip pens, fountain pens, fiber tips, reservoir, or ballpoint, the line and the dot offers limitless textures

Tempera—any kind of paint containing oils in emulsion that can be used with water as a medium

Pencil—a thin cylindrical instrument consisting of a rod of graphite inside a wooden or metal sheath

Woodcuts—process used in textile printing where the design is executed on a smooth block of wood; parts to not be printed are cut away, leaving the design standing in relief

An Overview of Twentieth-century Fashion Illustrators
Each illustrator covered in this chapter had a different angle or impact on the fashion drawings they created. Some focused on the creation of the garment; others translated fashion designers' finished basic garments into living, flowing creations highlighting silhouette, color, texture, and details. Still others created art that represented fashion designers' works and included the artistic movements, body attitudes, social statuses, and aesthetic directions of the times.

The publication and brand clients list enables students to easily discern who are the trendsetters in visual presentation. Early in the twentieth century Paul Poiret realized that the art of fashion and the art of promotion were intrinsically bound. He employed leading artists of the day (Iribe, Lepape, and so on) to collaborate on everything from textile design to advertising. Elsa Schiaparelli, fashion's ambassador of surrealism, worked with Salvador Dalí, Marcel Vertes, and Christian Bérard. Christian Dior's choice of linking exclusively with René Gruau for his advertising campaigns was a visual feast of two amazing artists. Antonio's various translations of 1960s, 1970s, and 1980s fashion via pencil, marker, and acrylics kept fashion illustration in a powerful position in spite of photography's encroachment in the advertising industry. Thierry Perez took photography's challenge by incorporating it into illustration, creating something truly personal and original.

Chapter 2 highlights these new communication tools and identifies the leading fashion illustrators *crossing over* to the "screen side." (No, not the "dark side!") The drafting table, easel, and sketchpad of fashion's past will now share design room space with the Mac or PC screen—the same screen no longer the sole domain of graphic artists. It is the canvas of all artists. The fashion designer has these tools to make sure no boundaries are up to inhibit the textile choices, color combinations, and exercising all possibilities in the development of garments and accessories.

Here follows an overview of the illustrators who inspired those today, providing an interesting reference to begin one's personal investigation of varied styles (See Table 1.1).

Table 1.1

Illustrator (AKA/signature)	DoB	DoD	Publishing Client/Designer (overview)
Léon Bakst	1866	1924	*Vogue*; Ballets Russes, House of Paquin
Charles Dana Gibson	1867	1944	*Tid-Bits* (now *Time*), *Collier's Weekly*, *Harper's Bazaar*
Raoul Dufy	1877	1953	Paul Poiret, Le Petit Usine textile factory, artistic director of Bianchini-Ferier (textiles); authored *Raoul Dufy: Paintings and Drawings*
Umberto Brunelleschi	1879	1949	*La Gazette du Bon Ton, Femina, Flit, Le Journal*; authored "Umberto Brunelleschi: Fashion Stylist, Illustrator, Stage and Costume Designer"
André-Edouard Marty	1882	1974	*Vogue, La Gazette du Bon Ton, Fémina, Modes et Manières*; Doeuillet
Georges Babier	1882	1932	French *Vogue, Fémina, Feuillets d'Art, La Gazette du Bon Ton, Journal des Dames et des Modes, Guirlande de Mois*
Paul Iribe (Iribe)	1883	1935	*Les Robes de Paul Poiret*, founded *Le Témoin*; Jacques Doucet, Paquin, Chanel
Bernard Boutet de Monvel	1884	1949	*Femina, La Gazette du Bon Ton, Vogue, Harper's Bazaar*; authored "Bernard Boutet de Monvel, 1881–1949"
Charles Martin	1884	1934	*Vogue, La Gazette du Bon Ton, Journal des Dames et des Modes, Vanity Fair, Harper's Bazaar, Fémina*
Pierre Brissaud	1885	1964	*Gazette du Bon Ton, L'Homme Élégant, Vogue, Monsieur*; Les Galéries Lafayette
Adrien Désiré Étienne (Drian)	1890	1965	*La Gazette du Bon Ton, Fémina, Harper's Bazaar*; Printemps, Max, Revillion
Helen Dryden	1887	1981	*Vogue* covers and editorials—1910s and 1920s
Georges Lepape	1887	1971	*Les Choses de Paul Poiret, Harper's Bazaar, Vanity Fair, Vu, Lu, House & Garden, Fémina, L'Illustration*; Paul Poiret
Jean Cocteau	1889	1963	*Harper's Bazaar*; designed for Diaghilev's ballets; Elsa Schiaparelli's embroidery motifs; collaborated with Chanel; authored *The Difficulty of Being*, and *Jean Cocteau: 129 Drawings from Dessins*
Eduardo Garcia Benito (Benito)	1891	1953	*L'Homme Élégant, Vogue*
Carl Erickson (Eric)	1891	1958	*Vogue*; Henri Bendel, Marshall Field
Romain de Tirtoff (Erté)	1892	1990	Costumes for *Ziegfield Follies, Ben Hur, La Bohème*; *Vogue, Harper's Bazaar, La Gazette du Bon Ton*; Poiret, Mata Hari, Henri Bendel
Ernesto Michaelles (Thayaht)	1893	1959	*Gazette du Bon Ton*; Vionnet logo
Gordon Conway	1894	1956	*Eve, Vanity Fair, Vogue*; set, costume, graphic design
George Petty	1894	1975	*Esquire*, the *New Yorker, Vogue, Collier's*

Illustrator (AKA/signature)	DoB	DoD	*Publishing Client*/Designer (overview)
Marcel Vertès	1895	1961	*Harper's Bazaar, Vanity Fair*; Saks Fifth Avenue, Schiaparelli perfumes; authored *Art and Fashion*
Alberto Vargas	1896	1982	*Esquire, Playboy*; Early fashion, pin-up art, calenders
Count René Bouët-Willaumez (R.B.W.)	1900	1979	French & American *Vogue*; Mainbocher
Christian Bérard	1902	1949	*Vogue, Harper's Bazaar*; Dior, Schiaparelli
Cecil Beaton	1904	1980	British *Vogue*; Ballet Russes, Le Pavillon; designed for 13 films and won Oscars for *My Fair Lady* and *Gigi*; book illustrations and numerous publications
Salvador Dalí	1904	1989	*Vogue*; Schiaparelli; authored "The Secret Life of Salvador Dalí" and "My Unspeakable Confessions"
Ruth Sigrid Grafstrom	1905		*Vogue*; Saks Fifth Avenue, Molyneux
René Bouché	1906	1963	English, French, American *Vogue*
René Gruau	1909	2004	*Vogue, Harper's Bazaar, Flair, L'Officiel, Figaro, Marie Claire*; Pierre Balmain, Christian Dior, Givenchy; posters for *Moulin Rouge*
Edmond Kirazian (Kiraz)	1923		*Glamour*, French *Vogue, Playboy*; Nivea Beauty, Canderel; published a dozen books of his cartoons, including "Kiraz in Playboy 2002"
Joe Eula	1925	2004	*Herald Tribune, New York Times* magazine, *Vogue*, Italian & French *Harper's Bazaar*; creative director of Halston; sets for Diana Vreeland and Costume Institute, Yves St. Laurent
Antonio Lopez	1943	1987	French *Elle*, all *Vogue* editions, *WWD, New York Times*; Charles James, Karl Lagerfeld, Chloe, Versace; authored "Antonio's Girls" and "Antonio's Tales from the Thousand and One Nights"
Steven Stipelman	1944		*WWD*; Henri Bendel, Estée Lauder, Charles of the Ritz, Clairol, Orlane, Lord & Taylor, Marshall Field, Adele Simpson, Hanes, Helga, Ralph Lauren
Hippolyte Romain	1947		*Vanity, La Mode en Peinture, Vogue, Stern, Vanity Fair*
Michael Roberts	1947		*Sunday Times, Nova, Tatler, Vanity Fair*, British *Vogue* and all editions; *L'Uomo Vogue, GQ, Harpers & Queen*, the *New Yorker, Esquire, Interview, Independent*; and is the author of *The Snippy World of New Yorker Fashion Artist Michael Roberts*.
Gladys Perint Palmer	1947		*Vogue*, London *Sunday Times, Harper's Bazaar, San Francisco Examiner, New York Times* magazine, *Mirabella, Self, Town & Country, Los Angeles Times, L'Officiel, Elle*; Missoni, Vivienne Westwood, Oscar de la Renta, Geoffrey Beene, Lancome, Estée Lauder; authored "Fashion People"
Ruben Alterio	1949		*La Mode en Peinture, Mirabella, Marie Claire*, German *Vogue*; Neiman-Marcus

Illustrator (AKA/signature)	DoB	DoD	*Publishing Client*/Designer (overview)
Mats Gustafson	1951		British *Vogue*, American *Vogue*, French *Marie Claire*, *Interview, New York Times, Marie Claire, Marie Claire Bis*; Henri Bendel, Bergdorf Goodman, H & M, Burberry, Tiffany's, Club Monaco, Bloomingdales, Nike, Shiseido, Printemps, Chanel, L'Oreal, Revlon, Comme des Garcons, Geoffrey Beene; www.artandcommerce.com
Hélène Tran	1954		American *Vogue, GAP, La Mode en Peinture*; www.helentran.com
Lawrence Mynott	1954		*Tatler, Harpers & Queen*, British *Vogue, Observer, Radio Times, Le Mode en Peinture, Madame Figaro, Harper's Bazaar*; Hermès, Rifat Ozbek, Christian Lacroix, Yves St. Laurent, Ungaro, Comme des Garcons, Karl Lagerfeld; www.lawrencemynott.com
Lorenzo Mattotti	1954		*The Face*, the *New Yorker, Deutsche Vogue*; Le Printemps, Kenzo, Vivienne Westwood, Fumetti comic strips
Michel Canetti	1955		*Vogue* Australia, *Madame Figaro, Elle, Joyce*; Chanel, Neiman-Marcus, Estée Lauder, Waterman, Perrier, DeBeers; www.michelcanetti.com
Zoltan	1957		*New York Times*, American *Vogue, Interview*, Italian *Vogue, Donna*; J. Walter Thompson, Young & Rubicam; Shiseido, later worked in photography
Jean-Philippe Delhomme	1959		British *Vogue, La Mode en Peinture, World of Interiors, Elle*, the *Observer*, the *New Yorker, Glamour, GQ, Condé Nast Traveler*; Volvo, Club Med, Le Printemps, BarneysNewYork; authored "Visit to Another Planet"; www.jeanphilippedelhomme.com
Stefano Canulli	1959		*Vanity*; Roberto Capucci couture, Valentino
Ruben Toledo	1960		*Visionnaire, Details, New York, L'Uomo Vogue, Vogue, Madame Figaro, Esquire*; mannequin designs for Pucci; painter, sculptor, reporter, chronicler; authored "Fashion Dictionary"
Tony Viramontes	1960	1988	*Vogue, Lei, The Face, Marie Claire, Le Monde*; Yves St. Laurent, Valentino, Versace, Chanel, Perry Ellis, Claude Montana, Hanae Mori
François Berthoud	1961		Art director of *Vogue Sposa, Vanity, Vogue Bambini*, Italian *Vogue, Visionnaire*; Mondi, Jean-Paul Gaultier, Missoni, Moschino, Krizia, Lacroix, Romeo Gigli, Prada, Vivienne Westwood
Robert Wagt	1962		*Vogue Sposa, Marie Claire, Bis, Playboy, Vanity, GAP, Donna*; Pierre Cardin, Jean-Paul Gaultier
Thierry Perez	1964		French and Italian *Glamour, Vogue, Elle, Vogue Hommes*; Versace's ad campaigns and books; Alaïa, Versace, Dolce & Gabbana's catalogues, Jean-Paul Gaultier, Jeremy Scott, Madonna/*Sex* collateral

Review Questions

1. Which designer led the concept of documenting their fashions by illustrations, much like today's "look book"?

2. What harsh realities does the illustrator's hand correct that original photography does not?

3. Name three art movements affecting fashion illustration's style.

4. Name three traditional media used by illustrators of the twentieth century.

5. Name the Surrealist artist and the Surrealist fashion designer who collaborated on artistic projects.

2

New Tools for the New Millennium:
Fashion Images That Relate to
the Technology of the Times

What You Will Learn in Chapter 2

This chapter chronicles the late-twentieth century's embrace of computer technology and explores several artistic leaders of the movement. It also reviews the work of those whose illustration styles can be generated and manipulated by Photoshop or Illustrator, whether software actually entered their creative processes.

Some prominent illustrators crossed over from hand-drawing to using computer software like Photoshop or Illustrator, while others have always used the computer. Present-day illustrators' exposure and attraction to American and Japanese comic books, cartoons, and television and their assimilation into computer technology as they honed their art skills have all directly influenced the growing importance of the pen *and* the pen tool.

Introduction

Whether used as a stepping-stone in the creative process or as a way to promote the three-dimensional end product, technology has definitely aided in allowing concepts to reach consumers faster. The pencil or pen initiates the creative process of fashion illustration and allows the illustrator to communicate in this visual language. Watercolor, gouache, pastels, and ink function as adjectives in this visual language. Today the new fashion language is "computereze"—Adobe Photoshop and Illustrator. It was once considered de rigueur for haute couture designers to speak French. Communicating in Italian, Chinese, or Spanish used to be a must for manufacturers. Now familiarity with computer software, a keyboard, screen, mouse, and pen tool is essential in jumpstarting the creative process.

Computer technology allows for change—immediate change—with just a click. Artwork can be recolored, resized, reshaped, and/or distorted. As discussed in Chapter 1, photography captured the reality of the live model, with all the flaws, shocking many. The kinder hand of a fashion illustrator got rid of flaws such as excess pounds or wrinkles.

The twenty-first century has seen the proliferation of high-definition television (HDTV). The details of actors' pores, moles, or expression lines are not blurred out as they were by prior lower-definition television reception. Now the real reality show—part visual horror, according to some—exposes the once believed perception of televised perfection. Actors on camera now appear as they really look, especially in focused close-ups. Photoshop allows an artist to mask imperfection in a printed photograph when the camera lens is not as kind, just as fashion illustrators did by hand.

Advertising and Illustration

The digital arena has brought the graphic and fashion worlds together. Fashion illustration has indeed evolved, as evidenced by the use of stylized illustration and cartooning in advertising, including ads for Wheat Thins, travel, liquor, and TiVo and in ads for clothing and accessories from haute couture to street. Some ad campaigns use illustration as a way to stand out among countless slick photographs. Other campaigns combine the art of photography with illustration by using illustration as a background or canvas on which to superimpose traditional photographs of models showing off garments. These skills will be detailed step-by-step later in the text.

Fashion illustrations that incorporate new technology have transcended the norm of exclusively portraying haute couture, fine jewels, and designer accessories so often inaccessible to the mainstream public. Fashion illustrations now also present products for the mainstream consumer. Cosmetic companies that long relied on live beautiful models to sell their products now include stylish sketches to attract attention. Stila's advertising and Benefit's packaging receive as much attention for its fashion illustration branding as it does for its contents.

Despite, and perhaps because of Photoshop and Illustrator, fashion illustration has recaptured its prominence as an amazing medium in itself, just as the early twentieth century recognized the strength of it as art. Design professionals acknowledge the definition of fashion illustration's purpose with its assimilation of the new technology: to increase the speed, efficiency, and creativity of a designer in the design room and to aid in the image presentation of the clothing.

Technology and the Actual Building of Fashion

Fashion illustration enters the life of fashion first by making an intangible idea tangible by laying the building blocks and later by aiding the design presentation in promotional advertisements. As mentioned before, creativity, whether it's by way of a brush, pen tool, or mouse, is not optional. Steps in design development (technical flats, colorways, textile designs, design editing, embellishments, and so on) also benefit from technology.

Textile design—whether used as a strategic way to create interest in an illustration or whether it's integral to a design—benefits the most from Photoshop and Illustrator. Scanning an existing motif from any source, then modifying it to create unique colorways and textures saves costly artwork that would have been done by hand. It affords the ability to show countless variations to clients. In advertising, the saying is: "Show them three slogans, even if you know you have one great one." In the design world, when presenting a collection to decision-making personnel, showing a variety of options is ideal.

Seeing a T-shirt sample in various colorways with various scales of the graphic image emblazoned on it before it hits the sewing room is a sure way to cut costs . . . and see different creative possibilities. Designers are no longer limited by

the previous time constraints of redrawing and recoloring. Advertising art directors now have the luxury of reviewing fashion layouts and are able to request different scales of a drawing or changes in background color so they can insert more readable copy. Graphic designers who have fashion clients (magazine editorials, advertorials, and so on) share this ability to play with their images before creating a final product.

This ability to explore various design choices is also shared by Internet consumers. Many people turn to store Web sites as online shopping continues to gain popularity. Web sites such as nikeid.com, vans.com, polo.com, and target.com allow consumers to experience some of the power the computer affords to clothing designers. Just as designers can show many variations of a great idea, consumers visiting the Nike Web site can customize the color design of their sneakers. On certain clothing store Web sites, consumers can change the color of a garment on the model so they can decide which color best suits their personal tastes.

Technology and the Presentation of Fashion

There are some designers who use the computer as their primary source of creating artwork. With every click, something new comes into view. Other designers use traditional media; they use the computer primarily because of convenience.

The G5 as Shared Canvas

Illustrator Sara Singh has always painted and drawn by hand but began using Photoshop to reformat scanned originals so she could e-mail her work to clients rather

Figure 2.1   Illustration by Sara Singh.

than deal with the inconvenience of packing and shipping originals. It is important for her to keep the hand-crafted feel of the work, which is why she paints and draws by hand. The computer comes into play so she can change colors, dye areas, and cut and paste images together. The computer does bring a new sense of color to the screen, so Sara works in black-and-white washes, then scans into the computer to add color digitally. The beauty of this combination speaks for itself (see Figure 2.1). Her work for LeSport-sac propelled an overwhelming interest in the relaunched design line and set a new precedent for illustrated products and models.

Jeffrey Fulvimari's (b. 1963) inter-esting blotchy pen-and-ink cartoon-like images, enhanced by Photoshop and Illustrator, are fluid and curvi-linear. The purity and innocence of the human hand is never overshad-

Figure 2.2   Illustration by Jason Brooks.

owed by technology. Madonna chose him as the illustrator for her first children's book, *The English Roses* (Callaway Editions, Incorporated). His style, desired by many book and music publishers and fashion clients, is also merchandised on calendars, notepads, and related accessories for the buying public.

Jason Brooks (b. 1969), a leader in combining traditional fine art media with Photoshop and Illustrator, loved drawing and painting from an early age. His treks through Europe and Central America inspired him to research the people, their personalities, their clothing, and their attitudes toward their surroundings. Brooks's early inspirations were as widespread as his travels, with the artists Michelangelo, David Hockney, Egon Schiele, and Pablo Picasso providing artistic influence. His love of 1960s and 1970s American comic books is evident in his clean, slick style. Brooks's work has been seen in all the top fashion magazines in Europe and the United States, including *Vogue, Elle, Visionaire,* and *The Face,* with corporate clients including Nike and Coca Cola (see Figure 2.2).

Figure 2.3 Illustration by Izak Zenou.

Izak Zenou's painterly quality, with India inks and watercolors as his favored mediums, creates subtle yet intense, whimsical characters rich in textures. He translates his influences of art, culture, fashion, and beauty to the individual character and beauty of women (see Figure 2.3). Clothing textures come to life with the use of his traditional media. Izak has created corporate identities as well as ad campaigns for Henri Bendel and Printemps Japan. Celine commissioned him to create a series of scarves; he thus created "wearable" art in the most stylish sense. Although the artwork may be done in traditional methods, the print reproduction utilizes computer technology to the fullest.

Monsieur Z (b. 1968) is a true artist as well. He draws by hand, but he does use software to manipulate his work. Monsieur Z's personal interest is to find the graphic line based in a modern composition, with the computer allowing the clear shapes and colors to come together in aesthetic perfection. The hair, bodies, and interiors all create a dreamlike world where fashion and lifestyle are one. This symbiosis has sparked the interest of both fashion and interior design businesses, where his work is commissioned for advertising campaigns as well as editorial content in numerous publications including *Wallpaper** and *Vogue*. Monsieur Z's 2-D life never looked better (see Figure 2.4).

Anja Kroencke (b. 1968) is a fashion illustrator whose skills have gone from promoting fashion, cosmetics, and lifestyle to designing Pucci mannequins. Her unique side-view silhouettes of hip hair, clothing, and body attitudes placed against stylish backgrounds bring to her clients that include Ann Taylor, Estée Lauder, Bergdorf Goodman, and Motorola. Her graphic design background and keen eye as an agency art director is evident in the major companies that want to commission her vision for their campaigns. Kroencke's work has appeared in *Allure*; British, French, and German *Vogue*; *Travel & Leisure*; *Wallpaper**; and *W* (see Figure 2.5).

Robert Clyde Anderson (b. 1950s) has a sophisticated cartoonlike approach in his portrayal of stylish people in realistic yet angular forms. He usually depicts them in stylish interiors. Each person he illustrates possesses specific characteristics and varies in age and physicality, with hipness being the common denominator.

Illustrators Go 3-D with Mannequins

Ralph Pucci, president of Pucci International (a fine furniture and mannequin design firm), has made an impact in the display world by revolutionizing the mobility of the human form with his mannequins. He created body forms that took on

Figure 2.4   Illustration by Monsieur Z.

Figure 2.5   Illustration by Anja Kroencke.

activities that include running, swimming, and diving. These generated attention, interest, and most important, the sale of clothing. Pucci's next inventive step was to bring in top fashion illustrators to design mannequins. What could be a better collaboration than having illustrators—who render apparel on idealized 2-D figures that help to generate image and sales—join Pucci's forces? Inspired by the creative minds of Ruben Toledo, Anja Kroencke, Jeffrey Fulvimari, and Robert Clyde Anderson, Pucci has created a new breed of mannequins that have adopted the stylized look and detail representative of these creative minds.

Some artists do not work with computer software and work exclusively with traditional media; however, their styles would translate themselves effectively with the clean, crisp lines of Illustrator or the shadings of Photoshop. One such artist is Jordi Labanda (b. 1968), who works in gouache on paper. His work has appeared in *W, American Vogue, Visionaire,* and *Wallpaper** and has been used by corporate clients that include American Express, Knoll International, Zara, and JVC. His scene-setting and detailed characterizations of fashionable people provoke social commentaries and promote the client brand in the freshest way.

The Gen X and Y Visual Style
The Gen X consumers, born between the years of 1965 and 1979, prefer a cohesive and stylish lifestyle—from clothes to travel to furnishings to food. The outgrown grunge of their early years is gone. This attitude is also shared by the Baby Boom generation born between the years of 1946 and 1964.

The Gen Y consumers, also known as the Net Generation, react to fashion and advertising in a different way. The Gen Y style is a little more organic and natural, with free-flowing linear motifs, graffiti-like patterns, and a more guerrilla-marketing style of presentation, similar to street tagging. The cartoon image is popular, but not in the stylized tradition of beauty evident in the cartoonlike images used in years past.

Art director and graphic illustrator Graham Rounthwaite (b. 1968) has a multitude of advertising and fashion clients, including Fabergé, recording companies, MTV Europe, and publishing firms. He has done editorial work for fashion magazines, including *Details* and *Elle,* and his creative eye for detail led to his current commission of revitalizing and promoting Levi Strauss & Co.'s high-end Silver Tab clothing line to the Gen Y generation. His colorful multicultural, urban characters (100 in the series) successfully attract the target market so necessary to Levi's future success. His process of creating everything from the rough sketch to the final artwork for client approval by hand, then scanning and redrawing in Photoshop, clearly shows the relationship between traditional hand-drawing and computer software (see Figure 2.6).

Kristian Russell (b. 1968), an artist heavily involved in the music scene, has made quite an impact in the fashion world. His sought-after work has appeared in *Arena, Dazed & Confused, Jane, Mademoiselle, Nylon,* and *Spin.* Forward-leaning companies like Diesel also commission his unique perspective on image and style. Although Russell's work appears as the stylish epitome

Figure 2.6   Illustration by Graham Rounthwaite.

of computer-generated images, all of it starts with his pencil sketches of faces, bodies, and clothing. Clothing takes the compositional lead, with its inherent shape and angularity directing the body's pose and angle. He uses pen and ink to clarify the images, then scans and vectorizes so he can finalize in Illustrator. Russell is then able to add other components of his signature style, including strong colors, cityscapes, and flowers. To this illustrator, every decision on background and perspective stems from the clothing item for the particular fashion story. Artists can change the whole

Figure 2.7   Illustration by Kristian Russell.

perception of reality on the computer (see Figure 2.7).

Thierry Perez (b. 1964) is an illustrator and photographer who excels in portraying the pure exquisiteness of the body, as witnessed by his commissions with Azzedine Aläia and the late Gianni Versace—two designers who reveled in the sculptural attributes of the human form (see Chapter 1). His interests in incorporating photography with illustration, in both collage and decomposition, have led to a whole new world of appreciating reality with a twist. Thierry closed the twentieth century as one of the gatekeepers of traditional fashion illustration and

opened the twenty-first with a new compositional mix. He didn't consider computers to be otherworldly but keys to experimentation (see Figure 2.8).

American and Japanese Comics

The comic book world is realizing the importance of using fashion to attract consumers. Likewise, the fashion world realizes the importance of reaching consumers in more nontraditional venues. New York designer Anna Sui teamed up with illustrator Billy Tucci, creator of the character "Shi," to blend the best of both worlds. Tucci's stylish cartoon girl wore Anna Sui's runway collection on her adventures, which proved to be a great way to

Figure 2.8 Illustration by Thierry Perez.

increase the designer's exposure and both retain regular and draw new readers of the comic book series, half of whom are young women.

Manga

Manga are Japanese comic books with Manga-style characters. Due to the world's growing interest and obsession with anime, or Japanese animation, manga has expanded to movies and video games. Today's

artists who work in this manga style were raised watching television cartoons, including reruns of cartoons, from the 1930s to the 1960s.

Many people believe that almost everything about a person's character is gathered from their facial features. We can make guesses about a person's age, gender, race, and attitude, from his or her face. Thus, the American animation artists tend to use facial expressions to

Figure 2.9   Illustration by Ed Tsuwaki.

same features: extremely large eyes, very small noses and mouths, and sharp chins. This manga style has become popular in stylized ads and iconic advertising images. Michael Economy's (b. 1960) cartoons with large eyes, japanimation, and heavy outlines are clean and stylish. His work for Anna Sui—he created the first Anna Sui Dolly Head Icon— and Screaming Mimi's exemplifies this look.

Ed Tsuwaki (b. 1966) has honed his style by experimenting with Illustrator. His work for *Vogue* Nippon and Anna Sui bears his signature mark: alienlike beauties with slender, elongated necks and expressive eyes. It is science-fictional surrealism to a tee (see Figure 2.9).

Anna Sui has collaborated with some of the leading artists of the day. Her Web site, www.annasui.com, provides a glossary of illustrators she has worked with, including Tsuwaki, Michael Economy, Jeffrey Fulvimari, Karen Kilimnik, Michelle Kim, Sara Schwartz, and others.

Adobe Photoshop and Illustrator in the Art Box
Both fashion illustration and fashion designing involve creativity. An illustrator creates an interesting way to present a garment, while a fashion designer uses illustration to create the actual garment. Both benefit from incorporating various computer programs in their "art box."

Vector-based Programs
The desire to create the cleanest linear illustrations in an animation-cel style similar to those of Michael Economy, Jason Brooks, Monsieur Z, or Shag is by working on the

differentiate good characters from bad ones. The characters have childishly innocent or fierce expressions, all caught in various circumstances and look relatively real. Japanese manga artists have a different approach from American artists. Almost all the faces of manga characters have nearly the

computer with object-oriented vectors, called simply vectors. PostScript, developed by Adobe, is the vector language for drawing lines, curves, and geometric shapes. In Illustrator, artists scan in hand-drawn work and convert it into vector drawings that can then be filled with vivid colors and textures. An overview of how to use Illustrator and how to master the Pen Tool will be covered later in the text.

Raster-based Programs

Bitmap, or raster-based, programs are best suited to realistic, 3-D images such as photographs that have shadows and light. A bitmapped image is made up of tiny square dots called pixels. Photoshop is the raster-based program that many of the illustrators discussed in this chapter use to manipulate bitmapped images. An overview of how to operate Photoshop and how to learn to create and enhance flats, illustrations, and textile patterns will be covered later in the text.

Even More Technology

Having exposure to technology isn't limited to what is seen on a computer screen. The future promises to bring apparel and accessories equipped with wearable computers that have the ability to direct other technology. According to Alex Lightman, author of *Brave New Unwired World* and the CEO/founder of Charmed Technology, this "smart" technology will be able to enter the fashion world with the technology already available. For example, clothing will have nodules throughout specific areas whereby the wearers can connect their iPods and feel vibrations sent from currents through these nodules and massage them to the beat of the music. The phrase "Feel the music" will definitely have more tangible validity.

Fiber optics woven into textiles will allow customers to transmit video clips or still shots of what they want to wear. Fashion designers will not only build the base garment but also have a hand in creating and providing the visual image to be "worn" on that garment. Remember how Jason Brooks was inspired by David Hockney and Picasso? Wearing a T-shirt emblazoned with their image is one thing, but creating one-of-a-kind personalized imprints is now possible. Artists can use Photoshop and Illustrator to create garments and to create the composition of images that will print on those garments (Alex Lightman, "Wearable Computers Make for Funky Fashion," Special Section in *The Road Ahead*).

SIGGRAPH (Special Interest Group Graphics) holds yearly conventions to share the latest developments in graphics technology. Once the domain of photographers and graphic designers, this convention is now attended by fashion illustrators and designers. SIGGRAPH communicates the latest in wearable technology with yearly cyberfashion shows. "Techno-fashion" is no longer an empty journalistic adjective used to denote something that is far in the future. It is already here.

An Overview of Twenty-first-century Fashion Illustrators

Table 2.1 chronicles some of the leading artists of the twenty-first century who inspire users of the present and future technology. Their creations direct the image and clothing design aesthetics of the future.

Table 2.1

Illustrator	DOB	Website/View	Publishing Client/Designer (overview)
Robert Clyde Anderson	1950s	www.art-dept.com	*Vogue, Wallpaper*, Details, Fortune, New York* magazine, *Travel & Leisure*; Bergdorf Goodman, Barneys New York, The Gap, IBM, J.Crew, Neiman Marcus, TBS, Kenneth Cole, Absolut, mannequin line for Pucci
Amy Davis	1960	www.amydavis.com	*Teen People, Seventeen, Composite*, "Style Fiends" in *Paper*; Yohji Yamamoto, Thierry Mugler, Calvin Klein, Pucci, Nine West, Reebok, Jean-Charles Castelbajac
Michael Economy	1960	www.annasui.com	Screaming Mimi's, Anna Sui
François Berthoud	1961		Art director of *Vogue Sposa, Vanity, Vogue Bambini*, Italian *Vogue, Visionnaire*; Mondi, Jean Paul Gaultier, Missoni, Moschino, Krizia, Lacroix, Romeo Gigli, Prada, Vivienne Westwood
Tobie Giddio	1963	www.tobiegiddio.com	*Glamour, Harper's Bazaar, Interview, Marie Claire, Mode*, the *New Yorker, Vogue*; Bergdorf Goodman, Barneys New York, Ann Taylor, Armani, Norma Kamali, Calvin Klein, Tocca, Revlon, Max Factor, mannequin line for Pucci
Piet Paris	1962	www.unit.nl	*Cosmopolitan, Elle, Marie Claire*; Estée Lauder, MAC Cosmetics, Oilily, Olivier Theyskens, Studio Edelkoort
Josh Agle A.K.A. "Shag"	1962	www.shag.com	Author of *Shag: The Art of Josh Agle*; also a painter and artist
Jeffrey Fulvimari	1963	www.jeffreyfulvimari.com	*Vogue, Allure, Glamour, Harper's Bazaar, Interview, New York Times, Elle, Seventeen, Travel & Leisure, Visionaire, The English Roses* (Madonna); Louis Vuitton, Anna Sui, Helmut Lang, Neiman Marcus, Barneys New York, The Gap, Anna Sui, Hush Puppies, mannequin line for Pucci; authored *It's OK* and *Everything Is Gonna Be Alright*; calendars
Thierry Perez	1964	www.thierryperez.com	French and Italian *Glamour, Vogue, Elle, Vogue Hommes*; Versace's ad campaigns and books; Alaïa, Versace, Dolce&Gabbana's catalogs, Jean Paul Gaultier, Jeremy Scott, Madonna/*Sex* collateral
Maurice Vellekoop	1964		*Vogue*; collaborated with Cindy Crawford on *Basic Face*, authored *Vellevision, A Men's Room Reader, Maurice Vellekoop's ABC Book*
Ed. Tsuwaki	1966	www.art-dept.com	*Vogue Nippon, Wallpaper**; Anna Sui, Omega

Illustrator	DOB	Website/View	Publishing Client/Designer (overview)
Tanya Ling	–	www.tanyaling.com	*Elle, Nylon, Zoo, The Face, Harper's Bazaar,* British *Vogue, Vogue* Japan; Bis, Harrod's, Selfridges, Jil Sander, Diane von Furstenberg
Maxine Law	1967		*Flaunt, Jane, Esquire, Sky*; Paul Smith
Demetrios Psillos	1967		*Vogue, Wallpaper*, Harper's Bazaar,* the *New Yorker, London Times* magazine; Missoni
Sara Singh	1967	www.sarasingh.com	*Vogue, Elle, Marie Claire*; LeSportsac, Shiseido, Donna Karan
Kareen Iliya	1967	www.art-dept.com	*Mademoiselle, Metropolitan Home,* the *New Yorker, Visionnaire, W, Harper's Bazaar*; Bergdorf Goodman, Barneys New York, Kenneth Cole shoes, Katherine Malandrino, Romeo Gigli, Armani
Hiroshi Tanabe	1967	www.larkworthy.com	*Arena,* American, French, Japanese *Vogue, Glamour, Jane, Harper's Bazaar, Marie Claire, New York,* the *New Yorker, Rolling Stone, Visionaire, Vibe, Wallpaper**; Ann Taylor, Barneys New York, HBO, Redken, Shiseido, doll designs for Anna Sui, mannequin designs for Pucci, authored *Hiroshi Tanabe: Blue Mode*
Anja Kroencke	1968	www.anjakroencke.com	*Allure,* British, French, German *Vogue, Madame Figaro, Marie Claire,* the *New Yorker, New York Times, Travel & Leisure, Wallpaper*, W, Femme*; art director at GGK, Stein Rogan & Partners, Estée Lauder, Ann Taylor, Isetan, Motorola, Le Printemps, Bergdorf Goodman; mannequin line for Pucci
Jordi Labanda	1968	www.art-dept.com	*New York Times, Vogue, Marie Claire, Seventeen, Wallpaper*, Allure, Elle, Visionaire, Tatler, W, CosmoGirl, Details*; Abercrombie & Fitch, Neiman Marcus, Zara, JVC, Knoll International, Geffen Records, Pepsi, American Express; authored *Hey Day*
Monsieur Z (Richard Zielenkiewicz)	1968	www.unit.nl www.leouergue.com www.jeunesse/monsieur_Z	*Wallpaper*, Vogue, Man, Casa Brutus*; Evian, Ferragamo, Amstel Light
Kristian Russell	1968	www.art-dept.com	*Arena, Frank, Dazed & Confused, Spin*; Coca-Cola, Diesel, Saatchi & Saatchi, Time Warner
Kime Buzzelli	1969		*Bust, Paper*; owner of L.A.'s ShowPony clothing store; custom T-shirts, art prints
Jason Brooks	1969	www.jason-brooks.com	*Detour, InStyle, Elle, The Face,* the *Guardian,* the *Independent; Visionaire,* British and American *Vogue*; Katharine Hamnett, British Airways, Fabergé, Mercedes-Benz, Virgin Atlantic, Finlandia, L'Oreal, Olgivy & Mather

Illustrator	DOB	Website/View	Publishing Client/Designer (overview)
Julie Verhoeven	1969		*The Face, London Sunday Times, Nova, Independent, Dazed and Confused*; John Galliano, design consultant for Jasper Conran, Martine Sitbon, Richard Tyler, Guy Laroche, Jean Colonna, Clements Ribeiro, Byblos, designer for Gibo, Marc Jacobs/ Louis Vuitton, music graphics; authored *Fat-Bottomed Girls*
Graham Rounthwaite	1968		Art director of *Trace* magazine; *The Face, Details, Elle, Raygun*, the *Guardian*, the *Telegraph*; Levi's Silver Tab ad campaign, Fabergé, Top Shop, RCA, EMI, Virgin, HarperCollins, MTV Europe, National Aids Awareness Campaign
Rebecca Antoniou	1971	www.art-dept.com	
Liselotte Watkins	1971	www.art-dept.com www.liselottewatkins.com www.agentform.com	*Vogue, Elle, GQ, Marie Claire, Self, Travel & Leisure, Wallpaper**; Barneys New York, Anna Sui, Bergdorf Goodman, Estée Lauder, MTV, Ogilvy & Mather, Sony, Target, Victoria's Secret, American Movie Classics; authored *Watkin's Heroine*
Stina Persson	1972	www.stinapersson.com	*Elle, Gourmet, Gotham, Hamptons*
Shiv	1973	www.bigactive.com	Nike
Nawel	1973	www.unit.nl	Guy Laroche, Hermès, Jalouse
Bee Murphy	—	www.larkworthy.com	*Allure, Flaunt, Marie Claire, Fast Company, Lucky, Vogue*, German *Cosmopolitan, In Style, Town & Country, Wall Street Journal*; Federated Department Stores
Tomer Hanuka	—	www.thanuka.com	*New York Times* magazine; BiPolar
Margarete Gockel	—	www.larkworthy.com	*Elle Decoration UK*; *Elle Quebec*, the *New York Times, Cosmopolitan*; Neiman Marcus, Toyota, VW, Sony, Hewlett Packard
Izak Zenou	—	info@trafficnyc.com	Celine, Printemps, Henri Bendel

Review Questions

1. What is the process that fashion illustrators use today? What do they draw by hand, and what happens after they scan their work in?

2. Name three illustrators whose styles are cartoonlike.

3. What is manga? How does it differ from American comic book illustration?

4. Name two illustrators who have worked on mannequin design.

5. What does SIGGRAPH stand for, and what does it do?

3

The Elements of Design Development

What You Will Learn in Chapter 3

This chapter reviews the basic elements, or building blocks, of design necessary to fully utilize the digital technology now available to the fashion industry. It provides an overview of the key elements involved in creating anything from a single fashion item to a complete collection. Understanding the who, what, when, where, and why of developing fashion designs further clarifies how the elements of silhouette, color, texture, and detail (SCTDs) are used. Knowing the principles of balance, emphasis, harmony, proportion, radiation, and repetition—combined with the guidelines for tweaking these—gives to artists an infinite number of design alternatives.

Introduction

It is important to remember that current technology is a tool that allows artists to explore silhouette, color, texture, and detail options. A computer does not design; a designer does. It is still a designer's ability to formulate a concept and draw an initial fashion sketch that drives the entire process, even when it includes technological assistance. Scanning an original sketch or illustration into the computer for manipulation just gets the ball rolling. If there is nothing to scan, the computer won't be much help at all.

A fashion designer's ability to create has been immeasurably enhanced thanks to software such as Photoshop and Illustrator. Countless design options that were once unthinkably time-consuming are now possible with a click of the mouse. Options for color variations (called colorways), silhouettes (adjusting to make objects longer, shorter, or narrower), textures (adjusting existing textures, adding new ones, and fabricating and printing all choices), details (creating or duplicating pockets or decorative stitching), and scale (scaling prints or other details from large to small) can be executed and viewed immediately. These endless possibilities raise the bar of efficiency and aesthetics, empowering designers to enter unrestricted levels of creativity.

Elements of Design: Silhouette, Color, Texture, and Details

The four key elements to every aspect of garment or accessory design are creating it, costing it, evaluating it on the runway for fashion publications, and answering the most basic question: whether it appeals to the consumer.

Silhouette, color, texture, and details are what set apart the interesting from the mundane. SCTDs make it possible to sell yet another T-shirt to a consumer who may already have dozens. The first step to understanding design development is to briefly define SCTDs.

Silhouette is the overall shape of the garment, defined by its outline or form. The description of a garment's silhouette is often a geometric shape such as circular, rectangular, and squared/boxy, although it can also be described as narrow or wide.

Color refers to the visible light waves perceived according to the hue spectrum. Colors have not only visual appeal but also visual weight.

Texture describes the actual fabrication of each design, including the tangible and visual weight as described by the hand or feel of the fabric.

Details include aspects of the design that add functional or decorative qualities, such as zippers, fringes, pockets, appliqués, and buttons.

The integrity of SCTDs is strongly evident when developing successful items, groups, or collections. SCTDs are also the reasons why certain garments work on some bodies while others do not. Stylists and wardrobe consultants use these evaluation points as well. Fashion professionals have an innate habit of evaluating garments worn by the general public, so much so that it has become a national pastime for people outside the fashion industry. This phenomenon is evidenced by the popularity of television shows, including the BBC's and TLC's *What Not to Wear* and Bravo's *Queer Eye for the Straight Guy* and *Queer Eye for the Straight Girl*, and their companion how-to books. These shows evaluate the appropriateness and attractiveness of garments that people wear. SCTDs are often the points of discussion and critique. It is important to remember that designers have no control over whether consumers have made appropriate choices. Their responsibility is the integral quality of the design, whatever the price point. Thankfully, however, with today's digital communication networks, consumers have more access to fashion information. Trend information from Paris to Peoria is but a mouse click away.

The Fashion Cycle and SCTDs
Throughout each decade of the twentieth century, the overall silhouette, color, texture, and details of clothing designs changed just enough to make them obsolete in the next decade, but interesting the decade after that. This continuous fashion cycle of disdain and desire propels the factor of clothing obsolescence, so necessary in the fashion business to fuel the constant array of new clothing and accessories designed and merchandised each season. Garments aren't replaced because they wear out (physical obsolescence), but rather because of diminished desire (emotional obsolescence). SCTDs play an important part in this visual turnover.

The acceptance or rejection of garments can generally be measured by decades. In other words, what looks appealing to the eye for a few seasons or even several years can look dated when it nears the ten-year mark. Saying that something is "so fifties" or "so eighties"

becomes part of the cultural vernacular, adjectives to describe interiors, music, hairstyles, and clothing. Each decade becomes a means of classification.

The Billion-Dollar Question: Is It a Classic? Fad? What's the Trend?
The question of knowing which garment or accessory will provoke the public's frenzied desire to buy (or steady desire to buy and replenish) is the key to success. This key is often a mystery, but tracking the reactions of the public is one way designers can predict the life of a garment. **Classic** refers to a style that remains popular for long periods of time, with subtle changes in the silhouette, color, texture, and details. **Fad** refers to a short-lived fashion that has a distinct identity and usually enjoys a surge of interest that later wanes. A **trend** refers to the path and direction a particular style takes during this peak of intense interest and popularity before eventually settling into obscurity or steady acceptance.

The twenty-first century opened with the thrift-store grunge look fad of the 1990s that included ripped plaid shirts and Doc Martens. The desire to wear 1990s fashion was not present early in the millennium because consumers could recall it too easily, thereby rendering fashion dated ("so nineties"). Some consumers may not have such a quick recall of 1980s fashions. Some people may be too young to remember the eighties. Instead of seeing *Flashdance* in the movie theater in 1983, they may have seen it on DVD or perhaps seen Jennifer Lopez's 2003 "Glad" music video homage to it. The workout wear, leg warmers, and off-the-shoulder necklines seemed fresh and interesting once again. Consumers needed about twenty years to find 1980s fashion interesting again; ten years was not enough. Fashion, indeed, is cyclical.

Creative directors, fashion stylists, and trend forecasters who are looking for "the next big thing" don't wait for stores to carry the next look. Their world exists on a faster calendar than that of the retail world. To effectively compose exciting photographs that inspire consumers to buy that next big thing, artists often fish for ideas by looking to the past perhaps sometimes well before the public is ready to wear styles inspired from that period. Often the finished product looks so curious that only fellow creative minds and extremely innovative consumers get it.

Other key players need to also live by a faster calendar than the retail world for operational reasons. Photographs for magazines may need to be coordinated and shot from four to twelve weeks ahead of the publication or on-sale date. The same often holds true for television. Styling for movies pushes the concept date back even further, often a year or more before the finished product is seen by the public. It is up to fashion forecasters to identify the images that people will want to watch, as well as other expressions of high and low pop culture. They break down the messages into tangible silhouette, color, texture, and details ideas for designers and merchandisers to appropriate—for a price.

Television as Fashion Archives of the Cycle and SCTDs

Reruns of syndicated television shows known for their style quo-tient give a history of mid- to late-twentieth-century design. Shows of iconic fashion stature, including *I Love Lucy* (1950s), *The Dick Van Dyke Show* (1960s), *The Mary Tyler Moore Show* (1970s), *Miami Vice* (1980s), and *Sex and the City* (1990s/2000s) function as moving visuals of creative inspiration just as costume or fashion history books. The clothes of each decade are preserved in their pristine forms, becoming more familiar to present-day audiences. SCTDs of yesteryear assimilate into present-day SCTDs, with improved fabrics allowing for sharper silhouettes, truer colors, more comfortable textures, and better quality details.

Lucille Ball's Lucy Ricardo character in *I Love Lucy* (1951–1960) changed the impression of how a housewife dressed during the 1950s, giving stylish attention to detail from head to toe (see Figure 3.1). The limitations of black-and-white television did not hamper translating the amazing silhouettes, colors (seen in contrast), textures, and details.

Mary Tyler Moore as Laura Petrie in the *The Dick Van Dyke Show* (1961–1966) left behind the lady-like dresses of the 1950s and introduced sleeveless shells, turtlenecks, ballet flats, and sleek capri pants, thought to be revolutionary for housewives at the time. The feminine body silhouette was the most closely seen and well-defined on mainstream television thus far. Again, the black-and-white televised format highlighted the clean lines of Laura's wardrobe. Her physical similarity to Jacqueline Kennedy, as well as her overall fashion choices, were also of added interest to the American public who

Figure 3.1   Lucille Ball's character in *I Love Lucy* revolutionized the way housewives dressed during the 1950s.

Figure 3.2   On *The Dick Van Dyke Show,* Mary Tyler Moore was a trendsetter for the American public, with her fashion choices of sleek capri pants, turtlenecks, and ballet flats.

emulated the stylish First Lady (see Figure 3.2).

Mary Tyler Moore retained her title as fashion plate of the 1960s in the 1970s as Mary Richards in The *Mary Tyler Moore Show* (1970–1977). Her fashion choices were feminine yet professional, with A-line skirts, shirtdresses, and knit separates emulated by the newly emerging group of career women.

Figure 3.3   In the 1970s, Mary Tyler Moore kept her title as "fashion plate of the 1960s" and wore feminine, professional clothing, with A-line skirts, shirtdresses, and knit separates emulated by the women entering the workforce. This is an interesting contrast to her friend Rhoda.

These looks were an interesting contrast to her friend Rhoda Morgenstern (Valerie Harper), who embodied the bohemian artist look with her fringed ponchos, head scarves, boots, and bell-bottoms, all identifiable with SCTDs of the 1970s as well (see Figure 3.3).

Miami Vice (1984–1989) made it acceptable for men and women to wear vivid colors and textures in the 1980s. Detectives James "Sonny" Crocket and Ricardo Tubbs, played by Don Johnson and Philip Michael Thomas, had

Figure 3.4   Don Johnson and Philip Michael Thomas, stars from *Miami Vice,* made it acceptable for men and women to wear vivid colors and textures in the 1980s.

wardrobes that were anything but plain. The extreme pastel color palette, so new to menswear at the time, owed its popularity to Miami's architecture and ocean hues. The strong jewel and metallic tones of the women's costumes represented the flashy, nouveau-riche quality of the time. Naturally wrinkled linen and rich silk textures were the antitheses of the man-made polyester of the 1970s (see Figure 3.4). The movie version, currently in preproduction and slated for release in 2006, will later reintroduce the looks for old and new fans to appreciate.

Sex and the City (1998–2004), starring Sarah Jessica Parker and her three distinctly different fashion-able costars, closed the twentieth century and opened the twenty-first by paying tribute to haute couture and hot New York street style so eclectic in look and price point that women began coordinating $500 shoes with $20 nameplate neck-laces and $2 thrift-store scarves wrapped around $800 bags. The cable series was led by costume designer and wardrobe wonder Patricia Field's fresh eye (see Figure 3.5). Appreciation of vintage pieces as a viable commodity not only for inspiration but also for actual inclusion in wardrobes was fully achieved with *Sex and the City*. SCTDs of several decades were introduced by each character, including 1980s brights, 1970s textures, 1940s silhouettes, and 1950s details.

These five television shows are but an overview of strong fashion mes-sages communicated through tele-vision. Fashion standards set by other shows, such as the 1960s slick Euro style of *The Avengers* (1961–1966) or the youth culture of *Mod Squad* (1968–1973), define many looks explored by designers today. Other shows that have tar-geted audiences with fashion mes-sages include *Happy Days* (1974–1984), which sparked renewed interest in 1950s culture; *The Sonny and Cher Comedy Hour* (1971–1974), which showcased the artistry of Bob Mackie; *Charlie's Angels* (1976–1981), which showed 1980s fashion; *Dynasty* (1981–1989), which showed over-the-top fashions; *Murphy Brown* (1988–1998), which showed the professional look of the 1990s; and *Friends* (1994–2004), which showed the casual look of the late 1990s and new millennium.

Figure 3.5   Sarah Jessica Parker's look combines haute couture and hot street style.

Identifying the Elements of Design: Silhouette, Color, Texture, and Details (SCTDs)

Since a silhouette can be classified as the general overall outline of the entire body, described as a shadow cast of the entire figure from head to toe, it applies not only to clothing but also to hairstyles and shoe shapes. The silhouette alone can update the familiar aesthetic level of desire or create a whole new one. A men's or women's blazer may be a classic, but nuances in the shape of the waist, shoulder lines, and length are areas where designers can create interest and make a classic stand out (see Figure 3.6).

Perhaps of all the four elements, silhouette most identifies the look of a decade, with its evolution dictating the direction of each season. It also defines the true shape of the human body with relation to the shape of the clothing adorning it. Silhouette definitely relates to the fabrications (texture) available at the time. What may be considered formfitting in one decade may seem much less clingy in the next. Since silhouettes are often referred to as an overall geometric shape, marketing an A-line (think triangular) or a long and lean look (think rectangular) is also dependent on fabrication. Details can further give the impression of a long, lean rectangle by placing rows of buttons or banding vertically.

The power of color can take an average design and make it marketable. Phrases that include "brown is the new black," "think pink," and Diana Vreeland's declaration that "pink is the navy blue of India" all refer to the act of focusing on color in a new way. The marketing of color is as cleverly planned as garment designs. Gray becomes anthracite or gunmetal, brown becomes bark, and red becomes ruby. This strategy crosses over to interior design and cosmetic markets as well. Urban Decay, a trend-forward makeup line, stood out in the marketplace for using names such as gash (evoking red blood). This imagery clearly identified Urban Decay's target market as Gen X and Y and not so much Baby Boomer, who might find ruby a more palatable nail polish choice.

Many designs are not overtly extreme; what makes them interesting is purely the color quality they use, be it classic or unique. A red

Figure 3.6   This basic black blazer with sharp shoulders creates a strong silhouette.

Figure 3.7a and 3.7b   Compare the colors, silhouettes, and textures of these two skirt suits from Celine's fall 2004 Ready to Wear collection.

suit may be a red suit, but with the right mix of silhouette, texture, and details, the color stands out. Red becomes cherry, a character of the design (see Figure 3.7a and 3.7b). If the suit were rendered in a neutral color, perhaps the hanger appeal would not be as strong. The computer now makes available the Pantone color palette and pattern libraries for experimentation. How does it look in gray, navy, black, or blue? The answer is immediately available with just a click of the mouse.

The texture of a garment is both visible and tactile. The quality of the surface fabrication, whether soft or hard, rough or smooth, or hairlike or slick, can affect the overall silhouette. Texture can add visual weight (bulk) or suggest slim, curved lines that hug the body. It also affects color translation, with a wet-looking red appearing much different from red velvet. Visible and tactile qualities can suggest seasons, events, or provide the element of surprise depending on the surface that is chosen. Texture lends itself to working with or against itself. Strong contrast in textures alone can create a design message. Leather may be dull or shiny and mixed with fur (see Figure 3.8), fuzzy angora may be mixed with vinyl, lace may be overlaid on tweed, and fine mesh may be mixed with tattoo artistry that disappears onto the skin so only close inspection can reveal the tattoo's impermanence.

Details are the spices of design. They have the function of affixing garments to the body (buttons, bows, lacing, and zippers) but also

add an interesting aesthetic to a fashion basic. Often details are the strongest identification point of a group. As the designers create related pieces to their initial core concept, the dominant detail is used in other pieces. The silhouette, color palette, and textures chosen for each blouse, top, skirt, or pants will reference this dominant detail.

Fringes, appliqués, snaps, braids, and embroidery can be used either in moderation or excess, depending on the desires of the designer and the expectations of the target consumer. Details often become synonymous with a particular event or ethnic origin, as seen in the highly ornamented bolero jacket (see Figure 3.9) synonymous with Spanish culture. Intricate braiding

Figure 3.8 A black leather jacket mixed with fur by Balenciaga.

Figure 3.9 An ornamented, denim bolero jacket by Jean-Paul Gaultier.

Figure 3.10a   Classic black blazer with white chalk pinstripe.

detail can be used on the hem of capri pants, the panel of a skirt, or the lapel of a blazer.

Utilizing SCTD Components to Develop Fresh Design Ideas

The recipe for extracting countless ideas for developing items (stand-alone fashion garments or accessories), groups (garments related in theme of SCTDs), or an entire collection (groups of garments defined by a season) is illustrated by using the template of the classic black pinstripe jacket (see Figure 3.10a). It is shown as an item for womenswear, but the parallel steps can be executed for menswear as well. Experimenting with silhouette, color, texture, and details can multiply the possibilities of coordinating pieces, such as pants, skirts, vests, and shirts, thus creating a group.

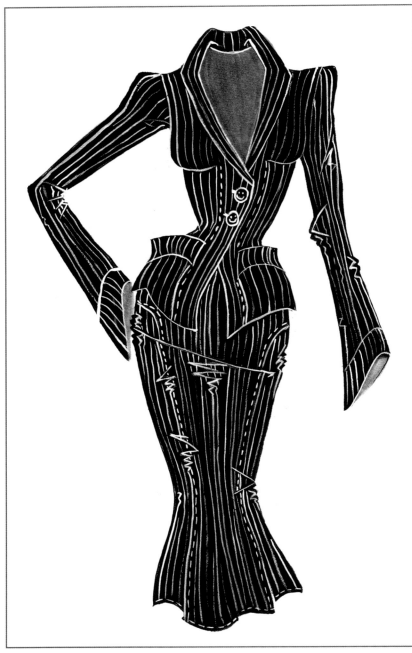

Figure 3.10b   Silhouette change: same classic blazer with sharper shoulder line
and nipped-in waist.

The Classic Pinstripe Jacket
The classic black blazer with classic
white chalk pinstripes is rendered
with the traditional tailoring components.

Sharply raising the shoulder line of
the blazer, as well as highly defining
the waistline, can change the silhouette dramatically, creating a
fashion-forward garment (see
Figure 3.10b).

Figure 3.10c Color change: classic black blazer now brown and pink.

The color of the blazer can be changed from classic black with white chalk stripes to brown with pink chalk stripes, creating interest with color (see Figure 3.10c).

The classic black pinstripe blazer can be rendered in velvet fabric to give a plushy, blurred effect to the classic stripe, adding a new visual and textural dimension (see Figure 3.10d).

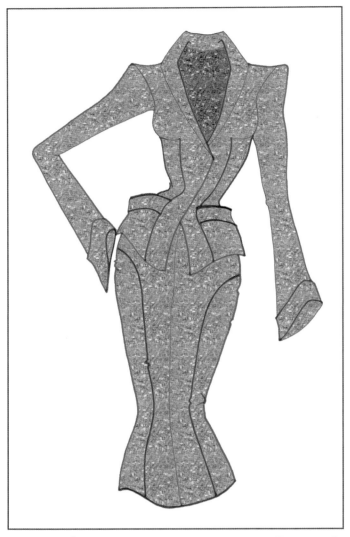

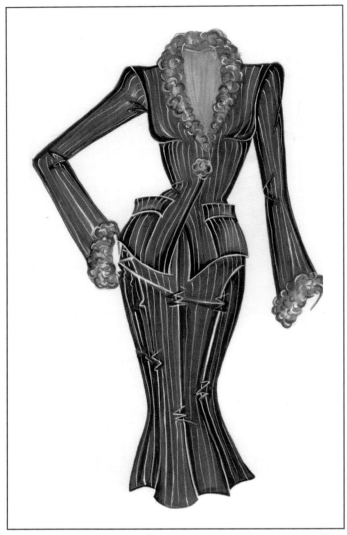

Figure 3.10d   Texture change: classic blazer with a different visual and textural dimension.

Figure 3.10e   Details change: classic blazer with decorative detail added.

A new garment can be created from a classic by simply changing the scale of the details. Enlarging and clustering the traditional buttons and buttonholes in twos or adding elements for decorative detail rather than functional necessity is attractive to the eye (see Figure 3.10e).

The Principles of Design: Balance, Emphasis, Harmony, Proportion, Radiation, Repetition, and Unity
Balance refers to a garment's visual weight. A sense of stability is created when the visual weights are equally distributed on both sides of a garment. The two types of balance are formal and informal. Formal balance, also known as symmetrical balance, occurs when one side of a design mirrors the other side, hence the predictable stability (see Figure 3.11).

Informal balance, also known as asymmetrical balance, exists when objects on either side differ, yet maintain a balance of visual weight and impact (see Figures 3.12 and 3.13).

Emphasis denotes the focal point or center of interest in a garment. It can be used as a means to strengthen the features of silhouette,

Figure 3.11 Ruffed jacket and low-rider pinstripe bell pants with symmetrical balance.

color, texture, or detail. One strong feature, or dominant detail, can accentuate not only the design but also the wearer's figure (see Figure 3.11). Drawing attention to one area

Figure 3.12   Green ruffle-burst skirt with purple asymmetrical top.

Figure 3.13   This pagoda-sleeve jacket, mesh top, and pouf skirt create an informal balance.

can deemphasize another weak area, taking unwanted focus away.

Harmony exists when the function, structure, and decorative details of a design all work together. This does not mean that uniformity is the rule. The cohesion of opposite elements within a garment or outfit, such as contrasting fabrications or varying scales of prints, can energize the total design (see Figure 3.14).

Proportion is the pleasing interrelationship of all aspects of a design. While each aspect of a design should individually hold its own, the effectiveness of a design is in the power of the whole design (see

Figure 3.11 through Figure 3.14). Scale is an aspect of proportion. Fabric textures and print patterns can be enlarged or diminished while ensuring that the proportion of silhouette and details relates to the color and fabric choices, all with the aid of the computer (see chapter 13).

Radiation is the outward energy disseminating from a central point. The source of energy can come from a decorative detail in construction (see Figure 3.12) or from a cinched waist that comes out to a full petticoat skirt silhouette (see Figure 3.13). Likewise, something as simple as an appliqué with a sunburst design can topically create a source of radiation on an otherwise overlooked portion of the garment, creating a new fashion message for an otherwise classic item.

Repetition occurs when a line, color, texture, or detail is used more than once in the execution of a design concept. This can include pockets, buttons, or braiding or construction of pleats, clusters, or panel lines (see Figure 3.12). It may also include repeating portions of construction for purely decorative reasons, such as several collars layered over one another or multiple bows or belts (see Figure 3.11).

Unity exists when every component of the elements and principles of design reviewed in this chapter upholds the central philosophy of the designer. The success of each designer's personal philosophy, be it "less is more" or "more is more," is contingent on the awareness that everything works together. Creativity emerges when the rules of design are respected, yet knowingly tweaked for the sake of experimentation.

Figure 3.14   The lace used in this skirt creates a nontraditional design.

Tools for Tweaking SCTDs and the Principles of Design

There is a formula to ensure every possible combination of the SCTDs and the principles of design are utilized. Traditional SCTDs + principles of design + one added ingredient: the ten creative commandments of fashion, also known as the tools for tweaking = endless options for creativity. The ten are as follows:

1. Exaggerate the elements of silhouette, color, texture, details, or any combination of these.
2. Exaggerate the principles of design: balance, emphasis, harmony, proportion, radiation, repetition, and unity.
3. Blur garment stereotypes; for example, use a garment that is traditionally for men and tailor it for women, as Coco Chanel did with her signature suit.
4. Break the rules of construction.
5. Use nontraditional or extreme fabric choices.
6. Play on the extreme social mores of modesty.
7. Mix time periods or eras in a single design.
8. Mix details synonymous with various ethnicities in a single design.
9. Inject popular culture into a mainstream design.
10. Combine the unexpected with the familiar.

The following breakdown of each creative tool for tweaking relies on the concept of hyperdesigning. Hyperdesigning eliminates the traditional boundaries or rules of what should be done in fashion, which is not to suggest a careless approach. Breaking rules merely for the sake of breaking them does not produce effective design. Thinking outside of the rules, however, frees the designer to use options never before explored.

Exaggerate the Silhouette, Color, Texture, Details, or Any Combination of These

Silhouette: Enlarging the shoulder line or extremely sloping it can transform an outfit. Exaggerating the leg line of pants from tapered to a thirty-inch-circumference bell will also completely change a design (see Figure 3.11).

Color: Using utilitarian signage colors such as bright orange or yellow rather than neutral colors can enliven a traditional item or accessory.

Texture: The tactile quality of fur (or faux fur) can be exaggerated by utilizing extremely long-haired fur rather than a short-haired, denser variety. Exaggerating the embossed quality of leather with oversize alligator scales or oversize zebra prints also transforms an outfit.

Details: Extremely exaggerated cuffs or collar sizes can transform the most basic or classic design. Buttons or other premade trimmings can be used in excess to make a bold statement.

Exaggerate the Principles of Design: Balance, Emphasis, Harmony, Proportion, Radiation, Repetition, or Unity

The power of every principle of design can be used to make a forceful statement. Aggressively repeating a ruffled layer (see Figure 3.11) or enlarging circular folds radiating from a knee-length skirt (see Figure 3.12) can create strong yet feminine lines.

Blur Garment Stereotypes

Using pinstripes for bra tops or lace print for men's shirt collars brings about unexpected designs. Feminine palettes of pinks, violets, and yellows with masculine palettes of blues, grays, and browns represent the traditional gender roles of color. Switch them for a fresh look (see Figure 3.14).

Break the Rules of Construction

Sewing and construction manuals of the past can be used as templates for what *not* to do to add life to a garment. Lining fabric with exposed construction details that are frayed and hanging used as the outer shell of a jacket, haphazard topstitching, asymmetric lengths, or even frayed and unfinished cuff hems push the envelope in a refreshing way.

Use Nontraditional or Extreme Fabric Choices

Experimenting with fabrics that seem too delicate or dense, too utilitarian or luxurious, or too masculine or feminine in ways that break tradition often result in some of the most dramatic designs (see Figure 3.14).

Play on the Extreme Social Mores of Modesty

Exposing parts of the body through different textures can be provocative. The mores of a particular culture played in opposition to others can create interesting looks on the runway and can be later toned down for broader consumption. These efforts can still open up a world of options once thought of as taboo (see Figure 3.13).

Mix Time Periods or Eras in a Single Design

Designers of the twentieth century were greatly influenced by the past but kept a singular time frame from

Figure 3.15 Greco-Roman goddess, combining early-twentieth-century looks with highlights from the past.

which to draw inspiration for collections. Today, mixing eras is what sets the standard of high fashion, as evidenced by combining early-twentieth-century looks with early Greco-Roman highlights (see Figure 3.15).

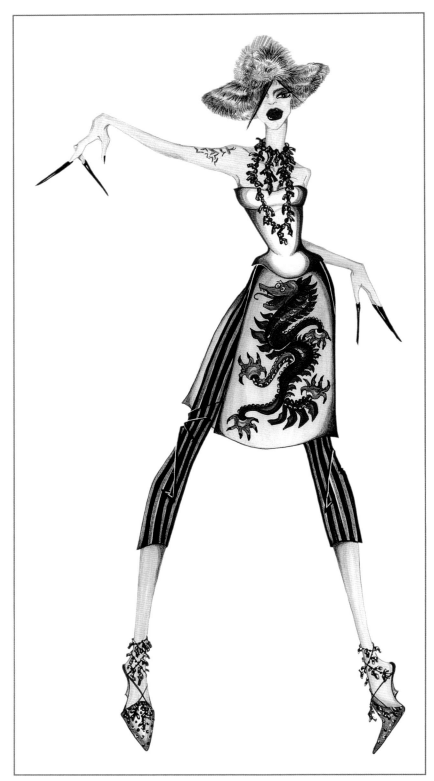

Figure 3.16 The global goddess, mixing different ethnic inspirations in one outfit.

country or ethnicity was always the sole focus. Today, mixing several ethnic inspirations on one garment or outfit defines great design (see Figure 3.16).

Inject Popular Culture into Mainstream Design

Mainstream SCTDs are wonderful canvasses that designers can add popular culture to, including cartoon messages or social commentary in any form (Figure 3.16).

Combine the Unexpected with the Familiar

Whatever is expected—do the unexpected. This general thought process is what maintains steady turnover in fashion. This process also encourages designers to keep taking risks for the sake of creativity. Due to current software, this experimentation can often be done at the computer screen.

The Masters of Tweaking

The geniuses of late-twentieth- and early-twenty-first-century hyper-designing include, but are not limited to, Jean Paul Gaultier, Viktor & Rolf, Rei Kawakubo of Comme des Garçon, Hussein Chalayan, John Galliano, and Alexander McQueen. They use the traditional SCTDs as a base for intensive experimentation with historical, cultural, and futuristic elements. Viktor & Rolf made their mark by playing on extreme repetition and exaggeration of silhouette and details. The end of the twentieth century, as with the end of every century, embraced the extreme. The following examples of several of these masters show the principles of extremes in action.

Jean Paul Gaultier's spring 1993 line included a switching of gender roles. He took a pair of men's

Mix Details Synonymous with Various Ethnicities in a Single Design

Designers of the twentieth century were also greatly influenced by other continents, and exploration went beyond Europe, but one

Figure 3.17 Jean-Paul Gaultier switched gender roles with his trouser skirt from 1993.

Figure 3.18 Jean-Paul Gaultier's summer 1998 white tailored suit for women shows a historical reference to the 1500s.

trousers, turned them upside down, and created a woman's skirt; he used classic tailoring details for decorative interest. It does not look like spring 1993; it looks stylish and thought-provoking (see Figure 3.17).

He also tailored a classic men's suit to create a woman's suit, once again switching gender roles while including the historical reference to the bum roll of the 1500s or panniers of the 1800s (see Figure 3.18).

Figure 3.19   Viktor & Rolf's 1999 ruff jacket breaks
the rules of construction, creating a
sophisticated, yet raw, focal point.

Figure 3.20   Comme des Garçon's dress from spring 1997 shows extreme proportions.

Viktor & Rolf's historic referencing, shown by their use of exaggerated collars with frayed edges, breaks the rules of construction, creating a sophisticated, yet raw, focal point (see Figure 3.19).

Rei Kawakubo for Comme des Garçon takes the simplicity of line but pushes the silhouette to extreme proportions, exaggerating not only the bustle-shaped posterior but also adding a backbone hunch as well (see Figure 3.20).

Hussein Chalayan uses extreme textures and silhouettes as the distinctive theme of his collections. He uses the clean, organic line of polished wood with exaggerated screw fixturing to lock in the very feminine silhouette of his bustier over a classic pencil skirt (see Figure 3.21).

Alexander McQueen stylishly breaks every rule in the book while still respecting the traditions of Savile Row by using the clean tailoring of a men's suit, but hyperfeminizing it with a midriff-baring pencil skirt and see-through plastic mold top, decorated with butterflies (see Figure 3.22).

None of these designers' work is dated by the year it was created. The designs stand alone as creative inspiration for ready-to-wear fashion designers and stylists.

The Who, What, When, Where, and Why of Fashion

The building blocks of reporting a story, taught in every Journalism 101 class, always include the five W's: who, what, when, where, and why. These same principles apply to fashion design. Every collection is a story, every garment or accessory is physical evidence of desires and needs. Answering the five W's is vital to success. These five W's can be reviewed for sourcing inspiration and for developing every aspect of design appropriate for the wearer.

A consumer may need a simple, inexpensive T-shirt but may desire one made of the finest combed cotton by Chanel and produced in limited edition. Both T-shirts function as wearable apparel, but each answers different consumer needs. Here is where the five W's

Figure 3.21   Hussein Chalayan's fall 1995 wooden bustier.

Figure 3.22   Alexander McQueen's breast and butterfly suit from spring 1998.

come into play. The *who* represents the designer, consumer, and fashion leader or celebrity wearing it. The *what* represents the actual style of the T-shirt itself and what influenced the desire for it. The *when* represents the desire for a limited edition before the design is copied and the time it can be worn throughout the year. The *where* represents the location where consumers can purchase the T-shirts, be it through specialty stores or boutiques; it also represents the source of the next design inspiration. And the *why* represents what makes one T-shirt create such a sensation when others do not.

The Who of Design Inspiration

The who of design inspiration includes the haute couture designers—the masterminds of limitless fashion possibilities, who incorporate high art and creative street style. It also includes the people who are wearing the leading fashions; at the end of the twentieth century and the beginning of the twenty-first, celebrities are the ones wearing the fashions. Lastly, it includes the target consumer and their reliance on who else is wearing it.

Haute Couture

Every ready-to-wear or mass-produced item has an origin or point of inspiration. This origin can usually be traced to the highest level of fashion design—the haute couture. *Haute couture* is the French term for "highest quality of dressmaking," under the auspices of the Chambre Syndical of the Fédération Française de la Couture (Chambre Syndicale de la couture Parisienne).

The fashion cycle feeds on the worlds of creativity and commerce.

The haute couture designers are freed from confines in the world of commerce. Each piece is a work of art, built as a concrete compilation of their inner visualizations. Their curiosity about other cultures, materials, and workmanship knows no bounds. The growing costume collections and many fashion exhibitions in art museums throughout the world serve as evidence of haute couture existing as art.

Twenty-first-century Haute Couture

Some of the leading haute couture designers still relevant in the twenty-first century include John Galliano (House of Dior), Christian LaCroix (House of LaCroix), Karl Lagerfeld (House of Chanel), and Jean-Paul Gaultier (Hermes). These designers begin the fashion cycle with concepts that are often five or more years in advance. Their one-of-a-kind couture pieces, shown twice a year in spring and fall at fashion shows and special events, receive international attention (see Figure 3.23). The garments are later archived by their respective design houses and gathered by private collectors, waiting to be acquired by costume departments of museums through donations, loans, or purchases. They are the Picassos and Van Goghs of the fashion world. They do not generate profit directly for their design houses but do generate interest in the ready-to-wear collections and licensed merchandise, including sunglasses, fragrances, and accessories.

Haute couture designers also show their ready-to-wear collections twice a year. Unlike their couture lines, these collections need to conform to the world of commerce. These garments are meant to be sold to retailers worldwide, giving

Figure 3.23   John Galliano's fall 1997 haute couture Princess Afsharid suit.

visible and tangible direction to the balance of the design world. Other respected designers who are not part of the haute couture take part in the leading collections.

Prêt-à-porter / Ready-to-Wear
Prêt-à-porter, the French term meaning "ready-to-wear," is apparel made in factories with standard size measurements. These garments are often pared-down versions of the haute couture designs, simplified in all aspects so they conform to everyday wearability. Adaptations for various price points are taken from this group (see Figure 3.24).

Figure 3.24   An adaptation of a Dior ready-to-wear suit.

Leading mass merchandisers, including The Gap and GUESS?, as well as specialty boutiques, including bebe, are inspired by haute couture and ready-to-wear designers. These merchandise design teams target their retail audience by putting out fashions that the retail audience likes as well as fashions to attract new customers. Leading designers actually become adjectives; for example, "the bebe customer is very 'Marc' or very 'Dolce&Gabbana' this season." Marc Jacobs and Dolce&Gabbana are not only designers but also descriptions.

The Celebrities

The success of designers has always included having the right exposure. The person who wears the garment can be the deciding factor of whether the garment is a success. This has been especially true from the 1990s to today because of the focus on celebrities. The term **celebrity** encompasses personalities of interest from our high culture (fine artists, classical musicians, and literary writers), pop culture (film and television stars, fashion designers, and models), and low culture, also known as street culture (underground musicians, skateboarders, taggers, and just the plain infamous).

Models once graced the majority of all fashion magazine covers. Actors and actresses now outnumber them. Abundant twenty-four-hour media coverage on cable channels and the Internet document every move these celebrities make. Magazines such as *InStyle* focus on celebrity lifestyles and purchasing habits. These magazines often have a broader readership than *Elle, Harper's Bazaar,* or

Vogue, which have a more specific readership.

The plethora of entertainment award shows, including the Oscars, Golden Globes, Grammys, MTV Music Video or Movie Awards, and People's Choice Awards, provides visual documentation of fashion that the public will want for themselves. Designers create direct adaptations of select red-carpet looks. The successful Allen Schwartz, owner of the A.B.S. label and retail stores, openly admits to this treasure trove of ideas. He directs the collection along with his design team while watching the Oscars so the first samples are completed the very next day. This is not only limited to which evening gown or tux will be popular for proms or weddings but also to which silhouette, color, texture, and detail will predominate in ready-to-wear pieces. Designers and retailers acknowledge this relatively fail-safe forecasting of what will sell, but *who* dresses the celebrities in these garments in the first place?

The Fashion Stylists

Fashion stylists are people who have professional expertise in sourcing clothing and accessories for clients. They are hired for their abilities to fulfill their clients' tastes with the next new look. Leaders in the industry, including Phillip Bloch, Jessica Paster, Adrianne Phillips, and Rachel Zoel, create fashionable images for their clients that become objects of desires for the viewing public.

Costume Designers

The power and influence of the movie industry is immeasurable. Films are available twenty-four hours a day. Classic films are as accessible as the latest blockbuster showing at the neighborhood movie theater. The fashion industry is well aware that more people watch movies than read the latest fashion magazines. The actors/celebrities wearing the costumes in a film bring to life the clothing for two hours of the audience's undivided attention. This cultivates consumer interest.

The Catch-22 Question: Who Actually Propels a Style?

If a fashion designer didn't create a dress, there would be no dress for a stylist to pick for a celebrity to wear on the red carpet, an outfit that would then be photographed in numerous periodicals. There would be no dress for lesser-priced labels to adapt or knock off.

However, if a stylist selects a show-stopping design by an unknown designer, a currently popular one, or a long-established designer who is not on the hip barometer, that stylist can orchestrate a media frenzy for the label, igniting or reigniting an onslaught of publicity.

When a top actress appears for promotional purposes in costume between scenes of an upcoming period movie, often the intriguing silhouette, color, texture, and detail of her period garments (and hair and makeup) appeal to her audience. Did the costume designer generate a look and style that will inspire fashion designers before the actual movie premieres?

If celebrities are admired for their talent, personal style, and the people they surround themselves with creatively, they can instigate a look that fashion designers will copy. Many celebrities are creating their own fashion lines. Some celebrities who have launched their own lines include singer/producer Sean Combs's SeanJean lines and singer Gwen Stefani's L.A.M.B. label. Others include Jennifer Lopez, Eve, Serena Williams, Mary Kate and Ashley Olsen, and Britney Spears.

The media, in its print, televised, and online formats, brings fashion information to the public around the clock. Cable channels' fashion runway coverage and numerous award shows with red-carpet style commentary round out the daily celebrity news programs on network television. Fashion and gossip magazines present their summarized information weekly or monthly, but what is gaining increased momentum is the *blog*. A blog is a Web site where people can post thoughts, share links to other Web sites, and interact with people online. They are mostly used by amateur and professional journalists as well as aspiring fashion editors who, in reality, are consumers with a hyperinterest in fashion. The powerful word-of-mouth advertising is building with first-hand observations immediately hitting the Internet daily or hourly, rather than weekly or monthly. The phrase "all news, all the time" is now a reality in the world of fashion.

The Fashion Consumer

Clothing designers initially create items with appealing silhouettes, colors, textures, and details for their consumer market. The challenge is to keep the aesthetic and commercial directive. These consumers are defined as the target market. A target market is a group of people with similar needs (defined by age, body type, and pre-vious purchasing patterns), the ability to afford the product, and the availability to be reached in the marketplace.

Some designers have a direct mission to create mass-produced garments for an established target market, offering many choices or groups of interrelated pieces. Other designers are not so restricted and create unique and interesting art pieces that cater to a specific consumer market, often aesthetically driven. These consumers are referred to as a niche market. Each piece has singular integrity.

Certain accessories often fall into this niche category of being created for creativity's sake rather than for mass consumption; therefore, they have fewer restrictions on fit. A necklace or purse has more leeway than a pair of shoes. An oversized necklace or extremely large purse with pockets and zippers might be the wrong scale for a petite wearer but will still fit on her shoulder or around her neck. It is up to the consumer to determine whether an item is aesthetically appropriate for her body size. This freedom from size restriction does not exist with shoes or foundation garments. No matter how attractive a pair of shoes may be, a size 6 shoe will not fit on a size 8 foot.

The ready-to-wear clothing design process is geared around sales. No matter how much analysis of the creative process is done, if the garments are not desired and purchased, the line has failed. The primary directive in design is knowing who the target market is. A target market has certain common requirements: size, cost, and ease of availability. Their demographic profile (vital statistics of age, income, education, marital status, and so on) further gives clues to their wants and needs. Cultural referencing to past and present high, low, and popular cultures also points a designer in the appropriate creative direction.

The following age segments break the population into five groups. These groups generally define the target markets by age and exposure to high, low, and popular cultures, as well as the general aging patterns for figure types. The years are generalized since many demographic reports characterize each category with several years' discrepancies.

Gray market: Born before 1945, this group requires ease of access and larger sizing.
Baby boomers: Born between the years of 1946 and 1964, this group has an interest in fitness so they can maintain or improve their figures. Their motto is "50 is the new 40."
Generation X: Born between the years of 1965 and 1979, this group prefers a natural style coupled with career.
Generation Y: Born between the years of 1980 to 1999, these are the children of the baby boomers who have high school and college needs.
Generation Next: Born in the new millennium, these are the consumers of the future.

Each group is identified as a target for various fashion design firms. Designers are fully briefed on the brand's consumer profile.

The What of Design Inspiration
It is crucial to know what cultural force in communication is leading the way for the fashion consumer today, be it film, television, or theater. Practically speaking, deciding what the key pieces are to design for a group or collection is crucial. The question of what instigates the creative process—the fabric or the vision—is akin to the question of what came first: the chicken or the egg? The question of what gives birth to a design can be answered differently with each piece or collectively as the way each designer works. Some designers begin with their imaginations, pencils, and paper. The options of experimentation grow on the page. Other designers survey the available textile samples, with a color palette or fabric hand setting their creative wheels in motion. Where the intangible meets the concrete is affected by how much of the who, what, when, where, and why is put into the mix. A swatch of wafflelike steel-gray knit may elicit an image of medieval knights, Roman gladiators, or even *Star Trek*'s final generation. It may also elicit nothing of practical use to a designer who is aware of what his or her consumer wants and needs. This simply comes down to identifying the categories and price points of the target consumer.

The Categories and Price Points
Concerns of designing for various body types bring the art of design down to the practical reality of comfort, fit, and the art of camouflage. Men, women, and children all prioritize these needs differently. The following categories designate the amount of leeway in creativity and practicality. Playing up or paring down SCTDs for economic parameters is part of designing for each category. All the creative ideas combined are ineffective if

the garment does not follow pricing, quality, and fit standards.

Womenswear: Clothing and Pricing Categories

Following is a list of womenswear clothing and pricing in categories that include designers whose products fall within the specified category.

Haute couture—custom-designed garments of the highest quality for clients. Designers within this category include John Galliano for Dior and Karl Lagerfeld for Chanel.

Designer custom—custom-designed garments offered by designers in limited availability or for select clients. Ralph Lauren's Purple Label Custom Collection and Isaac Mizrahi's Custom Collection are two well-known collections that fall within this category.

Designer/prêt-à-porter—quality ready-to-wear designs by signature designers, such as Donna Karan, Ralph Lauren, and Jean-Paul Gaultier.

Bridge—creations designed to give consumers an affordable version of designer lines. The work of Ellen Tracy, Tahari, Dana Buchman, and Eileen Fisher is representative of this category.

Diffusion line—lower-priced, pared-down versions of designer's own lines, such as Donna Karan's DKNY and Marc by Marc Jacobs.

Contemporary—stylish merchandise with a particular trend direction. The designs of Shelli Segal, Cynthia Rowley, and Vivienne Tam fall within this category.

Better—fashion at affordable prices from designers such as Liz Claiborne, Karen Kane, and Jones New York.

Moderate—included in this category are products by Levi Strauss and J.G. Hook.

Promotional/mass market—mass-produced items, formerly known as budget. Wrangler and Kmart's Jaclyn Smith are two brands representative of this category.

Designer for mass market—nationally known designers producing mass market–priced lines, including Mossimo and Isaac Mizrahi for Target, Nicole Miller for JCPenney, and Karl Lagerfeld's limited edition for H&M.

Womenswear: Clothing Classifications

Following is a list of womenswear clothing categories and their definitions.

Accessories—includes footwear, handbags, small personal goods, belts, socks, hosiery, scarves, hats, hair accessories, gloves, umbrellas, eyewear, fine and costume jewelry, and watches.

Activewear—apparel items designed to be worn for active sports, such as yoga, running, and other exercises.

Blouses—clothing for the upper part of the body; softer and less tailored than a shirt.

Bridal—clothing and accessories worn by brides; sometimes includes bridesmaids' attire.

Dresses—one-piece garment extending at least to below the hips, ending in a skirt.

Eveningwear—clothes worn primarily in evening for formal or informal occasions.

Furs—apparel, accessories, or trimming made from the pelts of an animal (coats, hats, scarves, muffs, and boots). Making apparel out of fur is often controversial.

Intimate apparel—lingerie and underwear.

Maternity—garments designed with fullness in front to accommodate pregnant women.

Outerwear—raincoats, dress coats, all-weather coats, hoodies, Windbreakers, and parkas.

Prom—targeted to teenage girls; eveningwear/formal wear worn to high school event.

Sportswear—casual wear for leisure time and when participating in spectator sports.

Swimwear—general category of apparel for swimming and related activities, including swimsuits (one-piece, two-piece, and bikini) and cover-ups.

Uniforms—any specific type of apparel required for special occupations, schools, or competitive team sports.

Womenswear: Sizing Categories

Following is a list of women's sizing categories and their ranges.

Missy—0 to 18 or S, M, L, XL
Junior—3 to 15, average 5'6" with shorter torso than missy
Women's—16W to 26W (can go to 52) or 1X to 4X
Petite—2P to 16P, under 5'4"
Women's petites—14WP to 20WP, shorter figure with overall larger girth
Tall—10T to 18T, from 5'9" to 6'1"

Children: Pricing Categories

Following is a list of pricing categories for children's wear.

Better—trendy designs and quality fabrications that include labels such as Polo by Ralph Lauren, Oilily, and Tommy Hilfiger.

Moderate—average price points between better and budget that includes clothing lines from Esprit, Gap, Osh Kosh B'Gosh, and Quiksilver.

Popular—most affordable of the brand offerings (also known as budget), including Healthtex, Carter's, Wal-Mart, and Target private labels.

Children: Sizing Categories

Following are the sizing categories of children's clothing and their ranges.

Infants—preemie/premature, newborn, 3 months, 6 months, 12 months, 18 months.
Toddler—2T to 4T.
Children's—3 to 6X.
Boys—8 to 20, husky or chubby.
Girls—7 to 14.
Preteen/subteen—6 to 14.
Young junior—3 to 13.

Menswear: Pricing Categories

Following are some menswear pricing categories.

Custom-tailored/bespoke—finest construction and fabrication custom-made for clients (women's counterpart is haute couture). Labels within this category include London's Savile Row and Ozwald Boetang.

Designer ready-made suits—fine quality overall but not made-to-measure. Designers in this category include Donna Karan, Giorgio Armani, and Ralph Lauren.

Bridge—suits and sportswear with lesser price points than designer clothing. Clothing designed by Kenneth Cole and Jones New York falls within this category.

Moderate—priced below bridge but above popular-priced

discount merchandise. Clothing from private labels at Nordstrom's and Macy's I.N.C. falls within this category.

Popular priced—most affordable of all categories; private label discount and mass merchants provide bulk of availability. Clothing from this category can be found at Wal-Mart and Target.

Menswear: Sizing Categories

Following are some standard sizing categories for menswear and their ranges.

Men's suits—36 to 50 (chest measurement); lengths: S for short, R for Regular, L for Long.

Active sportswear—S, M, L, XL, XXL, XXXL (may include Tall).

Furnishings—S, M, L, XL, XXL, XXXL; dress shirts sized by collar measurements and sleeve lengths.

Sportswear—S, M, L, XL, XXL, XXXL (may include Tall).

Uniforms/work wear—S, M, L, XL, XXL, XXXL (may include Tall).

The When of Design Inspiration

The when implies looking outside the current time, both to the past and the future. Designers understand the rich inspiration that is to be found in designs of the past. There are countless amounts of design inspiration today found in plentiful art and costume history books. These resources are necessary and as effective as color forecasting and trend-predictive services. The great couturier of today visit libraries as fervently as they study the archives of past fashion designers. The costume collections amassed by the great museums of the world have contributed to

the popular exhibitions where clothing receives the same cultural, social, and scholarly respect that paintings and sculpture do. The Metropolitan Museum of Art's Costume Institute presents yearly blockbusters that steer the direction of current fashion with salutes to history and sociology.

The "Goddess: The Classical Mode" 2003 exhibition generated a renewed interest in soft feminine curves and the beauty of the draped body. Every award show looked as if a trail of fashion goddesses had stepped off exhibit pedestals. Designs thereafter recreated the theme in various price points (see Figure 3.15). The most significant change in the twenty-first century is speed: speed of broadcasting the live runway via satellite, speed of digitally photographing selected favorites from the runway's front row and e-mailing them around the world, and the speed of scanning artwork to send to development teams. The ability of fashion-predictive services to translate and reinforce messages from the haute couture runway is equally as swift.

The fashion-predictive and reportage services (see Web site listings under trend predictive/reportages/analyses/news services) provide silhouette, color, texture, and detail information twelve to twenty-one months in advance, with most color services averaging about eighteen months in advance.

When the haute couture and ready-to-wear collections are presented in Europe, the knockoff cycle begins for designer brands and private labels alike. When the spring lines are shown in October, the summer lines in January, transition/fall in

February, fall II in April, and resort/holiday in August, each and every category and price point is assimilating silhouette, color, texture, and detail messages to sell to the right consumer, at the right place, at the right time, at the right price—the goal of successful fashion merchandising.

The Where of Design Inspiration

Many of the haute couture designers of the early twentieth century were part of social groups that traveled internationally, exposing themselves to new and different cultures. The designs of Paul Poiret brought the beauty of Asian themes to the traditions of the Western world. Coco Chanel's avant-garde social interactions with men and women throughout Europe and Russia were present in each collection, all while keeping true to the classic Chanel look.

The haute couture designers of the late-twentieth and early-twenty-first century are exposed to travel and technology as well. They look beyond the familiar integration of ethnic imagery when designing a collection. Rather than spinning the globe for a new cultural concept, they incorporate several ethnic directions in one garment or outfit. The world of high and low culture in ethnicity is also an oasis for endless design inspiration, where peasant and folkloric embellishments appear on the richest silks and velvets.

This mixing of high and low culture in both design and presentation generates interest season after season. The influence of pop culture inspires the origins of some designs. Traditionally it was thought that the majority of design inspiration came from the rich and rarified world of the elite, which then trickled down to the masses in watered-down versions. It was also acknowledged that fashion items traveled up the societal scale to reach the elite, as evidenced by the popularity of jeans, Doc Martens, or motorcycle jackets. Today design inspiration comes from all directions, and coexists with the extreme and classic. This mass dissemination of ideas reinforces endless exposure to the many things that will inspire the next new trend.

The Why of Design Inspiration

Simply stated, the interaction of the who, what, when, and where of design inspiration defines the why of the buying cycle. The why references what is needed emotionally and physically to generate interest in choices of dress, including the climate of the times (patriotism, sensuality, and economics, for example).

Why the public is willing to purchase items every season without needing to is part of human nature. It is the desire for the beauty of the new and different. It is fashion.

Review Questions

1. What are the four elements of fashion design? Define them.

2. What are the seven principles of design? Define them.

3. What are two sources of inspiration for fashion stylists?

4. What is hyperdesigning?

5. What are five of the ten tools for tweaking?

Key Terms

Across-the-board

Activewear

Achromatic

Anchor

Apparel

Alternation

Avant-garde

Balance

Bridge fashion

Classic

Color

Color palette

Collection

Colorway

Concept boards

Contemporary

Contrast

Cool colors

Couturier

Couturière

Croquis

Emphasis

Demographics

Diffusion line

Fabrication

Fad

Fashion cycle

Fashion illustration

Flats

Floats

Form

Gradation

Group

Hanger appeal

Harmony

Haute couture

High culture

Hue

Label

Line

Logo

Line-for-line copy

Low culture

Magalog

Neutrals

Palette

Pattern

Pop culture

Prêt-à-porter

Premiere vision

Primary colors

Private label

Proportion

Product type

Psychographics

Radiation

Ready-to-wear (RTW)

Repetition

Rhythm

Roughs

Saturation

Scale

Silhouette

Subcultures

Storyboards

Space

Shade

Shape

Stylist/designer

Swatch

Target customer

Technical flats

Texture

Tint

Tone

Trimming

Transition

Upward flow theory

Unity

Value

4

Fashion Sketching Basics:
Building the Fashion Croquis

What You Will Learn in Chapter 4

This chapter teaches the basics of fashion sketching anatomy in an easy-to-understand manner, breaking down the body into five basic shapes that can be manipulated to form anatomical structures. The ten-head fashion figure will be developed from front, back, and various moving poses. These figures can then be utilized as croquis or templates for designing garments and production flats.

There Is No Sketching Gene

Sketching is not an ability to which people are genetically predisposed. There is no sketching gene, at least none that has yet been discovered. Babies are not born with the ability to illustrate fashion. It is an accumulated skill set. Illustration is a hand-eye skill that requires constant training to develop, similar to the requirements of athletic pursuits. Inherent genius, creativity, or ability is a Victorian concept rooted in bigotry. Sketching and the ability to draw and stylize the human form are skills that anyone who is sufficiently motivated can learn.

Accomplished illustrators often make their achievements look easy, as if anyone can accomplish the same. This, in part, fuels misconceptions of talent. When marveling at these feats, people do not see the years of training critical to the development of the skill sets.

The most important initial step for anybody who wants to master fashion sketching is simply drawing 20 minutes daily. This exercise will strengthen hand-eye coordination, help to develop compositional perspective, and fine-tune the eye. Much discipline is needed, as it is important to be consistent with the exercises.

Basic Drawing Materials

Following are some of the supplies illustrators have so they can begin to sketch.

- Pencils with soft lead: 2B, 3B, or 4B
- Technical pencil with .05 lead
- Bond paper pads: 11 × 14 and 14 × 17
- Marker paper pads: 11 × 14 and 14 × 17
- Gray or white erasers
- .01 black fine line (permanent) ink pens
- Drafting brush

Drawing Leads

Sketching pencils come in several different leads. The type of lead dictates when an illustrator may use a specific pencil. Following is a list of the different leads and how they are best utilized.

2H A medium to hard lead used for finished work; as it is the hardest lead used for drawing, this lead does not erase easily.
F This is a medium or fine lead that is an excellent general-purpose lead weight used for quick sketching.
H and B These are soft leads that require control for fine line work. They erase easily and are good for shading. Press hard for better density.
2B to 6B These are very soft leads that smear easily. They are excellent for shading and drawing gestures.

Drawing leads are graded from a range of 9H, which is extremely hard, to 6B, which is extremely soft. The soft fine leads used in technical pencils tend to be brittle and break easily. Although the 6B pencil smears easily, most illustrators prefer a medium-grade, medium-density lead pencil such as a 2B or 3B. Experiment with a variety of pencils, leads brands, and weights to discover what works best for you.

Professional Markers

Following are some brands of markers that are widely used by professional illustrators. Please note that if you wish to do a final marker rendering before scanning it into the computer, it is required to use a

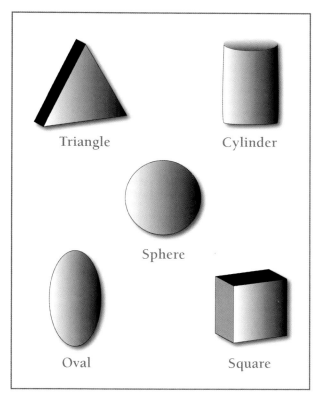

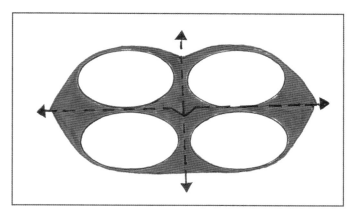

Figure 4.2   Lips created by strategically placing ovals together.

Figure 4.1   The five basic shapes used in art.

set of professional medium-nib-size markers.

Copic: The best thing about Copic markers is that they have a brush end and come in a natural range of skin tone colors. The drawbacks are that they quickly run out.

Pantone Tria: These great markers have a third (ultrafine) tip, which is good for small details. They offer a wide variety of colors and more options in the lighter pastel chroma range. They do tend to be a little tougher to blend with other brands. Overall this is a good marker but more expensive.

Berol Prisma Color: This is also a good double-sided marker that is less toxic smelling than other brands, if you are sensitive to marker smells. Every marker has a corresponding Prisma Color pencil number that it blends with.

Prisma Color Pencils: These color pencils are the best and most widely used. They were developed with marker technology in mind, as they have a low wax content. Wax is always the enemy of marker application since it repels the pigment.

**Mass Before Detail:
Basic Shapes**

Try thinking of the figure in terms of three-dimensional shapes. These shapes form a substructure or mass. Leonardo da Vinci is known to have said that all of art can be analyzed and broken down into five basic shapes (see Figure 4.1). Da Vinci noted that these shapes can be used to create the foundation of the human form. These shapes subdivide and break down major anatomical areas so the illustrator can better understand and develop the form. For example, lips can be seen as four simple ovals arranged side by side and one on top of the other (see Figure 4.2).

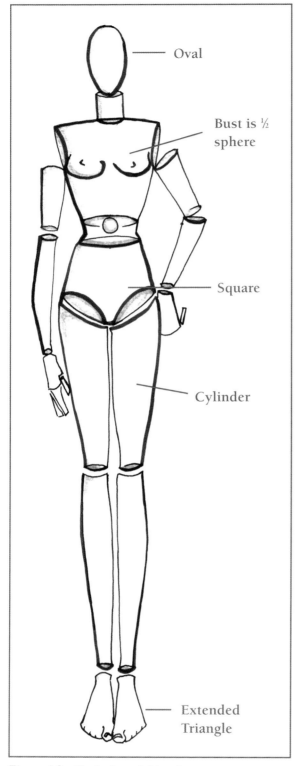

Oval

Bust is ½
sphere

Square

Cylinder

Extended
Triangle

Figure 4.3   Blocked-out fashion figure.

Circles used
for rotation
and muscle
form

Fingertips
are at 5 when
arms are
extended
straight

Note the center
front line used
to create
symmetry

The toes look
like a half
moon

half way point
(on head) for eyes

1 head

1½ shoulders, also
1½ heads wide

2 bust apex
and armpit

2¼ lowest part
of bust

3 waistline

4 hips
4⅛ crotch

5 fingertips

6 knees
6⅛ knee bone

7 calves
7⅛ upward hash marks
(red arrows) used
to designate highest
muscle point of calf

8 shin (flat)

9 anklebone is always
higher on the inside

10 bottom of foot

Figure 4.4   The ten-head fashion figure.

Blocking Out the Fashion Figure

The human form is composed of basic, elemental shapes. These shapes are used to form the primary part of a drawing. Blocking out a figure means manipulating these masses or shapes in various ways to create different poses (see Figure 4.3). The five shapes are as follows:

1. Oval
2. Sphere
3. Square
4. Cylinder
5. Triangle

The Ten-head Fashion Figure: Proportions

The fashion figure is based on a ten-head concept. This is a system of shapes and incremental measurements that are easily scaled and adjusted (see Figure 4.4).

The ease in manipulating the figure is attributed to the uniform barometers utilized and to the simple building block shapes that form the substructure. When thinking of the figure in terms of heads instead of inches or meters, balance and scale do not seem as rigid.

All the elements of a fashion figure can be measured with the head. Always begin by designating the size of the oval shape that will represent the head. This will dictate all the other landmarks and proportions on the figure.

Renaissance artists originated this concept of blocking out a figure. Fifteenth-century artisans and architects learned this from the ancient Greeks. These methods are centuries old. It is therefore logical to simply apply these theories and concepts to fashion illustration.

Developing the Fashion Figure: Front View

1. Begin by drawing a vertical line through the entire length of your paper. This line is known as the pit, symmetry, plum, balance, or center front line, and it should be perfectly parallel with the paper's vertical side edge.

   Notch and number ten equal spaces (see Figure 4.5). These ten increments are based on the box placed within the first notched area. This square represents the head and will be roughly one tenth of your paper, allowing for a small margin or border.

2. Draw an oval in the top box and tapered squares for the upper torso and lower hip area. Draw angled hash marks in at the

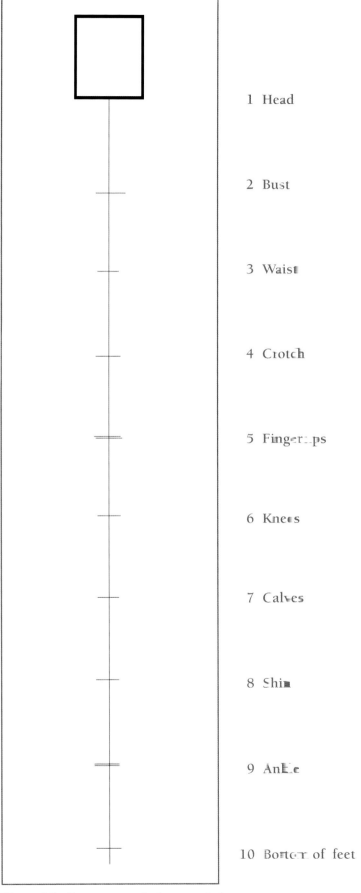

1 Head

2 Bust

3 Waist

4 Crotch

5 Fingertips

6 Knees

7 Calves

8 Shin

9 Ankle

10 Bottom of feet

Figure 4.5　Ten spaces notched on a vertical line.

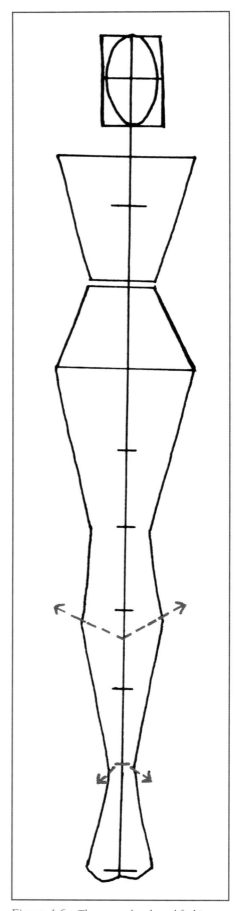

Figure 4.6   The more developed fashion
           figure.

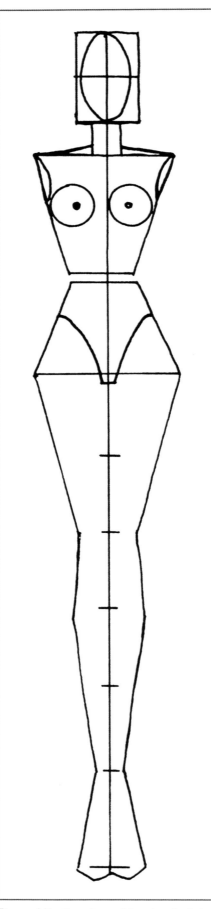

Figure 4.7   Step three of drawing the fash-
           ion figure.

seventh head. These will be used as a landmark to indicate the highest muscle and bone point on the calves and ankles (see the red broken lines in Figure 4.6). Draw outer leg lines and elongated pyramid shapes between the ninth and tenth head. This pyramid shape will form the feet.

3. Draw a tubular shape or cylinder for the neck. Draw a horizontal line one-and-a-half heads down that spans one-and-a-half heads across. This will be the shoulder line. Draw fried eggs at the second head mark to suggest the bust. Shape the panty line as desired (see Figure 4.7).

4. Erase the top part of the fried eggs to create the bust shape. Curve the waistline. Draw cylinder shapes that hinge at the second head mark to create the upper arm. The elbow socket should never be longer than the waist.

   Sketch tapered cylinders or cones for lower arms. Next draw the outer leg lines and place small squares at the sixth head for the knee bones. Invert the pelvic bone just past the curved waistline at the third head (see Figure 4.8).

5. To finish the fashion figure, place a piece of slightly transparent marker paper (please refer to the materials list on page 86) over the figure. This allows you to make refinements. Connect all the balls and boxes at the neck, shoulders, elbows, wrists, knees, and ankles. Smooth out sharp lines and curves where appropriate. Figure 4.9 can serve as a three-dimensional reference guide.

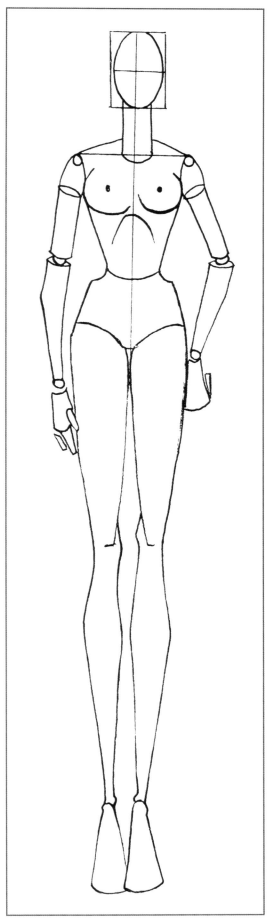

Figure 4.8   The waistline curved.

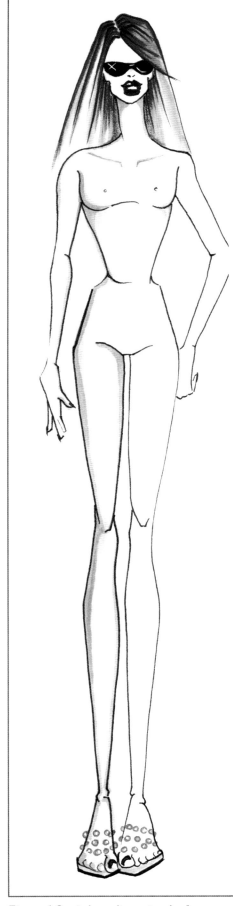

Figure 4.9   A three-dimensional reference guide.

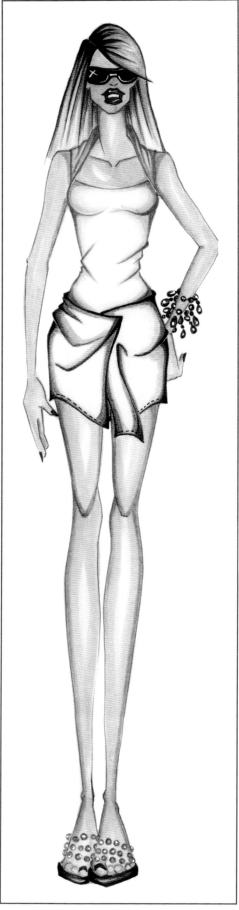

Figure 4.10 The completed fashion figure.

The Fashion Figure: Completed

6a. After developing the figure, draw in clothing details and accessories to the sketch (see Figure 4.10). The completed drawing can be utilized to show design concepts on the body and convey junior or contemporary fashions. This figure was rendered with Copic markers before being scanned into the computer. Line art can be scanned in and color or patterns applied using Photoshop. See Chapter 13 for a tutorial lesson on how to fill line art.

The Fashion Figure: With Style Lines

6b. The figure has style lines applied to it so that clothing can best be understood and designed on top of the figure. This figure can be used as a template for designing flat garments. This type of highly technical figure template is also referred to as a croquis (see Figure 4.11).

The Fashion Figure: Back View

1. The same blocking out technique to create substructure can be used to create different poses. For example, the proportions and measurements used for the front view can be applied to the back view of the fashion figure (see Figure 4.12).

2. Flesh in the back view using the same methods you employed for the front view (see Figure 4.9). Smooth out the lines around the blocked shapes. Sketch in the elements that will give the figure human qualities such as hair and other details (see Figure 4.13).

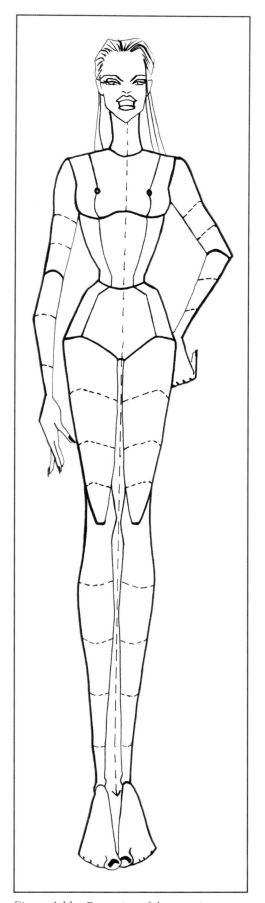

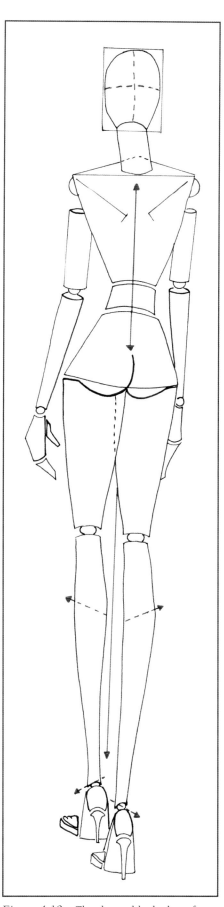

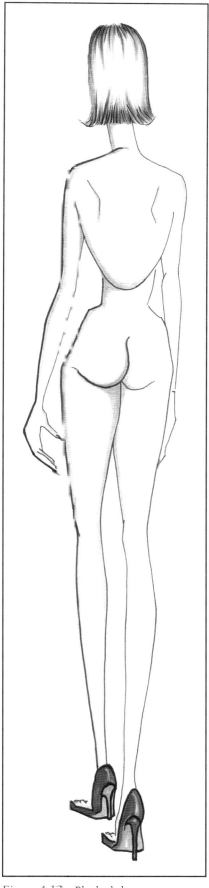

Figure 4.11   Front view of the croquis with style lines.

Figure 4.12   The shapes blocked out for the back view.

Figure 4.13   Blocked shapes are smoothed out to show human qualities.

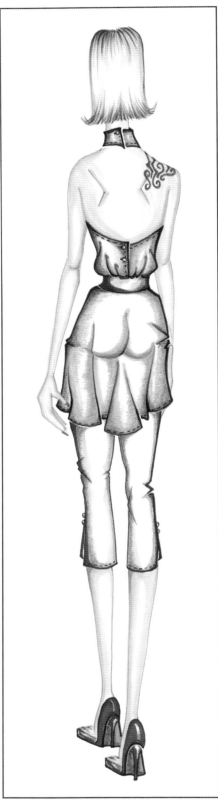

Figure 4.14 The back view of the fashion
figure completed.

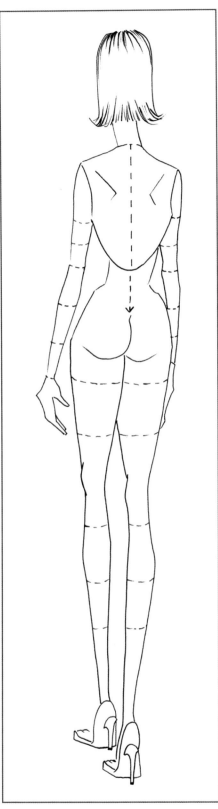

Figure 4.15 Back view of the croquis with
style lines.

The Back View: Completed

3a. Figure 4.14 was rendered with
Copic markers and Prisma
Color pencils.

The Back View: With Style Lines

3b. Figure 4.15 can be utilized as a
croquis or template on which
you can design garments.

Figure 4.16   Front view of the moving fashion figure.

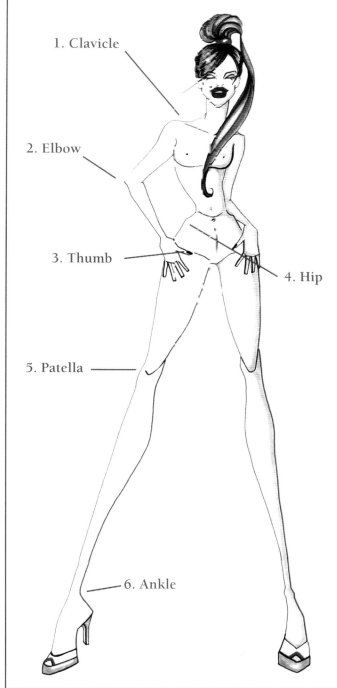

1. Clavicle

2. Elbow

3. Thumb

4. Hip

5. Patella

6. Ankle

Figure 4.17   The six most important parts of the croquis.

The Fashion Figure: Moving

1. Shift the hips slightly upward to create the illusion that the figure is shifting body weight. This will create a more relaxed-looking fashion figure. The weight of the body (plumb line) still falls directly under the pit of the neck; however, note the equal distribution of weight.

Equally distributing the body weight is an alternative to placing a load-bearing leg under the pit of the neck. These are the only options if the figure is to stand up straight and not tilt or sway (see Figure 4.16).

2. Fleshing in the fashion figure (any pose) requires sketching in the bones that stick out. It is critical to highlight these bones on your figure, as it will express more human qualities. The six most important topical landmarks are as follows (see Figure 4.17):

- Clavicle or collar bone
- Ulna or elbow bone

- Radius or thumb bone
- Hip bone
- Patella or knee bone
- Ankle bone

The Moving Figure: Completed

3a. Figure 4.18 was rendered with Copic markers and Prisma Color pencils.

The Moving Figure: Variation

3b. Figure 4.19 was rendered in Copic markers and Prisma Color pencils.

The Back View: Moving

1. Apply the same concepts from the front view on the moving fashion figure. Shifting the

Figure 4.18   Front view of the completed moving figure.

Figure 4.19   A variation of the completed moving figure.

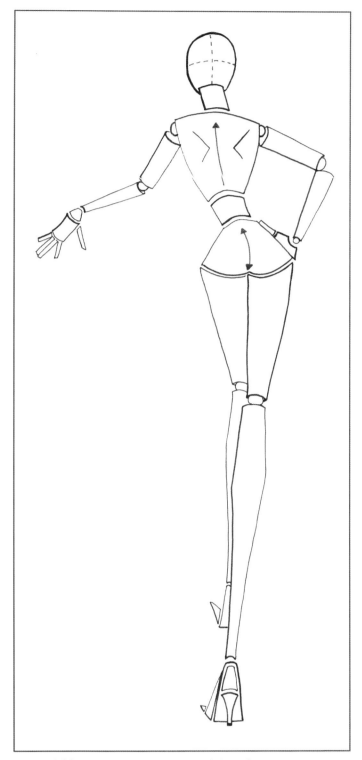

Figure 4.20   Back view of the moving fashion figure.

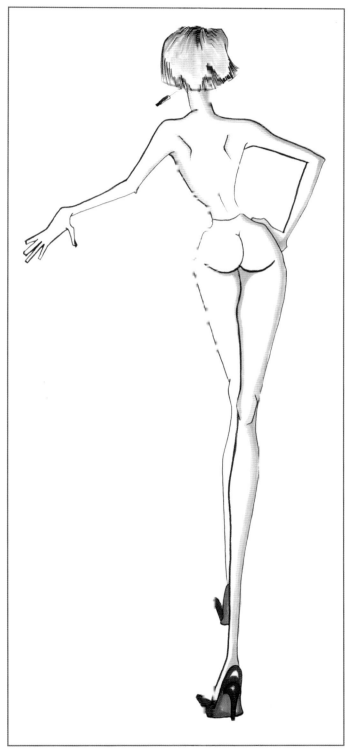

Figure 4.21   Blocked shapes smoothed out to show human qualities on the back view of the moving fashion figure.

weight and counterbalancing the upper torso with the pelvis is identical for the front and back views (see Figure 4.20).

2. Flesh in the fashion figure (see Figure 4.21).

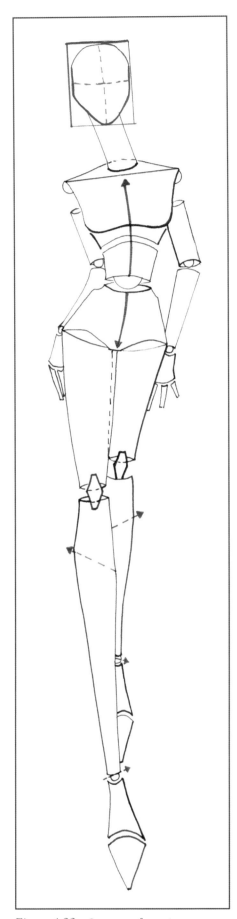

Figure 4.22   Back view of the completed moving figure. A fashionable pet can add
        interest to an illustration.

Figure 4.23   Step one of creating an
        action pose.

Figure 4.24 The fashion figure fleshed in.

Figure 4.25 The completed action pose.

The Back View Moving: Completed

3. Figure 4.22 was rendered in Copic markers and Prisma Color pencils. Note the accessories and how they lend personality to the illustration.

The Fashion Figure: Action Pose

1. Proportions remain the same for the action pose. The figure por-trays a more aggressive attitude, and she appears to be moving forward. This is achieved by a technique known as foreshortening. The illusion of foreshortening is achieved by drawing one leg shorter than the other (see Figure 4.23). The limb appears to be moving back in space.

This creates a sense of depth and dimension.

2. Flesh in the fashion figure (see Figure 4.24).

The Action Pose: Completed

3a. Figure 4.25 was rendered in Copic markers and Prisma Color pencils.

Figure 4.26   A variation of the completed action pose.

Figure 4.27   Step one of creating the three-quarter fashion figure and her pet.

The Action Pose: Variation

3b. Figure 4.26 was rendered in
   Copic markers and Prisma
   Color pencils.

**The Fashion Figure:
Three-Quarter View**

1. The three-quarter view is composed of blocks foreshortened
   on one side of the body, creat-

ing the illusion that the body is
rotating back in space. The
upper torso and pelvis can also
be counterbalanced to create a
sense of shifting weight.

The concept of mass before
detail, or working with shapes
to create figures, can also be
applied to animals. Our fashion

Figure 4.28   Details added to both the fashion figure and pet.

pet is simply composed of circles and cylinders (see Figure 4.27).

2. Flesh in the fashion figure.

   Add curls to the poodle, giving texture and detail to the dog (see Figure 4.28).

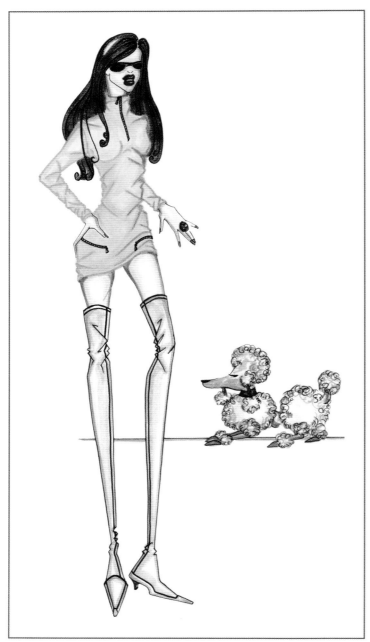

Figure 4.29 The completed fashion figure and pet.

Figure 4.30 Three-quarter variation of the completed fashion figure.

The Three-Quarter View: Completed

3a. Figure 4.29 was rendered with Copic markers and Prisma Color pencils.

Add minimal marker shading to complete poodle.

The Three-Quarter View: Variation

3b. Figure 4.30 was rendered with Copic markers and Prisma Color pencils.

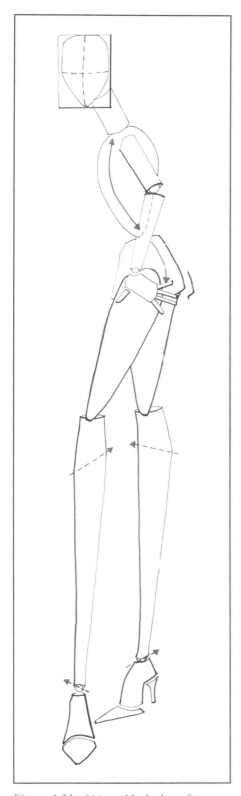

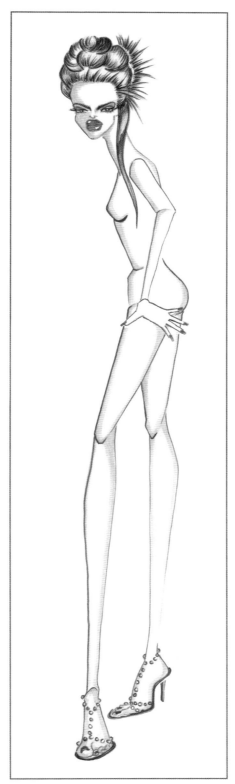

Figure 4.31 Using a blocked-out figure, one can create a figure in a side-view pose.

Figure 4.32 Flesh tones should then be added.

The Fashion Figure: Side View

1. The upper torso in the side view figure is created with an oval shape instead of the square used for other views (see Figure 4.31).
2. Flesh in the fashion figure (see Figure 4.32).

Figure 4.33   Once apparel and other details are added, the figure is complete.

The Side View: Completed

3a. Figure 4.33 was rendered in Copic markers and Prisma Color pencils. The tattoo was drawn on the finished rendering with a fine .03 dark blue Sakura brand micron ink pen.

Figure 4.34   The figure can also be dramatically varied, depending on the apparel added.

The Side View: Variation

3b Figure 4.34 was rendered in
    Copic markers and Prisma
    Color pencils.

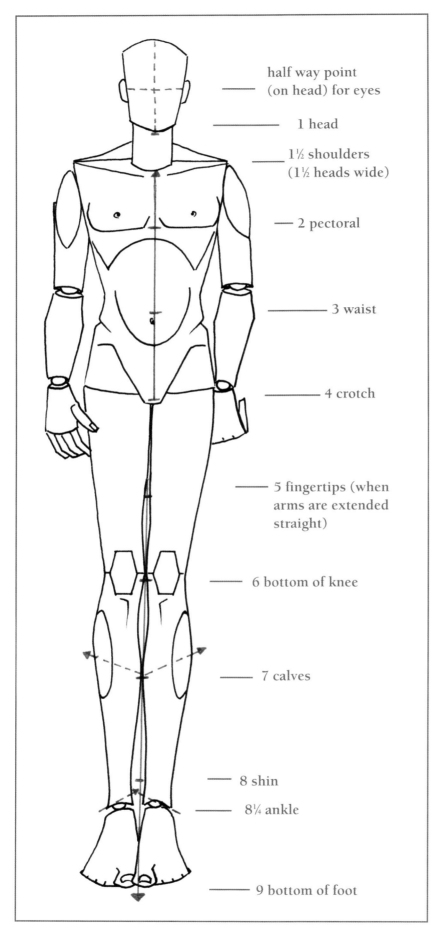

half way point
(on head) for eyes

1 head

1½ shoulders
(1½ heads wide)

2 pectoral

3 waist

4 crotch

5 fingertips (when
arms are extended
straight)

6 bottom of knee

7 calves

8 shin

8¼ ankle

9 bottom of foot

Figure 4.35   The nine-head male fashion figure.

Developing the Male Fashion Figure

You can employ most of the same techniques used to develop the female figure—mass shapes, blocking, symmetry, balance, pit lines, and fleshing—when drawing the male fashion figure.

The male figure does have certain distinct and specific differences that need to be incorporated. A critical component is the more angular quality of the line that needs to be drawn. For accuracy, visual and anatomical references are the key. Some differences to note are as follows (see Figure 4.35):

- The male figure is nine heads tall.
- The male neck is drawn thicker than the female neck.
- The male head shape is square and angular.
- The male upper torso forms a V shape with little delineation at the natural waistline.
- Hands are large (approximately one head) and broader than the female hand.
- The male breast or pectoral muscle area is square and flat.
- The male wrists and ankles are thicker than the female wrists and ankles.
- Male calf muscles are well defined and rounded.
- The male deltoid or shoulder muscles are round and well defined.
- Male feet are broad and square-shaped. Female feet tend to be delicate and triangular.

The Nine-head Male Fashion Figure: Proportions

The Male Fashion Figure: Front View

1. The blocking of the male figure corresponds to the same steps as

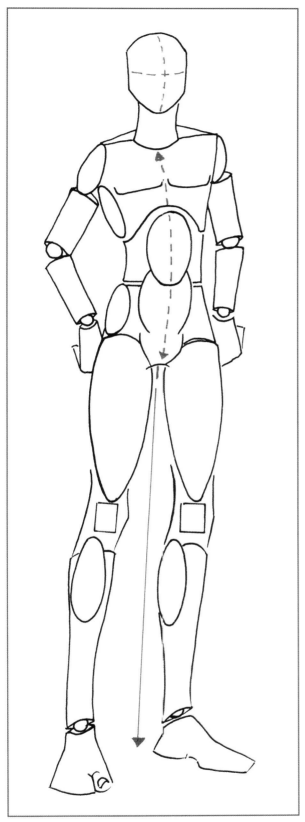

Figure 4.36   Front view of the blocked-out male
fashion figure.

the female figure (see pages 88–89). After notching and numbering the nine equal increments, place the boxes, cylinders, and shapes according to the male figure proportions in Figure 4.36.

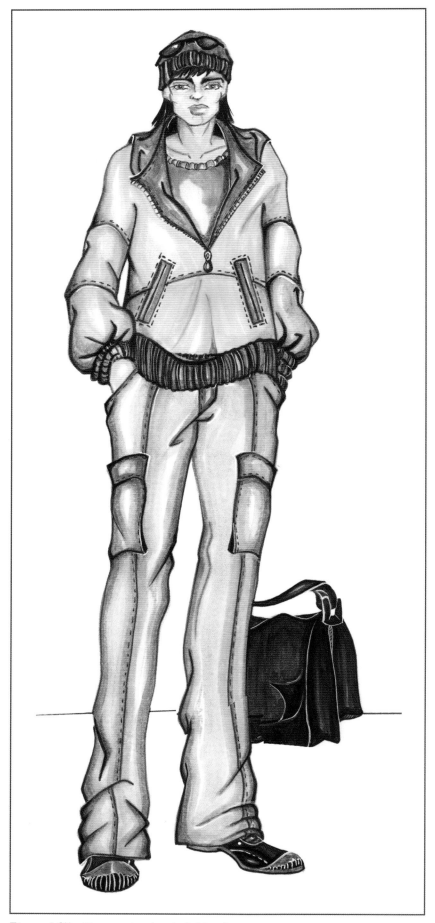

Figure 4.37   The completed male fashion figure.

The Male Fashion Figure: Completed

2. Clothing and accessories were added to complete Figure 4.37. The male figure was rendered with Copic markers and Prisma Color pencils.

The Male Fashion Figure: Three-Quarter View

1. The male three-quarter view is composed of blocks that are foreshortened on one side of the body, creating the illusion that the body is rotating back in space. The upper torso and pelvis can also be counterbalanced to create a sense of shifting weight (see Figure 4.38).

The Male Three-Quarter View: Completed

2. The male figure in Figure 4.39 was rendered with Copic markers and Prisma Color pencils.

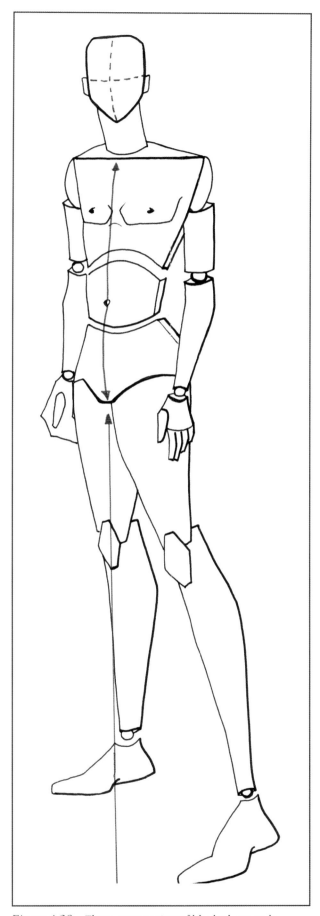

Figure 4.38   Three-quarter view of blocked-out male
fashion figure.

Figure 4.39   Completed three-quarter male fashion figure.

Review Questions

1. What does "mass before detail" refer to?

2. What does the concept of **blocking out** the figure mean?

3. How many basic shapes are required to form the initial block figure?

4. What are the basic shapes used to create the block figure?

5. What are some of the specific anatomical differences between male and female fashion figures?

6. Foreshortening is used to create the illusion of what?

7. What are the six bones that stick out?

8. Where are the ten incremental proportions located on the female fashion figure?

Suggested Practice Project

Insert the CD-ROM⊙ that comes with this book. In the Bonus Library on the CD-ROM⊙ you will find a croquis subfolder. Drag the folder to your computer desktop and print these out. Next trace your design ideas (or flats) over the printed croquis using a piece of translucent marker paper. Try creating four to six garments based on a theme or construction detail (see Chapter 5 for construction details). This is considered a design group.

Key Terms

Blocking out

Croquis

Foreshortening

Form

Mass

Pit line

Rendering

Symmetry

Substructure

5

Understanding Flats: A Visual Reference Index for Silhouettes and Styling Details

What You Will Learn in Chapter 5

Chapter 5 focuses on drawing the various types of flats and understanding the language of garment construction. Included with this chapter is a visual index of garment silhouettes: coats, jackets, pants, skirts, tops, and dresses. Styling details have also been included as a visual reference on the CD-ROM ⊙ as a vector library. The CD-ROM ⊙ styling details can be manipulated to create groups or individual items.

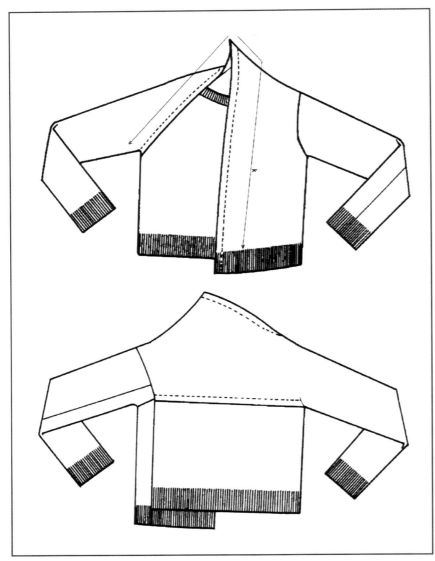

Figure 5.1   Example of a technical flat.

The Language of Construction

Understanding how garments are constructed is a critical component in the design process. Speaking the language of sewing, fitting, patterns, and silhouettes is part of being in the fashion industry. Every business has its own language, and learning the terminology is the first step toward being a successful professional. Much like a secret Masonic handshake, those who don't know the signs and symbols are limited.

Designers, patternmakers, buyers, production personnel, cutters, markers, seamstresses, and merchandise managers all understand the language of construction. Every detail drafted or draped onto a garment has a name. Sometimes these names are logical labels or associative words, but sometimes they are fanciful terms. Remember, all the specific sewing components in a garment are considered styling details; the **silhouette** of a garment is the outside shape minus the styling details.

Various Types of Flats

There are three main types of flat garment drawings utilized in the fashion industry: technical, spec, and stylized flats.

Technical Flats

Technical flats are manually or digitally created illustrations of a garment without the fashion figure (see Figure 5.1). These flats are used primarily for production purposes. They are considered the blueprints for sewing and producing articles of clothing. Accuracy is the key element when drafting a technical flat.

Spec Flats

Spec flats are identical to technical flats in appearance except that sewing measurements are included with the drawings (see Figure 5.2). Complex construction details are sometimes enlarged to the side or framed in a thought bubble next to the spec. All technical and spec flat drawings are outlined in black ink, or if computer-generated, they have black stroke lines to delineate them as objects. As with technical flats, accuracy is of key importance.

Stylized Flats

Compared with technical and spec flats, **stylized flats** are more free-flowing and animated. Stylized flats are used more as sales tools—so creative license is acceptable (see

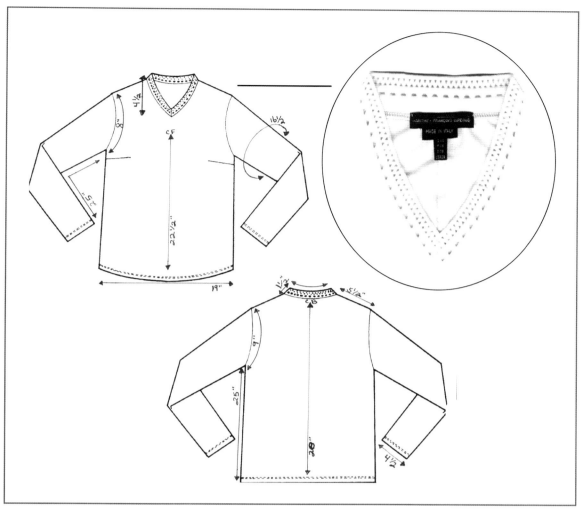

Figure 5.2   Example of a spec flat.

Figure 5.3). The aim is to make the drawing look desirable or to project a consistent and marketable image to a target customer. These types of drawings are also used internally at companies for a variety of purposes that include buying office bulletins, line sheets, trend forecasting, and sales and design presentations. Stylized flats are often utilized by designers as working sketches. It is acceptable to render them in either black and white or color. The rules for drawing stylized flats are distinctively less rigid than those for drawing technical flats.

Using the Pencil to Pen Tool Visual Index of Styling Details

The first part of this chapter illustrates key silhouettes used to clas-sify clothing. They provide a visual reference. These **Pencil to Pen Tool** silhouettes can serve as a starting point or guide for develop-ing your design ideas and new silhouettes.

The second part of this chapter is a visual index for specific styling and sewing details. This section can serve as both a visual reference and a terminology guide. All the details in this section have been included and converted to vector files. (Also see the flats library located in the Bonus Library folder on the CD-ROM ○ .)

The Digital Styling Details Library allows users to access and experiment with design details

Figure 5.3   Example of a stylized flat.

quickly. Access interchangeable components to test out ideas without having to draw, drape, draft, or sew (see Figure 5.4).

Creating a Digital Silhouette
To utilize the Digital Styling Details Library, launch the Adobe Illustrator software. Adobe Illustrator must be running on your computer

so you can work with the Digital Styling Details Library and complete tutorial lessons in Pencil to Pen Tool. Student or educational versions are widely available at

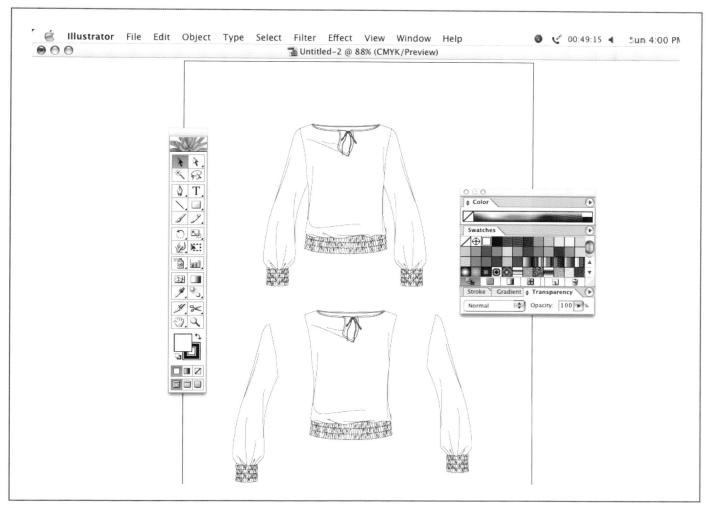

Figure 5.4 Design variation created using styling details.

discounted prices. Check with any college bookstore or on www.Adobe.com (click on educational software or student pricing).

After launching the program, open a new document through the Illustrator pull-down menu. Specify letter size in the dialog box that appears on the screen. There are multiple ways to create flat silhouettes digitally. The methods most commonly used today are the scanning method and the freehand method.

The Scanning Method

Once you scan your pencil-drawn flat into Adobe Photoshop, import it into Illustrator. In Illustrator, the pencil drawing is locked on a template layer and traced with the Pen Tool to create a **vector object**. Once the flat is converted to a vector object, you can manipulate, fill, scale, print, or upload it to the Web (see Figure 5.5).

One of the most common reasons for turning a flat into an .eps file format is to get the sharp, crisp lines that these vector images produce. Vector images or Illustrator files characterized with the extension .ai are resolution independent. See Lesson 2 in Chapter 12 for more tutorials and instructions. We do recommend that you complete these initial chapters and the Getting Started basic chapters

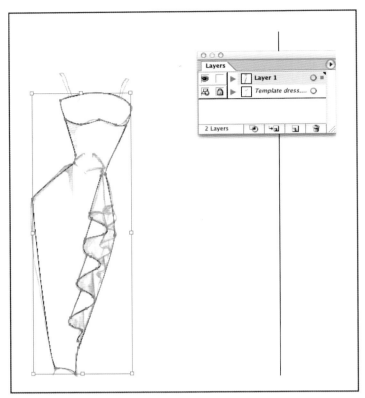

Figure 5.5   The scanning method.

before attempting more advanced silhouettes.

The Freehand Method

This method is more intuitive. A flat is developed from basic shapes directly on the computer screen. The Pen Tool is used in a free-form manner to create segments and anchor points that form a garment (see Figure 5.6).

You can lock a croquis or body on a separate template layer and utilize it as a reference or guide for the body's landmarks. Then trace the design or silhouette around the body. Experiment with these different methods to see which suits your skill level best. You can use the basic croquis on the CD-ROM ○ for this method or draw your own figure from the lessons in Chapter 4.

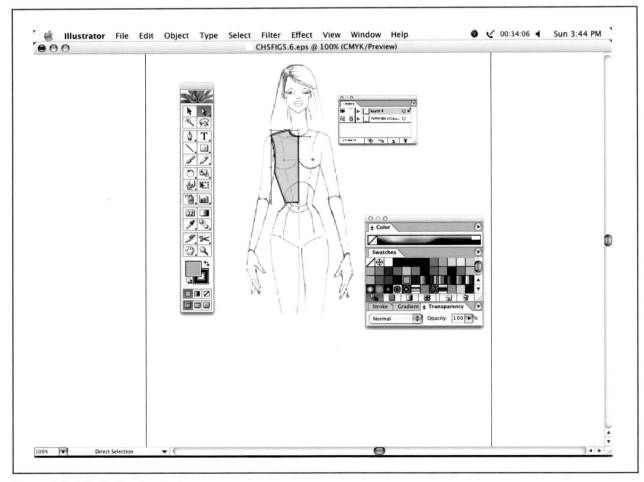

Figure 5.6   The freehand method.

The Pencil to Pen Tool Visual Index of Silhouettes (see figures 5.7a –5.11b)

Poncho

Hoodie

Trench Coat

Figure 5.7a Coats.

A-Line Swing Coat

Peacoat

Figure 5.7b   Coats (continued).

Bolero Jacket

Baseball/
Tour Jacket

Anorak Jacket

Figure 5.7c Jackets.

Cardigan Jacket

Eisenhower
Jacket

Blazer

Military/Double Breasted Jacket

Figure 5.7d   Jackets (continued).

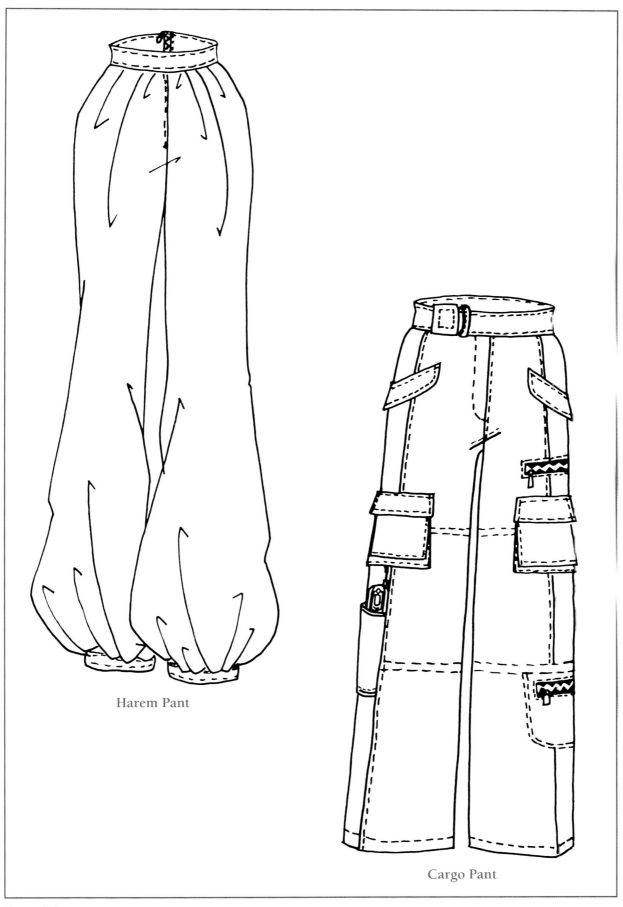

Harem Pant

Cargo Pant

Figure 5.8a Pants.

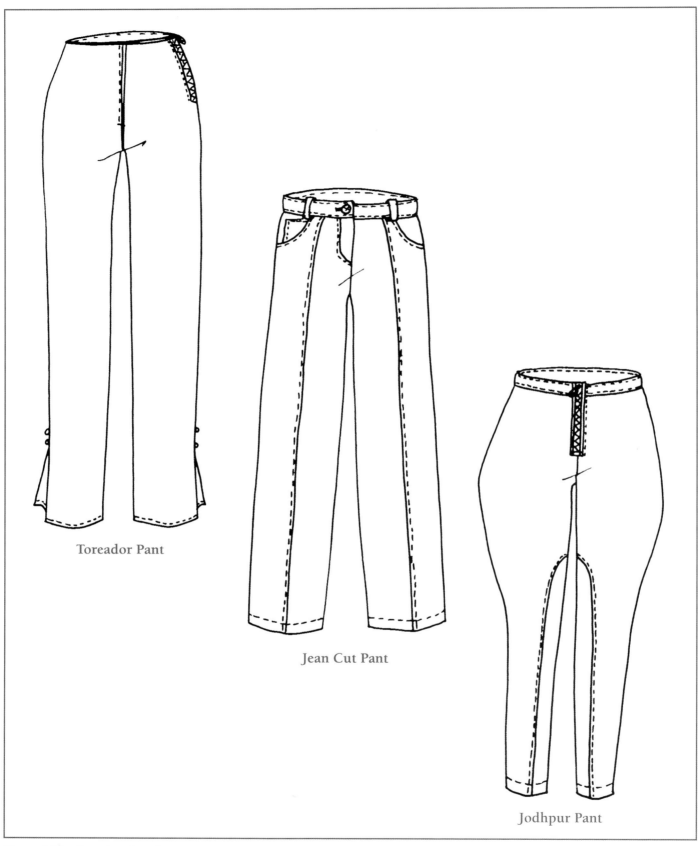

Toreador Pant

Jean Cut Pant

Jodhpur Pant

Figure 5.8b   Pants (continued).

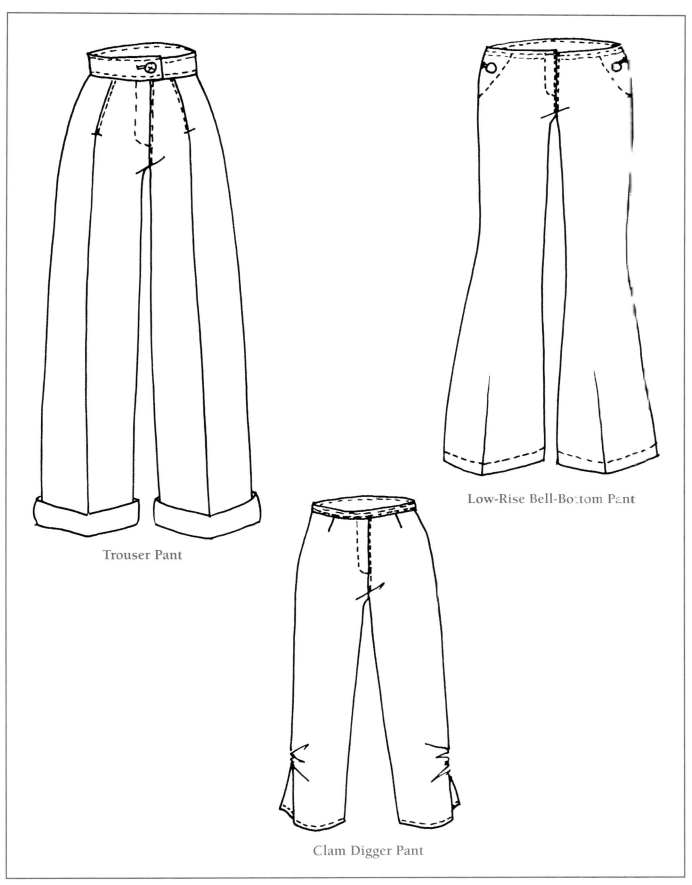

Trouser Pant

Low-Rise Bell-Bottom Pant

Clam Digger Pant

Figure 5.8c Pants (continued).

Figure 5.8d   Pants (continued).

Gored Skirt

Tiered Skirt

Basic Straight Skirt

A-Line Skirt

Figure 5.9a Skirts.

Tennis Wrap Skirt

Full Circle Skirt

Mermaid Skirt

Figure 5.9b   Skirts (continued).

Sarong Skirt

Pleated Skirt

Dirndl Skirt

Figure 5.9c   Skirts (continued)

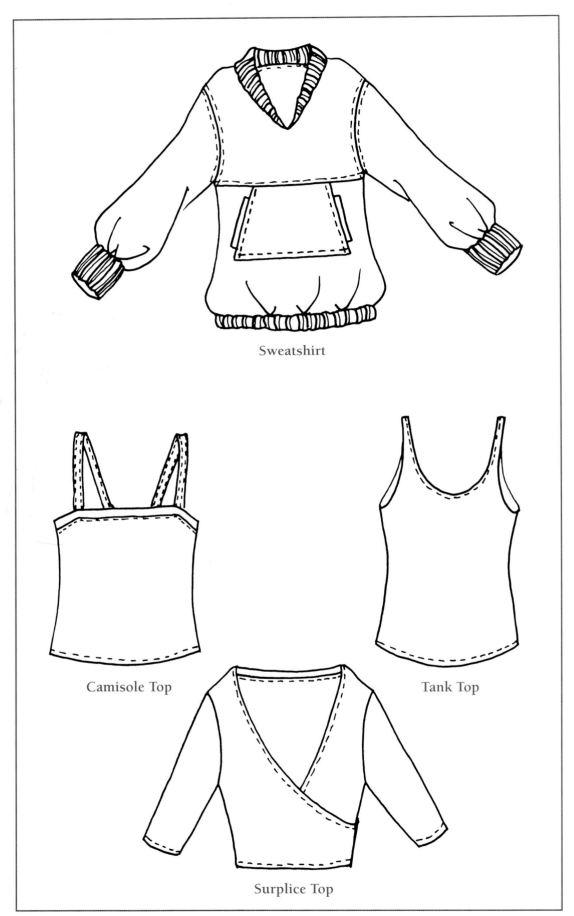

Sweatshirt

Camisole Top

Tank Top

Surplice Top

Figure 5.10a   Tops.

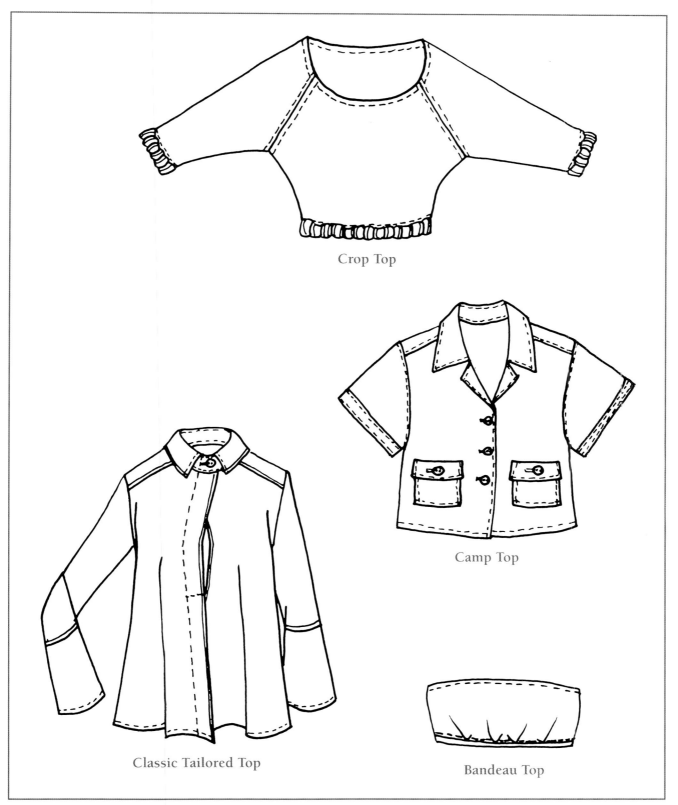

Crop Top

Camp Top

Classic Tailored Top

Bandeau Top

Figure 5.10b Tops (continued).

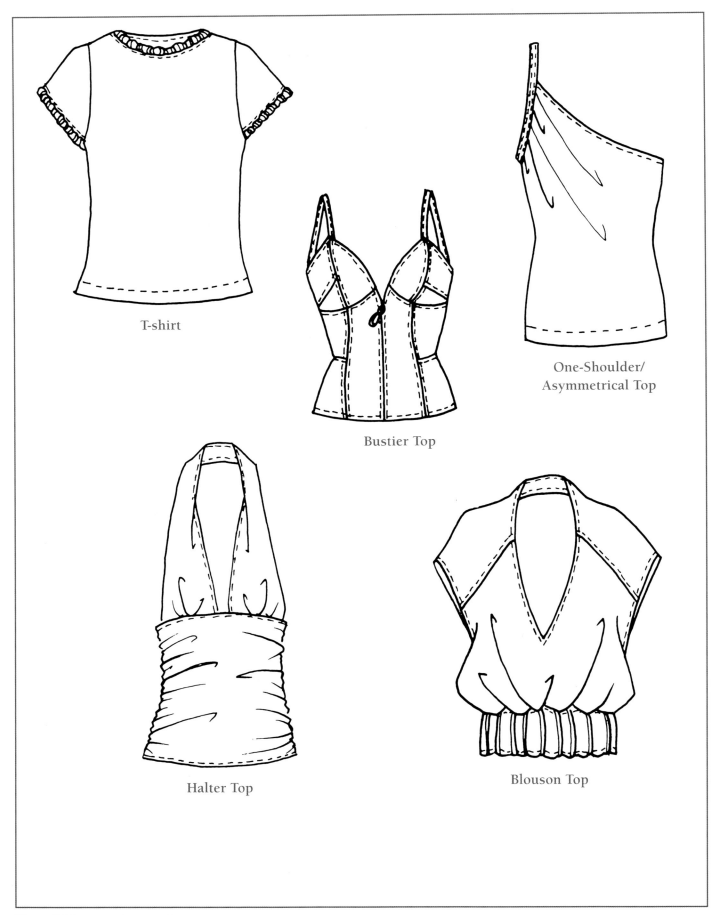

T-shirt

Bustier Top

One-Shoulder/
Asymmetrical Top

Halter Top

Blouson Top

Figure 5.10c   Tops (continued).

Tunic Dress

Wrap Dress

Empire Dress

Tent Dress

Figure 5.11a Dresses.

A-Line Dress

Drop-Waist
Dress

Sheath Dress

Chemise Dress

Hourglass-Style Dress

Figure 5.11b   Dresses (continued).

The Pencil to Pen Tool Visual Index of Styling Details with Corresponding Digital Library or CD-ROM

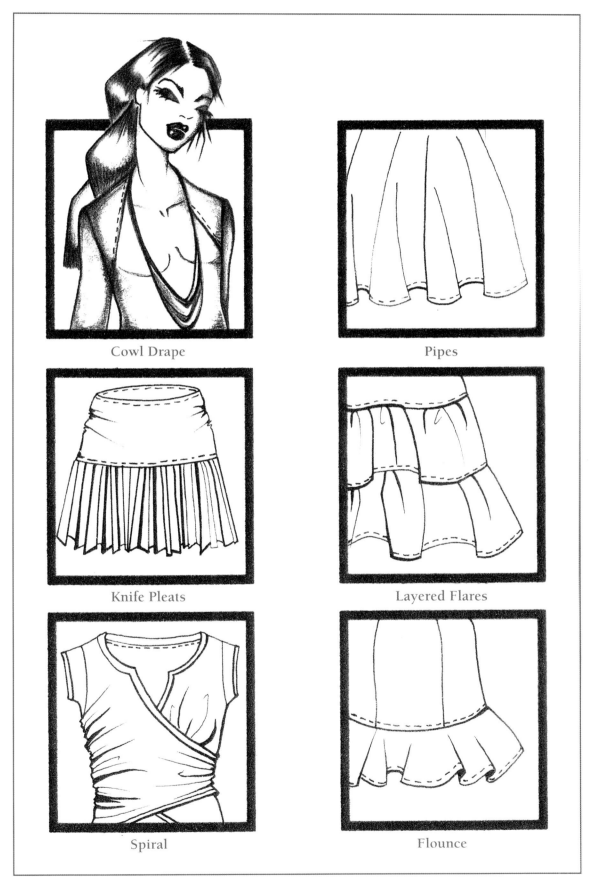

Cowl Drape

Pipes

Knife Pleats

Layered Flares

Spiral

Flounce

Figure 5.12a   Pleats, drapes, and folds.

Inverted Cluster

Fortuny Pleats

Box Pleats

Ruffled

Cascade

Shingled

Figure 5.12b   Pleats, drapes, and folds (continued).

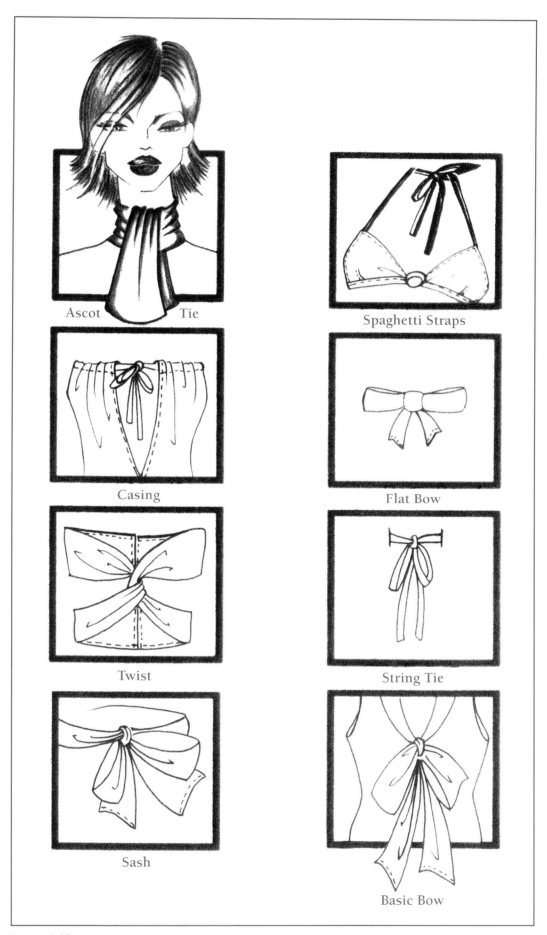

Figure 5.13a Ties, wraps, and bows.

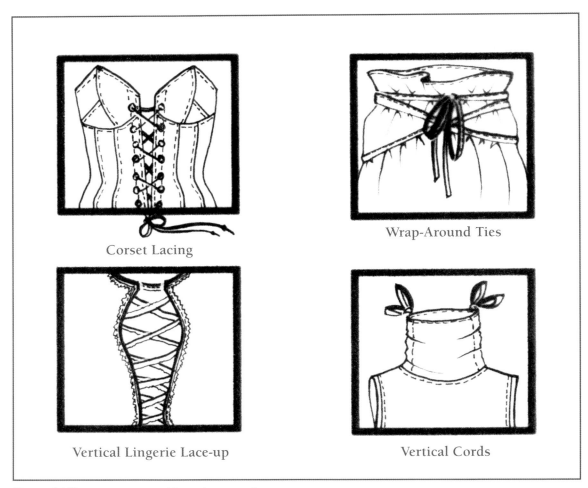

Corset Lacing

Wrap-Around Ties

Vertical Lingerie Lace-up

Vertical Cords

Figure 5.13b   Ties, wraps, and bows (continued).

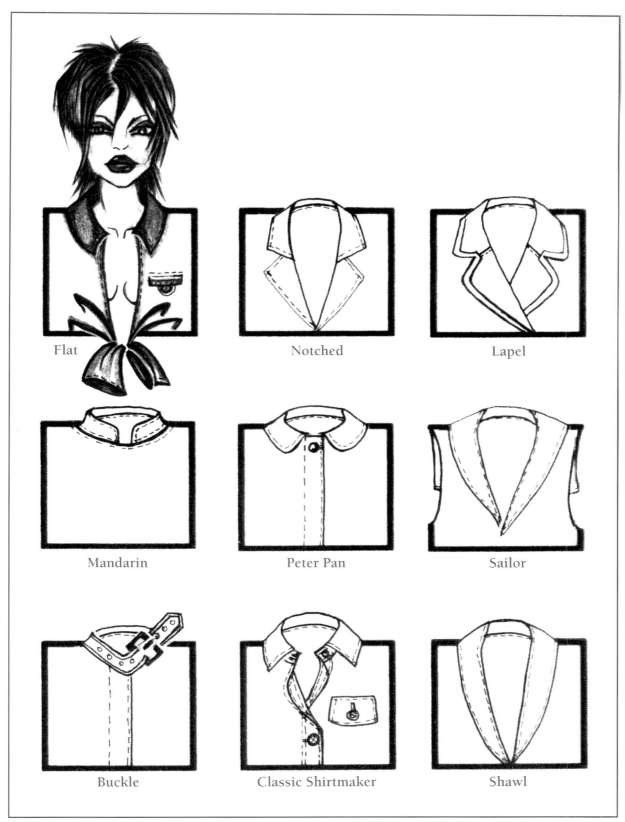

Figure 5.14a Collars and necklines.

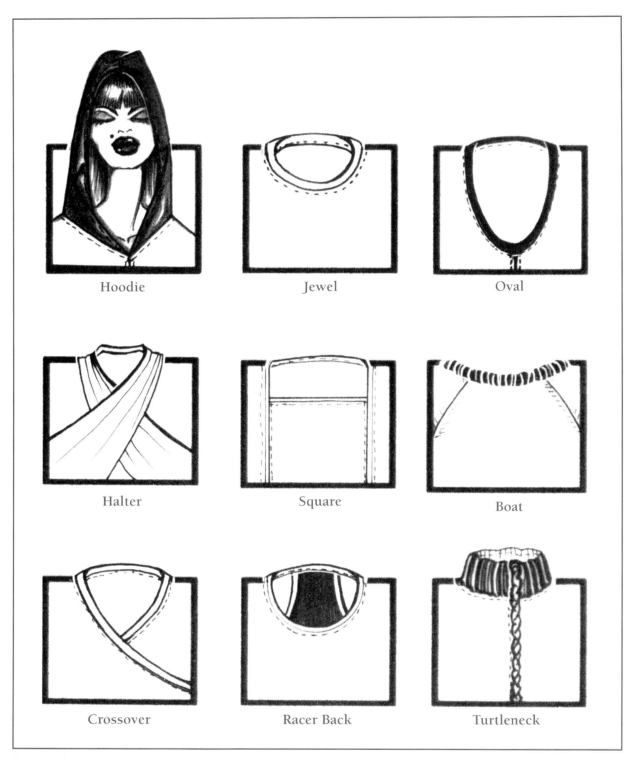

Figure 5.14b   Collars and necklines (continued).

Raglan

Kimono

Set-in

Three-Quarter

Leg-o'-Mutton

Slashed

Bishop

Placket

Figure 5.15a Sleeves.

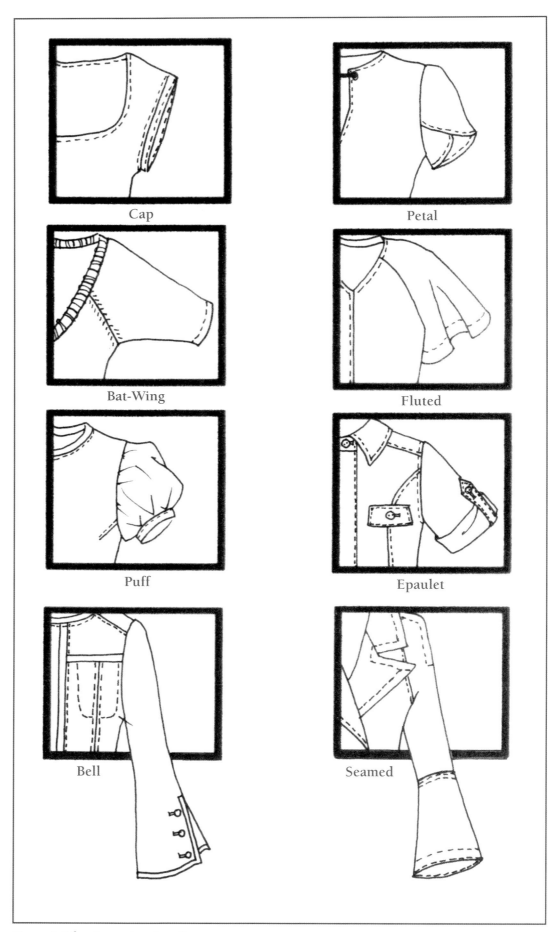

Figure 5.15b Sleeves (continued).

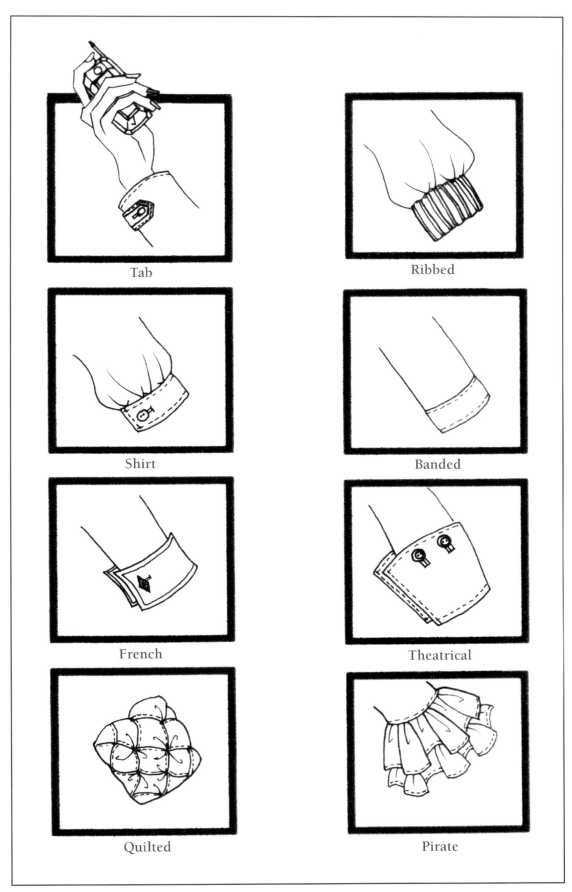

Figure 5.16a   Cuffs.

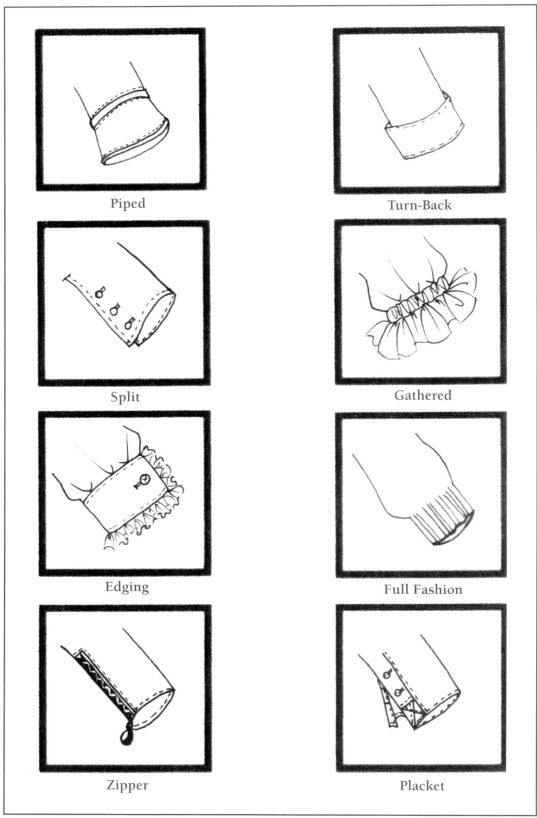

Piped

Turn-Back

Split

Gathered

Edging

Full Fashion

Zipper

Placket

Figure 5.16b   Cuffs (continued).

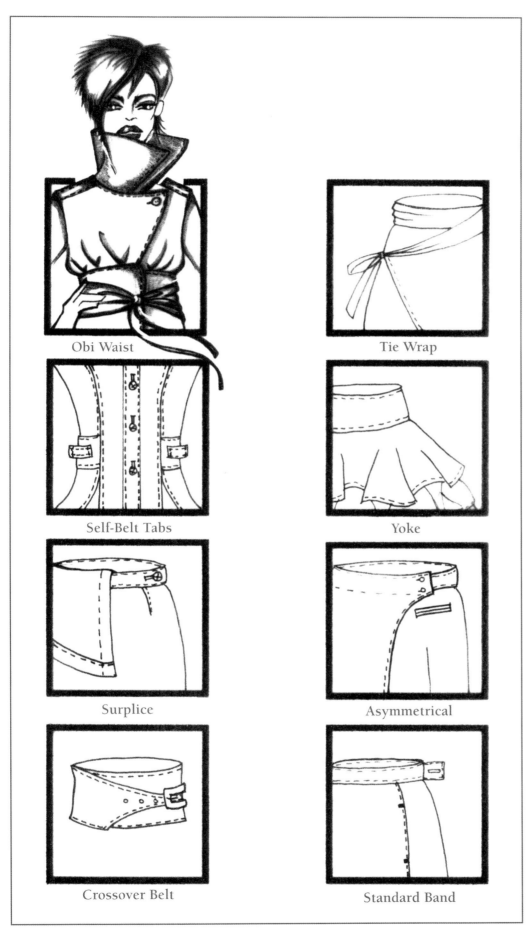

Obi Waist

Tie Wrap

Self-Belt Tabs

Yoke

Surplice

Asymmetrical

Crossover Belt

Standard Band

Figure 5.17a   Waist details.

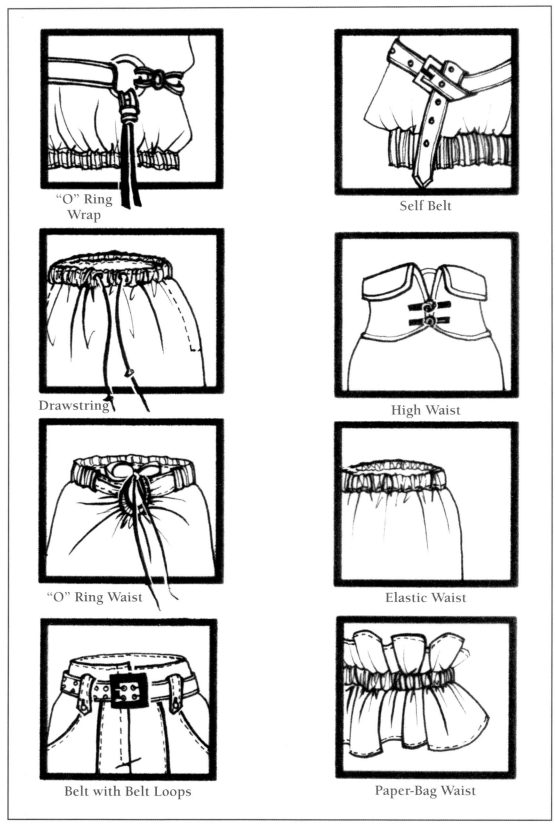

"O" Ring Wrap

Self Belt

Drawstring

High Waist

"O" Ring Waist

Elastic Waist

Belt with Belt Loops

Paper-Bag Waist

Figure 5.17b   Waist details (continued).

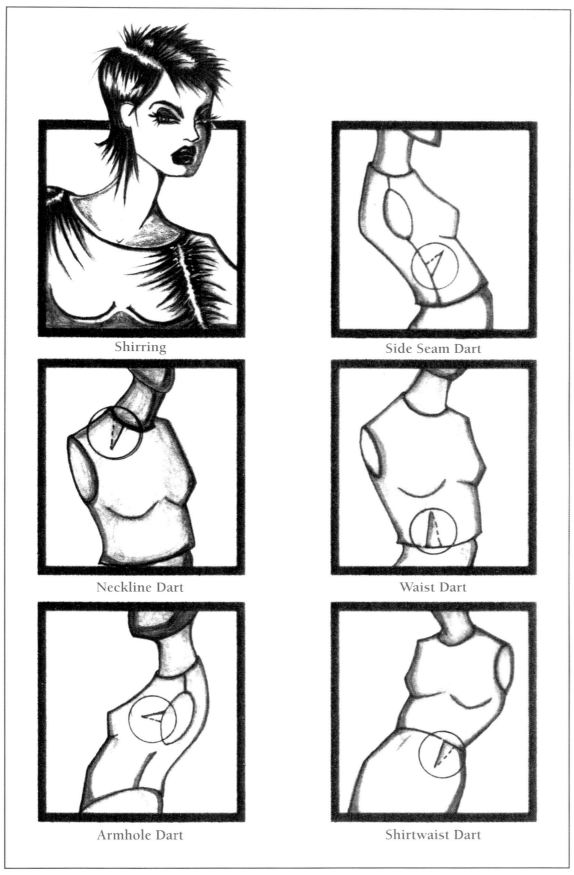

Shirring	Side Seam Dart
Neckline Dart	Waist Dart
Armhole Dart	Shirtwaist Dart

Figure 5.18a   Shape and control details.

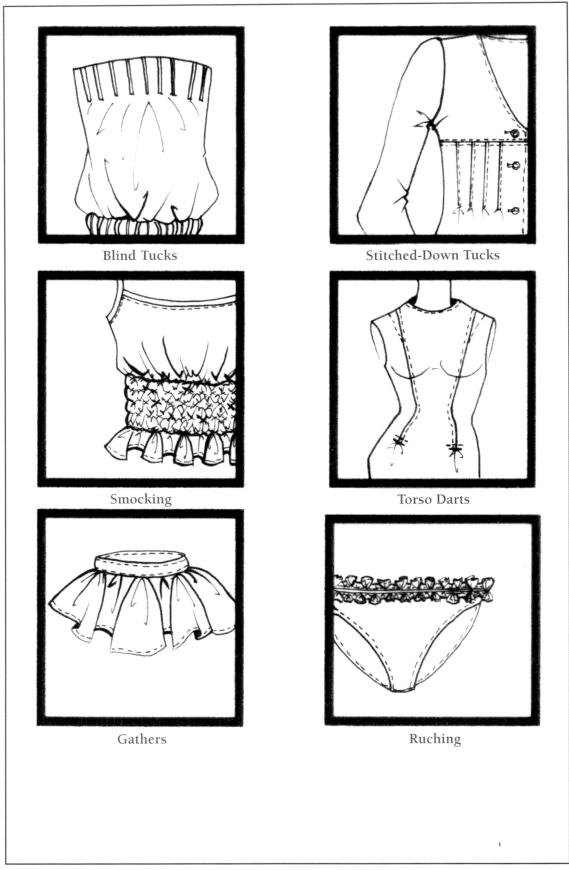

Blind Tucks

Stitched-Down Tucks

Smocking

Torso Darts

Gathers

Ruching

Figure 5.18b   Shape and control details (continued).

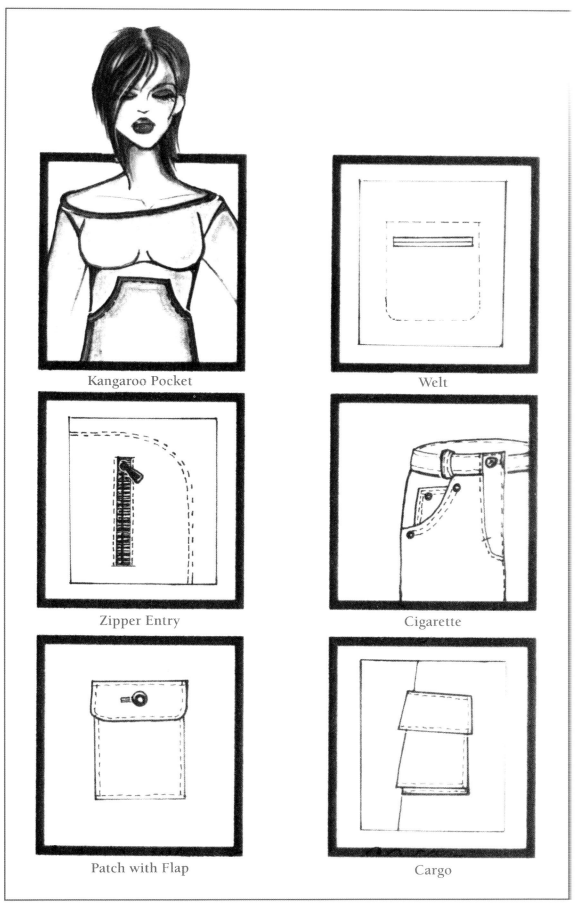

Kangaroo Pocket

Welt

Zipper Entry

Cigarette

Patch with Flap

Cargo

Figure 5.19a   Pocket details.

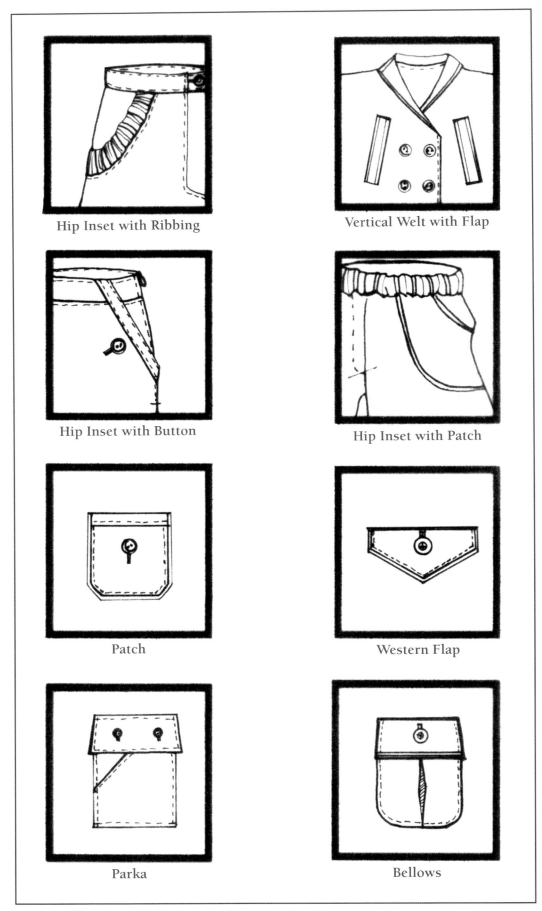

Hip Inset with Ribbing

Vertical Welt with Flap

Hip Inset with Button

Hip Inset with Patch

Patch

Western Flap

Parka

Bellows

Figure 5.19b   Pocket details (continued).

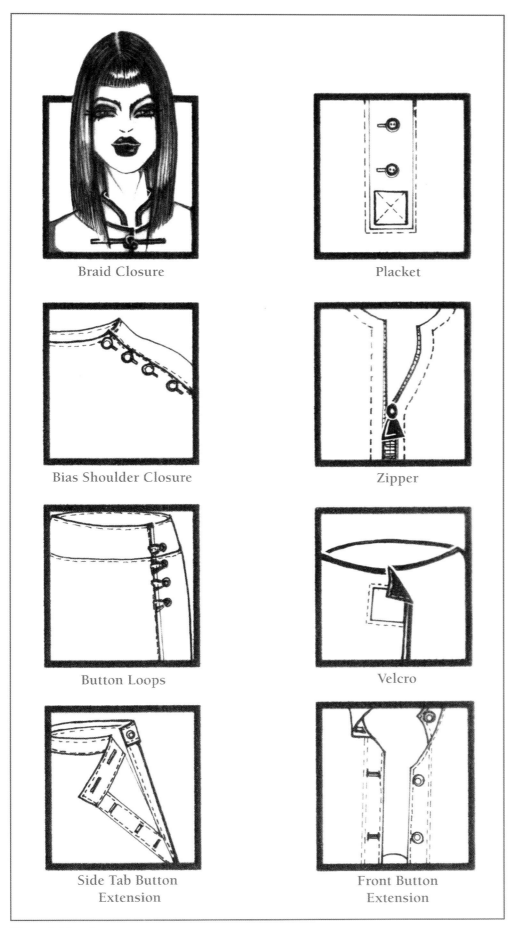

Braid Closure

Placket

Bias Shoulder Closure

Zipper

Button Loops

Velcro

Side Tab Button
Extension

Front Button
Extension

Figure 5.20   Closures.

Review Questions

1. For what purpose is a technical flat used?

2. For what purpose is a spec flat used?

3. Why is a drawing converted into a vector object?

4. What software application is used to scan a drawing?

5. What are three ways a stylized flat can be utilized to generate sales?

Suggested Practice Project

Scan a pencil-drawn flat (any silhouette) into Photoshop, and import the scan to Illustrator. Lock the scan on a layer and trace around it with the Pen Tool. Click on the eye icon in the Layers palette next to the scan layer to eliminate the pencil scan. This converts the flat into a vector object that can now be filled or manipulated. Open the Flats Library folder located on the CD-ROM ◌ in the Bonus Library folder. Choose details from the library that will enhance or alter your silhouette. Design a variety of items from the one original silhouette you created in Illustrator using the Pen Tool or scan method.

Key Terms

Resolution Independent

Silhouette

Spec Flats

Style Details

Stylized Flats

Target Customer

Technical Flats

Vector Object

6

Fashion Technology Overview: Pixel Versus Vector for the Mac and PC

What You Will Learn in Chapter 6

This chapter gives an overview of the basic vocabulary used to discuss hand-drawn and scanned images. Traditional vocabulary, such as pen-and-ink, charcoal, and bristol board, is replaced by vocabulary that identifies scanned images in vector-based or raster-based programs.

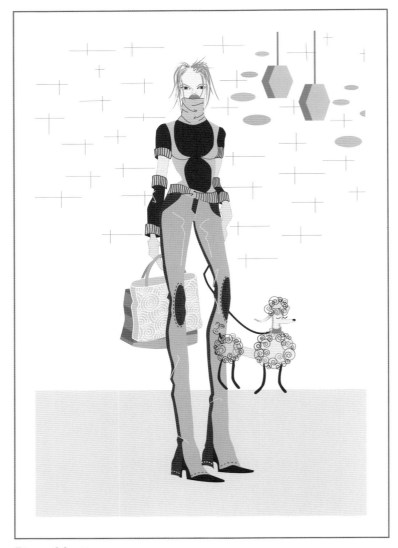

Figure 6.1   Vector image.

Introduction

The fashion industry, defined by its very existence, leads by innovation and change. It is, therefore, curious that this same industry was so slow to utilize the innovations of computer technology in the early 1990s, whether in two-dimensional or three-dimensional forms. As the twentieth century drew to a close, more people in the industry started switching to computers. Today designers are given newfound creative freedom with the advent of many time-saving innovations. Digital fabric printing, for instance, allows users to print any image onto fabrics without being hindered by the limitations of conventional printing and dyeing techniques. This new technology enables designers to include anything that can be drawn or scanned onto a surface. Now users can place, position, scale, or repeat an infinite number of images in any direction.

Mac or PC? Haute Couture or Prêt-à-Porter?

The choices in fashion are endless. The choices in computer platforms are two: Mac or PC. When a program is identified as **cross-platform**, it means the program can be used on either a Mac or PC. Graphic designers prefer to use Macs. It was designed from the ground up as the ideal tool for graphics. Advertising agencies, magazines, and newspapers almost always use Macs, as do professional photographers and digital video designers. In contrast, 3-D design is built around PC hardware and software, with systems allowing for virtual modeling and coordination of clothes and accessories.

Vector or Pixel?

The decision to work with **vectors** or **pixels** depends on what a fashion designer wants to convey with an image. Is it a flat image (such as a technical flat) or a three-dimensional illustration that has shades and shadows?

Vector Images

The vector drawing program creates curve and line images that appear flat (see Figure 6.1). The most important feature of vector drawings is that they are resolution independent. This means that changing the size does not change the quality or clarity of the line (see Figure 6.2). Blurring or jagged edges do not occur. Vector graphics are great for designing T-shirt graphics, flat renderings of garments, typography, and textile prints. Enlarged typography of a company name or logo can be scaled to encompass the entire front of a T-shirt or minimized and repeated to create unique patterns of multiple clusters.

Vector drawings (object-oriented drawings) are images defined by mathematical formulas. The drawings are easy to select, color, move, and resize without degrading the image. Vector graphics use very little memory for storage but are not as realistic as raster-based images.

Figure 6.2   Enlarged vector image.

Illustrator is the most commonly used vector-based program. Fashion designers create their technical flats (see Chapter 11) with Illustrator due to the sharp and well-defined edges that are generated with this software. The designs can then be edited, redesigned, and scanned into Photoshop for textile sampling (see Chapter 13).

Raster Images
Raster-based images (the technical term for bitmapped images) are composed of pixels that form images on a grid system (see Figure 6.3). Each pixel has a color value and a particular location. These color values make up the seamless lights and darks in a photograph. Due to their particular location, however, pixels lose detail and create aliasing—the jagged edges, or "jaggies," when scaled up (enlarged) on the screen or printed at lower resolutions (see Figure 6.4a and 6.4b). The advantage is that they are realistic images that can be transformed with other image-editing effects.

Fabrics can be color reduced and colors can be changed in raster

Figure 6.3   Raster image.

Figure 6.4a   Raster image scaled up to 300 DPI.

Figure 6.4b   Raster image printed at a low resolution of 72 DPI.

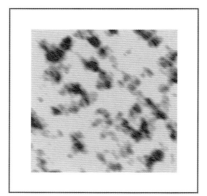

Figure 6.5a   Raster image of original fabric coloration.

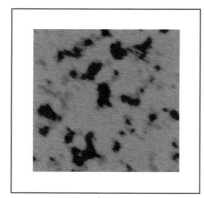

Figure 6.5b   Raster image of fabric color change.

programs (see Figure 6.5a and 6.5b). This feature allows for unlimited experimentation with various textile prints and color-ways.

Raster (bitmapped) images are resolution dependent, meaning that the user must specify a resolution. A common mistake users make is to scale up bitmapped images, which results in severe image degradation, although reducing the image size does not result in as severe an image degradation. Photoshop is the most commonly used raster-based software program. Many of the clean, crisp illustrations of the twenty-first century are drawn in Illustrator but textured and shaded in Photoshop. Any 2-D sketches, photographs, fabric swatches, buttons, trimming, or any flat found objects can be scanned into the computer and saved as image files. Chapters 7, 8, 9, and 12 detail the basics of Photoshop as well as its applications involving trend boards/ mood boards, textile prints, and other applications used in the fashion industry.

File Formats

Every graphics program defaults to its own native format; therefore, to ensure that a designer's work is readable in other applications, it must be assigned a special identify-ing code. This three-character code is called an extension. For example, if you have designed a corset and saved it in a Tagged Image File Format (TIFF), the file would be saved as corset.tif. If you saved the corset design in Photoshop, the extension would be .psd, and the file would be saved as corset.psd. If you want to reopen a file on a PC that was originally saved to a Mac, add .tag to the file name.

Following are some common file format extensions:

TIFF stands for Tagged Image File Format and is a cross-platform file format that can contain multiple images. It is successful with scanners and image-editing programs.

PSD is the native Photoshop file format and is the only format supporting most of the Photoshop features. It is wise to do most of your Photoshop work in this format. The Photoshop CS format allows other users to open your file even if they are working in an earlier version of the program.

BMP stands for bitmapped images. They are common to PC IBM-compatible computers. The BMP file format stores pixels or grids of dots in Windows format. It codes color information as 1, 4, 8, 16, or 24 bits.

EPS stands for Encapsulated Post-Script and is a standard cross-platform graphics file format primarily used for storing vector (object-oriented) graphics files generated by drawing applications such as Illustrator. It is a resolution-independent file format, meaning the file output will default to the printing device's highest possible resolution rather than being dependent on the pixel-per-inch resolution of the file itself. EPS is the best format for transferring files to a page layout or illustration program. It can contain both vector and rasterized images. An EPS file has two parts: the PostScript code directing the printer how to print the image and an on-screen preview in PICT, TIFF, or JPEG formats. EPS files will support clipping paths but not alpha channels (saved selections). Photoshop Desktop Color Separations (DCS) allows users to save spot colors and each of the color plates separately in CMYK mode. CMYK stands for cyan, magenta, yellow, and black, respectively, and all colors can be derived from this four-color process.

CompuServe GIF (Graphics Interchange Format) is a format commonly used for Web images containing flat colors and transparencies.

JPEG stands for Joint Photographic Image Experts Group and is the standard format for displaying continuous tone or photographic images on the Web. It can hold images using millions of colors and can save a broad color range and variations of continuous tone (contone) images.

PCX is a PC IBM-compatible format.

PDF stands for Portable Document Format and is a cross-platform, cross-application format that can embed fonts and images. It has a number of compression options.

Photoshop Raw is a format used for transferring large files between platforms, but they cannot contain layers. The large document format can contain up to 300,000 pixels and be any dimension. It can also contain layers but is only supported by Photoshop CS.

The PICT format is a Mac format and is most often used for on-screen presentations. Pixar is used for animation and 3-D programs.

PNG stands for Portable Network Graphics and is a lossless compression. Although some browsers do not support this format, it is most often used for display on the Web.

CT is a format used by Scitex computer systems for storing continuous tone (contone) scanned images for high-end productions such as fashion ads.

Targa is a digital image format for 24-bit image files used for MS-DOS applications.

Review Questions

1. What does "vector-based" denote?

2. What does "raster-based" denote?

3. Is Photoshop vector-based or raster-based?

4. What is meant by cross-platform?

5. What are three file formats and their corresponding three-character extensions?

Key Terms

Application	PC
Bitmapped	PCX
BMP	PDF
CMYK	PICT
Cross-platform	Pixels
DPI	PSD
EPS	Raster-based image
Extension	Raster-based software
File	Resolution
File format	Resolution independent
GIF	Scale
Image degradation	Scanner
Jaggies	TIFF
JPEG	Vector
Layers	Vector images
Mac	

7

Software Basics:
Getting Started with Adobe Photoshop CS

What You Will Learn in Chapter 7

It is crucial to understand the basics of Photoshop in order to progress to more complicated Photoshop techniques. This chapter explains the basics and also serves as a review tool for intermediate Photoshop users. It covers Photoshop basics, the environment, the toolbar, and pull-down menu items. System requirements for Macintosh and PCs are outlined along with setting preferences.

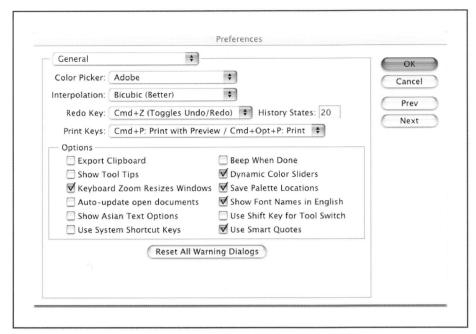

Figure 7.1   Setting Photoshop CS General Preferences.

Systems Requirements for Photoshop 7.0 and Photoshop CS
Photoshop runs effectively with a Windows Pentium-class (or faster) operating system and a Windows 98 (or later) or Windows NT 4.0 or Millennium operating system. Photoshop needs the Macintosh system with a PowerPC (or faster) processor running OS 8.5, 8.6, or 9.0 (or later). Photoshop CS needs 10.3 (or later).

The monitor should be capable of displaying 800 X 600 pixels and at least 8-bit color (256) or more. Most monitors today are capable of 16-bit color (thousands of colors). Your computer should have a minimum RAM (Random Access Memory) of 64 MB (megabytes), although 128 MB is suggested for running Photoshop CS and Image Ready together. This does not include any memory required for the operating system or for running other programs at the same time. The virtual memory option or scratch disk is used when Photoshop doesn't have enough room or memory to handle a file entirely in RAM. You'll want as much space in RAM plus at least five times the size of any file you work on.

Setting Photoshop CS Preferences
Photoshop CS Preferences can be accessed through the Photoshop pull-down menu. Set the General Preferences according to Figure 7.1. General Preferences in Photoshop refer to the basic work environment interface. Manipulating keyboard commands and navigation ease levels are also set in this panel.

Click on the button marked Next in the Preferences sidebar after becoming familiar with and setting the General Preferences according to Figure 7.1. Move through the panels and set the other Preferences according to the Pencil to Pen Tool options. Preferences, such as language, can be changed for individual considerations. You may want to reset the Preferences to suit your individual needs as you become more proficient in Photoshop CS.

Color Picker: Setting the Color Picker to Adobe will give you more options than the Apple System Color Picker.

Interpolation: Interpolation chooses how resampling (adding or taking away pixels) will occur. Bicubic interpolation is the most accurate.

Export Clipboard: Turn off the Export Clipboard option to make the switch from one application to another much faster.

Show Tool Tips: Check the Show Tool Tips option if you are a novice. When this is checked, tips can be easily accessed when you roll the mouse over the toolbar. Other tips show up for palettes and dialog boxes. This is a good way to memorize the toolbar functions. You can turn off this option once you become familiar with Photoshop CS.

Keyboard Zoom Resizes Window: Check this option. It allows you to use the keyboard commands to resize the screen window.

Dynamic Color Sliders: Check this option. The Dynamic Color Slider allows you to see all the possible colors in the Color Palette as you change colors.

Use shift key for Tool Switch: Keep this option unchecked. You won't have to use the shift key when moving through each tool.

Figure 7.2   File Handling Preferences.

File Handling

Click on the button marked Next in the sidebar. You should be in the File Handling dialog box. Preferences should be set according to Figure 7.2. The File Handling Preferences are set to facilitate the handling of file formats, folders, and file memory size.

Image Previews: Select the Ask When Saving option. An icon will be created automatically if this option is not activated. The file size is increased when a preview icon is created. You should take this into consideration when saving for the Web.

Append File Extension: Keep this checked. This option appends the correct three-character file extensions so they can be opened on a PC platform.

File Compatibility: Keep Ask Before Saving Layered TIFF Files

and Always Maximize Compatibility for Photoshop (PSD) Files checked. You will have the option of flattening TIFF files. This will result in smaller memory use and file size.

Enable Workgroup Functionality: Keep this option checked when file sharing on a network.

Displays & Cursors

Click on the button marked Next in the sidebar. The dialog box for Displays & Cursors will appear. This panel will affect Photoshop brushes, cursors, and color options. Set these Preferences according to Figure 7.3.

Color Channels in Color: Turn this option off. The channels will then appear in gray scale, which is a more accurate display. Channels store color information and Alpha Channels store selections.

Use Diffusion Dither: Keep this option checked. This allows for a smoother transition on colors that

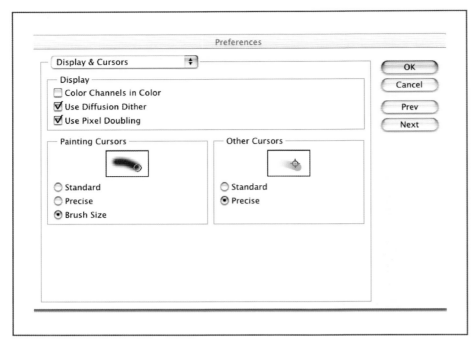

Figure 7.3   Displays & Cursors Preferences.

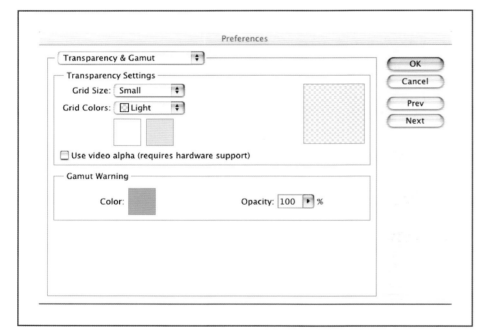

Figure 7.4   Transparency & Gamut Preferences.

are not in the Photoshop color palette.

Use Pixel Doubling: Check this box. This option speeds up the preview of tools and commands and has no effect on an image.

Painting Cursors: Check the Brush Size option. This option will display the size of the brush. Other Cursors should be set to Precise.

Transparency & Gamuts
The next Preference dialog box is Transparency & Gamut (see Figure 7.4). A Transparency preference setting refers to the area on a Photoshop layer that appears as a checkerboard. A Gamut is the range of colors a particular color mode will display. A Gamut warning occurs when there is a large variable between the screen and possible print color. This warning appears as a yellow triangle in the color picker.

Grid Size: Set this option to Small. The grid size determines the size of the gray squares on the Photoshop layers. The background is transparent. You can experiment with this option to see which one you prefer.

Grid Colors: Gray is the default color. This option can be adjusted by double clicking on the gray color box. A color wheel will appear, allowing the user to select a new Grid Color.

Use video alpha: Use video alpha is not checked. You should check this option if you want a transparent background to export to video.

Gamut Warning: This allows the viewer to see which areas of an

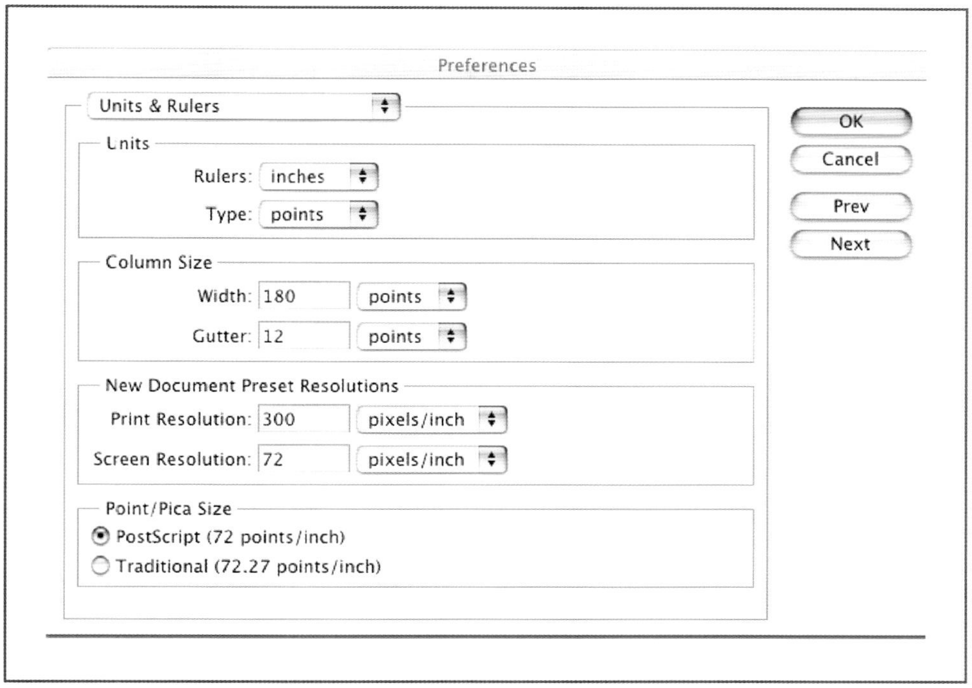

Figure 7.5   Units & Rulers Preferences.

image will not be Gamut safe printable colors.

Opacity: The Opacity slider in the Gamut Warning box allows users to adjust opacity when they are checking colors for Gamut Warnings and printability.

Units & Rulers

Click on the button marked Next to access the Units & Rulers options. Units and Rulers in this Preference panel aid the Photoshop user with measurements, point sizes, pixel sizes, file or image resolution, and document Grids (see Figure 7.5).

Units: These options can be set to display the way Rulers and Type measure print or Web documents, respectively.

Rulers: We recommend inches or millimeters.

Type: The choice of points, pixels, or millimeters is available. Based on

the final output and your personal preference, select one of these options. We suggest you use the point scale for print and the pixel option for the Web.

Column Size: Set these options based on the size of your page and number of columns required. You can select the measurement system you prefer, either points or inches.

Width: This box allows you to type in a value amount.

Gutter: This option refers to the width between two columns. Type in a value.

New Document Preset Resolutions: These two settings are the default sizes that come up when you open a new Photoshop document.

Print Resolution: Use the default option setting of 300 pixels/inch.

Screen Resolution: Use the default option setting of 72 pixels/inch.

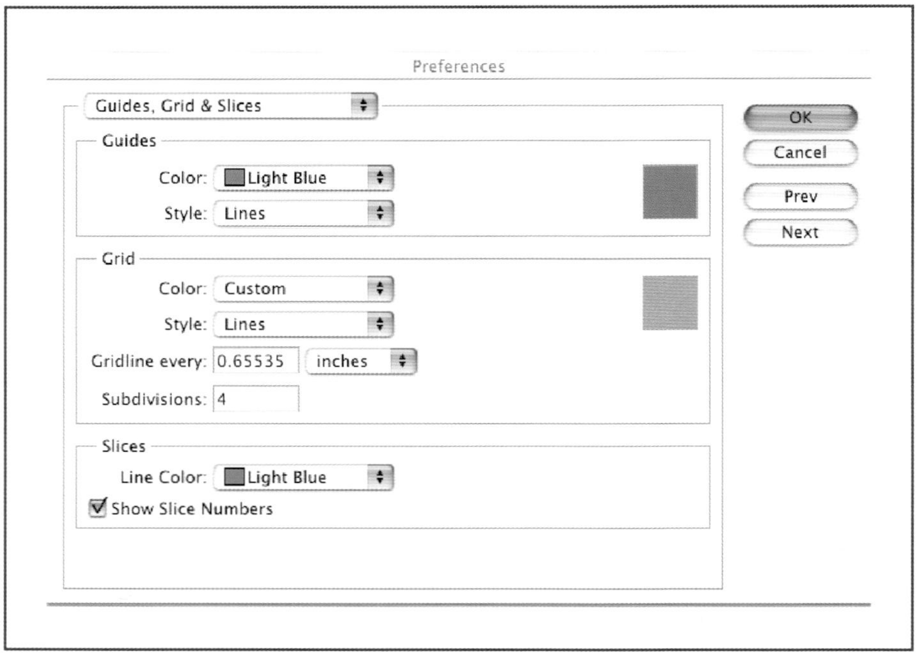

Point/Pica Size: Click the PostScript (72 points/inch) option setting.

Guides, Grid & Slices

The next dialog box to appear is Guides, Grid & Slices (see Figure 7.6). Guides and Grid allow you to change the appearance of the Guides and Grid you are using. Slices affect Web pages.

Guides: This allows you to change the way Guides are displayed. You can double click on a Guide when the move tool is selected. This will bring up the Guides Preferences panel.

Color: Set the Guide color by clicking the color box on the right.

Style: This allows you to select the line style for a Grid. Options are dashed lines, dots, or straight lines.

Gridline every: This option box allows you to type in a value for the space between Gridlines or subdivisions.

Slices: Slices are a way to optimize images for the Web.

Line Color: This is the color that your line guides will appear while you are laying out slices on a Web page.

Show Slice Numbers: Keep this box checked; it will help keep you organized when working on a Web page.

Plug-Ins & Scratch Disks

Click the button marked Next to access the Plug-Ins & Scratch Disks dialog box. This option refers to the Plug-Ins Folder and reserve memory options. Set these Preferences according to Figure 7.7.

Figure 7.6   Guides, Grid & Slices Preferences.

Additional Plug-Ins Folder: Check this box. The Plug-Ins Preferences tell Photoshop where to find Plug-Ins filters and actions. Click the button marked Choose to find the Plug-Ins Folder located in the Photoshop CS application.

Scratch Disks: The Scratch Disk Preferences tell Photoshop where to store temporary files on disk. Use the disk drive with the largest amount of memory for the First option. Any additional drives may be used for the Second, Third, and Fourth options.

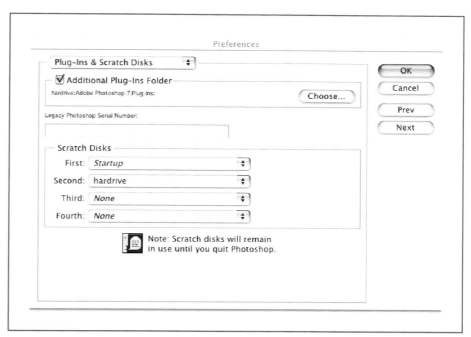

Figure 7.7   Plug-Ins and Scratch Disks.

Memory & Image Cache

The next dialog box is Memory & Image Cache (see Figure 7.8). Cache Settings will increase Photoshop's effectiveness when working with larger files. The larger the cache setting, the more RAM and disk space Photoshop uses when opening a file.

Cache Settings: We recommend setting this option to 4.

Use cache for histograms: Keep this box unchecked. This will give a more accurate histogram reading.

Memory Usage: Devote at least 50 percent to the Maximum Used by Photoshop setting.

Color Settings

The Color Settings dialog box can be accessed through the Photoshop CS pull-down menu (see Figure 7.9).

Settings: Click on the Custom option to customize or reset these Preferences.

Working Spaces: This allows you to set color output Preferences accord-

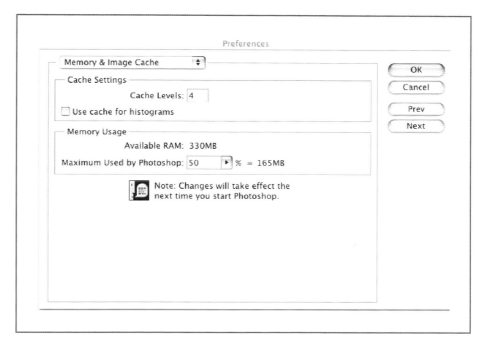

Figure 7.8   Memory & Image Cache Preferences.

ing to the Preferences that are enabled in these bars.

RGB: Set this option to ColorMatch RGB. This is the industry standard for print work and gives the most reliable screen color.

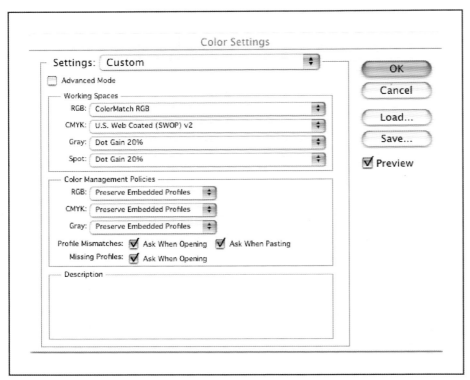

Figure 7.9   Color Settings.

CMYK: Set this to U.S. Web Coated (SWOP) V2. SWOP stands for Standardized Web Offset Printing. This is the industry standard for print work.

Gray: Set this to Dot Gain 20 percent as the default amount. Dot Gain determines how much black ink is to be distributed. The higher the percentage, the more black is distributed.

Spot: Set this option to Dot Gain 20 percent.

Color Management Policies: These setting options affect the way a file opens to default Preference settings. When you open a file that was not set up for current configurations, you will be notified.

RGB: Set option to Preserve Embedded Profiles.

CMYK: Set option to Preserve Embedded Profiles.

Gray: Set option to Preserve Embedded Profiles.

Profile Mismatches: Check these two boxes.

Missing Profiles: Check this box.

Preview: Check this box.

File Browser Preferences
The next dialog box is the File Browser Preferences box. This allows you to control the size and appearance of preview icons, files, and folders that appear on your desktop or laptop in the Photoshop environment.

Do Not Process Files Larger Than: We recommend setting this value at or no larger than 200 MB.

Display: Set this to the number 10.

Custom Thumbnail Size: Set this to 256 in the numbers field.

High Quality Previews: Check this box.

Keep Sidecar Files with Master Files: Check this box.

Navigating Around the Photoshop CS Work Environment
Learning the quickest ways around the Photoshop interface will help you to save time and money (see Figure 7.10). Here are several important keyboard commands to remember.

- Press Command (CTRL for Windows) and 0 (zero) to bring the document into full view.
- Press Command (CTRL for Windows) and the − (minus) key to zoom out.
- Press Command (CTRL for

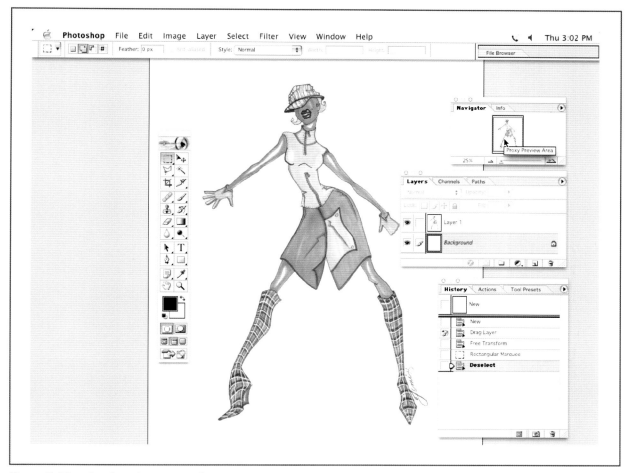

Figure 7.10 The Photoshop CS Interface.

Windows) and the + (plus) key to zoom in.

• Hold the space bar down to switch to the hand tool, which allows you to maneuver around the document.

Modes

There are three different modes you can work with in Photoshop: Normal Screen Mode, Full Screen Mode, and Full Screen Mode Without Menu Bar. By pressing the F key on your keyboard you can scroll through the different modes. It is preferable to work in Full Screen Mode because if you accidentally click down on the gray area you won't switch to some other application or the Finder. The gray area also serves as a neutral background to view colors against. Full Screen Mode Without Menu Bar has a black background and is useful for presentations.

Scrolling and Zooming

Holding down the space bar will switch the cursor to the hand tool, allowing you to scroll around your document even with dialog boxes (such as Levels or Curves) open. If you hold down the Option/Alt for Windows key with the space bar, the cursor will switch to the minus sign, allowing you to shrink the image on your screen. Holding down the Command/CTRL for Windows key and space bar together will switch the cursor to a plus sign, allowing you to zoom back to the original size. These are handy keyboard commands to use when a dialog box is open. The

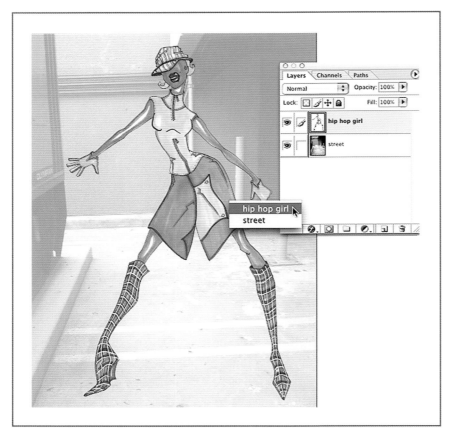

Figure 7.11   Control key or right click shortcut.

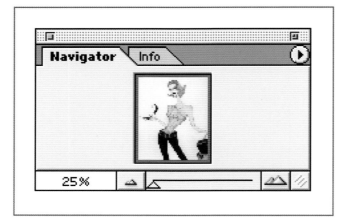

Figure 7.12   Navigator palette.

zoom tool is not automatically accessible when a dialog box is open. Pressing Command/CTRL for Windows and zero allows the entire image to fit on the screen. Pressing Command/Option and zero zooms the image back to 100 percent.

Control Key or Right Click

Holding down the CTRL key or mouse right click for Windows while working on a particular active layer will bring up a context-sensitive menu (see Figure 7.11). This shortcut allows you to visually identify the layer you are working on. The same CTRL/right click action can be utilized to access the transformation commands: scale, rotate, skew, flip, and perspective.

Navigator Palette

The Navigator palette allows you to adjust the view or to focus in on a particular detail (see Figure 7.12). The Navigator palette has four methods of operation.

1. The image viewing size can be numerically typed in via the percent field in the lower left corner of the palette.
2. Using the slider at the bottom will also scale your view.
3. Clicking on the double pyramids on either side of the slider will increase or decrease the document size.
4. You can grab the red outline around the image with the hand tool (access the hand tool by pressing the spacer bar) to scale or manipulate the image around the Photoshop document.

File Browser

The File Browser allows you to open, view, delete, rotate, copy, sort, rename, and move a file (see Figure

7.13). You can also view file information in the File Browser feature. The highlighted file shows it is selected and can now be renamed, rotated, opened, and manipulated in any other way. Click the flag icon to flag a file you have selected. This is a way to organize a large number of files. Metadata shows a file's information, including size and modification dates. The Automate menu lets you batch and run actions on files chosen through the File Browser. You can run a number of other automated functions, such as Web Gallery, Photomerge, and Contact Sheets.

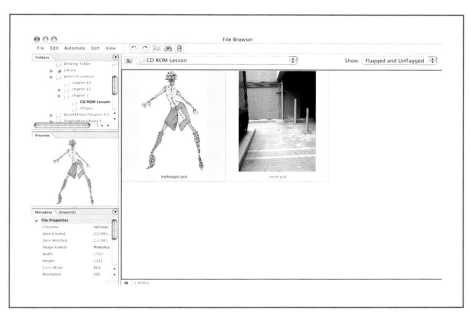

Figure 7.13   File Browser.

The Photoshop Toolbar

To access the Photoshop toolbar, go to the pull-down menu and click on Window-Tools. Click once on the tool icon in the toolbar to select an individual tool. Place the cursor over the arrow located in the lower right corner of some of the tools. This displays a subfunction list.

Tools can be grouped into five categories. The selection tools select pixels. The crop and slice tools isolate objects. The painting tools fill, create, and change color. The retouch tools are used to improve and correct pixels. The other tools are native to Photoshop and help you to navigate the work environment. Memorize the keyboard commands in Figure 7.14 and Table 7.1 to use the tools more efficiently.

The Options Bar

The options bar as shown in Figure 7.15 is located on your computer screen directly under the pull-down menu. It is an adjunct function that works in conjunction with the tools in the toolbar. This feature allows you to view and activate preset toolbar options.

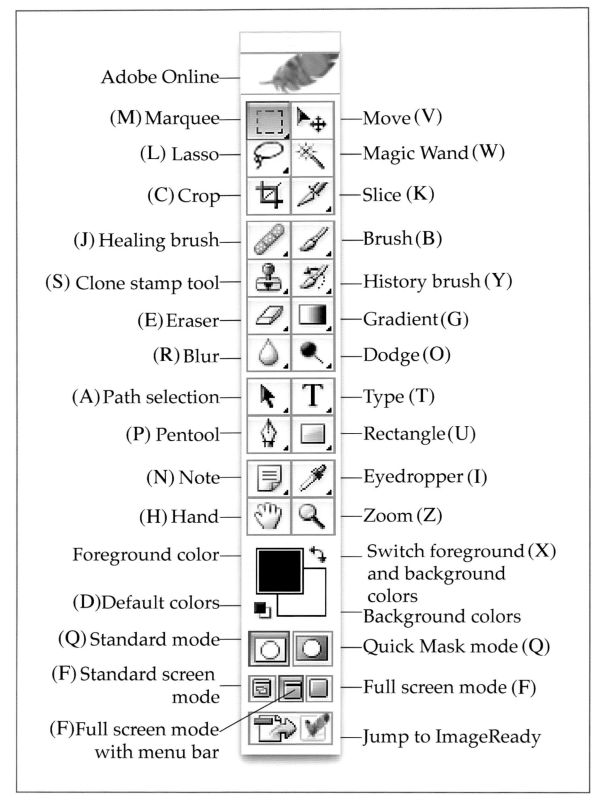

Adobe Online

(M) Marquee — Move (V)

(L) Lasso — Magic Wand (W)

(C) Crop — Slice (K)

(J) Healing brush — Brush (B)

(S) Clone stamp tool — History brush (Y)

(E) Eraser — Gradient (G)

(R) Blur — Dodge (O)

(A) Path selection — Type (T)

(P) Pentool — Rectangle (U)

(N) Note — Eyedropper (I)

(H) Hand — Zoom (Z)

Foreground color — Switch foreground (X) and background colors

(D) Default colors — Background colors

(Q) Standard mode — Quick Mask mode (Q)

(F) Standard screen mode — Full screen mode (F)

(F) Full screen mode with menu bar — Jump to ImageReady

Figure 7.14   Retouch tools.

Figure 7.15   The options bar.

Table 7.1 Toolbox Shortcuts and Corresponding Keyboard Commands
The toolbox, toolbox submenus, and corresponding keyboard commands are listed below. Using these keyboard commands whenever possible will save time.

Pressing the Shift key and the corresponding keyboard command allows you to cycle through the tools submenu.

M = Rectangular Marquee Tool M / Elliptical Marquee Tool M / Single Row Marquee Tool / Single Column Marquee Tool	Rectangular Marquee Tool: Creates rectangular selections Elliptical Marquee Tool: Creates oval selections Single Row Marquee Tool: Creates selections that are 1 pixel high Single Column Marquee Tool: Creates selections that are 1 pixel wide
V =	Move Tool: Moves a layer, selection, text, or guide
L = Lasso Tool L / Polygonal Lasso Tool L / Magnetic Lasso Tool L	Lasso Tool: Creates freehand selections Polygonal Lasso Tool: Creates polygonal selections Magnetic Lasso Tool: Creates snap-to freehand selections
W =	Magic Wand Tool: Selects pixels that are similar in color
C =	Crop Tool: Crops the Photoshop canvas
K = Slice Tool K / Slice Select Tool K	Slice Tool: Slices images for the Web Slice Select Tool: Selects slices
J = Healing Brush Tool J / Patch Tool J	Healing Brush Tool: Applies and blends pixels from one area to another Patch Tool: Selects areas to blend pixels from one area to another
B = Brush Tool B / Pencil Tool B	Brush Tool: Applies brushstrokes Pencil Tool: Draws freehand lines
S = Clone Stamp Tool S / Pattern Stamp Tool S	Clone Stamp Tool: Clones and repositions pixels Pattern Stamp Tool: Applies patterns
Y = History Brush Tool Y / Art History Brush Y	History Brush Tool: Restores pixels from a designated history state Art History: Paints a history state or snapshot
E = Eraser Tool E / Background Eraser Tool E / Magic Eraser Tool E	Eraser Tool: Erases pixels Background Eraser Tool: Erases sample color Magic Eraser Tool: Erases areas of color
G = Gradient Tool G / Paint Bucket Tool G	Gradient Tool: Creates color blends Paint Bucket Tool: Fills areas with color
R = Blur Tool R / Sharpen Tool R / Smudge Tool R	Blur Tool: Blurs pixels Sharpen Tool: Sharpens pixels Smudge Tool: Smudges pixels

Table 7.1 Toolbox Shortcuts and Corresponding Keyboard Commands (*cont.*)

O = [Dodge Tool O / Burn Tool O / Sponge Tool O]	Dodge Tool: Lightens pixels Burn Tool: Darkens pixels Sponge Tool: Saturates or desaturates pixels
A = [Path Selection Tool A / Direct Selection Tool A]	Path Selection Tool: Selects paths Direct Selection Tool: Selects segments and points of a path
T = [Horizontal Type Tool T / Vertical Type Tool T / Horizontal Type Mask Tool T / Vertical Type Mask Tool T]	Horizontal Type Tool: Creates editable type on its own layer Vertical Type Tool: Creates vertical type Horizontal Type Mask Tool: Creates horizontal type in the form of a mask Vertical Type Mask Tool: Creates vertical type in the form of a mask
P = [Pen Tool P / Freeform Pen Tool P / Add Anchor Point Tool / Delete Anchor Point Tool / Convert Point Tool]	Pen Tool: Draws curved or straight paths Freeform Pen Tool: Draws freehand paths Add Anchor Point Tool: Adds points to a path Delete Anchor Point Tool: Deletes points from a path Convert Point Tool: Converts points into curves or corner points
U = [Rectangle Tool U / Rounded Rectangle Tool U / Ellipse Tool U / Polygon Tool U / Line Tool U / Custom Shape Tool U]	Rectangle Tool: Draws rectangular shapes Rounded Rectangle Tool: Draws rectangular shapes with rounded corners Ellipse Tool: Draws oval shapes Polygon Tool: Draws polygonal shapes Line Tool: Draws straight-line shapes Custom Shape Tool: Draws predefined custom shapes
N = [Notes Tool N / Audio Annotation Tool N]	Notes Tool: Creates non-printing annotations Audio Annotation Tool: Creates audio annotations
I = [Eyedropper Tool I / Color Sampler Tool I / Measure Tool I]	Eyedropper Tool: Samples colors from the image Color Sampler Tool: Places color sampler points Measure Tool: Measures distance
H = [Hand Tool icon]	Hand Tool: Moves the image around the document
Z = [Zoom Tool icon]	Zoom Tool: Enlarges and reduces the viewing size of an image
X =	This keyboard command switches the foreground and background colors.
D =	Activates the black-and-white default colors in the fill boxes
Q =	This command activates Quick Mask Mode.

Figure 7.16   File menu.

The Photoshop CS Pull-down Menus

Photoshop contains nine pull-down menus. They are file, edit, image, layer, select, filters, view, window, and help. This part of the chapter provides a comprehensive break-down of the options located within each menu. Please note that commands followed by ellipses (three periods) means a dialog box with options will appear.

File Menu

Following are some of the options available under the File pull-down menu (see Figure 7.16):

New: A dialog box containing presets and options for creating a new file

Open: Open a browser to find a file

Browse: Has advanced browser capabilities

Open Recent: Shows the most recent files opened

Edit in ImageReady: Opens the file up in ImageReady so it can be edited

Close: Closes the file that is active and open

Close All: Closes all open files

Save and Save As: Saves your files in a number of different formats

Save a Version: Manages files between the different Adobe applications

Save for Web: Saves images for the Web while viewing different options in a dialog box

Revert: Reverts to the last saved version

Place: Places EPS, PDF, and PSD files

Online Services: Connects remote service providers to send Photoshop images

Import: Import Anti-aliased PICT, PDF Image, PICT Resource, and Annotations

Export: Exports paths to Illustrator and Zoom view, creating an image for the Web

Automate: Batch, which allows you to run an action on multiple files and store them in a specified folder

PDF Presentation: Lets you open multiple images and turn them into a PDF slideshow

Create Droplet: Command creates an icon, which represents an action that you created, so when an image is dragged onto this icon the action is activated

Conditional Mode Change: Changes the color mode from the original to the specified one

Contact Sheet 11: Creates a sheet of thumbnail images from a selected folder

Crop and Straighten: Lets you crop and straighten multiple images

Fit Image: Allows you to fit an image into a size you choose without changing its aspect ratio (the ratio between the height of an image and the width).

Multipage PDF to PSD: Converts PDF pages to PSD files

Picture Package: Puts multiple copies of an image on a single page at different sizes

Web Photo Gallery: Creates a Web site with thumbnails linked to individual JPEG pages

Photomerge: Creates a panorama from multiple images

Scripts: Includes Export Layers as files, which lets you export individual layers as files in various formats

Exporting Layers to Files: Allows you to export layer comps as files in various formats.

Layer Comps to PDF: Turns layer comps into PDF files

Layer Comps to WPG: Turns layer comps into a Web picture gallery

File Info: Enters information about a File, Page Setup, or Print Preview

Page Setup: Provides choices for settings, format, and dimensions of a new page

Print with Preview: Shows how the page will print

Print: Opens a dialog box with options to print multiple copies

Print One Copy: Prints just one copy

Print Online: Allows you to open and print images online

Jump To: Opens the ImageReady application

Edit Menu
Following is a list of some of the options within the Edit menu (see Figure 7.17):

Undo Delete Action: Undoes the last step

Step Forward: Moves one step forward

Step Backward: Moves one step backward

Fade: Lessens the effects of most operations

Cut: Cuts the selection from the document and copies it to the clipboard

Copy: Copies the selection to the clipboard

Copy Merged: Copies all visible layers and pastes them into one merged layer

Paste: Pastes clipboard contents into a document

Paste Into: Pastes into a selection

Clear: Deletes selection

Check Spelling: Checks spelling of selected words

Find and Replace Text: Locates and replaces text

Fill: Fills a selection with foreground or background colors and patterns

Figure 7.17   Edit menu.

Stroke: Strokes a selection with a color

Free transform and Transform: Includes transformation scale, distort, skew, perspective, and rotate

Define Brush Preset: Creates a brush from a selection

Define Pattern: Creates a pattern from a selection

Define Custom Shape: Creates a custom shape from a shape, vector mask, or paths

Purge: Clears the clipboard and history. This is useful when Photoshop is running low on memory

Keyboard Shortcuts: Allows you to create custom keyboard shortcuts

Preset Manager: Manages brushes, swatches, gradient styles, patterns, contours, and custom shapes

Image Menu

Following are some of the options located in the Image pull-down menu (see Figure 7.18):

Mode: An image can be converted to eight different color modes: bitmap, gray scale, duotone, indexed, RGB, CMYK, lab color, and multichannel.

Adjustments: These commands can modify an image's hue, saturation, levels, brightness, contrast, color balance, levels, and curves. A variety of image-altering options can be created using the Adjustment commands.

Duplicate: Duplicates an image

Apply Image: Blends one image with another. using layers and channels

Calculations: Creates different blending effects by combining two individual channels from one or more images

Image Size: Changes the size of an image

Canvas Size: Allows you to add workspace area

Pixel Aspect Ratio: This option is used to create a proportioned file for video.

Rotate Canvas: Rotates the canvas 90 percent clockwise, counterclockwise, 180 percent, arbitrary, horizontal, or vertical flip

Crop: Activates the crop tool

Trim: Crops an image with added options

Reveal All: Reveals what is on a layer

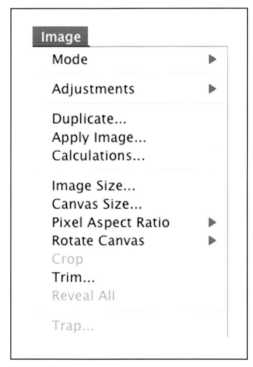

Figure 7.18   Image menu.

Trap: Overlaps images to prevent gaps from appearing

Layer Menu
Following is a list of some of the options found within the Layer menu (see Figure 7.19):

New: Creates a new layer

Duplicate Layer: Duplicates a layer

Delete: Deletes a layer, hidden layer, or linked layer

Layer Properties: Names and colors a layer

Layer Style: Adds effects such as drop shadow, bevel and emboss, stroke, pattern, and blending options

New Fill Layer: Creates a new color, gradient, or pattern fill layer

New Adjustment Layer: Creates a new layer that includes editable levels, curves, and image adjustment options

Change Layer Content: Changes the type of adjustment layer.

Layer Content Options: Edits properties of an adjustment layer.

Type: Converts type to shape, so you don't have to include the font when sending out to a printer. Anti-alias options convert to path and warp text.

Rasterize: Turns vector-based objects into pixel-based objects

New Layer Based Slice: Creates a new slice (an optimized area for the Web) based on a layer

Add Layer Mask: Adds a layer mask and can hide or reveal a mask

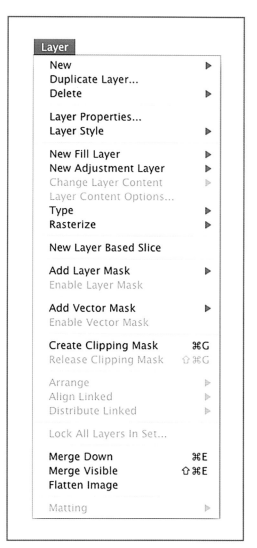

Figure 7.19   Layer menu.

Enable Layer Mask: Enables a layer mask

Add Vector Mask: Adds a vector mask—a sharp edged option to a layer mask

Enable Vector Mask: Enables a vector mask

Create Clipping Mask: A shape, text, or selection can be clipped to reveal an image

Release Clipping Mask: Releases the clipping mask

Arrange: Arranges layer order

Align Linked: Once layers are linked, they can be aligned through this command

Distribute Linked: Distributes layers evenly or unevenly

Lock All Layers in Set: Locks layers in a set so they cannot be edited

Merge Down: Moves selected layer down to merge with the layer below it

Merge Visible: Merges all visible layers

Flatten Image: Flattens image into one background layer

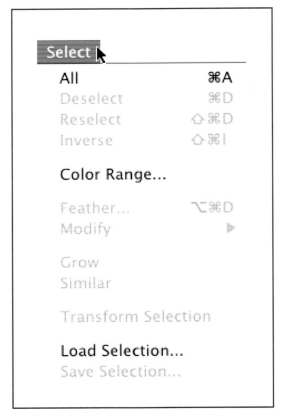

Figure 7.20   Select menu.

Matting: Removes unwanted pixels from a pasted image

Select Menu
Following is a list of some of the options within the Select menu (see Figure 7.20).

All: Selects everything on the highlighted layer

Deselect: Deselects all selections

Reselect: Restores the last deselected selection

Inverse: Authors to add text

Color Range: Creates a selection based on color

Feather: Softens the edges between the selection

Modify: Creates a border; smooths, expands, or contracts a selection

Grow: Expands the selection to include all adjacent pixels within the tolerance range specified in the magic wand option

Similar: Selects pixels throughout the image that falls within the tolerance range

Transform Selection: Distorts, rotates, skews, scales, or applies a perspective to a selection

Load Selection: Loads a saved selection that has been saved as an alpha channel

Save Selection: Saves a selection, creating an alpha channel

Filters Menu
The Filters Menu displays various image-editing functions organized into submenu groups. Following are some of the options available within the Filters Menu:

Extract: Creates a way to extract images from their background

Filter Gallery: Lets you view how various filters look combined with one another

Pattern Maker: Creates patterns from images

Artistic: Imitates artistic techniques, such as Colored Pencil, Cutout, Dry Brush, Film Grain, Fresco, Neon Glow, Paint Daubs, Palette Knife, Plastic Wrap, Poster Edges, Rough Pastels, Smudge Stick, Sponge, Watercolor, and Underpainting

Blur: Assorted techniques for softening images, such as Blur More, Gaussian Blur, Motion Blur, Radial Blur, and Smart Blur

Brushstrokes: Imitates brush and calligraphy techniques such as Accented Edges, Angled Strokes, Crosshatch, Dark Strokes, Ink Outlines, Spatter, Sprayed Strokes, and Sumi-e

Distort: Creates special effects, such as Diffuse Glow, Displace, Glass, Ocean Ripple, Pinch, Polar Coordinates, Ripple, Shear, Spherize, Twirl, and Wave

Noise: Alters the image with noise and median

Pixelate: Creates printing effects such as Color Halftone, Crystallize, Facet, Fragment, Mezzotint, Mosaic, and Pointilize

Render: Creates cloud effects and lighting effects

Sharpen: Sharpen Edges, Sharpen More, and Unsharp Mask are utilized to sharpen images

Sketch: Bas Relief, Chalk & Charcoal, Charcoal, Chrome, Conte Crayon, Graphic Pen, and Halftone Pattern, Note Paper, Photocopy, Plaster, Reticulation, Stamp, Torn Edges, and Water Paper can be utilized to create fine art techniques

Stylize: Diffuse, Emboss, Extrude, Find Edges, Glowing Edges, Solarize, Tiles, Trace Contour, and Wind add styles to an image

Texture: Craquelure, Grain, Mosaic Tiles, Patchwork, Stained Glass, and Texturizer add texture to an image

Video: Deinterlace, which smooths images captured by video, and NTSC Colors filter restricts the gamut of colors

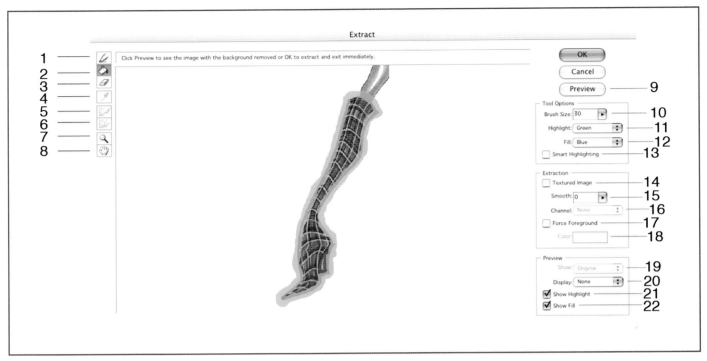

Figure 7.21   Extract Filter.

The Extract Filter

The extract command produces a dialog box with a secondary toolbox that contains the highlighter tool (see Figure 7.21 for number of references). This tool creates edges around the desired area. The fill tool will fill the areas you have indicated with highlights. Click on Preview to preview the selection.

1 Highlighter tool: Outlines the selection
2 Fill tool: Fills the selection
3 Eraser tool: Erases a highlight
4 Eyedropper tool: Samples foreground color when a forced foreground is selected
5 Cleanup tool: Erases background pixels of an extracted image
6 Edge touchup tool: Cleans up edges of an extracted image
7 Zoom tool: Magnifies an image
8 Hand tool: Moves the image in the preview window
9 Preview: Click to preview an extracted image
10 Brush Size: Drag slider bar or enter a number to adjust the brush size
11 Highlight: Selects a highlighted color
12 Fill: Selects the fill color
13 Smart Highlighting: Applies a highlight that adjusts automatically to the size of the edge
14 Textured Edge: Select this option if the area to be deleted contains a lot of texture
15 Smooth: Has a similar effect as a feather technique that softens the outline of an edge
16 Channel: Select this option if you base your highlight on a saved alpha channel
17 Force Foreground: Select this option for a difficult selection
18 Color: Selects color for a forced foreground
19 Show: Previews original or extracted image
20 Display: Options include showing extracted images against a colored, grayscale, white, or other matte background
21 Show Highlight: Check to show highlights
22 Show Fill: Check to show a fill

Filter Gallery

The Filter Gallery allows you to preview how multiple filters will look when they are applied to an image. By adding layers and selecting a filter, you can view how it affects the image in the image preview window (see Figure 7.22 for number references).

1 Chosen filter and options
2 Filter layer added
3 Base filter
4 Add filter layer
5 Delete filter layer
6 Selected filter option
7 Preview window
8 Magnification options

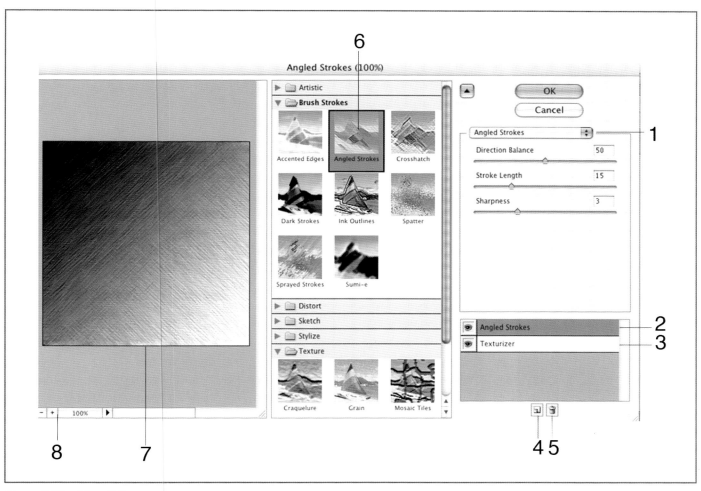

Figure 7.22 Filter Gallery.

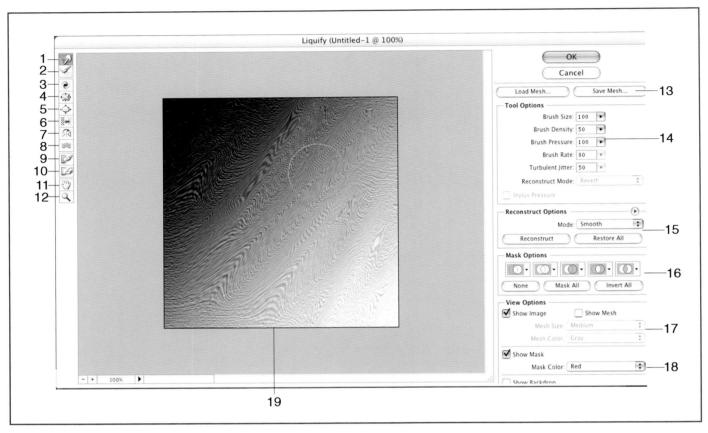

Figure 7.23   Liquify Filter.

Liquify Filter

The Liquify Filter allows you to push, bloat, warp, twirl, and distort pixels that can be used to create interesting effects with textiles as well as photographs (see Figure 7.23).

1 Forward warp tool: Pushes pixels

2 Reconstruct tool: Copies distorted areas

3 Twirl tool: Twirls pixels clockwise (Option key twirls counterclockwise)

4 Pucker tool: Pushes pixels toward the center

5 Bloat tool: Pushes pixels outward

6 Push left tool: Pushes pixels to the left

7 Mirror tool: Copies pixels to the brush

8 Turbulence tool: Mixes pixels

9 Freeze mask tool: Prevents selected areas from distortion

10 Thaw tool: Unfreezes areas selected by the freeze mask tool

11 Hand tool: Moves around the preview window

12 Zoom tool: Zooms in and out of preview window

13 Meshes are distortions that can be saved and loaded

14 Brush options

15 Reconstruct methods restore distortions to their normal state

16 Mask options for freeze tool

17 Show or hide mesh options

18 Show or hide mask options

19 Preview window

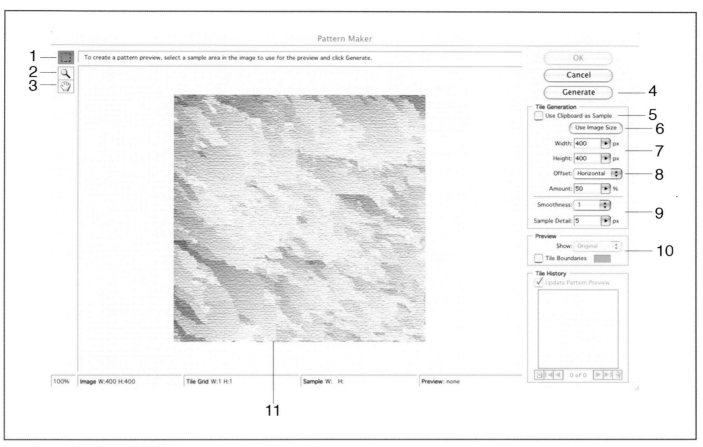

Figure 7.24   Pattern Maker Filter.

Pattern Maker Filter

The Pattern Maker feature lets you create patterns from photographs and textures. Choose Filter-Pattern Maker from the pull-down menu, select an area of the image you want to turn into a pattern, and click on generate (see Figure 7.24). Experiment with the various options until you get a pattern you like. Then click on the OK button. The Pattern Maker will only make a single repeat pattern. This pattern is not seamless.

To quickly make your pattern seamless, go into the ImageReady filters folder on your hard drive and copy the Tile Maker plug-in. (See Chapter 9 for more information about creating seamless patterns.) Paste this plug-in in the Photoshop filter folder. After placing the plug-in in the Photoshop filter folder, restart your computer and launch Photoshop. Choose Filter-Other-Tile Maker from the Photoshop pull-down menu, and choose the Blend Edges option in the dialog box. Choose or type in 10 percent for the width. Check the Resize Tile to Fit Image option.

1 Rectangular Marquee Tool selects area to be affected
2 Zoom tool
3 Hand tool
4 Generates pattern
5–9 Tile options include using the clipboard (the last item saved) as a source for the pattern and image size. The offsets will offset the image either horizontally or vertically. The higher the smoothing, the less the breaks between the tiles will appear.
10 Tile boundaries show tiles
11 Preview window

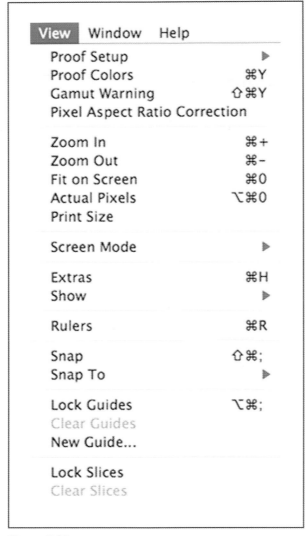

Figure 7.25   View menu.

View Menu

The View menu regulates how the screen displays itself (see Figure 7.25).

New View: Displays the same image in a second window

Proof Setup: Lets you see how an image will look in different output color spaces

Proof Colors: Allows you to see a soft proof of your document

Gamut Warning: Highlights colors that won't print on a four-color press

Pixel Aspect Ratio Correction: Shows the file after a pixel aspect ratio has been applied

Zoom In: Magnifies the image to the next preset percentage

Zoom Out: Reduces the image to the next preset percentage

Fit on Screen: Scales the window size to fit the available screen space

Actual Pixels: Shows number of pixels

Print Size: Displays a document's approximate print size; the size and resolution of your monitor affect the on-screen print size

Screen Mode: Switches between screen modes

Extras: Shows or hides guides, annotations, text bounds, text baselines, grid, target paths, selection edges, slices, and image maps

Show: Shows the individual extras

Rulers: Shows or hides rulers

Snap: Allows you to choose whether you want to snap to various elements in your document

Snap To: Gives you the various elements to snap to

Lock Guides: Locks the nonprinting lines that appear over the image

Clear Guides: Clears the image of guides

New Guide: Creates a new guide

Lock Slices: Locks the slices

Clear Slices: Clears the slices

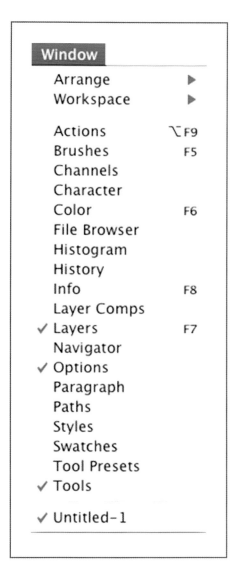

Figure 7.26   Window menu.

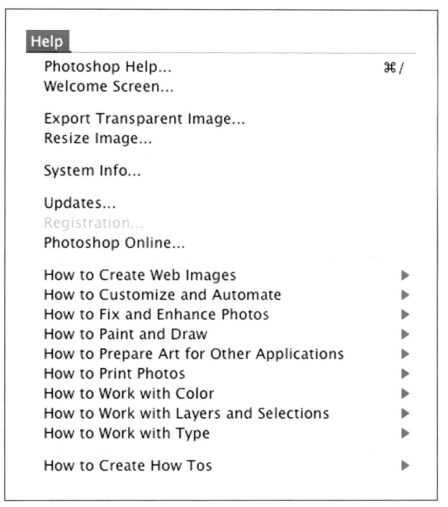

Figure 7.27   Help menu.

The rest of the options allow the user to hide or show palettes.

Window Menu

Following is a list of options located within the Window menu (see Figure 7.26).

Arrange

Cascade: Displays windows stacked from the upper left to the lower right of the screen

Tile Horizontally or Tile Vertically: Displays the document windows edge to edge

Workspace: Saves the workspace (how the palettes are arranged on the screen).

Help Menu

If you have any questions or run into difficulties while working with Photoshop, the Help menu is a good source to turn to (see Figure 7.27).

Photoshop Help: Access the Photoshop manual online

Export Transparent Image: Exports an image with a transparent background

Resize Image: Resizes an image for print or the Web

System Info: Tells you about your operating system

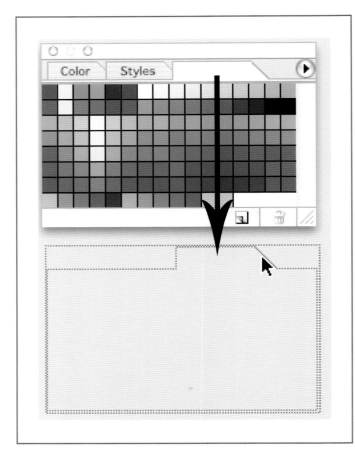

Figure 7.28   Palettes.

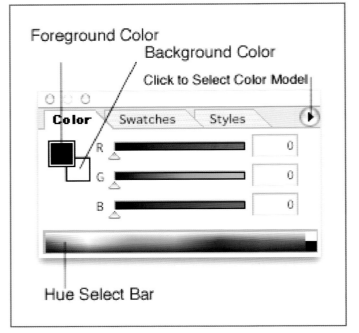

Figure 7.29   Color palette.

There are several how-to shortcuts that provide tutorials for common tasks. The rest of the commands connect you to Adobe Online for updates, support, and registration.

Palettes

Palettes let you check and adjust images. By default palettes emerge stacked together in groups (see Figure 7.28). To display a palette, choose the palette name in the window pull-down menu. To separate one palette from another, click on the name and pull it apart then release the mouse.

Color Palette

The Color palette is used for choosing and mixing colors (see Figure 7.29). Choose a color model by clicking on the right arrow. To open the Color Picker, click on the Foreground or Background Color square.

Layers Palette

The Layers palette allows you to add, delete, duplicate, group,

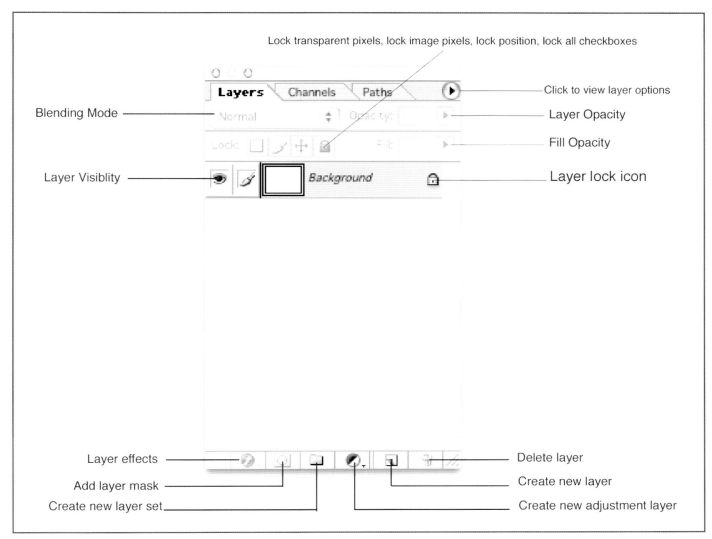

Lock transparent pixels, lock image pixels, lock position, lock all checkboxes

Click to view layer options

Blending Mode

Layer Opacity

Fill Opacity

Layer Visiblity

Layer lock icon

Layer effects

Delete layer

Add layer mask

Create new layer

Create new layer set

Create new adjustment layer

Figure 7.30   Layers palette.

link, and show/hide layers (see Figure 7.30). You can change the blending mode and opacity of each layer and also add a mask to a layer. You can add an adjustment layer, which is used for applying editable adjustments. The layer effects icon allows you to add layer effects such as drop shadows or outer glows.

Swatches Palette

The Swatches palette is used for choosing colors (see Figure 7.31). Swatches can be added or deleted from the palette. Other swatches can be loaded from the swatch libraries.

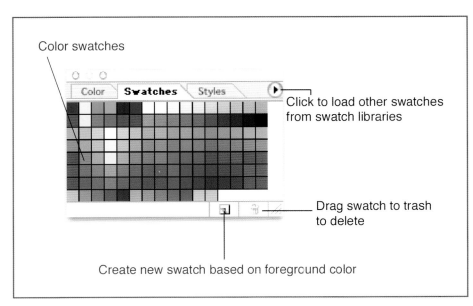

Color swatches

Click to load other swatches from swatch libraries

Drag swatch to trash to delete

Create new swatch based on foregrcund color

Figure 7.31   Swatches palette.

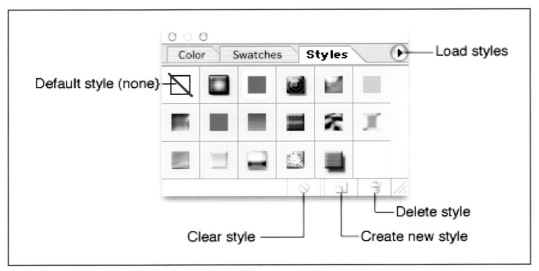

Figure 7.32   Styles palette.

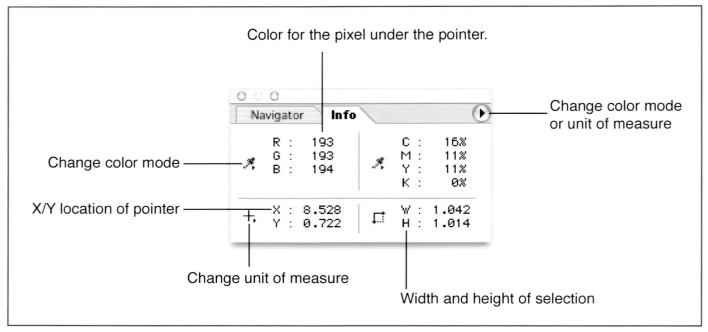

Figure 7.33   Info palette.

Styles Palette

The Styles palette is used to apply effects that have been previously created (see Figure 7.32).

Info Palette

The Info palette is used to display the color breakdown of the pixel under the pointer (see Figure 7.33). It also shows the X/Y position of the pointer on the image. More information can be obtained when the Measure Tool is used. When an exclamation point

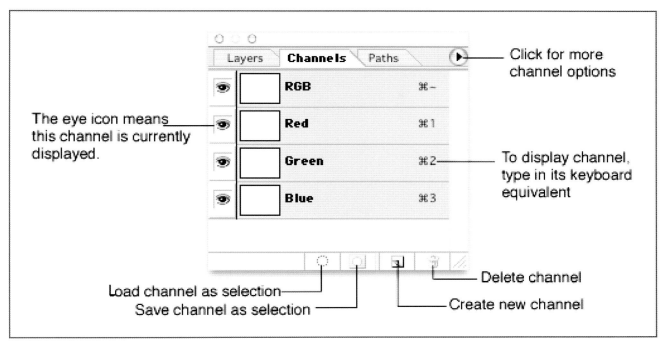

Figure 7.34   Channel palette.

appears next to a color readout, it means that color is outside the printable CMYK gamut.

Channel Palette

The Channels palette is used to display the channels that make up an image (see Figure 7.34). Channels will consist of Red, Green, and Blue in RGB mode. CMYK mode consists of Cyan, Magenta, Yellow, and Black channels. Lab mode consists of a lightness channel, a green-red axis channel, and a blue-yellow axis channel. Bitmap-mode, gray scale, duotone, and indexed-color images have one channel by default. Multichannel mode is useful for specialized printing. Spot color channels create spot color palettes. An additional channel called Alpha Channels can be used for storing and editing selections such as masks.

Paths Palette

Paths can be created by the Shape Tool or the Pen Tool and are stored and listed with a thumbnail image

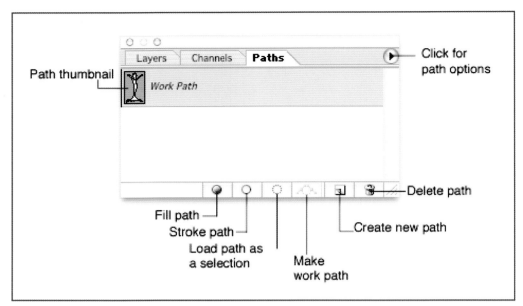

Figure 7.35 Paths palette.

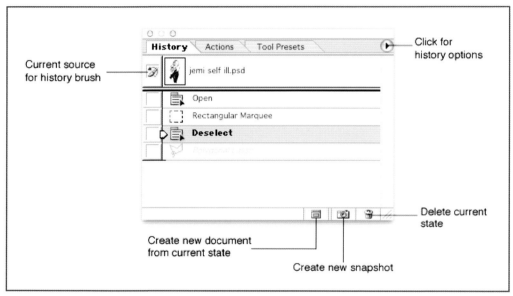

Figure 7.36 History palette.

in the Paths palette (see Figure 7.35). Selections can also be turned into paths and saved as clipping paths to be exported into a layout program.

History Palette

The History palette is used to revert to a previous step in an image (see Figure 7.36). You can also delete an image's states and create a document from a state or snapshot. A snapshot is a temporary copy of a state. The advantage of a snapshot is that you can name it and store it

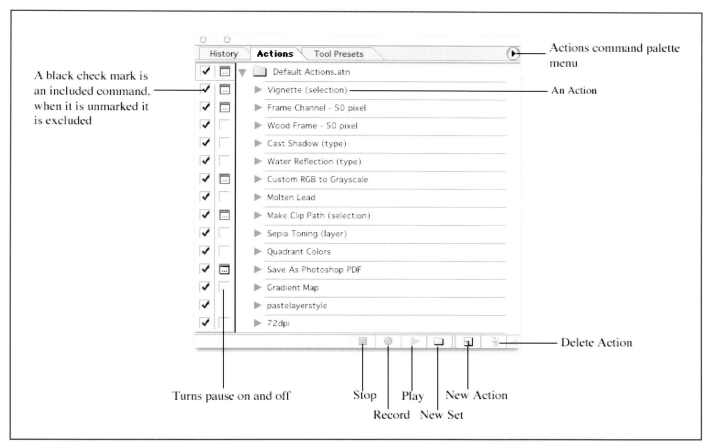

Figure 7.37 Actions palette.

for the work session. A snapshot is not saved once you close the file. To use the History brush tool option in the History palette, select the icon next to a palette step. You can then paint in parts of an image from previous snapshots.

Actions Palette

The Actions palette is used to record a sequence of image-editing functions that can be played back (see Figure 7.37). Actions can save you time when you have to deal with multiple images. The Actions palette is used to record, play back, edit, delete, save, and load actions. An action can be assigned its own keyboard shortcut.

Dialog Boxes

When a command is followed by an ellipsis (three periods), it means a dialog box will open with further

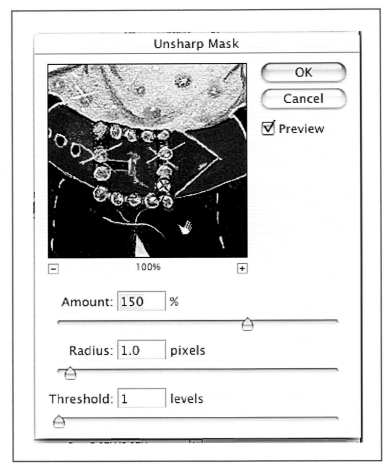

Figure 7.38 Dialog box.

options (see Figure 7.38). Holding down the ALT/Option key switches the Cancel button to Reset. The cursor becomes a hand when placed in the window, allowing you to maneuver around the document.

The Adjust Menu

Within the Adjust menu, you can find the dialog boxes for changing levels, curves, color, brightness/ contrast, and hue/saturation.

Levels

The Levels dialog box is used to adjust an image's highlights, mid-tones, and shadows (see Figure 7.39). You can make adjustments to an individual channel or to all the channels combined. A Levels adjustment can be saved and loaded later with the load option. Auto adjustments can be used when time is scarce. The Auto correction options allow you to automatically adjust the tonal range of an image.

The set black point eyedropper lets you manually darken the shadows

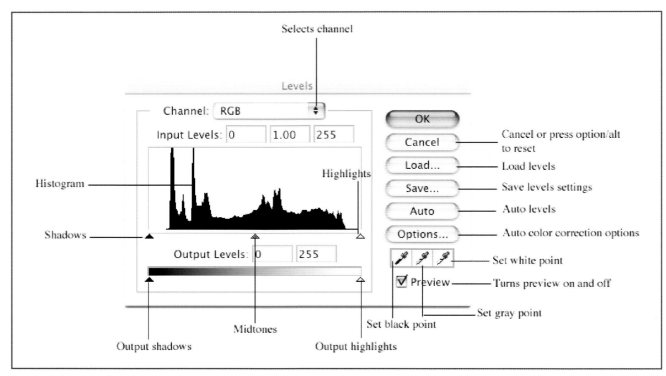

Figure 7.39 Levels dialog box.

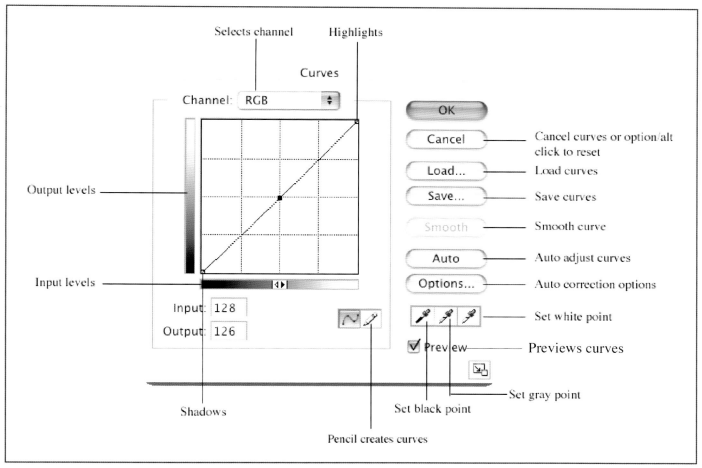

Figure 7.40 Curves dialog box.

of an image by clicking on the image's darkest point. The white point eyedropper does the same for the highlights of an image. The gray point eyedropper adjusts the mid-tones when you click on a neutral gray area of an image. To decrease contrast and lighten the image, move the output shadows slider to the right. To decrease contrast and darken the image, move the output highlights slider to the left. The Histogram graphs the pixels of an image, showing you if there is information (detail) missing in the shadows, midtones, and highlights for color correction.

Curves

Curves is similar to Levels in that it will adjust the image over the entire tonal range (see Figure 7.40). The

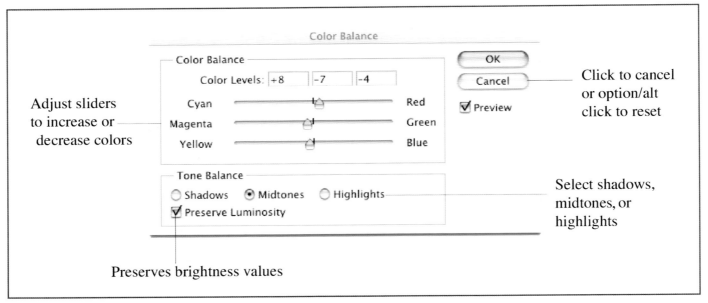

Figure 7.41   Color Balance dialog box.

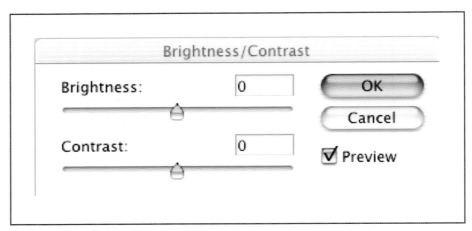

Figure 7.42   Brightness/Contrast dialog box.

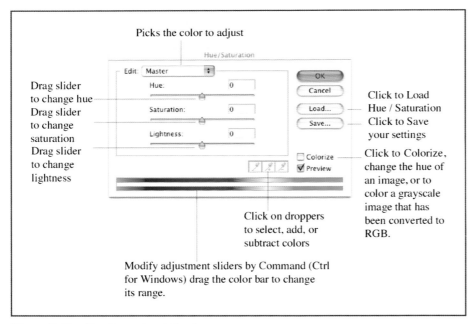

Figure 7.43   Hue/Saturation dialog box.

difference is that Curves allows you to make finer adjustments.

Color Balance
The Color Balance command changes the combination of colors in an image (see Figure 7.41).

Brightness/Contrast
The only time we use the Brightness/Contrast command is to adjust a mask (see Figure 7.42). Use Levels or Curves to adjust an image.

Hue/Saturation
The Hue/Saturation is used to change or adjust the hue and saturation of colors (see Figure 7.43).

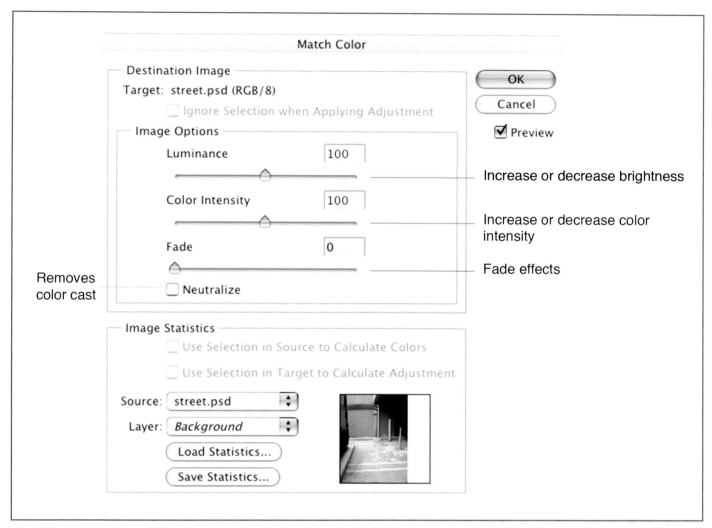

Figure 7.44   Match Color dialog box.

Check the colorize box to change the hue, color, or gray scale of an image. The desaturate command will turn an image into a gray-scale image without changing the color mode.

Match Color

The Match Color command lets you adjust the brightness, color intensity, and remove a color cast (see Figure 7.44). Match Color gives you the ability to match the color of one image to another by choosing a target source.

Replace Color

The Replace Color command lets you create a selection based on color and change the color of

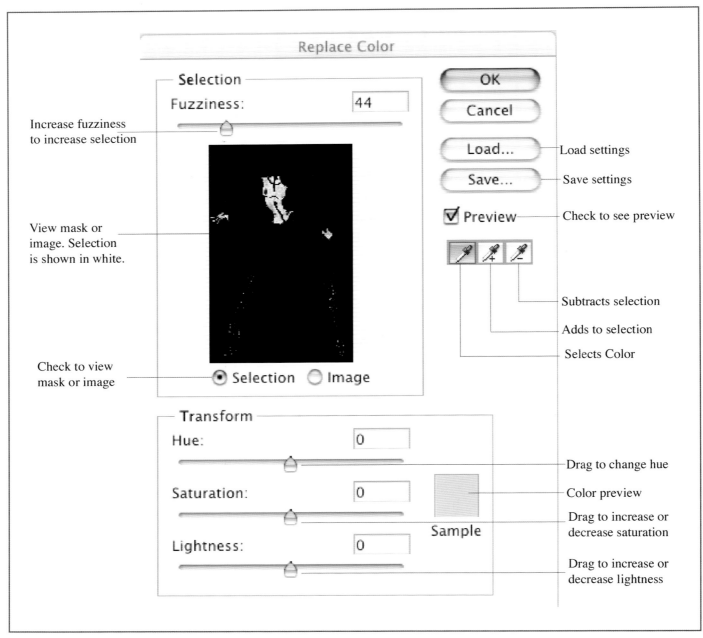

Increase fuzziness
to increase selection

View mask or
image. Selection
is shown in white.

Check to view
mask or image

Load settings

Save settings

Check to see preview

Subtracts selection

Adds to selection

Selects Color

Drag to change hue

Color preview

Sample

Drag to increase or
decrease saturation

Drag to increase or
decrease lightness

Figure 7.45   Replace Color dialog box.

whatever is selected (see Figure 7.45). You can make adjustments to the selection, hue, saturation, and lightness with the sliders.

Selective Color

Selective Color is used to increase or decrease the percentage of color and ink that is used (see Figure 7.46). This command is often used after an image has been changed to CMYK mode.

Channel Mixer

The Channel Mixer command is used to adjust a color channel using a mixture of different channels (see Figure 7.47).

Gradient Map

The Gradient Map command maps an image with a specified gradient fill based on the shadows and highlights of an image (see Figure 7.48).

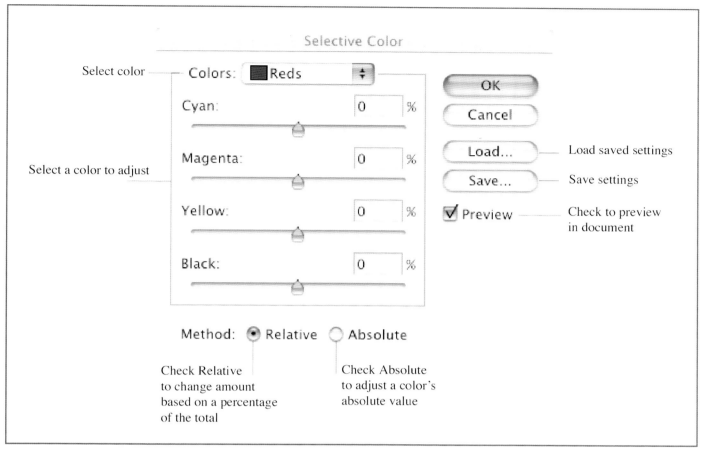

Figure 7.46   Selective Color dialog box.

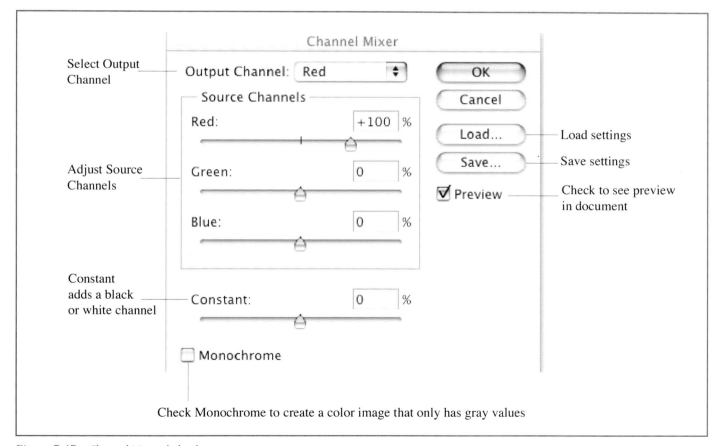

Figure 7.47   Channel Mixer dialog box.

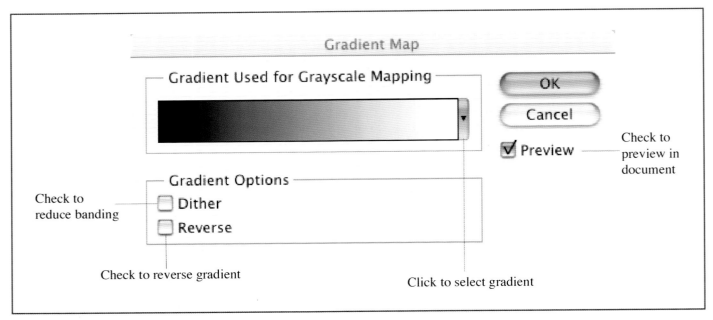

Check to
reduce banding

Check to reverse gradient

Click to select gradient

Check to
preview in
document

Figure 7.48   Gradient Map.

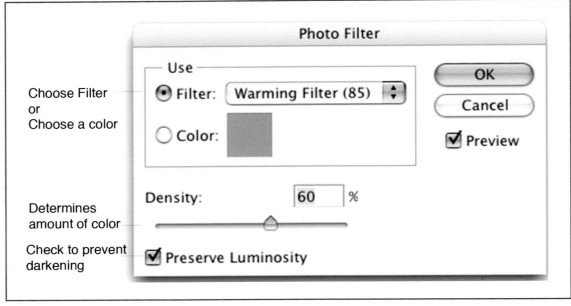

Choose Filter
or
Choose a color

Determines
amount of color

Check to prevent
darkening

Figure 7.49   Photo Filter dialog box.

Photo Filter

The Photo Filter lets you create a
warming or cooling color overlay
on any photo (see Figure 7.49).
Density determines the intensity of
the overlay. Check Preserve
Luminosity to keep the image from
darkening.

Shadows and Highlights

The Shadow/Highlight command
allows you to fine-tune shadows

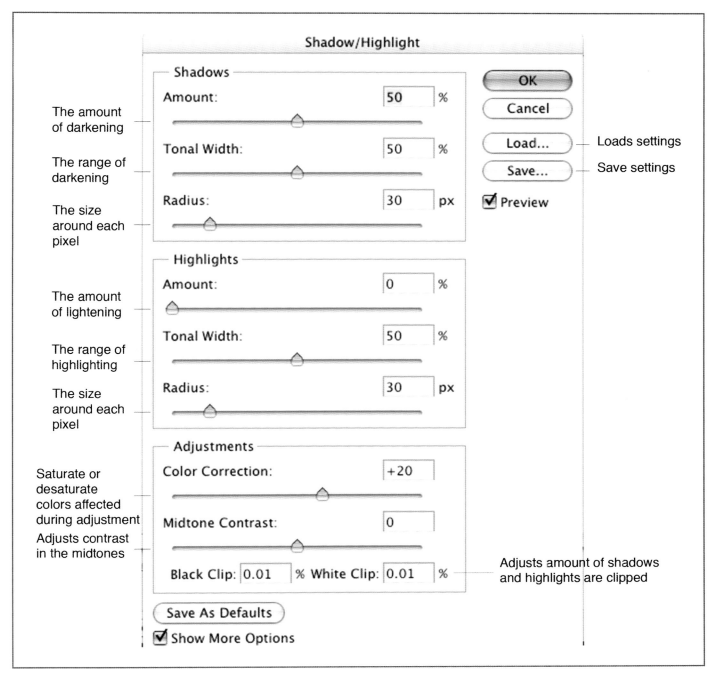

The amount of darkening

The range of darkening

The size around each pixel

The amount of lightening

The range of highlighting

The size around each pixel

Saturate or desaturate colors affected during adjustment

Adjusts contrast in the midtones

Loads settings

Save settings

Adjusts amount of shadows and highlights are clipped

Figure 7.50   Shadow/Highlights dialog box.

without affecting highlights and vice versa (see Figure 7.50). It also allows contrast control and black-and-white clipping adjustments to maintain detail in those areas.

Invert

The Invert command inverts the colors in an image. This command can produce a film negative appearance.

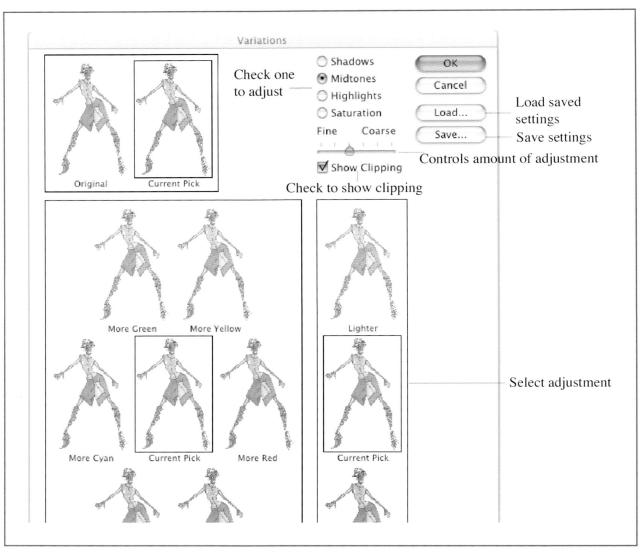

Figure 7.51   Variations dialog box.

Equalize

The Equalize command finds the brightest and darkest values in an image and redistributes them.

Threshold

The Threshold command will produce a high-contrast black-and-white image that can be adjusted. This command is useful for adjusting masks and determining the lightest and darkest areas of an image.

Posterize

The Posterize command will let you adjust the tonal levels in an image to produce special effects.

Variations

The Variations command lets you adjust color by using various adjustments (see Figure 7.51). This command is for quick adjustments and is not meant to replace Levels and Curves adjustments.

Apply Image

The Apply Image command lets you blend one image's layer and channel source with a layer and channel on another active image destination (see Figure 7.52).

Calculations

The Calculations command allows you to blend channels and layers

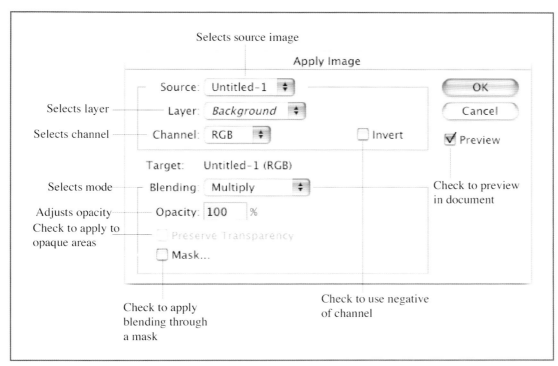

Figure 7.52   Apply Image dialog box.

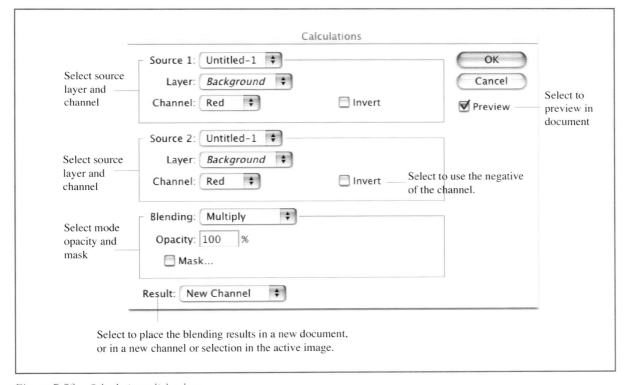

Figure 7.53   Calculations dialog box.

with two different images (see
Figure 7.53).

Image Size
The Image Size command is used
to change the size of documents
(see Figure 7.54). Check the

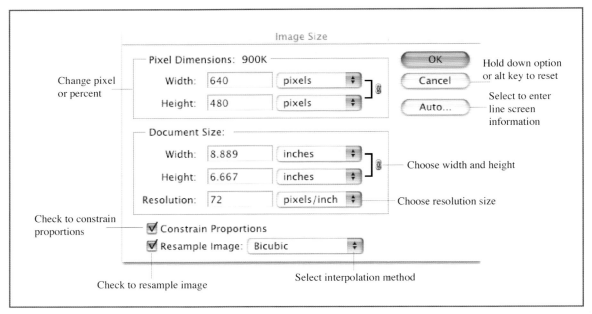

Figure 7.54   Image Size dialog box.

Resample Image box to resample an image, changing the pixel dimensions. When choosing an interpolation (creating color values for any new pixels created when an image is enlarged), you can choose from the following options:

- Nearest neighbor is the lowest quality but fastest
- Bilinear is medium quality
- Bicubic is the best quality for smooth gradations between colors
- Bicubic smoother is used for enlarging images that are resampled
- Bicubic sharper is for images reduced when Resample is checked in the box

Canvas Size

The Canvas Size command allows you to add or subtract an area around your image (see Figure 7.55). The background will be the same color as your background color swatch in the toolbar.

Trim

The Trim command allows a more specific way to crop an image by

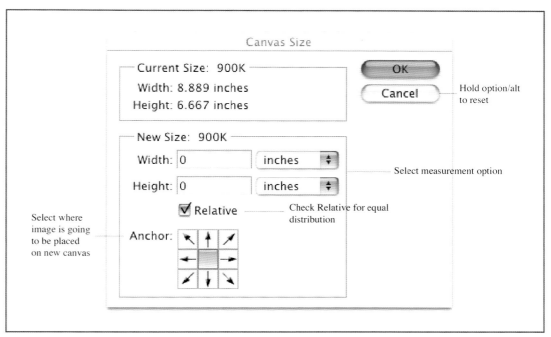

Figure 7.55 Canvas Size dialog box.

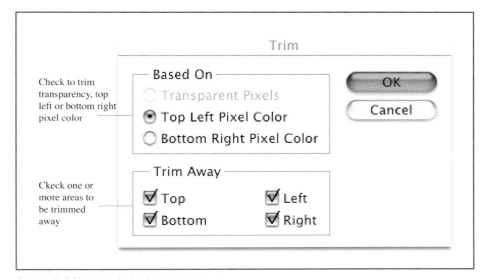

Figure 7.56 Trim dialog box.

determining the color and area to be trimmed away (see Figure 7.56).

Histogram

The Histogram shows a bar graph of the samples of settings from 0 pure black to 255 pure white (see Figure 7.57). In general, a good histogram would have values from one end to the other filling the graph. You can click and drag and see where shadow or highlight levels begin so you can adjust your color correction.

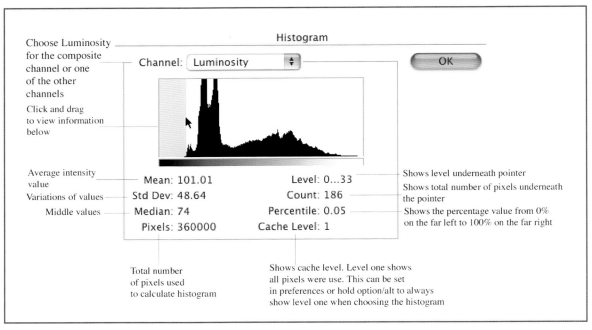

Choose Luminosity for the composite channel or one of the other channels

Click and drag to view information below

Average intensity value

Variations of values

Middle values

Shows level underneath pointer

Shows total number of pixels underneath the pointer

Shows the percentage value from 0% on the far left to 100% on the far right

Total number of pixels used to calculate histogram

Shows cache level. Level one shows all pixels were use. This can be set in preferences or hold option/alt to always show level one when choosing the histogram

Figure 7.57   Histogram dialog box.

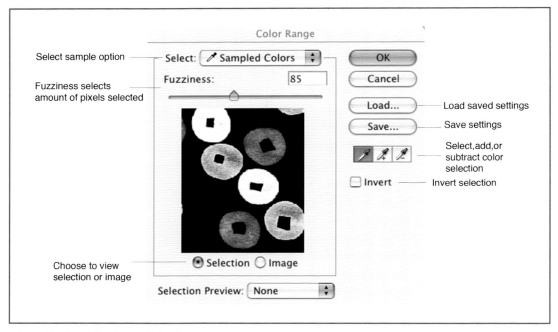

Select sample option

Fuzziness selects amount of pixels selected

Load saved settings

Save settings

Select, add, or subtract color selection

Invert selection

Choose to view selection or image

Figure 7.58   Color Range dialog box.

Trap

The Trap command becomes active in CMYK mode and is used to correct misalignment of solid colors. Consult your printer for trap amounts.

Color Range

Color Range allows you to make a selection based on the color in an image (see Figure 7.58). Fuzziness is the same as tolerance: the higher the fuzziness, the wider the ranges of pixels that are selected.

Learning the Basics Lesson: Getting Started With Photoshop

1. Before beginning this lesson you will need to set your Photoshop Preferences.

2. In the Photoshop pull-down

menu under File, select Preferences.

3. Select Transparency & Gamut.

4. Change the Grid Size to None (see Figure 7.59). This will create a solid white background so we can change opacity later in the lesson. Checkerboard squares will appear on the background layer if this step is eliminated.

5. Choose File: Browse and maneuver to the CD-ROM ◯ in the Chapter 7 lesson folder. When the two files street.psd and hiphopgirl.psd appear, hold down the Shift key and click on both files to select them.

6. After the files are selected, press return on your keyboard to open both files.

7. Select the street.psd file. Press Command/CTRL for Windows and 0 (zero) to view the file in full screen mode.

8. Choose Image: Histogram. Notice how detail information is missing in both the shadows and highlights that appear (see Figure 7.60).

9. Next choose Image: Adjustments: Auto Levels from the pull-down menu and look at the Histogram again (see Figure 7.61). Notice that more information is added at both ends.

10. Next choose Image: Adjustments: Desaturate from the pull-down menu. This will desaturate the colors without changing the image mode to gray scale.

11. Select the hiphopgirl.psd file, and choose Select: All in the pull-down menu. This will select the whole image.

12. With the street.psd file selected, choose Edit: Paste from the pull-down menu. The illustration is now on its own layer in the street.psd file. To get rid of

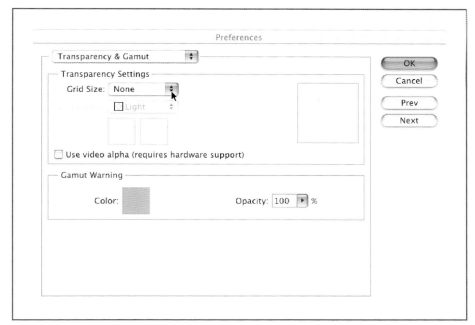

Figure 7.59 The grid size should be changed to None.

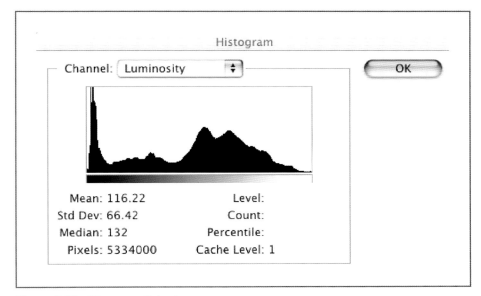

Figure 7.60 Histogram dialog box.

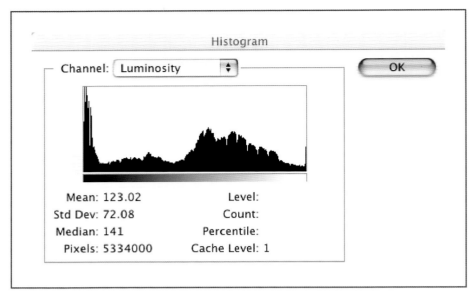

Figure 7.61   Histogram box with adjusted information.

the white background, make sure Layer 1 is the active highlighted layer.

13. Select the Magic Wand Tool (press W on your keyboard) and make sure the tolerance option is set to the default amount of 32. The contiguous option should be checked. Click on the white background. The file should look like Figure 7.57.

14. Press delete.

15. Choose Select: Deselect from the pull-down menu to deselect the "marching ants."

16. Double click on the Background layer and when a dialog box appears, click OK. This will turn the Background layer into a layer you can edit.

17. Drag the opacity slider to the left until it reaches 50 percent (see Figure 7.62).

18. Press D on your keyboard, then X. This action will choose the default colors of a black foreground and a white background. Then switch the colors so white is the foreground color.

19. Next select the text tool by pressing T on your keyboard. Select a font from the options bar. Type in the words "Street Couture," and move it with the move tool to the upper right-hand corner of the image. The cursor will change to the move tool when the mouse moves away from the text. You can change the font size by clicking and dragging over the text, then selecting a font and size from the menu.

20. Select the move tool to view the text. To hide the highlight while changing the font size, press Command-H /CTRL-H for Windows while the text is highlighted.

21. The final image should now look like Figure 7.63.

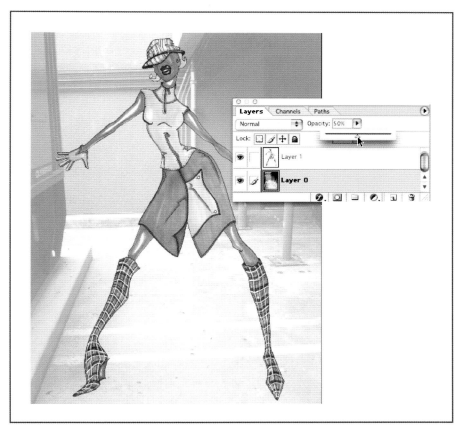

Figure 7.62   Opacity levels with layers palette.

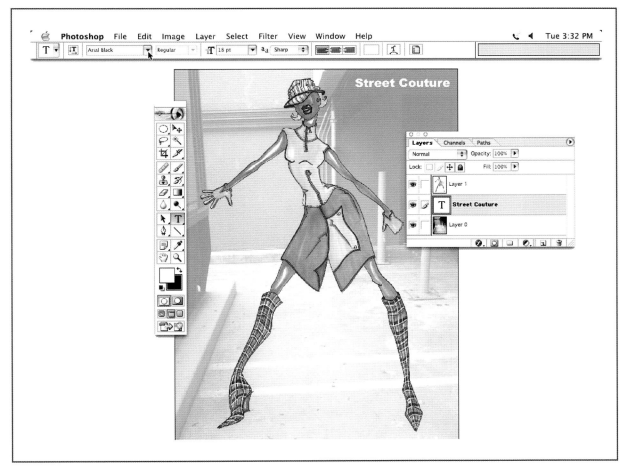

Figure 7.63   The final product with text.

Review Questions

What are the names of the selection tools?

How can you change a color in an image?

What are "marching ants"?

What happens when the letter "D" is pressed on the keyboard?

How do you add text to a document?

Suggested Practice Project

Scan in an image and replace a color.

Key Terms

CMYK

Image mode

Resolution

RGB

Selection

8

Working with Adobe Photoshop to Create Mood and Trend Presentation Boards

What You Will Learn in Chapter 8

This chapter utilizes the design elements integral to creating a fashion line or group with the documentation of what actually inspired the creative direction. The selling of the idea is as important as selling the designs themselves. Predictive services sell information and ideas to design firms. These firms then develop their own lines but must convey their ideas using visuals, including mood boards, trend boards, and color stories.

The process of creating a visual presentation of a company's predictive or reportage package and the actual mood and trend boards are covered in this chapter, along with the following Photoshop skills:

- Using Filters
- Photo Compositing
- Creating a Color Story using the Pantone Color System
- Fading Out a background photo
- Advanced Masking Techniques to add relevant photographic elements
- Polishing an illustration
- Scaling an oversize scan
- Modeling light areas using Dodge and Burn
- Smoothing Out flesh tones
- Creating Highlights with the Airbrush Tool

Predicting and Presenting Fashion Trends: An Overview

Ready-to-wear's immediate or gradual changes each season are presented for consumer approval. But where do these immediate or gradual changes come from? Who decides what the hot colors for spring are? Who sets the limits of how low the waistline will go? In other words, what elements dictate a trend?

Trends are not conjured up as new objects to sell but are dormant until creative minds dig them up. These creative minds have keen eyes for detail or hooks that will capture the attention of the buying public. Designers, stylists, insiders, futurists, trend spotters, merchandisers, and people who offer predictive services are faced with the task of how to best understand and present new trends every season.

The Mood Board

The first step in the design process is to understand the origins of what inspired a design, classified as conceptual. These conceptual inspiration points can best be presented and understood visually in the form of a mood board.

A mood board can be thought of as a visual tool used to present concepts or ideas that inspire and initiate a design concept by attempting to give the feel of a seasonal trend or theme. Inspirational materials are presented in a cohesive and palpable way that spells out the origins of the season's mood or feeling. This presentation format will frequently include color stories and fabric elements such as textures, weight, and print ideas. Descriptive buzzwords such as romantic, tailored, feminine, sexy, and modern are often associated with these conceptual presentation formats.

The second step is to derive the inspiration information from the fashion line's target consumer. This information is more succinct and specific and gives tangible details that translate the more ethereal conceptual elements of the original inspirational sources. The presentation format that proves most effective is a trend board.

The Trend Board

A trend board is a more targeted device used to telegraph specific silhouettes, colors, textures, construction details, and styling nuances. Mood boards are conceptual and generally convey a mood, while trend boards are more factual and definitive, explaining tangible details. Trend boards can be used to develop a look, style, or actual group of clothing.

Predictive Services

Predictive services translate and present trends to clients so they can glean new messages. These services pull together aspects that mainstream design companies can use. Selective pulling and presenting of concepts is dispersed throughout the major ready-to-wear corporations and interpreted at various price levels from prestigious to mass market. Predictive services generate a highly stylized and effective completion of mood and trend boards, finalized image illustrations, as well as fabric, print, and color stories. These formats are all digitally created.

Fashion companies create mood boards, trend boards, and color, fabric, and print stories internally as well. These presentation formats follow the dictates of their particular markets. The predictive color and style services provide the initial mapping. The company's design staff then articulates the elements relevant to their market. All facets of this undertaking depend on design professionals possessing both design skills and a keen knowledge of their market and competition. Today computer software and hardware has become an indispensable tool for blending all these elements seamlessly in the design room.

Creating a Mood Board

The following lesson shows some techniques to create a photo collage for a mood board (see Figure 8.1). This can be a useful design tool for expressing and justifying your ideas.

Using Filters

Filters are used to change a photographic element to achieve a desired result. The Filter Gallery

Figure 8.1   Chinoiserie Fall Mood Board.

allows you to preview and has controls so you can change a filter and see the results in real time.

1. Choose File: New in the pull-down menu. Under presets, choose letter to create a new file. Name the file "Mood Board."

Figure 8.2   Background Layer Art.

2. Open the file labeled 1.psd from the Chapter 8, mood board folder on the CD-ROM ○ .

3. Open the Layers palette by choosing Window: Layers from the pull-down menu. Drag the background layer from the Layers palette into the mood board file while holding down the Shift key to center the photograph in the mood board document (see Figure 8.2).

4. Choose Filter: Filter Gallery and go through the different filters by clicking on them to see a preview. Change the layer's opacity to 70 percent in the opacity pull-down menu located in the Layers palette.

5. Use the Crop Tool from the toolbox to drag the tool across the photo and press return to complete the crop.

6. Open file 2.psd from the Chapter 8, mood board folder on the CD-ROM ○ .

7. Drag the background layer of file 2.psd with the Move Tool from the Open Layers palette onto the mood board document while holding down the Shift key.

8. Choose Select: Color Range from the menu. A dialog box will appear. It is important to make sure Selection is checked. Click on a white area in the new layer and choose 80 for the Fuzziness in the open dialog box (the higher the fuzziness, the more pixels will be chosen). When you check Selection, it allows you to see the mask. A mask shows the area selected as well as the areas not selected. Black areas denote what is not selected, while white areas denote what is selected (see Figure 8.3).

9. Click OK in the dialog box, and press delete on the keyboard.

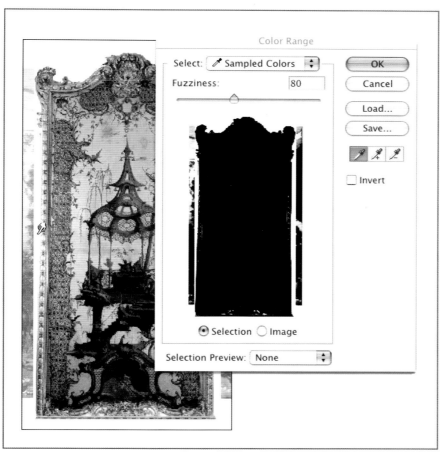

Figure 8.3 A mask showing selected and unselected areas.

This will delete the white areas of the layer. Choose Select: Deselect to deselect.

10. Choose Edit: Transform: Scale from the pull-down menu, and scale down the file until it is about one quarter of the original size. Add a layer mask by clicking on the Add Layer Mask icon at the bottom of the Open Layers palette (see Figure 8.4).

11. Choose the Gradient Tool from the toolbox or press G on the keyboard. Choose Window: Options if the Options toolbar for the Gradient Tool is not visible. The following options are to be selected in the Options toolbar: linear gradient, normal mode, 100 percent opacity. Now drag the Gradient Tool across the entire image on layer 2, starting at the bottom of the

Figure 8.4 Location of the Add Layer Mask icon.

Figure 8.5   Cropped image.

photo while holding down the Shift key and release. If too much of the image (or not enough) disappears, try again until it resembles Figure 8.5.

12. Open file 3.psd from the Chapter 8, mood board folder on the CD-ROM ◌, and follow the same steps for 2.psd.

13. Open the file marked 4.psd from the Chapter 8, mood board folder on the CD-ROM ◌. Crop the image at the point above the trees using the Crop Tool from the toolbox. Drag the file from its Layers palette onto the mood board. Use Select: Color Range as described in Step 8 to delete the white pixels.

14. Choose Edit: Transform: Scale from the pull-down menu to scale the layer down until it resembles Figure 8.6.

15. Change the Blend Mode in the Layers palette option to Multiply. The result should look like Figure 8.7.

Figure 8.6   Scaled image.

Figure 8.7 The Multiply blend mode.

16. Open file 5.psd from the Chapter 8, mood board folder on the CD-ROM ⊙, and drag the file from the Layers palette with the Move Tool onto the mood board. Change the Blend Mode to Multiply in the Layers palette pull-down menu. Choose Edit: Transform: Scale from the pull-down menu to scale the layer down.

17. Add a layer mask by clicking on the Add Layer Mask icon (second from the left) at the bottom of the Layers palette. Choose the Gradient Tool from the toolbar (make sure the options are set as described in Step 11). From the bottom of the carriage photo, drag one quarter of the way up. Drag the Layer Mask by moving your cursor over it and dragging it to the trash and choose apply (see Figure 8.8).

18. Add another layer mask by clicking on the Add Layer Mask

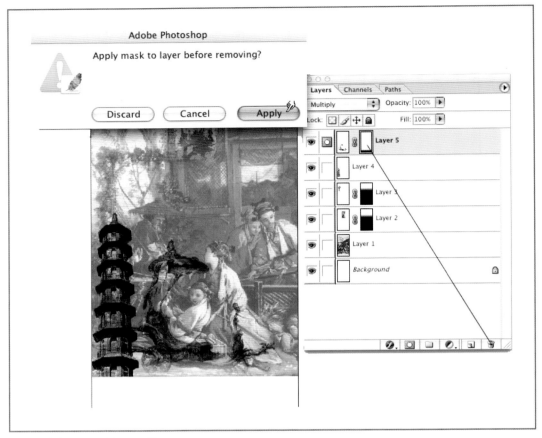

Figure 8.8   The addition of layer 5.

Figure 8.9   Layer 5 with Gradient Mask.

icon (second from the left) at the bottom of the Layers palette. Choose the Gradient Tool (make sure the options are set as described in Step 11). This time drag from the left, starting at the beginning of the image on layer 5, to the right (see Figure 8.9).

19. Open file 6.psd from the Chapter 8, mood board folder on the CD-ROM ○, and drag the background layer with the Move Tool onto the mood board document. Choose Edit: Transform: Rotate and rotate it slightly to the left. Choose Edit: Transform: Scale and scale the layer down until it is the size shown in Figure 8.10. Drag the layer down to the lower right-hand corner.

20. Add another layer mask by clicking on the Add Layer Mask icon (second from the

left) at the bottom of the Layers palette. Choose the Gradient Tool (make sure the options are set as described in Step 11). Drag the Gradient Tool from left to right while holding down the Shift key. (The Gradient Tool can be dragged several times until the correct effect is achieved.)

21. Select the Rectangular Marquee Tool or press M on the keyboard. Drag the Marquee Tool around the area where the coral layer runs into the white area at the bottom (see Figure 8.10).

22. Press delete with the marching ants active to get rid of the excess coral.

23. Open file 7.psd from the Chapter 8, mood board folder on the CD-ROM ⊙ , and drag the

Figure 8.10 Active layer.

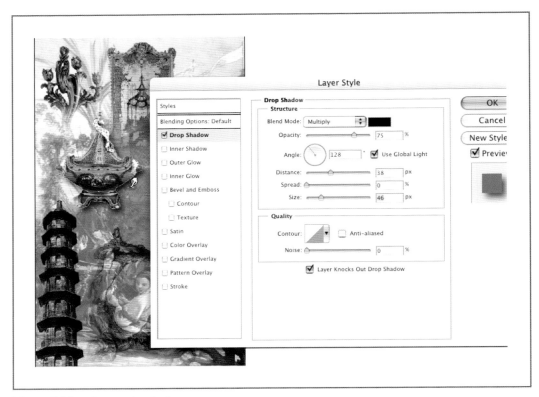

Figure 8.11   Blurring the shadow.

background layer with the Move Tool onto the mood board document while holding down the Shift key.

24. Choose the Magic Wand Tool (the tolerance option should be set to 32) or press W on the keyboard. Click once on the white background and press delete.

25. Choose Edit: Transform: Scale from the pull-down menu, and scale the layer until it resembles Figure 8.11.

26. Choose Layer: Layer Style: Drop Shadow from the pull-down menu. The drop shadow can be pulled directly into the document by moving the cursor over the document window and dragging it. Drag the size slider to the right to blur the shadow (see Figure 8.11).

27. Open file 8.psd from the Chapter 8, mood board folder on the CD-ROM ◯, and drag the background layer onto the mood board document with

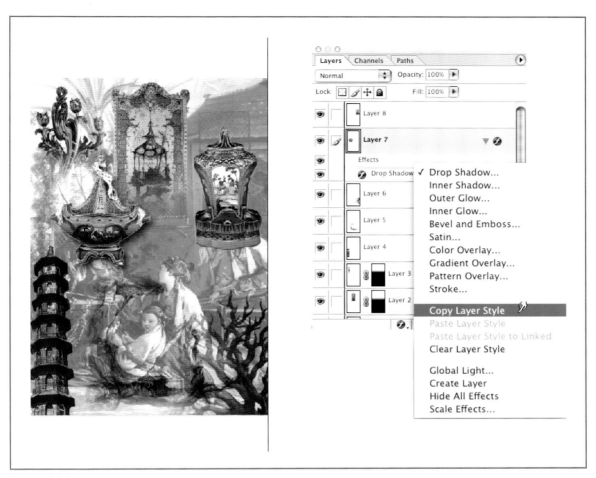

Figure 8.12   Copying Layer 7.

the Move Tool while holding down the Shift key. Choose the Magic Wand Tool and click on the white background with the marching ants active and press delete. Choose Edit: Transform: Scale to reduce the size of the layer. (Remember to drag from one of the corners of the bounding box while holding down the shift key to constrain the proportions).

28. While holding the Control key (or right click on a two click mouse), click on layer 7 (the previous layer where the drop shadow was applied), and choose Copy Layer Style (see Figure 8.12).

29. Click on layer 8 in the Layers palette (the newest layer) while holding the Control key (or right click on a two click

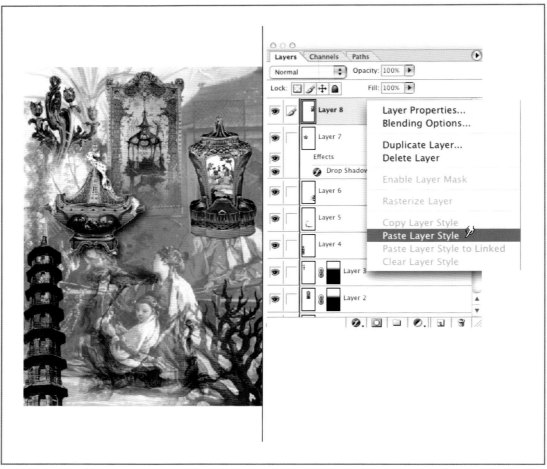

Figure 8.13   Duplicate Layer.

mouse) and choose Paste Layer Style. This will apply the same drop shadow style as on layer 7 (see Figure 8.13).

Creating a Color Story

New color stories are created every season to best complement silhouettes, textures, details, and overall themes. An individual color story will often have a chroma or range to build upon, such as pastels, jewel tones, or monochromatic themes. Color stories will often have specific formulas limiting the quantity of available choices. A traditional breakdown of colors may be four to six basic or base colors (such as black, brown, navy, white, or beige), two to four fashion colors (such as olive, burgundy, red, or khaki), and one to three accent colors (such as fuchsia, gold, or silver).

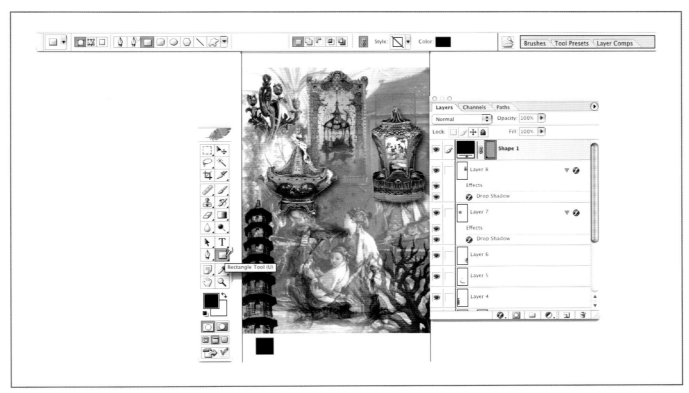

Figure 8.14　Shape Layer icon on the Options bar.

Names are then assigned to all the colors depicting the season's themes or trends. The Pantone Color System has the most extensive color palette universally recognized by designers, textile artists, and graphic artists; even costume designers are assured consistency when using a Pantone Color reference. This system also includes Pantone for Textiles, providing fabric swatch books showing how each color will look on a fabric swatch.

The first creative step begins at the computer screen, then follow these instructions to create a color story.

1. Choose the Rectangle Tool. In the Options bar, choose Shape Layer (the far left option), no style, and black for the color (see Figure 8.14).
2. To change the color, double click the Color Swatch in the Layers palette and choose a color

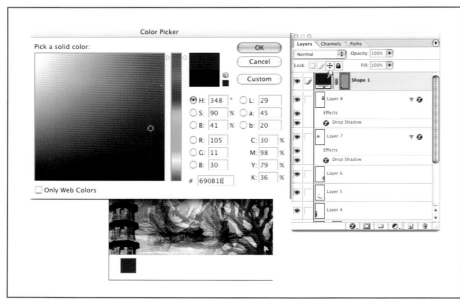

Figure 8.15   Color Picker.

from the Color Picker or click on Custom to select a Pantone Color (see Figure 8.15).

3. Create six more swatches by choosing the Move Tool and dragging the swatch to the right.

4. Change the color of the swatches. Link the swatch layers by clicking on the Link icons next to the swatch thumbnail. Evenly distribute the layers by clicking on the Distribute Horizontal Centers icon in the Options bar (see Figure 8.16).

5. Add text at the top of the document to complete the project. The final result will appear as in Figure 8.1.

Creating a Trend Board

The trend board is targeted toward communicating silhouettes, colors, textures, and styling nuances. All

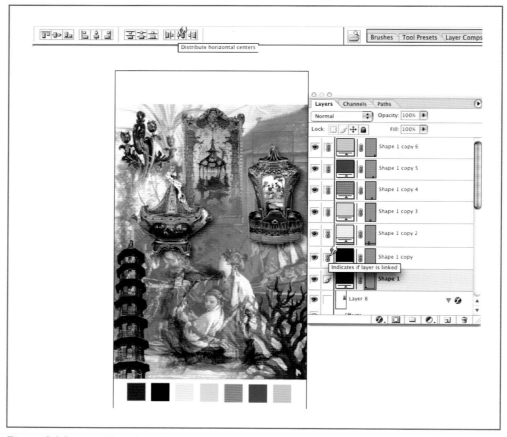

Figure 8.16   Mood board with color story.

Figure 8.17 Example of a trend board.

the elements of a trend are juxtaposed to create an interesting forecasting presentation (see Figure 8.17).

Fading the Background

Fading the background allows the elements in front to be prominent. It also allows special effects, such as drop shadows, to be visible. Follow these steps to fade the background.

1. In Photoshop, choose File: Open and maneuver to the Chapter 8 folder on the CD-ROM ○. Open the Trend Board folder and find file 1.psd. Click on Open.

2. Choose Window: Layers from the pull-down menu, and double click on the background layer in the Layers palette. When the Layers palette dialog box opens, type in 60 percent in the opacity

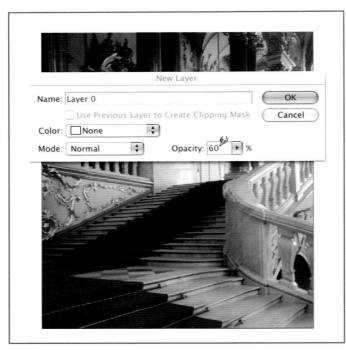

Figure 8.18   The Opacity field.

field and click on OK. Save the file, and name it "Trend Board" (see Figure 8.18).

3. Open file 2.psd from the Chapter 8, trend board folder on the CD-ROM ⟳ (Blackie the Boston Terrier). Drag Blackie's layer from the Layers palette onto the trend board document.

4. Choose the Magic Wand or press W on the keyboard. The tolerance should be set to 32. Click on the white area in the dog photo and press delete. Next choose Select: Deselect from the pull-down menu. Move Blackie to the bottom of the stairway using the Move Tool (see Figure 8.19).

5. Open file 3.psd from the Chapter 8, trend board folder on the CD-ROM ⟳, and drag the file

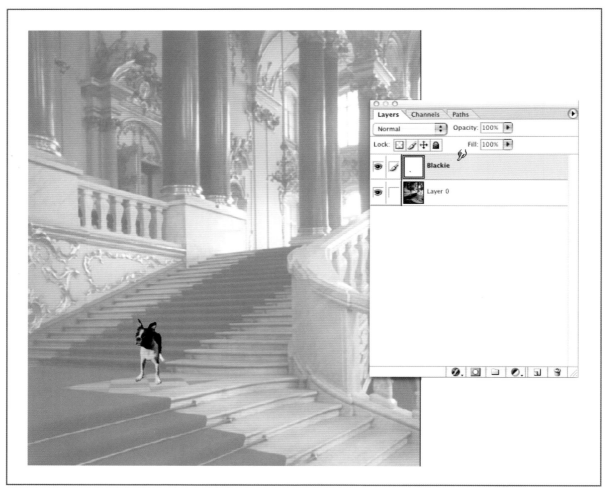

Figure 8.19   Position Blackie.

from the Layers palette onto the trend board document. Choose the Magic Wand Tool, and click on the white area around the illustration. Hold down the Shift key while clicking on the white inside of the arm (see Figure 8.20). Holding down the Shift key adds to a selection, and holding down the Option key will subtract from a selection.

6. Press delete on the keyboard to get rid of the white. Then choose Select: Deselect in the pull-down menu.

7. Open file 4.psd from the Chapter 8, trend board folder on the CD-ROM ⟳. Drag the background layer in the Layers palette (blue fan) onto the trend board document.

8. To remove the white area around the fan, choose the Magic Wand Tool, and click on the white area. Press delete on the keyboard, then choose Select: Deselect from the pull-down menu.

9. Use the Move Tool to position the fan in front of her right hand (see Figure 8.21).

Advanced Masking Techniques

Masking allows elements to be blended together seamlessly. The following will show how to blend a photographic element with an illustration.

1. Click on the Add Layer Mask icon at the bottom of the Layers palette (second icon from the left).

2. Choose the Brush Tool (or press B on the keyboard). Begin painting in black to reveal part of the hand underneath with a small brush. Switch to white by pressing X on the keyboard, which will paint back in the fan element on the layer. Continue to paint with both black and

Figure 8.20   Using the Magic Wand Tool.

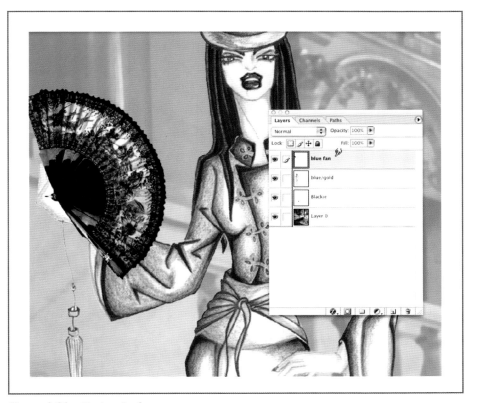

Figure 8.21   Placing the fan.

Figure 8.22   Painting the fan.

white until it looks like Figure 8.22.

3. Open file 5.psd from the Chapter 8, trend board folder on the CD-ROM ◯. Drag the background layer from the Layers palette onto the trend board document.

4. Choose the Magic Wand Tool, and click in the white area on the active layer highlighted in blue to select it. Press delete to eliminate the white areas, then choose Select: Deselect from the pull-down menu to eliminate the marching ants.

5. Open file 6.psd from the Chapter 8, trend board folder on the CD-ROM ◯. Drag the background layer from the Layers palette onto the trend board document. Choose the Magic Wand Tool, and click in the white areas. Click on the small areas

between the fan blades to add to the selection while holding down the Shift key. Press delete, then choose Select: Deselect. Position the fan over the left hand.

6. Add a layer mask by clicking on the Add Layer Mask icon at the bottom of the Layers palette.

7. Choose the Paintbrush Tool and begin painting with the black foreground swatch. This will reveal the hand. Paint with white (switch back and forth by pressing X on the keyboard) to show the fan (see Figure 8.23).

8. Open the file 7.psd from the Chapter 8, trend board folder on the CD-ROM ⊙. Drag the background layer from the Layers palette onto the trend board document. Choose the Magic Wand Tool, and click in the white background. Press delete on the keyboard, and choose Select:

Figure 8.23 Showing the hand and fan of the illustration.

Figure 8.24   Completed trend board.

Deselect from the pull-down menu. Use the Move Tool to position the illustration to the center of the file (see Figure 8.24).

Scaling and Joining Two Scans
Some large illustrations often need to be scanned in two parts because a large scanner may not be available. The following lesson will show

you how to scale and join two scans to fit into an 8.5 by 11 document.

1. Open files top.psd and bottom.psd from the Chapter 8, scaling a scan folder on the CD-ROM ⚪. The folder is called Scaling a Scan.
2. Click on the top.psd file to make it active.
3. Choose Image: Canvas Size, change the height to inches, and type 5. Choose the top middle Anchor and make sure the Canvas extension color is white and Relative is checked. This will make room for the bottom half of the illustration (see Figure 8.25).
4. Click on the bottom.psd file to make it active. Drag the background layer onto the top.psd file.
5. Use the Move Tool to position the file close to where the two illustrations meet (see Figure 8.26).

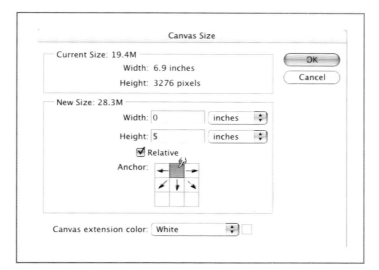

Figure 8.25 Set Canvas Size.

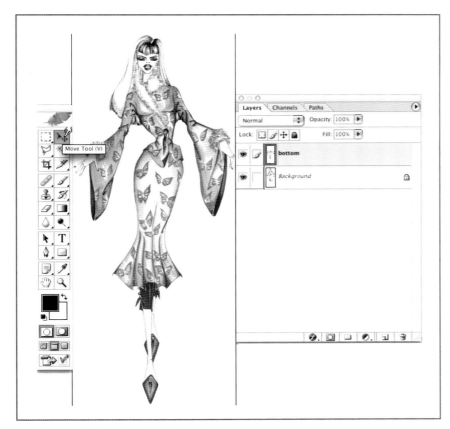

Figure 8.26 Position the top.psd file.

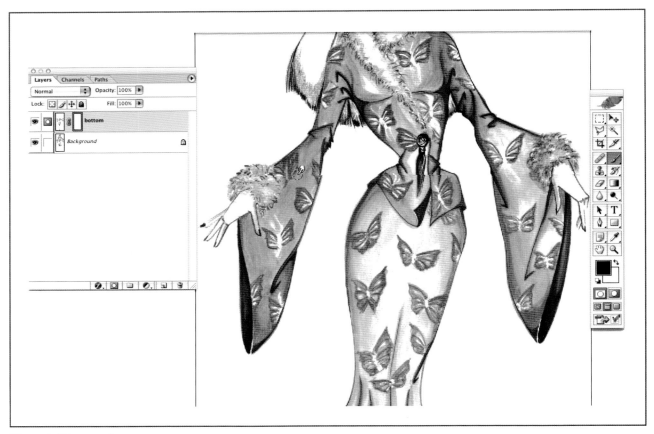

Figure 8.27 Partial scan.

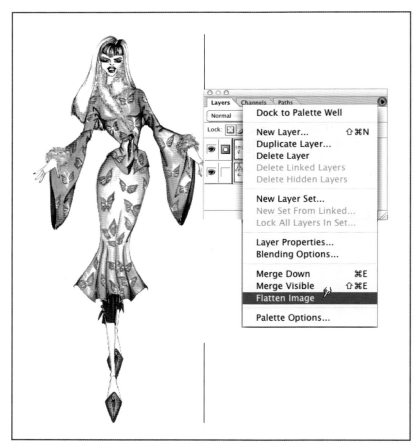

Figure 8.28 Completed scan.

6. Choose the Zoom Tool and zoom in on the area where the two scans meet.
7. Click on the Add Layers Mask icon at the bottom of the Layers palette, and choose the Paintbrush (or press B on the keyboard).
8. Begin painting away the hard edge where the two scans meet (see Figure 8.27).
9. Click on the arrow at the upper right-hand corner of the Layers palette, and choose Flatten Image (see Figure 8.28).

Creating Highlights

Creating highlights transforms flat illustrations into illustrations that have depth. The Dodge and Burn tools in Photoshop are two highlighting tools that effectively add depth to illustrations.

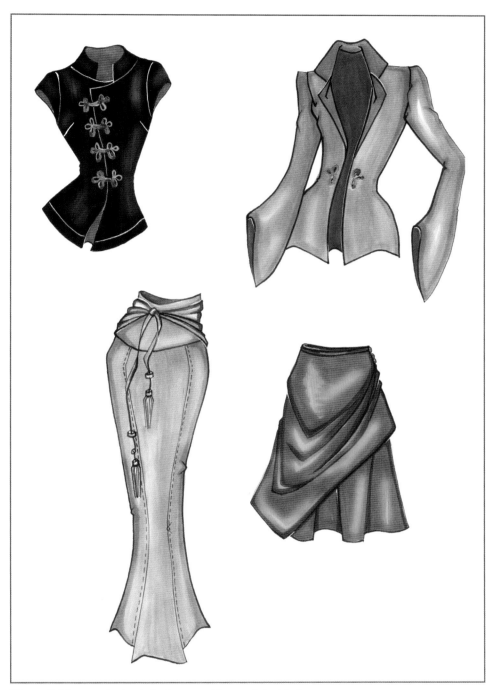

Figure 8.29   Finished polished group of flats with highlights.

1. Open flats.psd from the Chapter 8, creating highlights folder on the CD-ROM ◎ (see Figure 8.29).
2. Choose the Dodge Tool, set the range to Midtones and the Exposure to 50 percent (see Figure 8.30).
3. Begin painting on the flats with the Dodge Tool (see Figure 8.31).

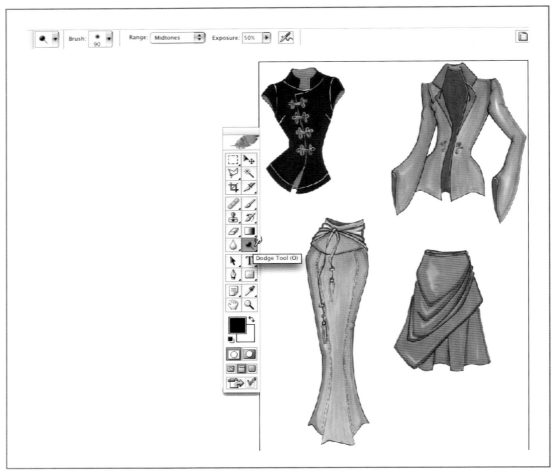

Figure 8.30 Using the Dodge Tool.

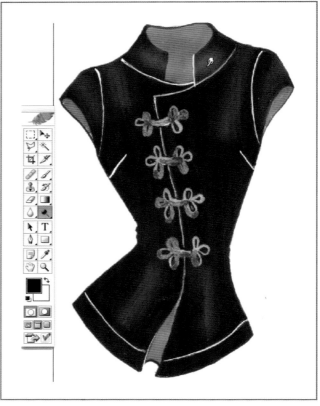

Figure 8.31 Completed illustration.

Polishing an Illustration

Polishing or smoothing out rough areas becomes necessary when scanning in an image. The following lesson will show you a few techniques to accomplish this. The techniques used for polishing an illustration, such as Dodge, Burn, or Airbrushed Highlights, can be applied to figures or stylized flats.

1. Open Asiantrend.psd from the Chapter 8, creating highlights folder on the CD-ROM ⟳, and zoom in on the face with the Zoom Tool (or press Z on the keyboard). Click and drag around the face (see Figure 8.32).

2. Choose the Smudge Tool (or press R on the keyboard); it resembles a pointing finger. Choose 20 percent for the strength. Begin painting over the rough areas to smooth them out (see Figure 8.33).

Figure 8.32   Original illustration.

Figure 8.33   Using the Smudge Tool, smooth out rough areas.

Figure 8.34   Completed illustration.

Figure 8.35   Select the Brush Tool to work on a close-up of the face.

3. Continue smoothing over the areas around the eyes, lips, hair, and anywhere else that looks rough until it looks similar to the final result (see Figure 8.34).

Creating Highlights with the Brush Tool

An important and fundamental rule to remember when adding depth to an illustration is "light always hits the highest point, and dark recedes." Creating depth is achieved by accentuating the light areas with the Airbrush Tool. The following lesson will show you how to create such highlights.

1. Open the Asiantrends.psd file from the Chapter 8, creating highlights folder in the CD-ROM ⊙. Zoom in on the face and choose the Brush Tool with white as the foreground color (see Figure 8.35).
2. Click once in the eye where the highlight is drawn in to accentuate it (see Figure 8.36).
3. Click in the lips. If the effect is ever too intense, lower the opacity on the Options bar.

The finished illustration will have lights and darks accentuated, and rough areas can be smoothed out (see Figure 8.37). These techniques are applied generally or to specific isolated areas of the illustration.

Figure 8.36 Select the eye that contains the highlight.

Figure 8.37 Completed illustration.

Review Questions

1. How do you add a Layer Mask?

2. How is the Gradient Tool used in a Layer Mask?

3. According to the fundamental rule of lighting, where will the lightest point be?

4. What does the Dodge Tool do?

5. What tool can be used to blend pixels?

Suggested Practice Project

Scan in a fashion figure illustration. Use the Smudge Tool to blend any rough pixels in the flesh tone areas.

Key Terms

Burn

Conceptual

Dodge

Exposure

Midtones

Mood board

Pixels

Predictive service

Smudge

Target consumer

Trend board

Trends

9

Creating Textile Patterns with Photoshop

Chapter 9 focuses on digital textile design and explains how to create fresh and vibrant textile patterns and prints. You will learn how to apply digital tools to the traditional process of color reduction and color replacements. The basic techniques of creating seamless patterns and saving these patterns within a preset manager are also covered.

Digital Printing

Traditional textile design tools such as watercolors, markers, and pens are being supplemented and often replaced by software such as Illustrator and Photoshop. The reason for this is the speed, accuracy, and lower cost in producing a digital image. Digital rendering on fabric allows companies to customize fabric designs and output the result for short-run production. Photoshop controls the dye droplet output in the digital printing process. This means the designer can have precise control over the amount of colors used and what percentages of process or spot colors are used.

Digital printing on textiles is not without its challenges. Textiles have greater absorbency than paper, which requires much more ink. Natural and synthetic fibers have their own requirements. Textiles often have highly textured and porous surfaces. Cotton is the most commonly printed substrate (the substance on which an image is printed), followed by cotton/polyester blends. The textile industry is working to combine its traditional screen printing method with digital printing. Before you attempt to work on this chapter, be sure to review Chapter 7, Getting Started with Adobe Photoshop.

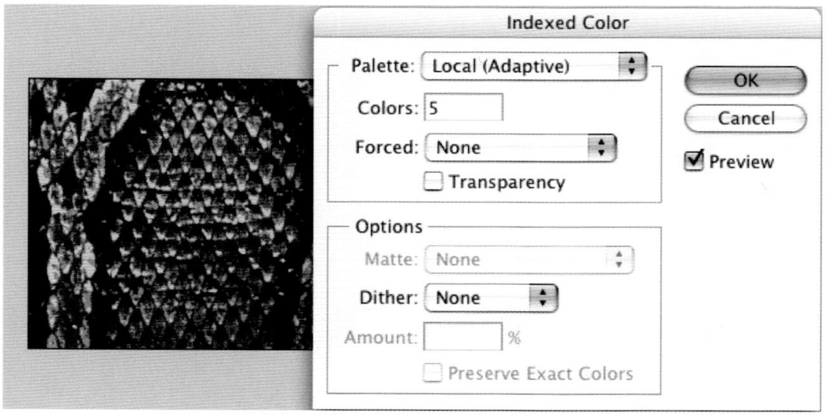

Color Reduction in a Textile

Color reduction of a pattern in Photoshop becomes necessary when scanning in a fabric because a scan contains thousands or millions of colors. When reducing the amount of colors in an image, it is easier to select and change specific colors. The printer will be thankful for the more manageable file that results.

1. Open snake.jpg from the Chapter 9 folder on the CD-ROM ⊙. This file was scanned in RGB mode, meaning it contains thousands of colors. Reduce the colors in the scan to only five, a significantly more manageable file for textile replication. Before color reducing a file, a slight Gaussian Blur of between 0.5 and 1.5, depending on the resolution of the file, will help keep the transition between colors smooth. The Gaussian Blur is found under Filter: Blur: Gaussian Blur in the pull-down menu.
2. Choose Image: Mode: Indexed Color (see Figure 9.1). Under Palette, choose Local (Adaptive). For Colors, type in 5. For Forced, choose None. Leave Transparency unchecked, and under Options, choose None for Dither. The fabric swatch has been reduced to five colors. Check and uncheck the Preview button for loss of quality.
3. Type in different color amounts, and see the update in the window.
4. Keep the Indexed Color palette open for the next lesson.

Every swatch will respond differently to the amount of colors

Figure 9.1   Indexed Color window.

deleted. Check and uncheck the preview button to determine how much color reduction you should trade off for image quality.

Replacing Color in a Textile

Replacing a color in a textile design becomes easier when it is color reduced. With the Indexed Color Custom Palette, color changes in the design can be modified. The colors are identified in CMYK or Pantone.

Method One

Method One shows how to replace color in a textile pattern. The color becomes easier to manipulate and modify if it is reduced prior to being changed.

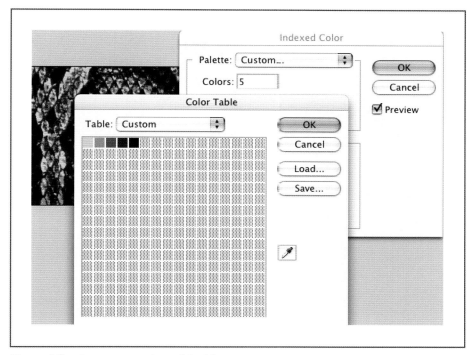

Figure 9.2   Customizing colors of the fabric.

1. If the Indexed Color palette isn't closed, change the palette option from Local (Adaptive) to Custom. If the Indexed Color palette is closed, open it back up (as described in the previous lesson). It may be necessary to switch to RGB mode and back to Indexed Color mode for the option to be available. Then switch from Previous to Local (Adaptive) to Custom.
2. The five colors in the fabric should be visible (see Figure 9.2).
3. Click on the second color from the left. The Color Picker will become visible. Select a new color. The old color will appear below the new one (see Figure 9.3).

Figures 9.4a and 9.4b show the before and after.

Method Two

Method Two shows how to modify or change specific isolated color areas or objects in a textile pattern. This method is employed when certain sections of the pattern do not require altering.

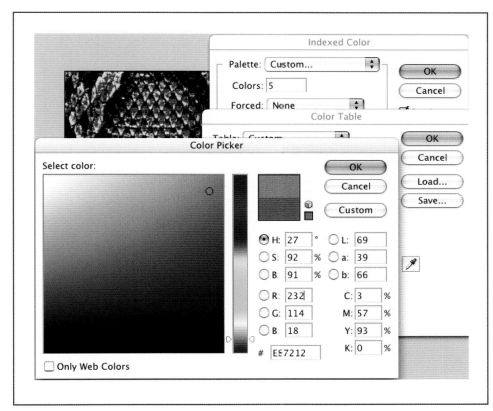

Figure 9.3   The new color is displayed.

Figure 9.4a The original color.

b The new color.

1. Open file flowers.psd from the Chapter 9 folder on the CD-ROM ○ . Choose the Lasso Tool, and drag it around the flowers but not the birds. Hold down the Shift key when adding to the selection (see Figure 9.5).

2. Choose Image: Adjustments: Replace Color, and click on a yellow area in one of the flowers. Drag the Hue slider to change the color and the Saturation slider to change the intensity. The original can be seen in the top yellow swatch. The result is the bottom swatch. Double click

Figure 9.5 An area selected using the Lasso Tool.

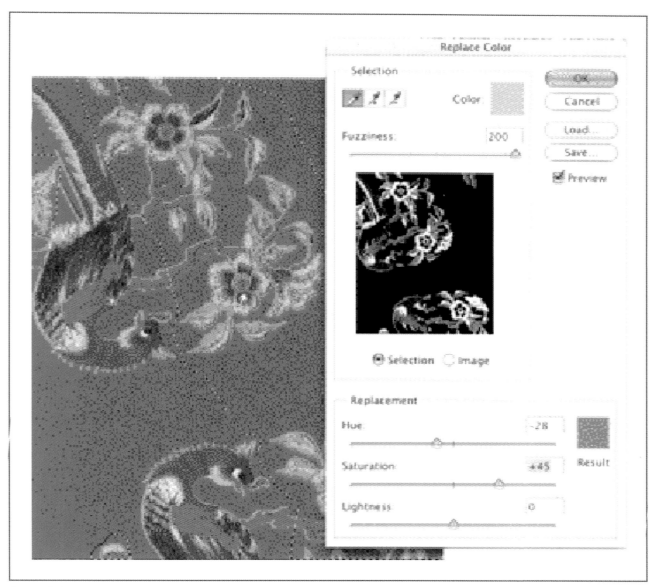

Figure 9.6 Access the Pantone Color palette.

on the bottom swatch to access the Pantone Color palette (see Figure 9.6).

Creating a Seamless Repeat Textile Pattern

To create a seamless repeat textile pattern, it will need to be "in repeat." The original motif (the single design from which a pattern can be created) will need to tile seamlessly to fill out the area. There are a few different ways to create a seamless textile pattern in Photoshop, with some techniques working better on certain textiles than others.

ImageReady Tile Maker Method

1. Create a new file that is 5" by 5", 72 dpi, and RGB color mode. Choose a light blue as the foreground color by clicking on it and choosing the color from the Color Picker. Keep white as the background color. Choose Filter: Render: Clouds. This will create a cloud pattern.
2. Click on the ImageReady icon at the bottom of the toolbox (see Figure 9.7).
3. Choose Filter: Other: Tile Maker while in ImageReady.
4. Check the Blend Edges option. Select Width 10 percent (sometimes 5 percent is enough to blur the edges), and check the Resize Tile to Fill Image option (see Figure 9.8).
5. Click on the Edit in Photoshop icon at the bottom of the toolbox to return to Photoshop. It is the same icon that brought up Image-Ready.

6. When back in Photoshop, choose Edit: Define Pattern.
7. Name the pattern "tile maker clouds."

Create a new file to view the pattern, choosing the 1024 × 768 preset. Click on the new adjustment layer icon at the bottom of the Layers palette and choose Pattern. Set the scaling to 50 to see a tighter pattern (see Figure 9.9).

After selecting OK, close the file without saving it because the pattern is stored.

Offset Filter Center Cross Method

1. Create a new file that is 5" by 5", 72 dpi, and RGB color mode. Choose a light blue as a foreground color, and keep white as the background color. Choose Filter: Render: Clouds. This will create a cloud pattern.
2. Choose Filter: Other: Offset. Choose +180 horizontal, +180 vertical, and Wrap Around. 180 and 180 are half the Horizontal

Figure 9.7   ImageReady Icon.

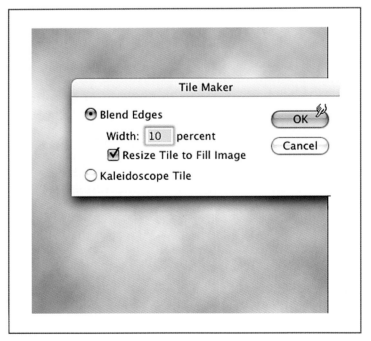

Figure 9.8   Resize Tile to Fill Image option.

Figure 9.9   Changing the scaling in the Layers palette.

and Vertical file size in pixels of the file that was 360 pixels by 360 pixels. For the Offset method, always choose half the size for Horizontal and Vertical (see Figure 9.10).

3. Drag a cross shape with the Lasso Tool as seen in Figure 9.11.

4. Choose Select: Feather from the pull-down menu. Choose 50 pixels for the feather. (Larger dpi files will require a higher number of pixels for the feather.)

5. Choose Offset again with the same amounts as on Step 2.

6. Choose Select: Deselect from the pull-down menu.

7. Choose Edit: Define Pattern from the pull-down menu.

8. Create a new file and fill the file with the cloud pattern (as described in the previous step) to see it tile seamlessly.

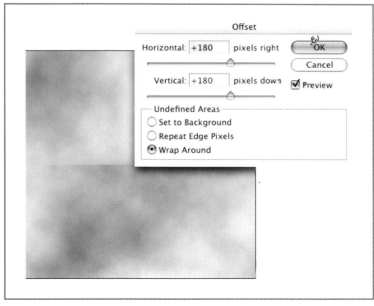

Figure 9.10   The Offset window with Horizontal and Vertical options.

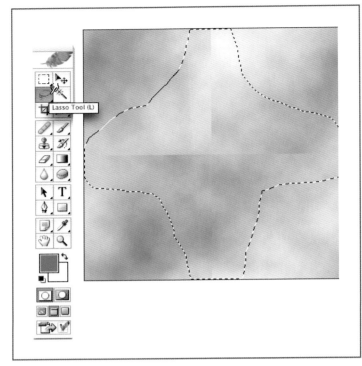

Figure 9.11   Cross-shape design using the Lasso Tool.

Mosaic Method

This method will create a mirror effect.

1. Create a new file that is 5" by 5", 72 dpi, and RGB color mode. Choose a light blue as a foreground color, and keep white as the background color. Choose Filter: Render: Clouds from the pull-down menu. This will create a cloud pattern.
2. Choose Select: All, then Edit: Copy from the pull-down menu.
3. Choose Image: Canvas Size from the pull-down menu. Click in the upper left corner, and choose 100 percent for both Width and Height options (see Figure 9.12).
4. Click on the Rectangular Marquee Tool and choose Fixed Size. Enter 360 pixels for both options. This is the size of the original file copied to the clipboard in pixels.
5. Click in the top right corner of the image and choose Edit:

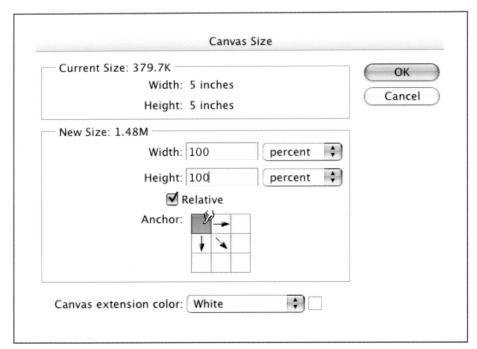

Figure 9.12   Canvas Size window with Width and Height options.

Figure 9.13   The clouds have been flipped horizontally.

Paste from the pull-down menu. This should paste the cloud file in the top right corner. If there is any white space at the top right or left side of the file, choose the Move Tool and nudge the cloud copy layer until no white space is visible.

6. Choose Edit: Transform: Flip Horizontal from the pull-down menu. The file should look like Figure 9.13.

7. Click the Rectangular Marquee Tool in the lower left-hand corner of the file, and choose Edit: Paste from the pull-down menu.

8. Choose Edit: Transform: Flip Vertical from the pull-down menu.

9. Click the Rectangular Marquee Tool in the lower right-hand corner, and choose Edit: Paste from the pull-down menu.

10. Choose Edit: Transform: Flip Horizontal from the pull-down menu.

Figure 9.14   The clouds have been flipped vertically to fill the area.

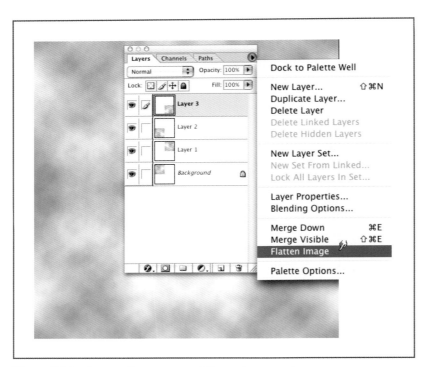

Figure 9.15   Layer pullout menu and Flatten Image option.

11. Then choose Edit: Transform: Flip Vertical from the pull-down menu. The file should look like Figure 9.14.

12. Choose Flatten Image from the Layer pullout menu (see Figure 9.15).

13. Choose Edit: Define Pattern from the pull-down menu to create a pattern from the mosaic cloud texture.

Straight Repeat Method

1. Create a new file that is 100 pixels by 100 pixels at 72 dpi.

2. Press D on your keyboard to change to the default colors: black foreground and white background.

3. Choose the Custom Shape Tool (it is a rectangle subtool) and make sure the Shape Layer option to the far left is selected (see Figure 9.16).

4. Choose the Fleur-De-Lis shape and drag it in the window to fill the file (see Figure 9.17).

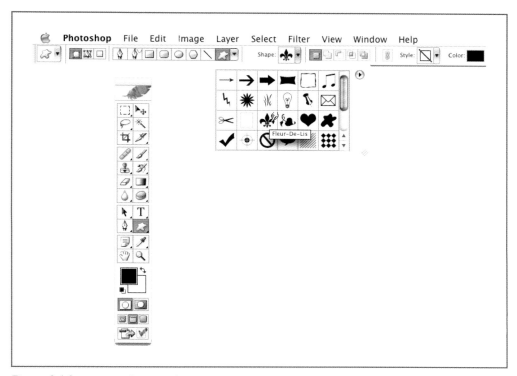

Figure 9.16   Custom Shape Tools.

5. Choose Flatten Image from the Layer pullout menu.
6. Choose Edit: Define Pattern from the pull-down menu.

Half-drop Repeat Method

1. Follow Steps 1 to 5 in the previous exercise.
2. Choose the Magic Wand Tool, and click once in the Fleur-De-Lis shape to select it.
3. Choose Edit: Copy, then Select: Deselect, both from the pull-down menu.
4. Choose Filter: Other: Offset from the pull-down menu. Enter 0 for the Horizontal and 50 for the Vertical and click Wrap Around. The Vertical will be exactly half the file size. Make adjustments by dragging the arrow sliders (see Figure 9.18). Click OK.
5. Choose Image: Canvas Size from the pull-down menu, and click the far left anchor point and enter 100 percent in the Width.

Figure 9.17   Fleur-De-Lis Shape.

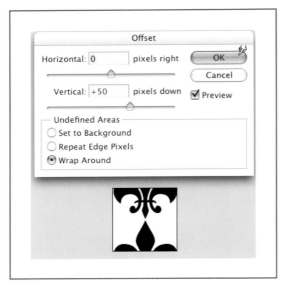

Figure 9.18   Offset window with Horizontal,
Vertical, and Wrap Around options.

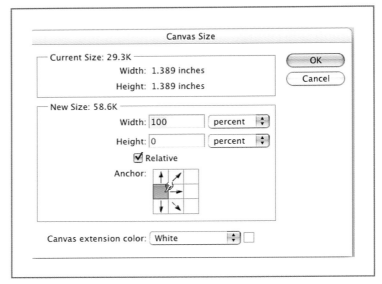

Figure 9.19   Canvas Size window with Width and Height options.

Figure 9.20   Image repeated once with the Paste Tool.

Leave the Height at zero. Click OK (see Figure 9.19).

6. Choose Edit: Paste from the pull-down menu, and move the motif to the empty space as shown in Figure 9.20.

7. Choose Edit: Define Pattern from the pull-down menu. Figure 9.21 is an example of the straight repeat pattern.

Figure 9.21   Straight repeat pattern.

An example of the half-drop repeat pattern is shown in Figure 9.22.

Toss and Repeat Method
Toss and Repeat creates a random pattern arrangement. Try the following steps to practice this method.

1. Create a new file that is 5" by 5", 72 dpi, and RGB color mode.
2. Using the Custom Shape Tool, lay out your design to resemble Figure 9.23. Vary the design later after mastering the basic principle.
3. Choose Flatten Image from the Layer pullout menu.
4. Choose Filter: Other: Offset from the pull-down menu and enter the following:

- Horizontal: +180 pixels
- Vertical: +180
- Check the Preview option
- Undefined Areas: Select Wrap Around
- Select OK

We chose 180 pixels because it is half the pixel dimensions of the original file. The design will now resemble Figure 9.24.

Figure 9.22   Half-drop repeat pattern.

Figure 9.23   Random pattern arrangement.

Figure 9.24   Pattern with 180 pixels.

Figure 9.25   The pattern has been copied to fill the design.

5. Choose the Magic Wand, and select the motif that is complete (in the lower right-hand corner). Choose Edit: Copy, then Edit: Paste from the pull-down menu. Move the pasted selection in the empty space, and rotate it to the right to fill the design. Choose Flatten Image from the Layer pullout menu. It should now look like Figure 9.25.

6. Choose Edit: Define Pattern from the pull-down menu, and name it "Toss Repeat."

Creating Pure Photoshop Textile Patterns

Creating pure Photoshop textile patterns involves using only Photoshop. No other images, such as scanned fabrics or photographs, are involved. This offers advantages due to resolution control, original design options, accurate color, as well as seamless pattern possibilities.

Denim

1. Create a new file that is 5" by 5", 72 dpi, and RGB color mode.

2. Press D on the keyboard to switch to the default colors: black foreground and white background. Then press X on the keyboard to switch to a white foreground and black background.

3. Click on the foreground swatch to bring up the color palette. Choose a blue for the denim. The example is cyan 77 percent, magenta 45 percent, yellow 0 percent, and black 0 percent.

4. Choose Filter: Sketch: Halftone Pattern from the pull-down menu. Choose 1 for the size and 10 for the contrast (see Figure 9.26). Click OK.

5. Choose Filter: Stylize: Diffuse from the pull-down menu. Choose Lighten Only for the setting (see Figure 9.27). Click OK.

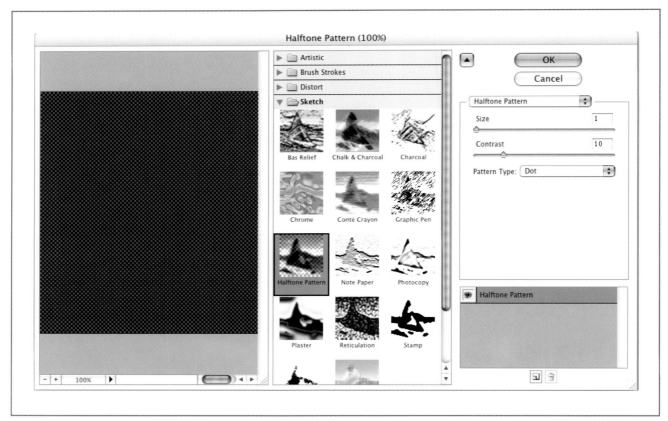

Figure 9.26   Halftone Pattern window.

6. Choose Image: Image Size from the pull-down menu. Make sure Constrain Proportions is selected, and choose 2.5 inches for the Width and 2.5 for the Height. This will tighten up the pattern.

7. Choose Edit: Define Pattern from the pull-down menu, and name it "Denim."

Quick Denim

1. Create a new file that is 5" by 5", 72 dpi, and RGB color mode.

2. Fill the file with a blue for the denim color.

3. Choose the Adjustment Layer icon at the bottom of the Layers palette, and choose Pattern.

4. Click on the Pattern Arrow and choose the Texture Fill option.

5. Choose Denim from the patterns, and click OK.

6. Change the Blend mode to Overlay from the Layers palette blend options.

7. Choose Flatten Image from the Layers palette pullout menu, and change the image size to 2.5 by 2.5.

8. Choose Edit: Define Pattern from the pull-down menu, and name it "Quick Denim" (see Figure 9.28).

Stripes

1. Choose File: New from the pull-down menu, and create a new file that is 5" by 5", 72 dpi, and RGB color mode.

2. Fill the file with black by choosing Edit: Fill from the pull-down menu and clicking on black.

3. Click on the foreground swatch, and choose cyan 14 percent and magenta 70 percent. Leave yellow and black at 0 percent.

4. Create a new layer by clicking on the New Layer icon at the bottom of the Layers palette.

Name this layer "Stripe."

5. Choose View: Rulers from the pull-down menu. Using the Move Tool, drag a guide out at the ½-inch, 1-inch, 2-inch, 3-inch, and 4-inch mark.

6. Choose the Rectangular Marquee Tool, and create a rectangle ½ inch wide and press Option: Delete to fill the selection (see Figure 9.29).

7. Duplicate the stripe layer by dragging it to the New Layer

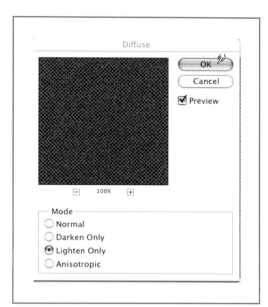

Figure 9.27 Diffuse window.

Figure 9.28 The "Quick Denim" pattern.

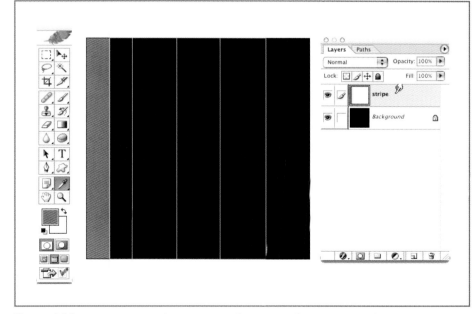

Figure 9.29 Creating vertical stripes using the Rectangular Marquee Tool.

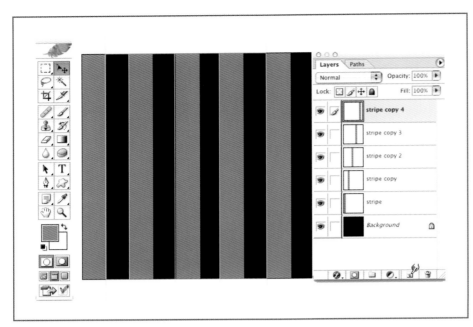

Figure 9.30   Repeat of the rectangular pattern.

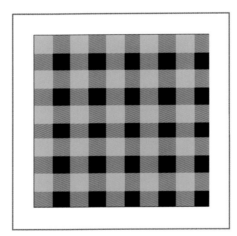

Figure 9.31   Check repeat.

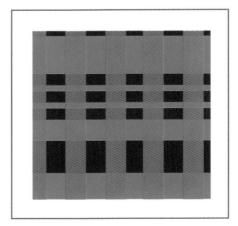

Figure 9.32   A plaid pattern.

icon at the bottom of the Layers palette.

8. Create four more stripes and drag them to each of the guides (see Figure 9.30).

9. Choose Flatten Image from the Layer pullout menu located at the arrow on the top of the Layers palette.

10. Choose Edit: Define Pattern from the pull-down menu, and name it "Vertical Stripes."

11. To create horizontal stripes, choose Image: Rotate Canvas: 90 degree CW, choose Edit: Define Pattern from the pull-down menu, and name it "Horizontal Stripes." Keep the file open for the next textile.

Check Repeat

1. With the horizontal stripe file open, choose Image: Duplicate from the pull-down menu.

2. Choose Image: Rotate: Canvas: 90 degree CW from the pull-down menu to make vertical stripes.

3. Drag the Layer icon of the vertical stripe file while holding down the Shift key to the horizontal stripe file. This will bring the file in the center of the horizontal file while creating a new layer.

4. Switch this Layer Mode to Screen from the Blending Mode option in the Layers palette, and choose Flatten Image from the Layer pullout menu to produce the check repeat (see Figure 9.31).

5. Choose Edit: Define Pattern from the pull-down menu, and name it "Check Repeat."

Plaid

1. Begin by creating vertical stripes and horizontal stripes on different layers and different sizes.

2. Use three or four colors and try different blending modes before flattening the image as shown in Figure 9.32.

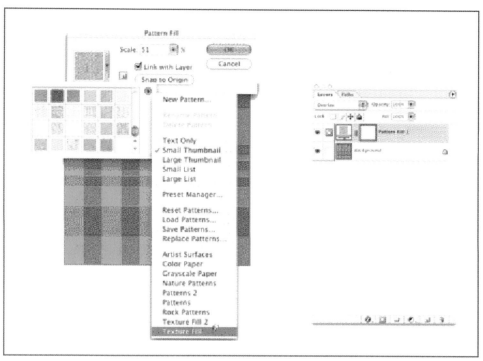

Figure 9.33 Pattern Fill window and Layer Mode options

3. To add a texture, go to the Adjustment Layer icon at the bottom of the Layers palette and choose Pattern. Experiment with the different patterns and layer modes. Try the different presets available in the pullout menu (see Figure 9.33).

Stripes 2

1. Choose File: New from the pull-down menu, and create a new file that is 10 pixels by 100 pixels, 72 dpi, and RGB color mode.
2. Choose the Rectangular Marquee Tool and choose Fixed Size in the Options toolbox. Enter 10 pixels by 10 pixels.
3. Click on the top and fill with a color (see Figure 9.34).
4. Continue to click down the stripe with multiple colors until it is filled (see Figure 9.35).
5. Choose Select: All, then Edit: Copy from the pull-down menu.
6. Choose Image: Canvas Size from the pull-down menu, and enter the following measurements:

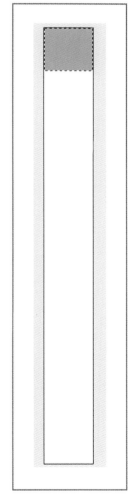

Figure 9.34 Beginning of a stripe pattern.

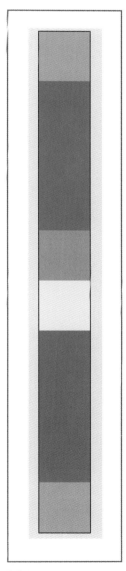

Figure 9.35 Filled in vertical canvas.

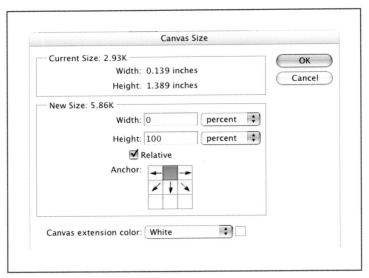

Figure 9.36   Canvas Size window with Width and Height options.

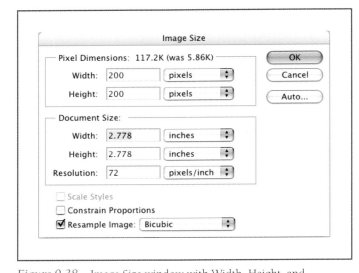

Figure 9.38   Image Size window with Width, Height, and
Resolution options.

Figure 9.37   The pattern has been
flipped vertically.

- Width: 0 percent
- Height: 100 percent
- Top middle anchor point (see
  Figure 9.36)

7. Choose Edit: Paste from the
   pull-down menu, and move the
   stripe copy to the bottom.
   Choose Edit: Transform: Flip
   Vertical from the pull-down
   menu (see Figure 9.37).
8. Choose Flatten Image from the
   Layers palette pullout menu.
9. Choose Image: Image Size from
   the pull-down menu, and turn
   off the Constrain Proportions
   check box. Enter 2.788 in the
   Width box, and click OK (see
   Figure 9.38).

The file should look like Figure
9.39.

To create a pattern from the stripe
file, choose Edit: Define Pattern
from the pull-down menu. Keep the
file open for the next lesson. To create vertical stripes, choose Image:
Rotate Canvas 90 degree CW from
the pull-down menu.

Plaid 2

1. Keeping the stripe file open,
   drag the background to the New

Figure 9.39   Completed horizontal stripe pattern.

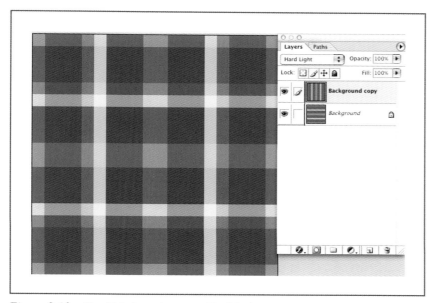

Figure 9.40 Blend Mode option set to Hard Light.

Layer icon at the bottom of the Layers palette to create a background copy.

2. Choose Edit: Transform: Rotate 90 degree CW from the pull-down menu.

3. Try the different blend modes from the Blend Mode options in the Layers palette for different plaid effects. In Figure 9.40, the Blend Mode is set to Hard Light.

Diamond Pattern

1. Use the finished stripe pattern before the plaid to create this pattern.

2. Choose Image: Mode: Index Color (exact palette) from the pull-down menu. This prevents anti-alias softening of the edges.

3. Choose Image: Rotate Canvas: Arbitrary (45 degree CW) from the pull-down menu.

4. Choose View: Rulers from the pull-down menu, and add a horizontal and vertical guide in the center of the image.

5. Select the Rectangular Marquee Tool, and set the style to normal with a feather of 0 in the Options bar while holding down the Shift Option key (see Figure 9.41).

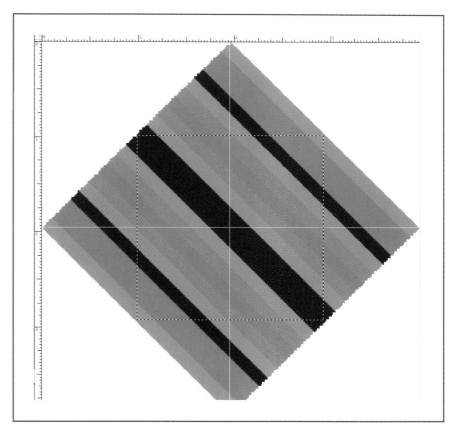

Figure 9.41 Creating a diamond pattern.

Figure 9.42   Cropped image.

Figure 9.43   Using the Mosaic Method makes this pattern seamless.

6. Choose Image: Crop from the pull-down menu (see Figure 9.42).
7. Use the mosaic method to make the pattern seamless (see Figure 9.43).
8. Choose Edit: Define Pattern.

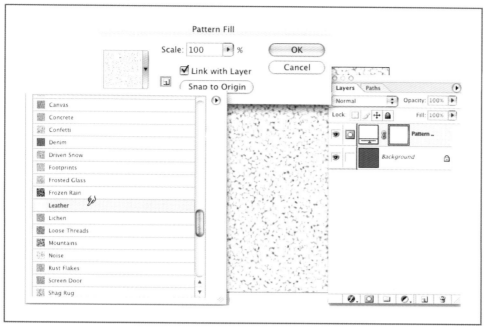

Figure 9.44 Small List window from the Option pullout menu.

Leather

1. Create a new file that is 5" by 5" at 72 dpi.
2. Click on the foreground swatch and choose cyan 38, magenta 63, yellow 100, and black 30 for the leather color.
3. Choose the Adjustment Layer icon from the Layers palette, and choose Pattern.
4. Choose Small List from the Option pullout menu (the small arrow on the side).
5. Choose Leather (see Figure 9.44). (If Leather is not visible, choose the arrow pullout and load the texture 1 and 2 presets from the options).
6. Change the scale to 50 percent, and click OK.
7. Change the Blend Mode of the pattern layer to Multiply (see Figure 9.45).
8. Flatten the image, choose Edit: Define Pattern from the pull-down menu, and name it "Leather."

Leather 2

1. Create a new file that is 5" by 5", 72 dpi, and RGB mode.

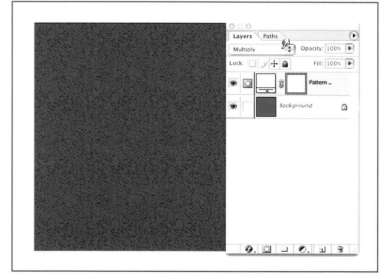

Figure 9.45 Blend Mode option set to Multiply.

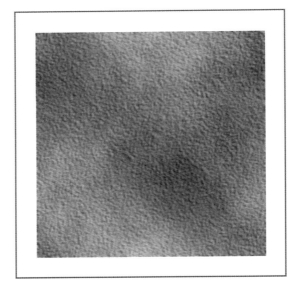

Figure 9.46   Completed leather pattern.

2. Create a new layer, fill it with white, and choose Filter: Noise: Add Noise (Gaussian, Monochromatic). Set the Amount to 175.

3. Select Filter: Stylize: Emboss. Set the Angle to 37, the Height to 3, and the Amount to 100 percent.

4. Select Filter: Blur: Gaussian Blur from the pull-down menu. Set the Radius Amount to 0.9.

5. Create a new layer and set the colors to their default settings by pressing D on the keyboard. Choose Filter: Render: Clouds from the pull-down menu. Change the opacity to 50 percent.

6. Create a new layer and set the foreground color to cyan 3 percent, magenta 42 percent, yellow 87 percent, and leave black 0 percent. Change the background color to white. Choose Filter: Render: Clouds from the pull-down menu.

7. Change the layer Blend Mode to Multiply and the opacity to 70 percent.

8. Use the ImageReady Tile Maker Filter (Click on the ImageReady icon at the bottom of the toolbox, and choose Filter: Other: Tile Maker from the pull-down menu) to make the leather seamless and choose Edit: Define Pattern. Name it Leather 2 (see Figure 9.46).

There are several plain weaves available in Photoshop. Using the same method as the leather method and choosing different colors make it possible to vary the weave and color of a plain weave textile.

Faux Animal Print

1. Create a new file that is 5" by 5", 72 dpi, and RGB color mode.

2. Create a new layer by clicking on the New Layer icon at the bottom of the Layers palette. Fill the layer with white.

3. Choose Filter: Texture: Stained Glass from the pull-down menu. Choose 16 for Cell Size, 8 for Border Size, and 0 for Light Intensity.

4. Choose Edit: Transform: Scale from the pull-down menu, and enlarge the layer until there is no black border.

5. Choose Image: Adjustments: Invert from the pull-down menu.

Figure 9.47 Faux animal print.

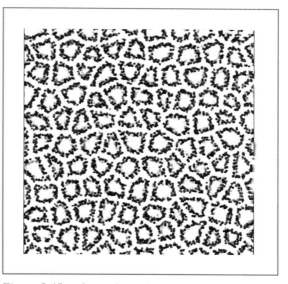

Figure 9.48 The pixilation has been adjusted.

6. Choose Filter: Sketch: Photo-copy from the pull-down menu. Set the Detail to 4 and the Darkness to 25 (see Figure 9.47).

7. Choose Filter: Pixelate: Pointil-ize from the pull-down menu, and set the Cell Size to 5 (see Figure 9.48).

8. Set the foreground color to black and the background color to cyan 9 percent, magenta 32 percent, yellow 77 percent, and black 0 percent.

9. Choose Filter: Sketch: Stamp from the pull-down menu and choose a Light/Dark Balance of 1 and a Smoothness of 4 (see Figure 9.49).

10. Choose Filter: Noise: Add Noise from the pull-down menu, and use a setting of 10 percent Gaussian and Monochromatic.

11. Choose Filter: Blur: Motion Blur from the pull-down menu, and use 90 for the angle and 5 for the distance.

12. Choose Filter: Distort: Ripple from the pull-down menu, and set the angle to 20 percent.

13. Choose Flatten image from the Layers palette pullout menu,

Figure 9.49 The contrast and smoothness of the pat-tern further adjusted.

Figure 9.50   Completed animal print.

and use the mosaic method (as described earlier in this chapter) to create a seamless pattern (see Figure 9.50).

Zebra Print

1. Create a new file that is 5" by 5", 72 dpi, and RGB color mode, with a white background.
2. Select the Lasso Tool, and begin drawing shapes similar to a zebra pattern (use a picture of a zebra for reference) (see Figure 9.51).
3. Fill the selections with black.
4. Choose Filter: Noise: Add Noise from the pull-down menu. Select 5 percent for Amount, Gaussian for Distribution, and check Monochromatic.

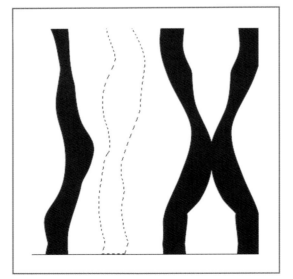

Figure 9.51   Zebra print.

Figure 9.52 Using the mosaic method makes this pattern seamless.

5. Choose Filter: Blur: Motion Blur from the pull-down menu, and use 90 degrees and 5 percent for the Amount.
6. Use the mosaic method to make the pattern seamless (see Figure 9.52).

Camouflage

1. Create a new file that is 5" by 5", 72 dpi, and RGB color mode. Fill it with a light color.
2. Create a new layer and choose Filter: Render: Clouds from the pull-down menu.
3. Choose Image: Adjust: Threshold from the pull-down menu to increase the contrast. Drag the triangle to the black area to adjust the contrast.
4. Select the black areas using Select: Color Range from the pull-down menu. Drag the layer to the trash can so that only the selection remaining is showing (see Figure 9.53).
5. Create a new layer.

Figure 9.53 The remaining selection.

6. Select: Modify: Smooth from the pull-down menu to soften the selection.
7. Fill this selection with a new color.
8. Select Filter: Blur: Motion Blur from the pull-down menu. Choose 90 degrees and 5 percent for the Distance.

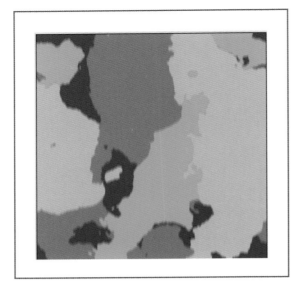

Figure 9.54   The results of using the Motion Blur option.

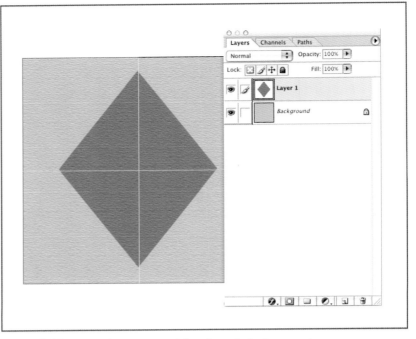

Figure 9.55   Using the Texturizer Filter through the Layers palette.

9. Repeat Steps 2 to 8 two more times (see Figure 9.54).

Argyle

1. Create a new file that is 5" by 5", 72 dpi, and RGB color mode.
2. Fill the document with red 200, green 202, and blue 17.
3. Choose Filter: Texture: Texturizer from the pull-down menu. Set Canvas and Scaling at 60 percent and Relief at 3 with the light direction coming from the top.
4. Choose View Rulers from the pull-down menu, and drag a vertical guide to 2½ and a horizontal guide to 2½.
5. Create a new layer, and change the foreground color to red 25, green 131, and blue 52.
6. Choose the Custom Shape Tool and click on the Diamond shape. Make sure the Fill Pixels option is chosen in the Option bar (it's the option on the far right).
7. Line up the crosshair in the middle and begin dragging while holding down the Option and Shift keys to create a diamond.

8. Apply the Texturizer Filter with the same settings (see Figure 9.55).
9. Select the Line Tool, and create lines along the edges of the diamond. Hold down the space bar to move and adjust the lines (see Figure 9.56).
10. Create four more diamonds, fill them with red, and apply the texturizer with the same settings (see Figure 9.57).

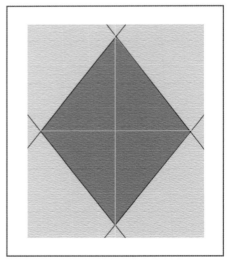

Figure 9.56   Lines that have been added to the pattern.

Figure 9.57 Overlapping the four new diamonds creates a distinct pattern.

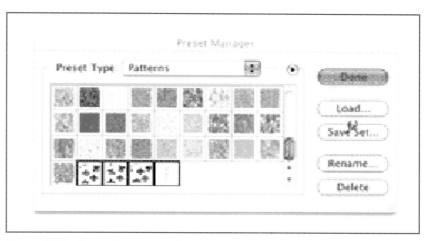

Figure 9.58 Preset Manager window.

11. Choose Edit: Define Pattern from the pull-down menu, and name it "Argyle."

Saving Patterns with the Preset Manager

Saving patterns with the Preset Manager makes it possible to save textiles that are created in their various repeat forms and to load them on different computers. The Preset Manager can also be used to organize, load, delete, and save brushes, swatches, gradients, styles, custom shapes, contours, and tools. Follow these steps when saving patterns.

1. To access the Preset Manager, choose Edit: Preset Manager from the pull-down menu. Choose Patterns in the Preset option.
2. To save your patterns, hold down the shift key while clicking on the patterns.
3. Click on the Save Set button (see Figure 9.58).
4. Name the patterns, which will have a .pat extension (see Figure 9.59).
5. To load patterns, click on the Load button, click the pattern set, and click on Load (see Figure 9.60).

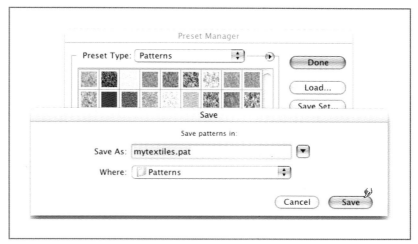

Figure 9.59 Save window.

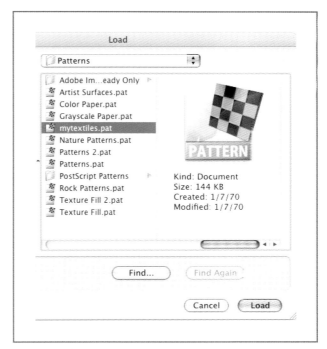

Figure 9.60 Load window.

Review Questions

1. What is a way you can replace a color in a textile?

2. How can you make a textile seamless?

3. What is the difference between a half-drop and a toss and repeat pattern?

4. How do you save patterns?

5. What does the Tile Maker do?

Suggested Practice Project

Create a half-drop repeat floral textile.

Key Terms

Half-drop

Mosaic

Toss and repeat

10

Software Basics:
Getting Started with Adobe Illustrator CS

Chapter 10 introduces the student to the core basics of the Adobe Illustrator CS environment. You will learn to set preferences, manage color settings, and utilize palettes and pull-down menus and commands. The basic toolbox functions are also covered in depth.

Figure 10.1   Color Settings window.

What Is Required to Run Adobe Illustrator CS

Adobe Illustrator runs effectively with Windows Pentium-class or faster and with Windows 98 (or later), Windows NT 4.0, or Millennium operating systems. A Macintosh system with a PowerPC processor Illustrator CS needs at least 10.3.

The monitor should be capable of displaying at least 800 × 600 pixels and at least 8-bit color (256) or more, although most monitors today are capable of at least 16-bit color (thousands of colors). The amount of RAM should be at least 64 MB, although 128 MB is suggested for running Illustrator CS together with Photoshop. This doesn't include any memory required for the operating system or for running other programs at the same time.

Setting Preferences for Adobe Illustrator CS

To locate the Illustrator preferences in a Windows PC system, launch the Illustrator program and choose Edit: Preferences from the pull-down menu. When the dialog box appears, you can set the various preferences according to your specifications. In a Macintosh operating system, choose Adobe Illustrator: Preferences from the pull-down menu after launching the application, and click on the button marked Next in the Preferences dialog box to set all the various preferences. We like to use the Illustrator default Preference settings. Illustrator preferences reactivate automatically every time the program is relaunched. To restore the program's default Preferences on a Macintosh computer, simply delete the Adobe Illustrator Preferences file located in the system's Preference folder and restart your computer. Then relaunch Illustrator. The file to be deleted from the system in Windows is called AIPrefs.

Managing Color Settings

Choose Edit: Color Settings from the Illustrator pull-down menu to manage the color settings. We recommend choosing the following settings: Custom, RGB, Color Match RGB, CMYK, U.S. Web Coated (SWOP) v2, Color Management Policies, RGB Preserve Embedded Profiles, and CMYK Preserve Embedded Profiles. Check the Profile Mismatches box so the "Ask When Opening" prompt is activated. Your settings should now appear as shown in Figure 10.1.

Navigating the Work Environment in Adobe Illustrator CS

The Navigator palette is accessed by choosing Window: Navigator in the pull-down menu. Click on the Zoom In or Zoom Out button at the bottom of the Navigator palette, or drag the slider to zoom in or out. The cursor turns into a hand when placed in the window of the Navigator palette and can be moved around to view different parts of the Illustrator document (see Figure 10.2).

In your document, as you press the space bar the cursor will turn into the Hand Tool, so you can move around the document by dragging the mouse. The lower right-hand corner of the document window shows the zoom percentages. These can be adjusted by clicking on the arrow and choosing a zoom percentage. The Zoom Tool can be accessed by pressing Z on your keyboard and clicking to zoom in. Hold the Option/ALT key to zoom out in Windows. Command/CTRL (Windows) and the minus sign will zoom out, and Command/CTRL (Windows) will zoom in. Holding the Control key or right clicking will show zoom in and zoom out options.

The Adobe Illustrator CS Toolbar

To select a tool in the Illustrator toolbar, click once on its icon. Holding down the mouse on an icon will display an arrow and the tool's subset or pop-out palette will appear. We recommend memorizing the keyboard commands in Figure 10.3 and Table 10.1. To run through the related tools press the shift and the shortcut keys.

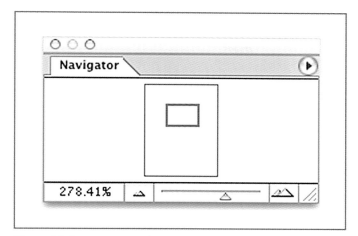

Figure 10.2   Navigator palette.

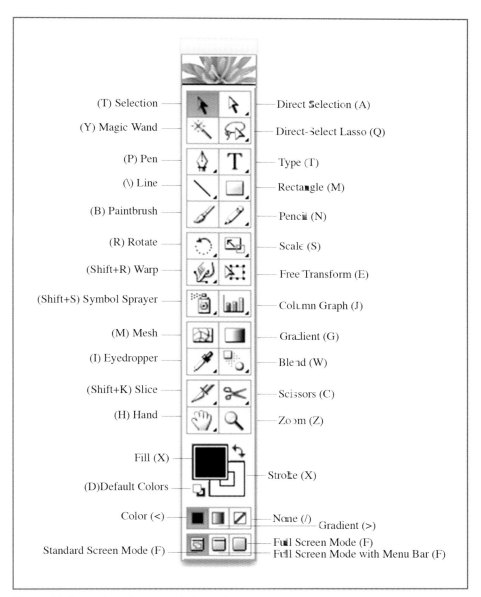

Figure 10.3   Keyboard commands for Tools.

Table 10.1 The Adobe Illustrator CS Tools with Corresponding Keyboard Commands

V =	Selection Tool: Selects entire objects
A =	Direct Selection Tool: Selects points or path segments Group Selection Tool: Selects objects and groups within groups
Y =	Magic Wand Tool: Selects objects of similar attributes
Q =	Direct Select Lasso Tool: Selects points or path segments within objects Lasso Tool: Selects entire objects
P =	Pen Tool: Draws Bezier curves and straight lines Add Anchor Tool: Adds anchor points to paths Delete Anchor Tool: Deletes anchor points from paths Convert Anchor Tool: Can change direction of paths
T =	Type Tool: Enters type that can be edited Area Type Tool: Enters type into closed paths that can be edited Path Type Tool: Enters type on a path you've created that can be edited Vertical Type Tool: Enters vertical type that can be edited Vertical Area Type Tool: Enters type in closed paths that can be edited Vertical Path Type Tool: Enters type on a path that can be edited
\ =	Line Segment Tool: Draws straight lines Arc Tool: Draws curved lines Spiral Tool: Draws spirals Rectangular Grid Tool: Draws rectangular grids Polar Grid Tool: Draws circular grids
M =	Rectangle Tool: Draws rectangles Rounded Rectangle Tool: Draws rounded rectangles Ellipse Tool: Draws circles Polygon Tool: Draws polygons Star Tool: Draws stars Flare Tool: Creates lens flares
B =	Paintbrush Tool: Draws freehand lines with a painterly appearance
N =	Pencil Tool: Draws and edits freehand lines Smooth Tool: Smooths paths Erase Tool: Erases paths and anchor points
R =	Rotate Tool: Rotates objects
O =	Reflect Tool: Reflects objects Twist Tool: Twists objects

S =	Scale Tool: Scales objects Shear Tool: Skews objects Reshape Tool: Alters a path while retaining the path's shape
Shift+R =	Warp Tool: Warps objects Twirl Tool: Twirls objects Pucker Tool: Puckers objects Bloat Tool: Bloats objects Scallop Tool: Adds details to the outlines of objects Crystallize Tool: Adds spikes to objects Wrinkle Tool: Adds wrinklelike details to objects
E =	Free Transform Tool: Rotates, distorts, and scales objects
Shift + S	Symbol Sprayer Tool: Sprays symbols Symbol Shifter Tool: Moves symbols Symbol Scrunches Tool: Separates symbols from one another Symbol Sizer Tool: Resizes symbols Symbol Spinner Tool: Rotates symbols Symbol Strainer Tool: Colorizes symbols Symbol Screener Tool: Changes opacity on symbols Symbol Styles Tool: Applies styles to symbols
J =	Column Graph Tool: Sets up columns vertically Stacked Column Graph Tool: Stacks columns one on top of the other Bar Graph Tool: Sets up columns horizontally Stacked Bar Graph Tool: Stacks columns horizontally Line Graph Tool: Uses lines instead of bars Area Graph Tool: Shows lines with a fill Scatter Graph Tool: Uses dots to show changes Pie Graph Tool: Shows a pie-shaped graph Radar Graph Tool: Shows a circle-shaped graph
U =	Mesh Tool: Creates meshes to apply gradients
G =	Gradient Tool: Changes the angle of an applied gradient
I =	Eyedropper Tool: Samples colors or type attributes
K =	Paint Bucket Tool: Fills objects with color or type attributes Measure Tool: Measures distance between points
W =	Blend Tool: Creates a blend between objects Auto Trace Tool: Traces raster images to create vector objects
Shift + K	Slice Tool: Creates Web-based slices Slice Select Tool: Selects Web slices

(continued next page)

Table 10.1 The Adobe Illustrator CS Tools with Corresponding Keyboard Commands (*cont.*)

C =	Scissors Tool: Cuts paths Knife Tool: Cuts objects
H =	Hand Tool: Navigates around the art board using the mouse Page Tool: Adjusts the grid to show where printed material will appear
Z =	Zoom Tool: Zooms in and out of window

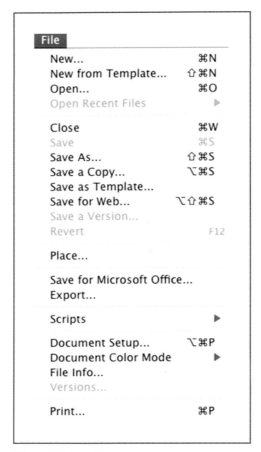

Figure 10.4   File menu.

The Adobe Illustrator Pull-down Menu Items

Following is a breakdown of the commands users can find within the Illustrator pull-down menus:

File Menu

Here is a list of commands located within the File menu (see Figure 10.4). Commands followed by ellipses (three periods) means an options dialog box appears.

New: A dialog box containing presets and options for creating a new file

New from Template: Creates a document based on a template

Open: Opens a browser to find a file

Open Recent Files: Gives a choice to open recently used files

Close: Closes a file that is open

Save and Save As: Allows you to save the file in a number of different formats

Save a Copy: Will save a copy of the file

Save as Template: Saves the file as a template that can be used over again

Save for Web: Allows you to save the image(s) for the Web while viewing different options in a dialog box

Save a Version: Used to manage files between the different Adobe applications

Revert: Reverts to the last saved version

Place: Places files such as eps and pdf

Save for Microsoft Office: Saves files in PNG (Portable Network Graphics) for use in Microsoft Office

Export: Exports the document with a number of options for export, including Macromedia Flash (SWF)

Scripts: A series of steps to automate repetitive tasks

Document Setup: Gives options for the setup and orientation of the Art Board as well as Type and Transparency

Document Color Mode: Option for CMYK mode or RGB

File Info: Allows you to include file information or metadata, such as copyright

Versions: For managing files between different Adobe applications

Print: Opens a dialog box with options to print multiple copies

Edit Menu
Following is a list of commands you will find under the Edit menu (see Figure 10.5):

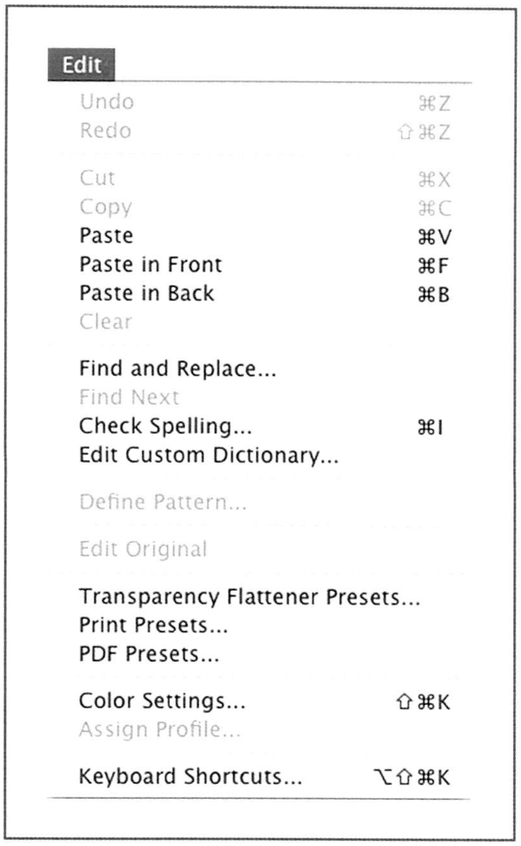

Edit	
Undo	⌘Z
Redo	⇧⌘Z
Cut	⌘X
Copy	⌘C
Paste	⌘V
Paste in Front	⌘F
Paste in Back	⌘B
Clear	
Find and Replace...	
Find Next	
Check Spelling...	⌘I
Edit Custom Dictionary...	
Define Pattern...	
Edit Original	
Transparency Flattener Presets...	
Print Presets...	
PDF Presets...	
Color Settings...	⇧⌘K
Assign Profile...	
Keyboard Shortcuts...	⌥⇧⌘K

Figure 10.5 Edit menu.

Undo: Reverses last step

Redo: Redoes last step

Cut: Cuts the selected object from the document and copies it to the clipboard

Copy: Copies the selected object and stores it in the clipboard

Paste: Pastes in document whatever is stored in the clipboard

Paste in Front: Pastes in front of other objects whatever is stored in the clipboard

Paste in Back: Pastes in back of other objects whatever is stored in the clipboard

Clear: Deletes selected objects

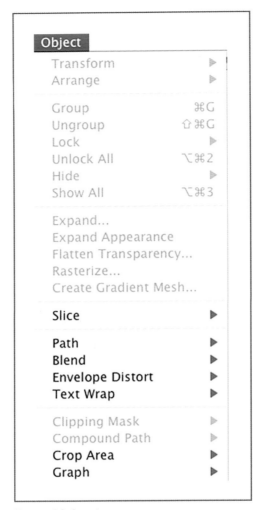

Figure 10.6   Object menu.

Find and Replace: **Finds and replaces text or text strings**

Find Next: **Finds next text or text string**

Check Spelling: **Checks spelling of selected word, words, or entire document**

Edit Custom Dictionary: **Adds, deletes, or modifies dictionary**

Define Pattern: **Creates a pattern from paths, compound paths, meshes, embedded bitmapped objects, clipping masks, or text with solid fills or no fill**

Edit Original: **Edits linked files**

Transparency Flattener Presets: **Presets for documents containing transparencies that require flattening printing**

Print Presets: **Creates print presets for different output devices**

PDF Presets: **PDF presets are included for different types of PDF output. You can also create your own.**

Color Settings: **Edits the color settings for RGB and CMYK**

Assign Profile: **Assigns new color profiles to a document**

Keyboard Shortcuts: **Shows keyboard shortcuts that can be customized**

Object Menu

Following is a list of commands within the Object menu (see Figure 10.6):

Transform: **Includes move, rotate, reflect, shear, scale. Transform opens a dialog box for more options. The reset bounding box option reorients the bounding box.**

Arrange: **Brings selected objects forward and backward, sends objects to the back and to the front, and sends objects to the current layer**

Group: **Groups all selected objects**

Ungroup: **Ungroups selected objects**

Lock: **Locks selected objects, all artwork, or other layers**

Unlock All: **Unlocks all**

Hide: Hides selected objects, all artwork, or other layers

Show All: Shows all

Expand: Divides an object into multiple objects that can be useful when modifying individual elements within an object

Expand Appearance: Divides appearance attributes such as pattern fills, strokes, transparencies, and effects into multiple objects to fine-tune the objects

Flatten Transparency: Used for exporting artwork containing transparencies for print. The medium resolution setting preset is useful for most output devices.

Rasterize: Changes vector objects into pixels with options for resolution and transparencies

Create Gradient Mesh: Creates a gradient mesh with options for the number of mesh lines that can be used for creating complex gradients

Slice: Creates, deletes, duplicates slices (Web-based objects). Slice options let you enter specifics for the slice.

Path: A path can be created with two existing anchor points. This option joins the two points to form a segment.
Outline Stroke: This option changes the stroke so a fill is easier to apply

Blend: Creates new objects between two objects by blending attributes of each

Envelope Distort: Reshapes objects by combining two objects and distorting them

Text Wrap: Wraps text around or within objects

Clipping Mask: Creates clipping masks that are objects or images masked within other objects

Compound Path: Creates paths that have holes where the paths overlap

Crop Area: Defines the area to be cropped

Graph: Displays options for the Graph Tool

Type Menu
The Type menu contains the following commands (see Figure 10.7):

Font: Displays available fonts

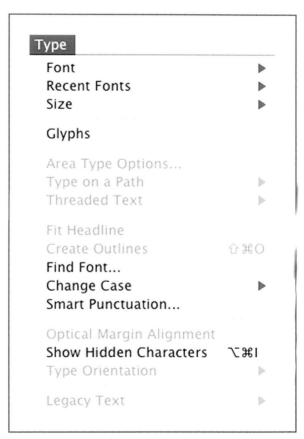

Figure 10.7   Type menu.

Recent Fonts: Displays recently used fonts

Size: Shows size options for type

Glyphs: Displays character forms to be inserted

Area Type Options: Shows area type options including rows and columns

Type on a Path: Shows options for type once it has been created on a path

Threaded Text: Links objects so area type or type on a path can continue from one object or path to the next

Fit Headline: Fits a headline along the full length of a type area

Create Outlines: Turns a font into an object

Find Font: Finds fonts within the document and can replace them with other fonts

Change Case: UPPERCASE will change all characters to uppercase,

lowercase will change all characters to lowercase, title case will capitalize the first letter of each word, and sentence case will capitalize the first letter of each sentence.

Smart Punctuation: Finds keyboard text symbols such as quotes and replaces them with publishing text symbols

Optical Margin Alignment: Keeps punctuation marks outside the paragraph margins so they appear more even

Show Hidden Characters: Displays nonprinting characters such as spaces, returns, tabs, and other nonprinting characters

Type Orientation: Type alignment options, such as left, center, right

Legacy Text: An option for Illustrator CS to display text as it was formatted in an earlier version of Illustrator; cannot be edited

Select Menu
Following is a list of commands found under the Select menu (see Figure 10.8):

All: Selects all objects in document

Deselect: Deselects all objects in document

Reselect: Reselects last selected object

Inverse: Selects all unselected objects and deselects all selected objects

Next Object Above: Selects the nearest object above the selected object

Figure 10.8 Select menu.

Next Object Below: Selects the nearest object below the selected object

Same: Selects all objects with the same style, tint, and so on

Object: Selects objects based on object attributes

Save Selection: Saves a selection

Edit Selection: Renames or deletes a saved selection

Filter & Effects

The difference between filter and effects is that effects can be modified in the Appearance palette and can be removed anytime. Filters change the object, but you can modify the anchor points. Effects must be expanded before you can modify the anchor points.

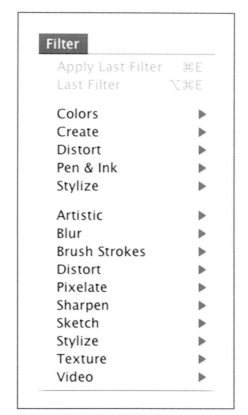

Figure 10.9   Filter menu.

Filter Menu

Following is a list of the commands found under the Filter menu (see Figure 10.9):

Apply Last Filter: Applies the last filter chosen

Last Filter: Opens dialog box of last filter chosen

Colors: Adjusts, blends, and converts color modes

Create: Object mosaic creates a mosaic tile effect to bitmapped images. Crop marks define where the document will be trimmed

Distort: Distorts vector objects

Pen & Ink: Drawing looks like it is created with ink

Stylize: Adds arrowheads, drop shadows, and rounds corners of vector objects

Artistic: Applies artistic effects to raster images

Blur: Blurs raster images

Brush Strokes: Applies fine-art effects to raster images

Distort: Creates glasslike effects on raster images

Pixelate: Affects the way color pixels interact with one another

Sharpen: Unsharp Mask option sharpens raster objects

Sketch: Creates sketchlike effects on raster images

Stylize: Adds arrowheads, drop shadows, and rounds corners of vector objects

Texture: Creates textures on raster images

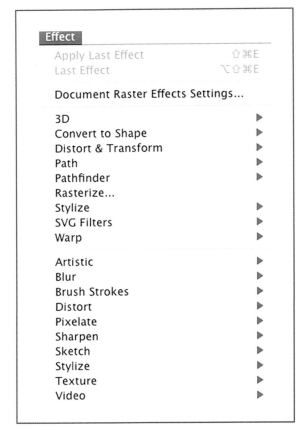

Effect	
Apply Last Effect	⇧⌘E
Last Effect	⌥⇧⌘E
Document Raster Effects Settings...	
3D	▶
Convert to Shape	▶
Distort & Transform	▶
Path	▶
Pathfinder	▶
Rasterize...	
Stylize	▶
SVG Filters	▶
Warp	▶
Artistic	▶
Blur	▶
Brush Strokes	▶
Distort	▶
Pixelate	▶
Sharpen	▶
Sketch	▶
Stylize	▶
Texture	▶
Video	▶

Figure 10.10   Effect menu.

Effect Menu

Following is a list of commands found under the Effect menu (see Figure 10.10):

Apply Last Effect: Applies last effect

Last Effect: Shows last effect applied

Document Raster Effects Settings: Raster settings include color model, resolution, background, anti-alias, creating clipping masks, and adding points around object

3D: Extrudes, revolves, or rotates an object to create a three-dimensional appearance

Video: Deinterlace smooths images captured on video. NTSC Colors restrict the gamut of colors to those acceptable for television reproduction.

Convert to Shape: Converts a vector or raster image to a rectangular, rounded, or elliptical shape

Distort & Transform: Distorts and transforms vector objects

Path: Offsets a path or turns type into a set of compound paths and can change the stroke of a selected object to a filled object

Pathfinder: Combines paths into new objects and shapes

Rasterize: Rasterizes selected vector objects with setting options

Stylize: Adds stylized effects to objects such as drop shadows, glows, and feathers

SVG Filters: SVG Filters are created especially for the Web. Use these filters if the final output will go on the Web.

Warp: Warps objects into arcs, flags, waves, twists, and many others

Artistic: Applies fine-art effects to vector objects

Blur: Applies Gaussian and Radial blurs to vector objects

Brush Strokes: Applies brush-strokes like spatter and ink outlines to vector objects

Distort: Applies glass effects to vector objects

Pixelate: Mixes color pixels to apply effects like Color Halftone to vector objects

Sharpen: Applies Unsharp Mask to sharpen bitmapped (or rasterized) objects

Sketch: Applies sketch effects like Chalk & Charcoal to vector objects

Stylize: Applies glow effects to vector objects

Texture: Applies texture like Canvas & Burlap to vector objects

Video: Deinterlace smooths images captured on video. NTSC Colors restrict the gamut of colors to those acceptable for television reproduction.

View Menu

Following is a list of commands found under the View menu (see Figure 10.11):

Outline: Shows the outline of objects without the fills

Overprint Preview: Shows approximately how ink will be distributed once printed

Pixel Preview: Shows how rasterized objects will appear on screen

Proof Setup: Shows soft proof of how an image would be displayed on various platforms such as Windows or Macintosh

Proof Colors: Shows colors with a specified color space

Zoom In: Zooms in at 50 percent increments

Zoom Out: Zooms out at 50 percent increments

Fit in Window: Fits document in window

Actual Size: Shows document at 100 percent

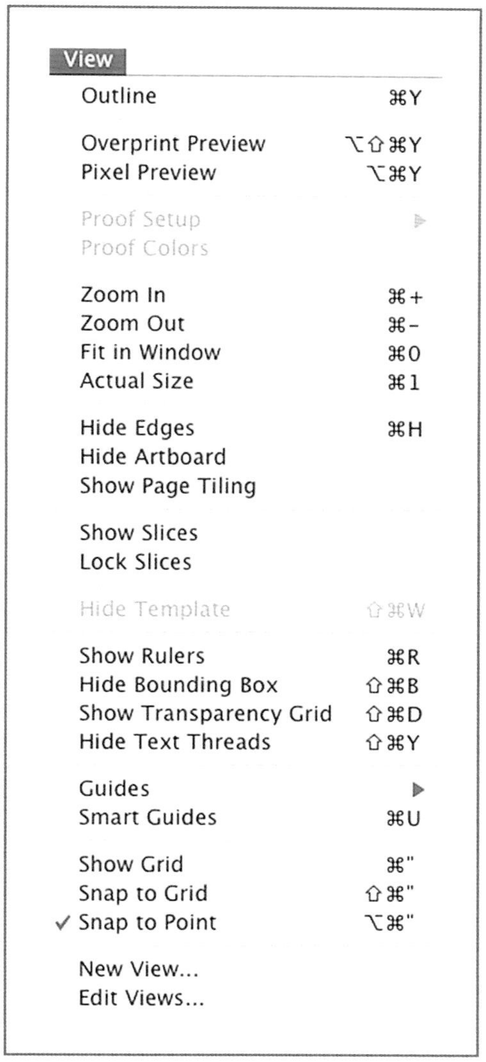

View	
Outline	⌘Y
Overprint Preview	⌥⇧⌘Y
Pixel Preview	⌥⌘Y
Proof Setup	▶
Proof Colors	
Zoom In	⌘+
Zoom Out	⌘-
Fit in Window	⌘0
Actual Size	⌘1
Hide Edges	⌘H
Hide Artboard	
Show Page Tiling	
Show Slices	
Lock Slices	
Hide Template	⇧⌘W
Show Rulers	⌘R
Hide Bounding Box	⇧⌘B
Show Transparency Grid	⇧⌘D
Hide Text Threads	⇧⌘Y
Guides	▶
Smart Guides	⌘U
Show Grid	⌘"
Snap to Grid	⇧⌘"
✓ Snap to Point	⌥⌘"
New View...	
Edit Views...	

Figure 10.11 View menu.

Hide Edges: Hides anchor points, direction lines, and direction points

Hide Artboard: Hides solid lines that represent the printable area

Show Page Tiling: Tiling divides artwork that is larger than the available size for printing output. This option shows or hides tiling.

Show Slices: Shows slices that are optimized areas of a page for Web output

Lock Slices: Locks slices

Hide Template: Hides template layer

```
┌─────────────────────────────────────┐
│  ▣ Window                            │
│  ─────────────────────────────────  │
│  New Window                          │
│                                      │
│  Minimize Window              ⌘M     │
│  Bring All To Front                  │
│                                      │
│  Actions                             │
│  Align                        ⇧F7    │
│  Appearance                   ⇧F6    │
│  Attributes                   F11    │
│  Brushes                      F5     │
│  Color                        F6     │
│  Document Info                       │
│  Flattener Preview                   │
│  Gradient                     F9     │
│  Graphic Styles               ⇧F5    │
│  Info                         F8     │
│  Layers                       F7     │
│  Links                               │
│  Magic Wand                          │
│  Navigator                           │
│  Pathfinder                   ⇧F9    │
│  Stroke                       F10    │
│  SVG Interactivity                   │
│  Swatches                            │
│  Symbols                      ⇧F11   │
│ ✓ Tools                              │
│  Transform                    ⇧F8    │
│  Transparency                 ⇧F10   │
│  Type                          ▶     │
│  Variables                           │
│                                      │
│  Brush Libraries               ▶     │
│  Graphic Style Libraries       ▶     │
│  Swatch Libraries              ▶     │
│  Symbol Libraries              ▶     │
│                                      │
│ ✓ Untitled–2 @ 72% (RGB/Preview)     │
└─────────────────────────────────────┘
```

Figure 10.12   Window menu.

Show Rulers: Shows or hides rulers

Hide Bounding Box: Shows or hides bounding box that surrounds objects

Show Transparency Grid: Shows or hides transparency grid that shows areas of transparency

Hide Text Threads: Shows or hides text threads, which are text that is linked between objects

Guides: Hides or shows guides, locks guides, makes and releases guides, and clears guides

Smart Guides: Smart Guides help you align and transform objects.

Show Grid: Shows or hides grid, which assists in lining up objects symmetrically

Snap to Grid: Snaps objects to the grid

Snap to Point: Snaps an object to a point. When you drag the object toward another point or guide, as it comes within 2 pixels of an anchor point or grid, it will snap to it.

New View: Creates a new window identical to the open one

Edit Views: Renames views

Window Menu
Following is a list of commands found under the Window menu (see Figure 10.12):

New Window: Creates a new window identical to the open one

Minimize Window: Sends window to dock

The rest of the Window options show (with check mark next to palette) or hides the palettes. The Brush, Graphic Style, Swatch, and Symbol libraries are also available.

Help Menu
Following is a list of commands under the Help menu (see Figure 10.13):

Illustrator Help: Opens Illustrator help for quick reference

Welcome Screen: Opens welcome screen

Tutorials: Makes step-by-step tutorials available

System Info: Shows your computer system information

Online Support: Connects you to online support

Updates: Connects you to the Internet for software updates

Registration: Connects you to the Internet to register the software

Illustrator Online: Connects you to Adobe Online

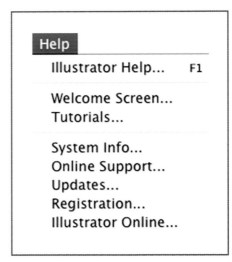

Figure 10.13   Help menu.

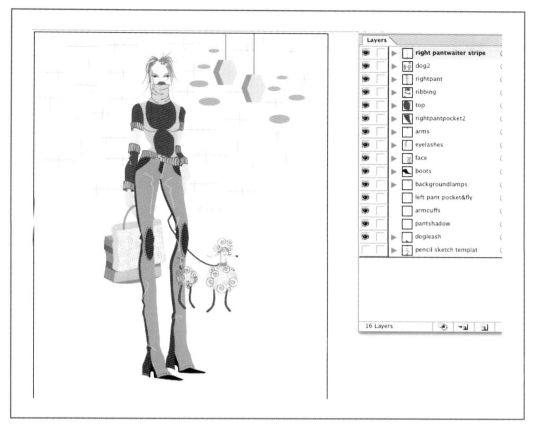

Figure 10.14 Using the Layers palette.

Learning the Basics: Adobe Illustrator CS Lesson

1. Open the file shoppinggirl.ai in the Chapter 10 folder on the CD-ROM ◯.
2. Open the Layers palette by choosing Window: Layers (see Figure 10.14).
3. Hold down the Option key while clicking on the bottom Layer Eye icon to see the illustration that was used as a template. You can show just that layer by holding down the Option key while clicking on a Layer Eye icon. By clicking on that layer again while still holding down the Option key, you can see all the layers again (see Figure 10.15).
4. Double click the pencil sketch layer, making sure the template option is checked. This allows you to trace over scanned-in line art. The Dimmed Images option

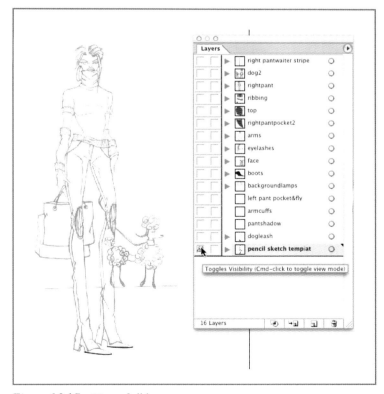

Figure 10.15 View of all layers.

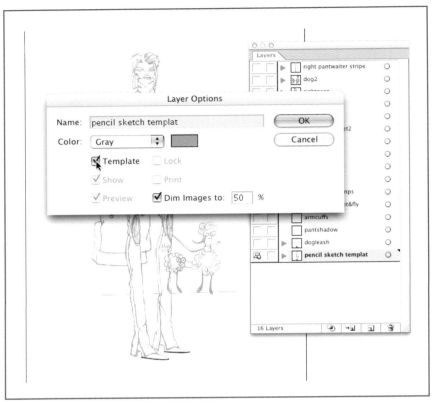

Figure 10.16   Dimmed Images option.

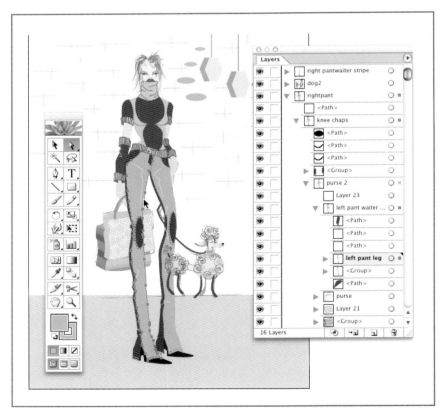

Figure 10.17   Direct Select Tool.

is set to 50 percent (see Figure 10.16).

5. Click on the Layer Eye icon again to view the Illustrator work. (Turn the Eye off on the pencil sketch template layer so you just see the Illustrator work.) Choose the Direct Select Tool (the highlighted tool in Figure 10.17) in the toolbar and select the left pant leg. Notice the fill and stroke colors change to reflect the color and stroke of the selected object.

6. Choose the Eyedropper Tool, and click on the figure's shirt (see Figure 10.18). The pant leg now becomes the color that the Eyedropper Tool selected. Do the same for the other pant leg.

7. Open the Layers palette by choosing Window: Layers. Click on the Target Icon in the boots layer (see Figure 10.19). This selects everything on the target layer.

Figure 10.18 Eyedropper Tool.

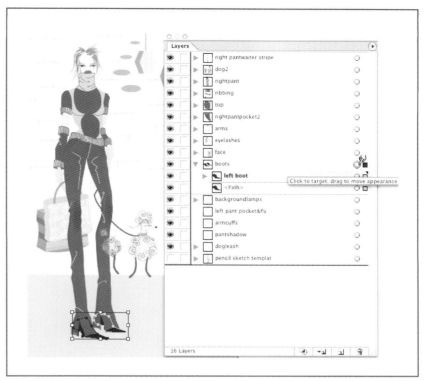

Figure 10.19 Target Icon.

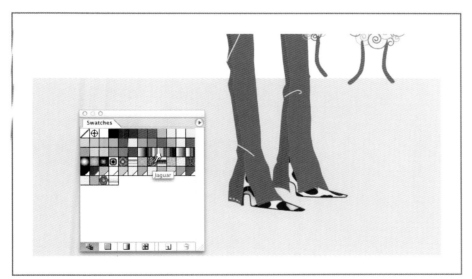

Figure 10.20 Jaguar swatch.

8. Select the Zoom Tool (press Z on your keyboard). Zoom in on the boots by clicking on them twice. Open the Swatch palette by choosing Window: Swatches. Select the swatch that says Jaguar (see Figure 10.20). The shoes are now filled with the Jaguar pattern.

9. Make sure the Layers palette is visible by choosing Window:

Layers. Select the dog layer by clicking on its target icon. Zoom in on the dog by clicking on it twice. Click and drag the dog layer down until it is behind the pant shadow layer (see Figure 10.21).

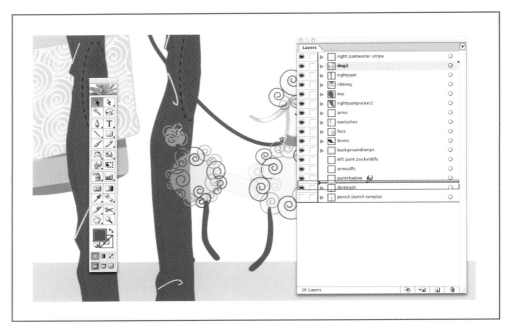

Figure 10.21 Selecting Zoom and the dog layer.

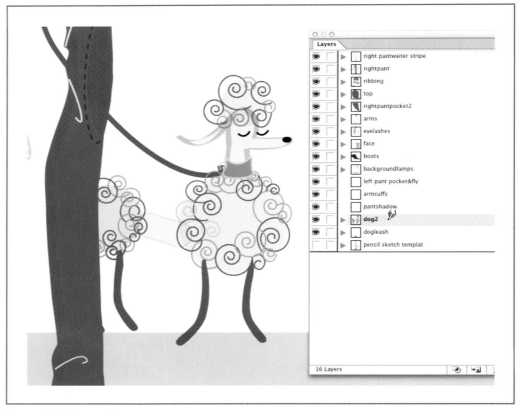

Figure 10.22 Pant leg layer.

Figure 10.23 Choosing the size and font (found under the type menu).

This will move the dog layer behind the pant leg layer as shown in Figure 10.22. The fur on the dog was created using the spiral tool.

10. Choose View: Fit in the Window menu. This will return the image to full view. Select the Text Tool by choosing the T in the toolbar. Choose a fill and stroke. Then type in "Fashion Forecast Trends." The size and font can be found under the Type menu (see Figure 10.23).

Notice the purse and lamps have been selected and the Jaguar swatch chosen.

Review Questions

1. What's the main difference between Illustrator and Photoshop?

2. What's the advantage (and disadvantage) of using Illustrator?

3. What are Pantone Colors?

4. What is the difference between filter and effects?

5. What is a font?

Suggested Practice Project

Sketch a personalized logo. Using the pen tool, outline your logo and apply to envelopes, stationery, or business cards.

11

Mastering the Adobe Illustrator Pen Tool

Once you have learned Illustrator basics (see Chapter 10), the most important skill is mastering the Illustrator pen tool. Drawing effortlessly with the pen tool will allow design ideas to take precedent and free you from focusing on technology. We have included examples, such as a line sheet, to show the many uses for vectorized flats; however, many more possibilities do exist.

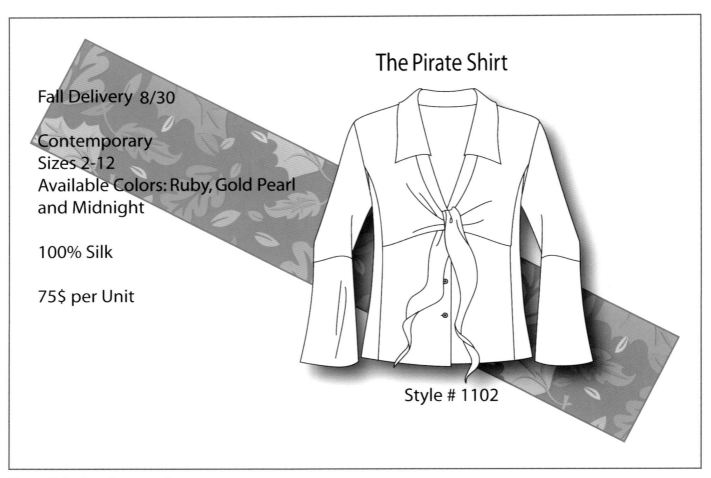

Figure 11.1   Line sheet example.

Raster Versus Vector

Raster images such as those created in Photoshop are made up of tiny squares of colored pixels. All scanning, color correction, reduction, and replacement is done in Photoshop. Vector images are made up of mathematical components or points, which makes them resolution independent. This means they can retain their sharp edges even when they are scaled and manipulated.

Illustrator produces vector images, which are used to create technical flats. Technical flats should have sharp, well-defined edges and appear to be hand-drawn. The advantage to having a computer-generated flat as opposed to having a hand-drawn one is that the designer can easily manipulate,

copy, scale, and print out consistent-looking flats. Once a flat is created in Illustrator, it can be easily imported to Photoshop if a certain special effect needs to be added that is beyond the capabilities of a vector program. These computer-generated flats can then be used for a variety of purposes in the design and marketing processes. The **line sheet** is just one example of how digital flats are utilized (see Figure 11.1).

Open Paths and Closed Paths

An open path (in which the lines of a flat are not connected) is most often used for topstitching and seams. Half of a flat is usually created first, resulting in an open path, and then reflected using the Reflect Tool (see Figure 11.2a). The two halves are then connected to form a

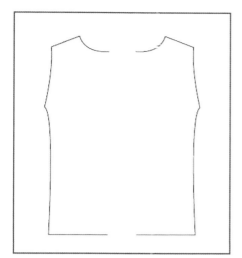

Figure 11.2a   Open path.

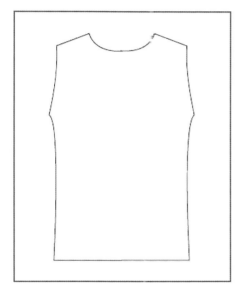

Figure 11.2b   Closed path.

closed path. Closed paths are used as flat outlines. A closed path can be filled with a color or pattern (see Figure 11.2b).

Working with a Croquis
A croquis that has been drawn and scanned into the computer serves as a template upon which you can design your flats. The croquis provided in this chapter is based on the ten-head fashion figure or six-foot supermodel. Refer to Chapter 4 to create your own croquis from scratch. Croquis can be customized for different markets, and they vary

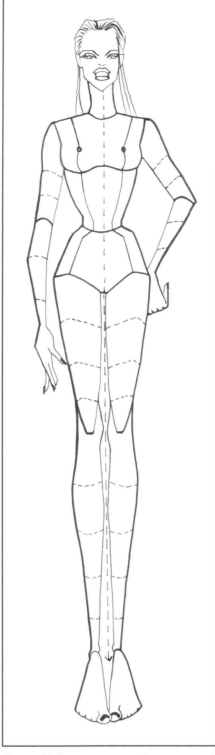

Figure 11.3a   Front view of a junior-sized croquis.

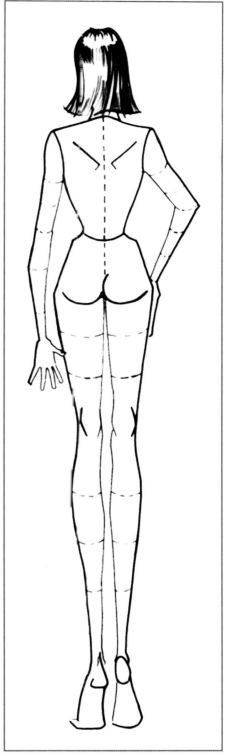

Figure 11.3b   Back view of a junior-sized croquis.

in proportions from company to company. The junior market, for example, will utilize a croquis that is slimmer in the hips and less full in the bustline (see Figure 11.3a and b).

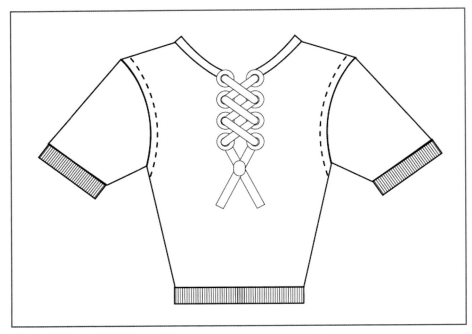

Figure 11.4   Modified basic T-shirt.

Creating Tops

Adding details such as topstitching, ribbing, and lace-up ties to a basic T-shirt will be created in the following lesson (see Figure 11.4).

1. Open up Illustrator and choose File: New. Choose Letter for the paper size and RGB for the color mode. Working in RGB mode makes all the filters and effects available.

2. Choose File: Place and select Template while opening the front and back croquis.psd files from the chapter 11 folder on the CD-ROM◯ (see Figure 11.5).

3. The croquis file opens as a **template** with a layer added to it. Choose the Pen Tool and make sure Fill is set to None and Stroke is set on Black.

4. Start clicking on point one, then click on points two and three. Click on point four and drag down and to the left to create the armhole. Click back on point four to bring the anchor point back. Click on point five, then hold down the Shift key and

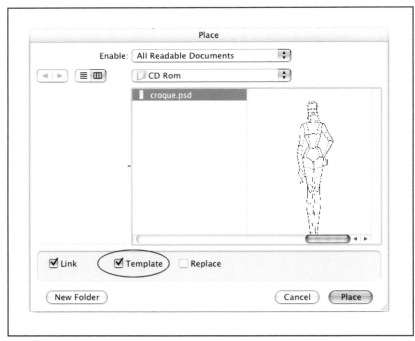

Figure 11.5   The opened croquis from the CD-ROM.

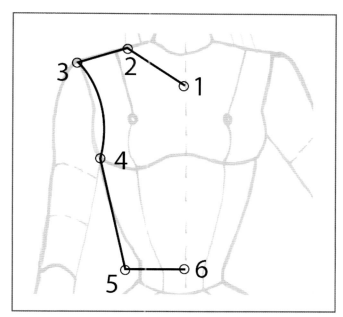

Figure 11.6   Creating the armhole.

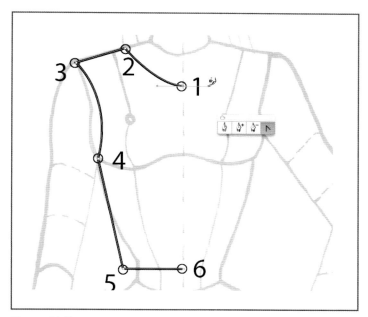

Figure 11.7   Creating the neckline.

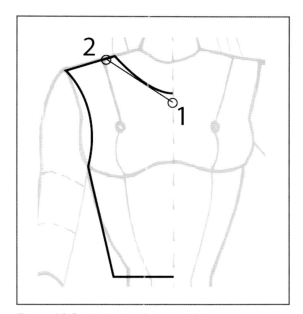

Figure 11.8   Beginning the topstitching.

click on point six (see Figure 11.6).

5. Choose the Convert Anchor Point Tool, and click and drag on point one while holding down the Shift key to create a curve for the neckline (see Figure 11.7).

Topstitching

6. To create topstitching, click on point one, then on point two (see Figure 11.8).

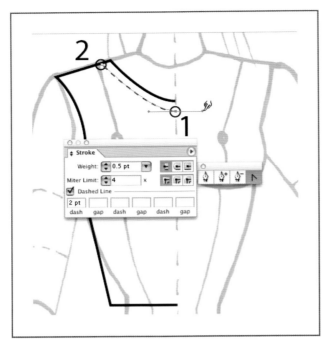

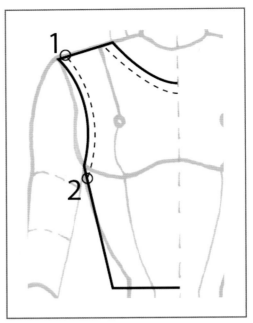

Figure 11.10   Topstitching along the armhole.

Figure 11.9   Topstitching created along the neckline.

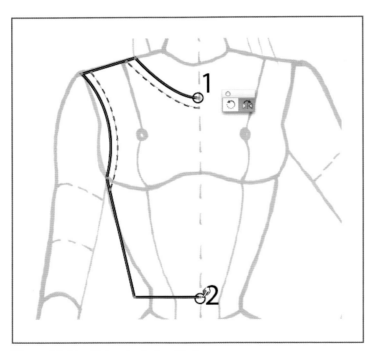

Figure 11.11   Using the Reflect Tool.

7. Choose the Convert Anchor Point Tool, and click and drag from point one to point two while holding down the Shift key to create a curve. Choose Window: Stroke, and select Dashed Line and two point for the size in the dash option box.

Weight is set to 0.5 (see Figure 11.9).

8. Follow the same process for the armhole stitching (see Figure 11.10).

9. Select the flat and choose Edit: Copy, then Edit: Paste to paste in front. Choose the Reflect Tool and click on point one. Then click on point two while holding down the Shift key and drag toward the right (see Figure 11.11).

10. Choose the Direct Select Tool and drag around where the two flats meet (see Figure 11.12).

11. Choose Window: Pathfinder, and select Add to Shape Area (the first option) (see Figure 11.13).

12. Turn off the croquis/template layer by clicking on the icon at the far left. To create the sleeves, choose the Direct Select Tool, and drag a square around the armhole (see Figure 11.14).

13. Choose Edit: Copy, then Edit: Paste (see Figure 11.15).

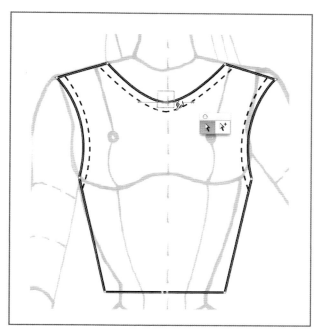

Figure 11.12　The topstitching has been mirrored on the other side of the croquis.

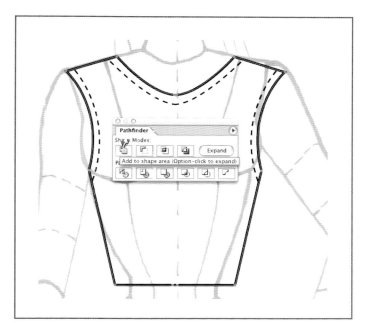

Figure 11.13　The Pathfinder window.

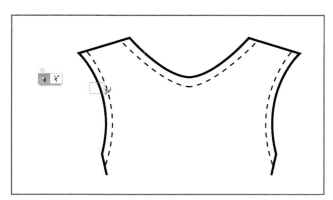

Figure 11.14　Use the Direct Select Tool to begin the sleeves.

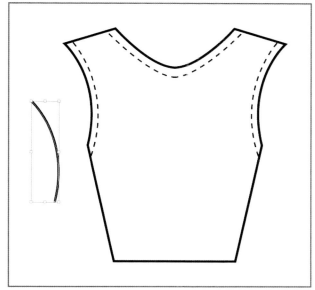

Figure 11.15　The selection from the armhole has been copied and pasted.

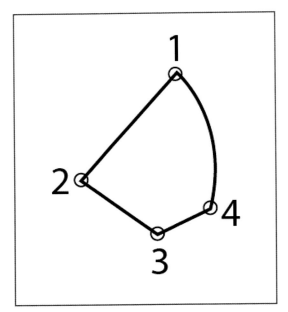

Figure 11.16   The shape of the sleeve.

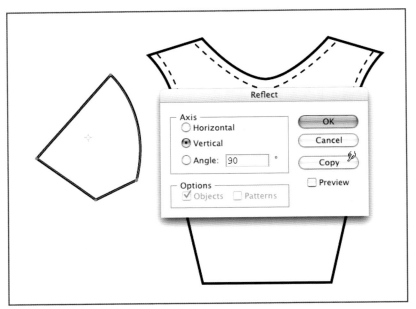

Figure 11.17   Use the Reflect Tool to mirror the original shape of the sleeve.

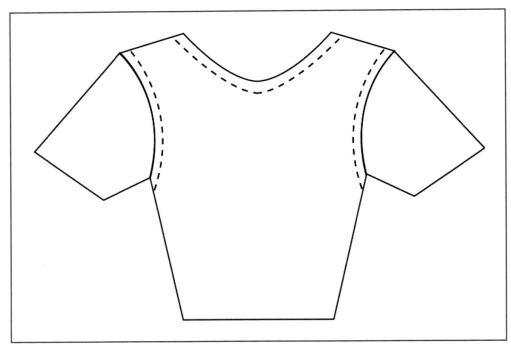

Figure 11.18   The sleeves added to the shirt.

14. To create the sleeve, click on points one, two, three, and four (see Figure 11.16).

15. Select the sleeve and double click on the Reflect Tool to bring up its dialog box. Check off Vertical, set Angle at 90 degrees, and click on Copy for the options (see Figure 11.17).

16. Line the sleeves up with the armholes (see Figure 11.18).

Ribbing

17. To create ribbing, hold down the Shift key to draw one straight line (with a stroke weight of 0.25). Make a copy by holding down the Option key and dragging the copy one half inch. Select one line, then hold down the Shift key and click on the second line. Double click on the Blend Tool, choose Specified Steps, and enter 30 for the amount (see Figure 11.19).

The result should look like Figure 11.20. If the lines are not aligned, go to Windows: Align: Distribute to fix.

18. Create a rectangle with a black stroke and no fill and drag it around the ribbing. Group the two by selecting both objects and choosing Object: Group. Guide, copy, and rotate the ribbing to the areas shown in Figure 11.21.

19. To create the neckline ribbing, drag the ribbing into the Brushes palette and choose New Pattern Brush in the dialog box (name the brush "Ribbing"). Select the neckline with the Direct Select Tool, and choose Edit: Copy, then Edit: Paste. Click on the new brush in the Brushes palette and the ribbing will be created. To scale the ribbing, double click on the brush in the Brushes Palette, and type in a new scale percentage (see Figure 11.22).

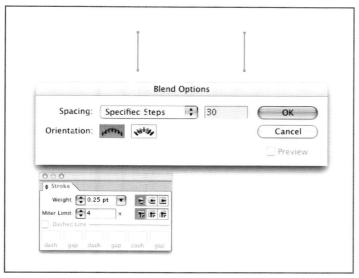

Figure 11.19   The beginning of the ribbing.

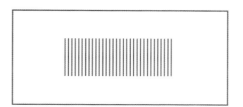

Figure 11.20   A line of ribbing.

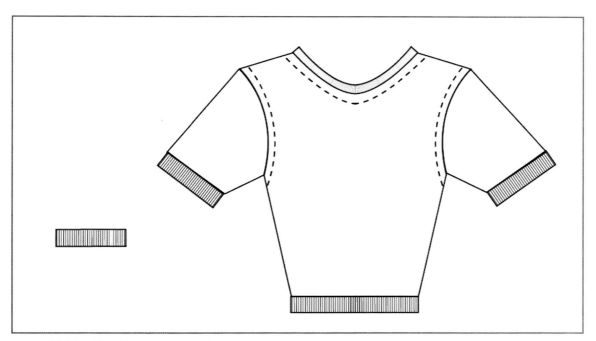

Figure 11.21   The ribbing applied to the shirt.

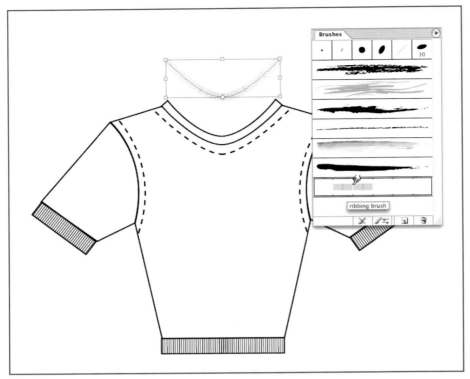

Figure 11.22   Adding ribbing to the neckline.

Figure 11.24a   Grommets with laces.

Figure 11.23   Grommets.

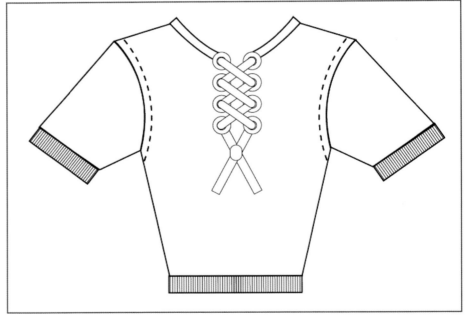

Figure 11.24b   Completed T-shirt with lacing.

Grommets and Lacings

20. Create a circle, copy it, and double click on the Scale Tool to choose 50 percent in the Uniform option. Place one circle inside the other.

21. Go to Window: Align to align the circles (see Figure 11.23).

22. Choose the Rounded Rectangle Tool, and rotate and place copies in the appropriate places (see Figure 11.24a and b).

Figure 11.25   Long-sleeved shirt with collar and buttons

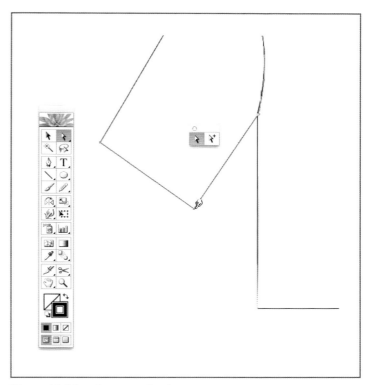

Figure 11.26   Elongating the sleeves.

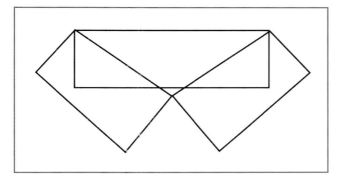

Figure 11.27   The collar.

The Sleeved Shirt

The basic long-sleeved shirt with collar and buttons will be created in the following lesson (see Figure 11.25).

The Sleeve

1. Start off with the basic T-shirt. Choose the Direct Select Tool, and click at both ends of one of the sleeves while holding down the Shift key. Press the down arrow key to lengthen the sleeve, and do the same for the other sleeve (see Figure 11.26).

The Collar

2. To create the collar, create three rectangles and arrange them as seen in Figure 11.27.

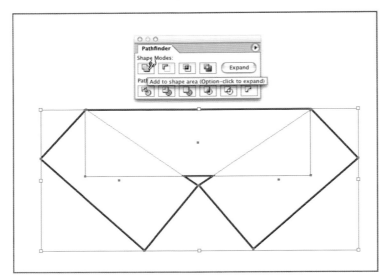

Figure 11.28 Adjusting the size of the collar.

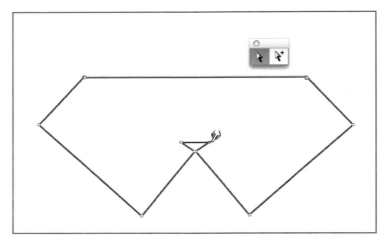

Figure 11.29 The neckhole.

3. Select all three rectangles and choose Window: Pathfinder. Click on Expand the Shape Area, then click on the Expand button (see Figure 11.28).

4. Choose the Direct Select Tool to grab the corners and pull out for the neck hole (see Figure 11.29).

5. Round off the corners by clicking on the corner and pulling one of the **anchor points** to create a Bezier curve using the Convert Anchor Tool (see Figure 11.30).

The Buttons

6. Create buttons using the Ellipse Tool to select the entire ellipse, then use the Align palette (see Figure 11.31).

7. Create the stitching with the Pen Tool, making sure to set the stroke to a dashed line. Create the shadow in the neckline using the Rectangle Tool with a black fill arranged behind the collar. Create the plackets with the Pen Tool (see Figure 11.32).

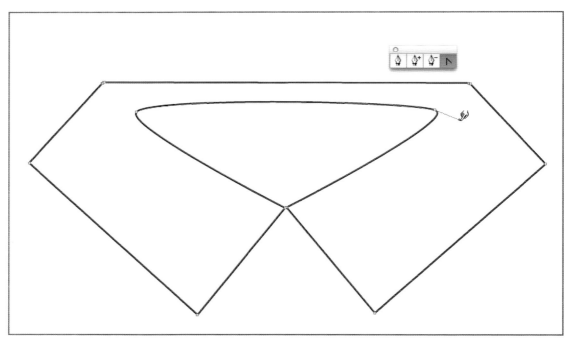

Figure 11.30 Bezier curve.

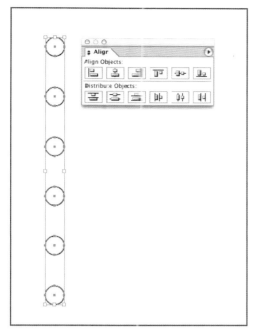

Figure 11.31 Creating buttons.

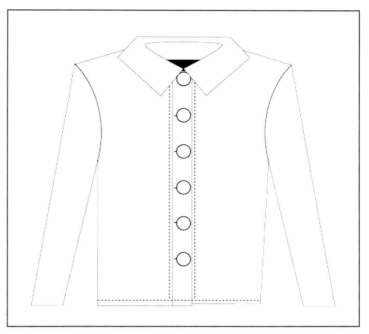

Figure 11.32 Completed sleeved shirt.

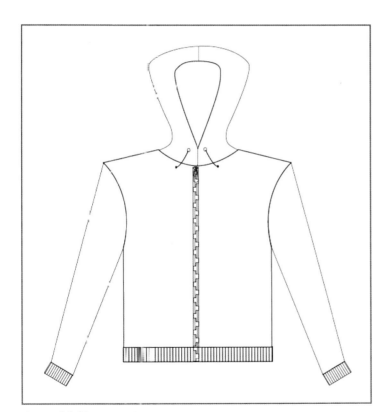

Figure 11.33 Sweatshirt.

The Sweatshirt

The basic sweatshirt with a zipper and hood will be created in the following lesson (see Figure 11.33).

1. Start out with a long-sleeved shirt. If you are not utilizing the provided croquis from the CD-ROM ◯, use the rulers and guides as shown in the following examples.

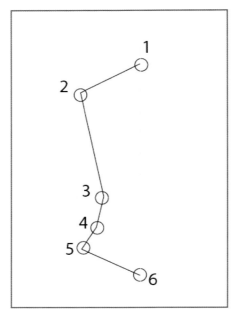

Figure 11.34   The beginnings of the hood.

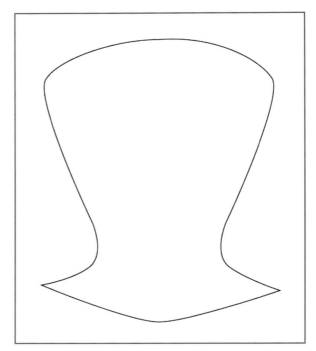

Figure 11.35   The outline of the hood.

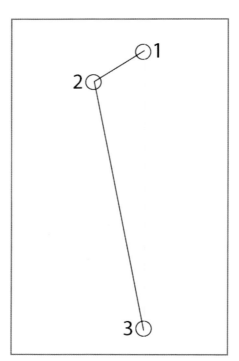

Figure 11.36   Creating the hood lining.

The Hood

2. To create the hood, choose View: Guides: Show Guides and View: Show Rulers. Pull out a guide and follow the points with the Pen Tool, starting at point one (see Figure 11.34).

   Curve anchor points one, two, three, and four, with the Direct Select Tool, and copy and paste in front. Choose the Reflect Tool and place the anchor on point one and drag to the right while holding down the Shift key (see Figure 11.35).

3. To create the hood lining, follow points one, two, and three with the Pen Tool (see Figure 11.36).

4. Curve anchor points one and two with the Direct Select Tool, and copy and paste in front. Choose the Reflect Tool and place the anchor on point one and drag to the right while holding down the Shift key (see Figure 11.37).

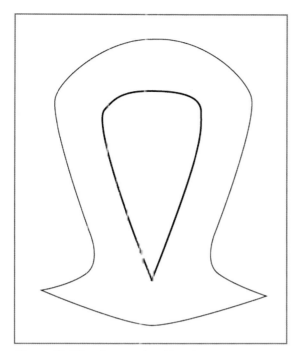

Figure 11.37   The completed hood.

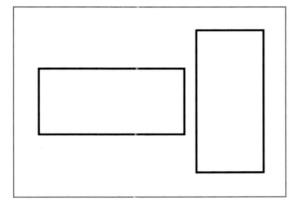

Figure 11.38   Beginning the zipper teeth.

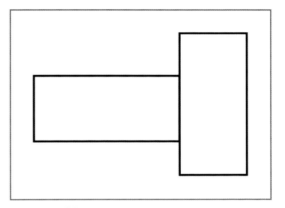

Figure 11.39   Shaping the zipper teeth.

The Zipper

5. Start with two rectangles, and rotate one 90 degrees (see Figure 11.38).

6. Center and overlap the rectangles (see Figure 11.39).

7. Select both rectangles and use Shape Modes in the Pathfinder palette to merge the two rectangles by choosing the Add to Shape Area option. Click the Expand button (see Figure 11.40).

8. Copy and paste the zipper tooth and rotate 90 degrees. Line up

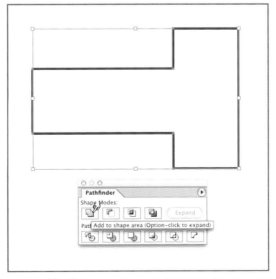

Figure 11.40   The two rectangles merged.

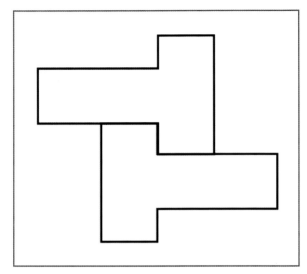

Figure 11.41 The completed teeth.

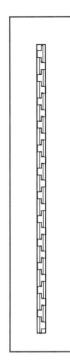

Figure 11.42 The completed zipper.

the two teeth (see Figure 11.41).

9. Continue with this process until you have a zipper, and surround it with a rectangle (see Figure 11.42).

10. Create different shapes and combine them to complete the zipper (see Figure 11.43).

11. Place the hood and zipper on the long-sleeved shirt to complete the hooded sweatshirt (see Figure 11.44).

Another way to create a zipper is to draw a straight vertical line with the Pen Tool and choose Effect Distort and Transform: Zig Zag. Set the font size at 1 point, set the ridges at 40 per segment, and select Corner for Points. Create a rectangle with no fill and a black stroke around it (see Figure 11.45).

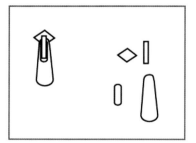

Figure 11.43 Shapes to add to the zipper.

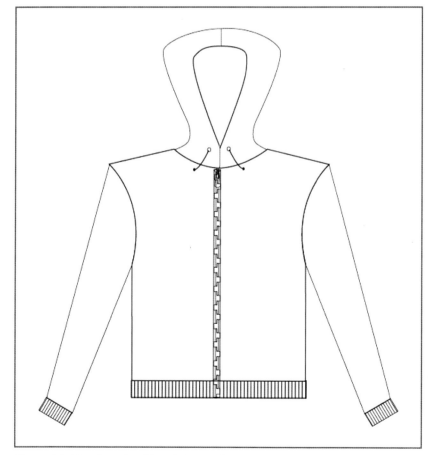

Figure 11.44 Completed hooded sweatshirt.

Creating Bottoms

The bottoms in the following section were created using a freehand method. Shapes and lines were drawn using the Pen Tool, measurements, Shape Tool, and guides in Illustrator.

The Straight Skirt

The straight skirt with patch pockets, darts, and a waistband will be created in the following lesson (see Figure 11.45).

1. Choose View: Show Rulers. Pull out a vertical guide for a centerline. Select the Pen Tool with a black stroke and no fill. Click on points one, two, three, four, and five (see Figure 11.47).
2. Using the Convert Anchor Point Tool, drag anchor point three to create a curve for the hip line (see Figure 11.48).

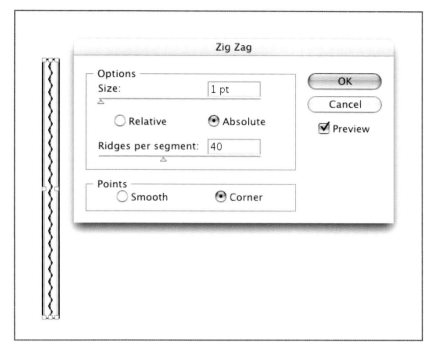

Figure 11.45   Zig Zag window.

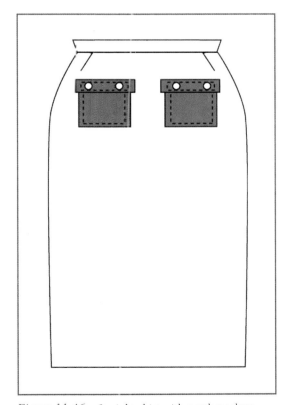

Figure 11.46   Straight skirt with patch pockets, darts, and a waistband.

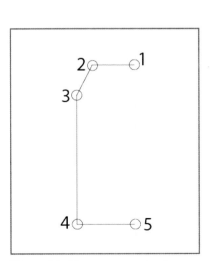

Figure 11.47   Beginning the skirt.

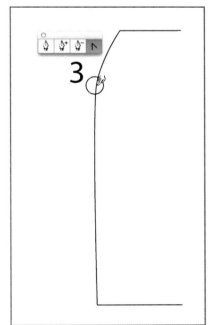

Figure 11.48   Curve for the hip.

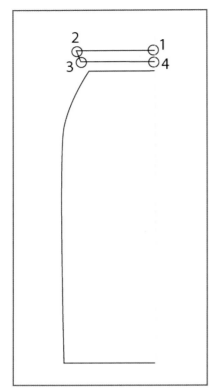

Figure 11.49   Add the waistband.

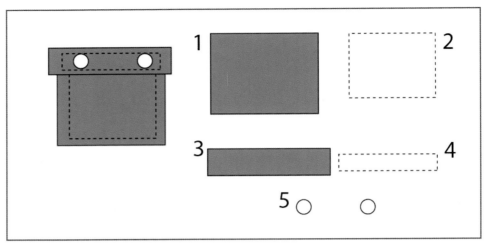

Figure 11.50   Pocket shapes.

The Waistband

3. To create the waistband, click on points one, two, three, and four (see Figure 11.49).

The Patch Pocket

4. Bring the waistband down to the skirt. Next add the patch pockets and fitted waist darts.
5. Create the pocket shapes by using the Rectangle Tool and the Stroke Tool, set to dashed line, for the stitching (see Figure 11.50).
6. Add the fitted waist dart with the Pen Tool. Add the completed pocket. Select all and copy and paste in the front. Choose the Reflect Tool and set the anchor point where one of the waistband points meets the center guide. Hold down the Shift key and drag the copied flat to the left from the bottom center point, not from the anchor point. Select all and group (see Figures 11.51 and 11.52).

The Fitted Pant

The fitted pant with inset hip pockets and fly front zipper will be created in the following lesson. To create the fitted pant, use the rulers and guides in the Illustrator pulldown menu (see Figure 11.53).

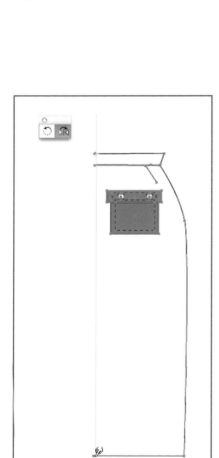

Figure 11.51   Using the Reflect Tool to finish the skirt.

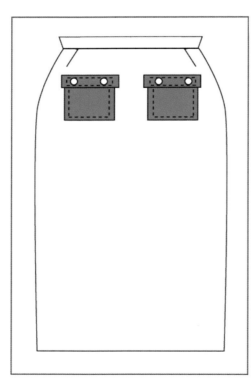

Figure 11.52   Completed straight skirt with patch pockets, darts, and a waistband.

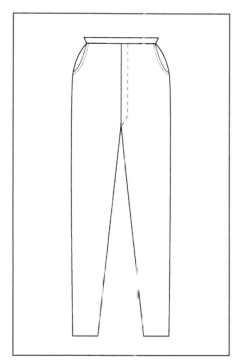

Figure 11.53 Fitted pant with inset hip pockets and fly front zipper.

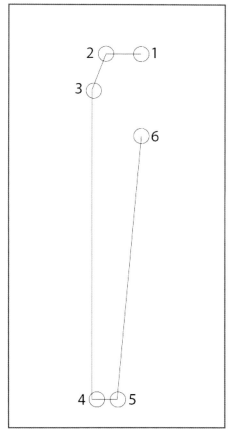

Figure 11.54 Beginning the pant.

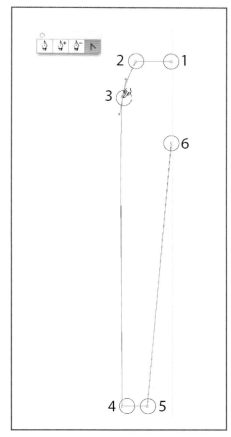

Figure 11.55 Creating the curve for the hip.

1. Choose View: Show Rulers and pull out a vertical guide for the centerline. Click on points one through s (see Figure 11.54).
2. Choose the Convert Anchor Point and pull point three into a curve (see Figure 11.55).
3. To create the waistband, click on points one through four (see Figure 11.56).
4. Bring the waistband down. To create the pocket with stitching, click on point one, then point two, and drag to create a curve.

Inset Hip Pockets

5. To create the hip inset pocket with topstitching, follow the previous steps on page 287, then choose Window: Stroke and create a dashed line (see Figure 11.57).
6. Select all and copy and paste in Front. Choose the Reflect Tool, and click the anchor point on the centerline to set up the Reflect Tool (see Figure 11.58).

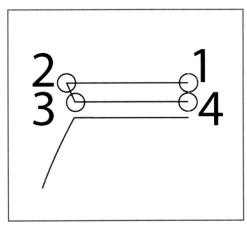

Figure 11.56 Add the waistband.

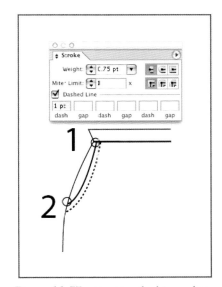

Figure 11.57 Creating the hip pocket.

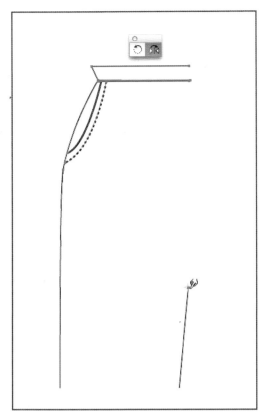

Figure 11.58 Set up the Reflect Tool.

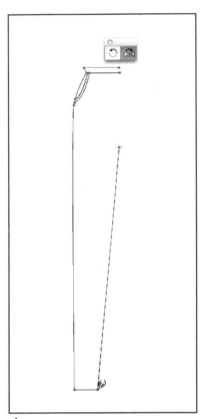

Figure 11.59 Creating the pant leg.

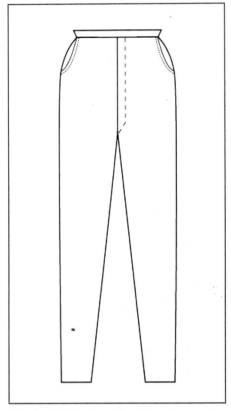

Figure 11.60 Completed fitted pant with inset hip pockets and fly front zipper.

7. While holding down the Shift key, drag the bottom anchor point to the right (see Figure 11.59).

8. Group the flat and add the fly front zipper with the Pen Tool and dashed line stroke (see Figure 11.60).

The Circle Skirt: Gathering and Lace Edge

The circle skirt with gathering and lace edging will be created in this lesson.

1. Select the Pen Tool and choose a black stroke and white (default) fill. Click on points one through twelve, dragging the Pen Tool to create the Bezier curves (see Figure 11.61).

2. Add the waistband and folds by using the Pen Tool with a black stroke and no fill (see Figure 11.62).

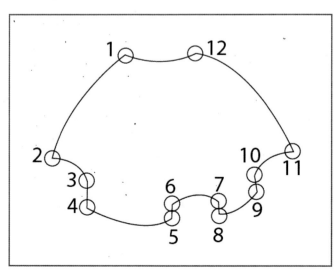

Figure 11.61 The Bezier curves of the skirt.

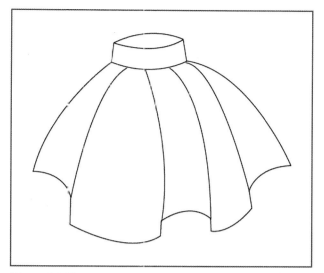

Figure 11.62   Add the waistband.

Figure 11.63   Creating the gathering.

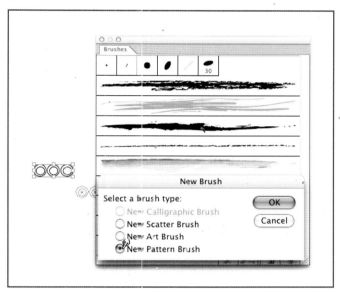

Figure 11.64   Creating the lace trim.

3. Add the gathering by using the Pen Tool with a black stroke and no fill (see Figure 11.63).
4. Create three circles and three corresponding smaller circles inside each by using the Ellipse Tool.
5. Choose Window: Brushes and drag the three circles with the smaller circles inside them into the Brushes palette. Choose new pattern brush (see Figure 11.64).
6. Choose the Direct Selection Tool and drag around the bottom corner of the circle skirt (see Figure 11.65).

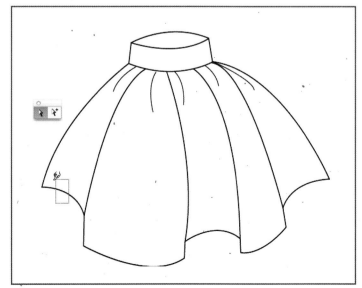

Figure 11.65   Begin to add the trim.

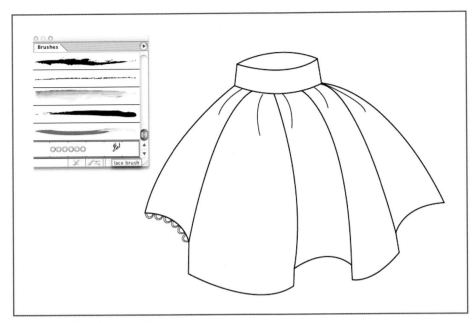

Figure 11.66   Apply the lace trim.

7. Copy and paste in back to apply lace to hem so it shows up on the underside of hem. Click on the lace brush (see Figure 11.66).

8. Repeat the same technique for the rest of the skirt (see Figure 11.67).

Creating Jackets

The notched-collar blazer is created with a long-sleeved T-shirt as the starting point. The elements are then added as design options. The swing coat was created by first scanning a pencil sketch and bringing it into an Illustrator document to be used as a template. These methods are different but are the two most common techniques used for creating flats.

The Tailored Blazer

The tailored blazer with notched collar, western pocket, welt pock-

Figure 11.67   Completed circle skirt.

ets, and cuffs will be created in this lesson (see Figure 11.58).

1. Start with a long-sleeved T-shirt (see Figure 11.69).

The Notched Collar

2. Create shapes for the back facing and the front collar (see Figure 11.70).

3. Place the back facing and front collar on one side and reflect a copy of both for the other side (see Figure 11.71).

The Western Pockets

4. Create the separate pieces of the pocket using the Rectangle Tool and the Pen Tool. Set the Stroke Palette to dashed line to create the stitching (see Figure 11.72).

Figure 11.68   Tailored blazer.

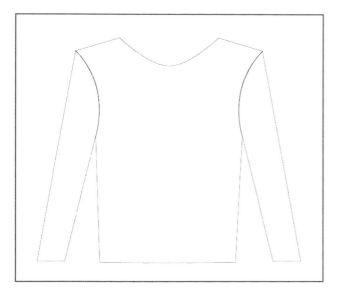

Figure 11.69   Basic long-sleeved T-shirt.

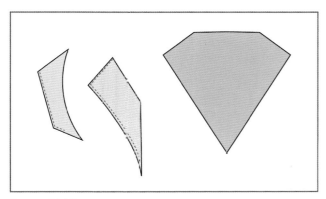

Figure 11.70   Shapes for the notched collar.

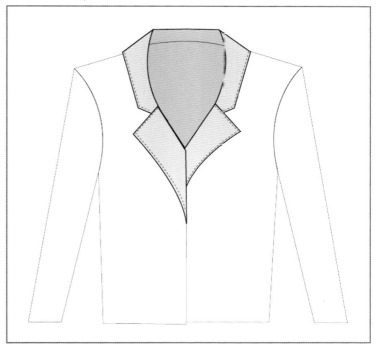

Figure 11.71   Placing the collar.

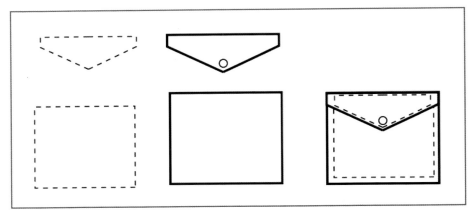

Figure 11.72   Shapes for the pockets.

Figure 11.73   Add the pockets and buttons to the blazer.

5. Use the Ellipse Tool to create the buttons and the Rectangle Tool to create the two pockets (see Figure 11.73).

6. Create the welt pockets with the Rectangle Tool using a black stroke and gray fill.

7. Use the Rectangle Tool to create a rectangle with a black stroke and a white fill. Choose the Add Anchor Point Tool and add points. Use the Direct Selection Tool to slightly move the points (see Figure 11.74 a and b).

8. Use the Pen Tool to add details (see Figure 11.75).

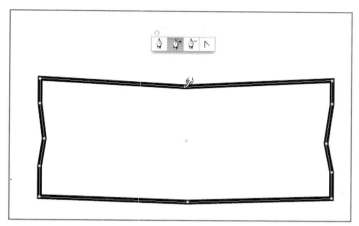

Figure 11.74a   Beginning of the cuff.

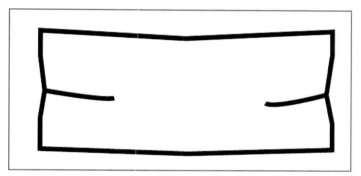

Figure 11.74b   Completed cuff.

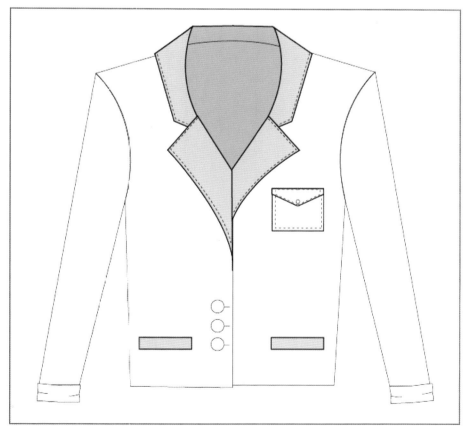

Figure 11.75   Completed tailored blazer.

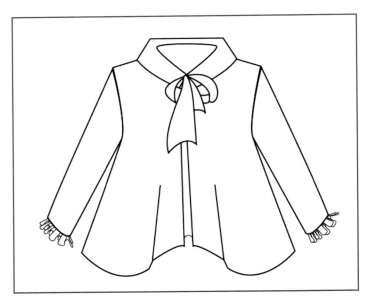

Figure 11.76   Swing coat.

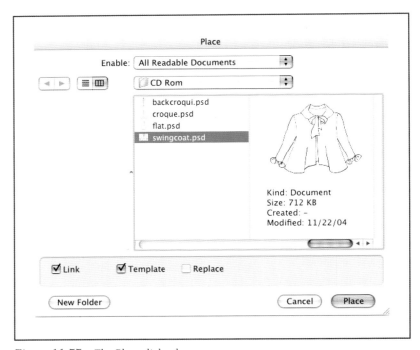

Figure 11.77   The Place dialog box.

The Swing Coat

The swing coat with ruffles and bows will be created in the following lesson (see Figure 11.76). Tracing a sketched flat with the Pen Tool will also be covered.

1. Choose File: Place and go to the Chapter 11 folder on the CD-ROM ◯ to find the swing coat sketch. Select the Template option and click the Place button (see Figure 11.77).

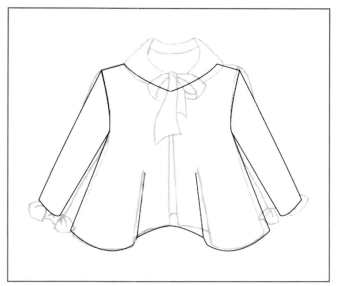

Figure 11.78   Half of the flat reflected.

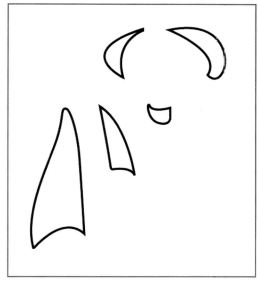

Figure 11.79   Shapes for the bow.

2. Choose the Pen Tool with a black stroke and no fill. Trace half the flat and reflect it to the other side (see Figure 11.78).
3. Create the bow by making the separate pieces and combining them. Use a black stroke and a white fill (see Figure 11.79).
4. Use the same technique described earlier in this chapter to create the collar. Place the bow in front of the collar (see Figure 11.80).
5. Create the ruffles by clicking on points one through sixteen (see Figure 11.81).
6. To create curves, choose the Convert Anchor Point Tool, and

Figure 11.80   Placing the bow.

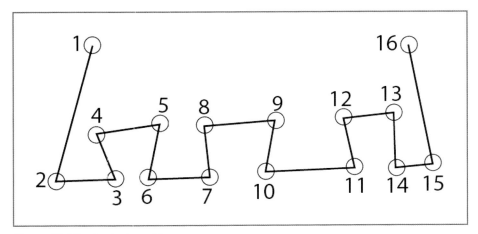

Figure 11.81   Begin the ruffles.

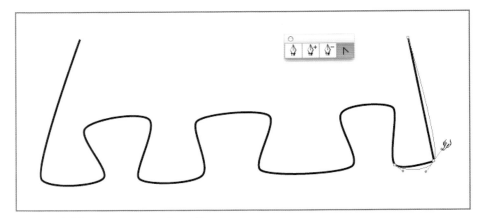

Figure 11.82   Add curves to the ruffles.

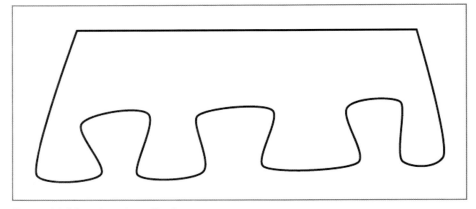

Figure 11.83   Close the ruffle shape.

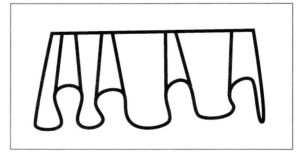

Figure 11.84   Add folds to the ruffles.

click on and drag each of the points (see Figure 11.82).

7. Close the shape by adding a line across the top (see Figure 11.83).

8. Add the folds using the Pen Tool with a black stroke and no fill (see Figure 11.84).

9. Choose Window: Brushes and drag the ruffle into the Brushes palette. Select New Pattern Brush, and name the brush "Ruffle Brush."

10. Select the bottom of the sleeve using the Direct Select Tool (see Figure 11.85).

11. Copy and paste in back.

12. Click on the lace brush in the Brushes palette (see Figure 11.86).

13. Copy the ruffle and drag it to the other sleeve. Rotate the ruffle until it fits correctly. For fuller ruffles, make copies and move them slightly to the right or left (see Figure 11.87).

Figure 11.85   Select the end of the sleeve.

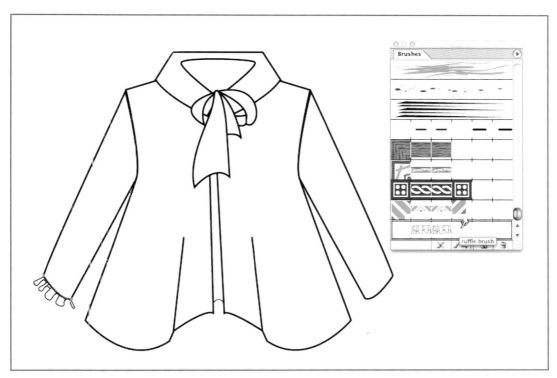

Figure 11.86 Apply ruffles to the sleeve.

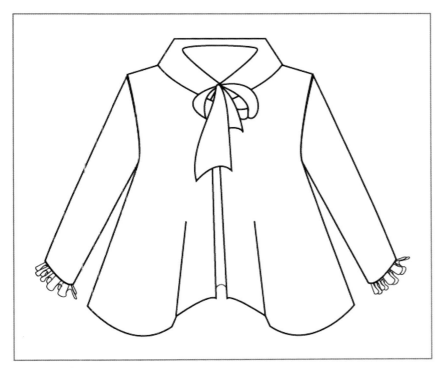

Figure 11.87 Completed swing coat.

Review Questions

1. What's the difference between an open path and a closed path?

2. What is a croquis?

3. What is a line sheet?

4. How do you create topstitching in Illustrator?

5. What is a Bezier curve?

Suggested Practice Project

Create a group of flats.

Key Terms

Anchor point

Croquis

Line sheet

Template

12

Creating Flats and Illustrations Using Adobe Illustrator and Photoshop

What You Will Learn in Chapter 12

Chapter 12 covers Photoshop and Illustrator skills as they are used together. The fundamentals of pixel images and scanning basics are explained. Understanding raw scans and how they are transferred to Illustrator documents, or kept as Photoshop files, is a key process. This chapter also outlines how these techniques are applied and utilized by fashion companies.

Introduction

The ability to create flats and illustrations with Illustrator and Photoshop requires familiarity with the basic skills of these software applications, which were reviewed in Chapters 7 and 10.

Lesson 1: Scanning Basics and Filling Flats with Printed Fabric or Solid Color

You need to be familiar with the fundamental terms involved in scanning images. Terms such as resolution are used differently in various industries. Web images or JPEGs are low-resolution files, usually 72 dpi, and do not print out well as a result. Graphic images should be scanned at 300 dpi or higher for clarity. Dots per inch, or dpi, refers to the number of ink dots in a square inch. The more dots per inch (the more ink), the higher the quality of the printed image. Every scanner is different. Hewlett-Packard and Astra make excellent-quality flatbed scanners that are reasonably priced. Make sure the scanner you purchase is compatible with your computer's platform.

Image, Monitor, and Printer Resolution

Image resolution is measured in pixels per inch (ppi). Image resolution is used to determine the actual number of pixels in an image. Pixels are the squares of color that make up the entire image on your monitor. For example, a 4" × 5" image with an image resolution of 300 ppi has pixel dimensions of 1200 pixels by 1500 pixels [300 ppi × 4" = 1200; 300 ppi × 5" = 1500]. A 15-inch monitor typically displays 800 pixels horizontally and 600 pixels vertically. An image with dimensions of 800 pixels by 600 pixels would fill that screen. On a larger monitor with a setting of 800 by 600 pixels, the same image would still fill the screen, but each pixel would appear larger. If you change the setting on the larger monitor to 1024 by 768 pixels, the image would appear smaller.

Monitor resolution is the number of pixels displayed on a monitor by a video card. This is important when developing a Web site, which is covered in Chapter 14. In regards to producing prints on an image setter or laser printer, it is important to know the printer resolution, measured in dots per inch (dpi).

The **printer resolution** is the number of physical dots produced by the printing device. The amount of detail in an image depends on its pixel dimensions in Photoshop, while the image resolution controls the printing space occupied by the pixels.

The Final Output

The most important factor in determining the resolution of an image is the final output of that image. Scanning an image for the Web differs greatly from scanning an image to create predictive books or line sheets. An image with 72 ppi (pixels per inch) will cover the same area as a file containing 300 ppi, but the pixels in the 300 ppi file will be smaller and therefore contain more detail for the printed page.

Print

For images that will be printed by using professional printing techniques, it is crucial to identify the line screen of those images. This requires asking the printer what the recommendations are and what the printing equipment is capable of producing. Professional printing resolution is measured in lines per inch (lpi). This is the number of halftone lines. Photoshop creates an illusion of gray tones by varying the size and spacing of tiny dots. The uniform density of these dots forms a bitmapped image. This differs from the ppi for the image resolution measured in Photoshop.

There are two dots or pixels for every line. You can determine the scanning resolution in ppi terms by doubling the intended line screen. For example, if you plan on printing at 150 lpi, you should scan at 300 ppi [150 lines per inch × 2 (double it) = 300]. But if you have a 4" × 5" image that you would like to double in size by printing at 8" × 10" at 150 lpi, you will need to scan at 600 ppi [300 ppi × 2 (double it) = 600 ppi]. Remember that an image can always be scaled down in Photoshop without causing much degradation. However, if an image is scaled without taking into account the preceding formula, image degradation (blurriness) will occur (see Figure 12.1a and b).

Web and Video

When scanning an image for use on a Web page or video application, the image is scanned at actual size. The image resolution should be set to 72 dpi. This is the standard image resolution for on-screen images. Most Web pages are between 640 by 480 pixels or 1024 by 728 pixels. Images on a television screen are typically 640 by 480 pixels. Web graphic file size is critical because of bandwidth considerations. File size is directly related to the number of pixels.

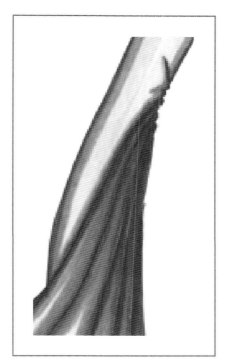 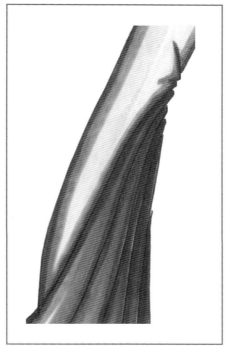

Figure 12.1a and b   Notice the blurriness of the image on the left compared with the image on the right.

Flats

The fashion industry utilizes stylized and technical flats for a variety of practical purposes. Chapter 5 provides an in-depth explanation of flats. A flat is simply a blueprint of a garment. Everyone involved in the design, construction, and production processes depends on these diagrams for visual reference. Today flats are often created digitally. Methods vary from company to company; however, Illustrator and Photoshop are the applications of choice used to create these digital flats (see Figure 12.2).

Preparing the Flat

1. Place the sketch or line art face-down on the scanner bed; choose the Advanced setting in the scanner dialog box (see Figure 12.3). Make sure the settings are correct for the final output; 300 dpi is used here for final print output in this example.

Figure 12.2   A group of flats filled with prints and solid fabrics.

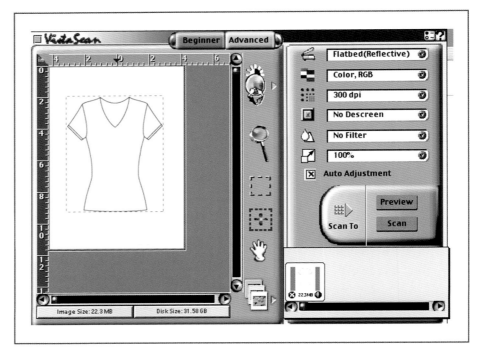

Figure 12.3   Scanner dialog box.

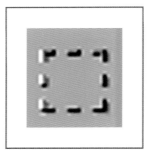

Figure 12.4   Marquee Tool.

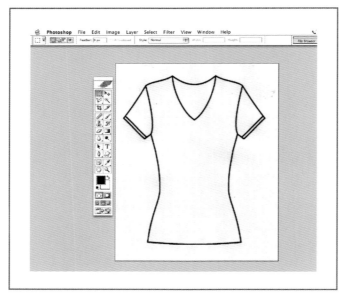

Figure 12.5   Image saved as a Photoshop .psd file.

2. Click on the Preview button in the scanner dialog box to see a preview of your image.

3. Click the Marquee Tool on the scanner toolbar. This will crop the image, eliminating unwanted negative space (see Figure 12.4).

4. Drag the Marquee Tool around the flat as shown in Figure 12.3. If you make a mistake, click the gray area outside the white scanning area and begin again.

5. Click the Scan button located in the scanner dialog box. The scanning software may be loaded independently of Photoshop. If this is the case, the file should be imported, or converted, to a Photoshop (.psd) file. The image should appear as shown in Figure 12.5. The scan may look quite gray and contain many artifacts or discolorations. See Step 7 to learn how to fix this.

6. Open the file before t-shirt.psd from the Chapter 12 folder on the CD-ROM ⊙.

7. A quick way to clean up undesirable marks is to access Image:

Adjust: Levels in the pull-down menu as shown in Figure 12.6.

8. The Levels dialog box will appear (see Figure 12.7).

9. Drag the right white triangle on the slide bar below the Histogram in the dialog box. Adjust the slider triangle to the left until it appears as shown in Figure 12.8. Since the artifacts are gone and the gray area has turned to white, this is now a clean scan.

10. Save the image using the File: Save option in the pull-down menu. Save the work as a Photoshop or .psd file. It is best to work on the files in the .psd file format, Photoshop's native format.

11. When the Photoshop file is complete, save it again as a .tif or .eps file, if it will be printed, or as a .jpg or .gif file, if it will be used on the Web. A .jpg file uses a compression method, which results in image degradation and is only suitable for print if saved at maximum-quality compression settings. PDF, or Portable Document Format, is also an option for print and is a cross-platform, cross-application file format. Always choose the maximum-quality compression for print.

Preparing the Fabric

This next section covers preparing existing fabric swatches. Refer to Chapter 9, Working with Photoshop to Create Textile Pattern Designs, to create custom seamless single repeat and in-repeat designs.

1. Place the fabric swatch facedown on the scanner bed. Choose the Advanced setting in the scanner dialog box. Make sure the settings are correct for the final output. In

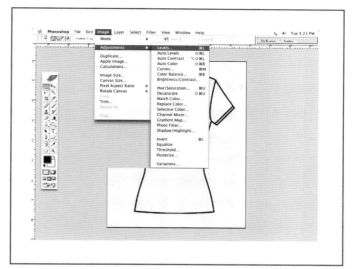

Figure 12.6 Image pull-down menu.

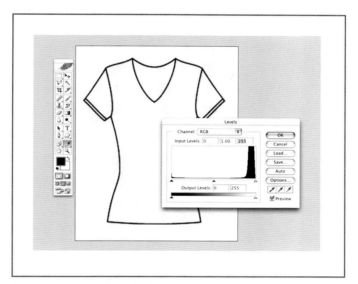

Figure 12.7 Levels dialog box.

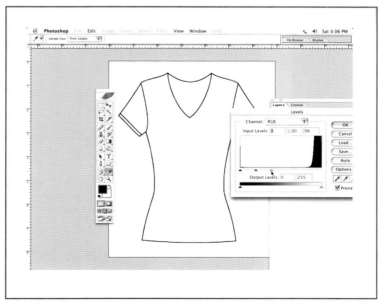

Figure 12.8 Adjusting the level.

this example, 300 dpi is used for final print output.

2. Click on the Preview button to see a preview of your image.

3. Click on the Marquee Tool in the scanning toolbar, and drag it around the fabric, isolating the section of fabric you will work on. Click on the Scan button in the scanner dialog box to complete the scanning process.

4. Open the file before fabric.psd from the chapter 12 folder on the CD-ROM ⊙.

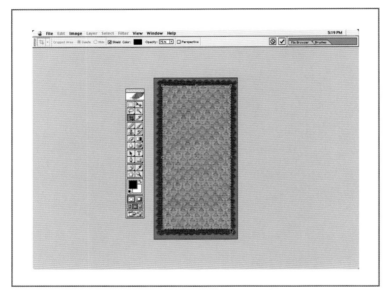

Figure 12.9   Selected area to be cropped.

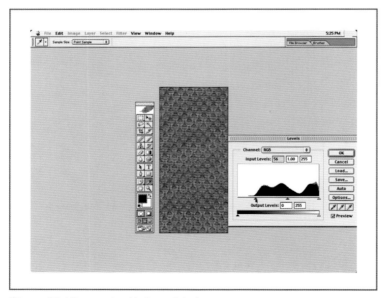

Figure 12.10   Levels of light and darkness in an image.

5. Click on the Crop Tool in the Photoshop toolbar, and drag it around the area you want to keep (see Figure 12.9).

6. The Crop Tool contains handles that can be dragged to adjust the cropped area.

7. Click inside the image to activate the adjustment.

8. To get an even distribution of lights and darks in the fabric, go to the Image: Adjust: Levels option in the pull-down menu and drag the black triangle on the slide bar to the right until it looks correct, as shown in Figure 12.10.

9. To reset the Levels amount, hold down the Option/ALT key on the keyboard and click on the Cancel button. Levels are the amounts of lights and darks within an image. Clicking on the Cancel button to reset will work for all the palettes (see Figure 12.10).

10. To sharpen the fabric, choose Filter: Sharpen: Unsharp Mask in the pull-down menu.

It is ideal to use the Unsharp Mask option to sharpen an image because it can be controlled through the Preview dialog box. Contrast, Radius, and Threshold can also be controlled.

The Radius setting determines the number of pixels surrounding the edge pixels that will be affected. A setting between 1 and 2 is recommended on high-resolution images. The Threshold is set at a default setting of 0, sharpening all pixels in the image with no regard to tonality and contrast. As the slider in the Unsharp Mask dialog box is moved to the right, more gray values in the shadows are excluded. The higher the setting, the more pixels are excluded from sharpening.

Click the minus (-) or plus (+) signs, located in the Preview window, to zoom in and zoom out. When the cursor is moved over the window notice it changes back into a Hand Tool, which, when dragged around the window, presents different views of the fabric.

Filling a Flat with Printed Fabric

There are three methods used to fill flats with fabric prints. The first method allows users to rotate the fabric swatch within a flat. The second method allows users to scale a fabric into a smaller area and adjust the color of a particular fabrication. The third method allows users to practice basic color fill and manipulation of Pantone colors.

Method One

1. Open the file t-shirt flat.psd from the Chapter 12 folder on the CD-ROM ◯.
2. In the file fabric for t-shirt.psd, choose the Select: All option in the pull-down menu, and choose Edit: Copy.
3. Go back to the file t-shirt flat.psd and select the Magic Wand Tool in the toolbar.
4. Click on the inside of the T-shirt so the marching ants are circling the inside, as shown in Figure 12.11.
5. To fill the sleeves, hold down the Shift key on the keyboard, and click inside the sleeves. Holding down the Shift key adds additional segments to the selection. Choose Select: Deselect from the pull-down menu to start again, if

you selected something incorrectly.

6. Choose Edit: Paste Into (not Paste) in the pull-down menu. The file should now appear as shown in Figure 12.12.
7. If the fabric covers the entire page, you incorrectly selected Paste. To correct, go back to the pull-down menu and choose the Paste Into option. To correct any mistakes, press Command plus Z on Macs or CTRL/Z on PCs. These commands are part of the operating system and allow

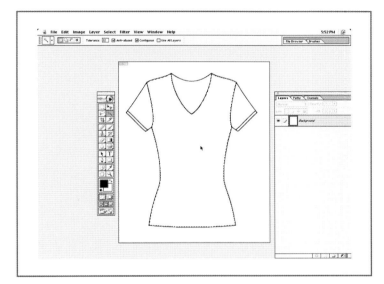

Figure 12.11 Filling a flat with printed fabric.

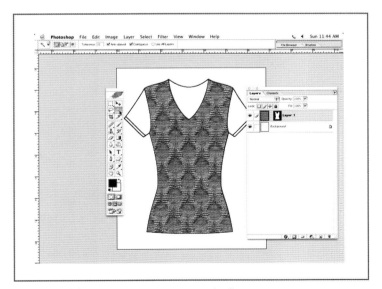

Figure 12.12 Pasting the pattern into the flat.

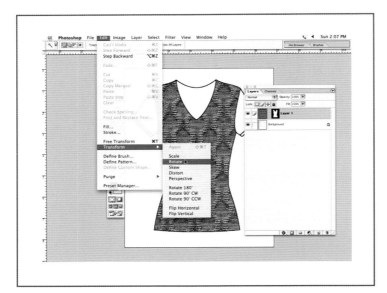

Figure 12.13   Using the Rotate option.

users to go back a step in any application.

8. To go back more than a few steps, choose Window: Show History in the pull-down menu. Click on any of the sequential steps in the open History palette, which reverts you to that step. Click on the arrow in the sidebar submenu, and choose New Snapshot to save your progress at any point. Note: The fabric swatch is imported into Photoshop on its own Layer with a Layer Mask. The **Mask** is a stored selection made earlier with the Magic Wand Tool. Clicking on the Background Layer Eye icon in the Layers palette makes the T-shirt line art disappear. Only the fabric will remain in view.

9. Choose Edit: Transform: Rotate from the pull-down menu. A box will appear around the fabric swatch (see Figure 12.13).

10. Click and drag the outer handlebars to rotate the image and change the fabric direction. This technique is especially useful with directional prints and stripes. The fabric can be manipulated in any direction by pulling and dragging the corner of the bars.

Method Two

1. Open the file fabric for shirt.psd from the chapter 12 folder on the CD-ROM ◉.

2. Choose Select: All from the Photoshop pull-down menu.

3. Choose Edit: Define Pattern. A dialog box will appear asking you to name your pattern. Type in a name, and click on the Save option.

4. Open the file t-shirt flat.psd from the Chapter 12 folder on the CD-ROM ◉.

5. Select the Magic Wand Tool. While holding down the Shift key on the keyboard, create a selection with the Magic Wand Tool as discussed in Method One.

6. Continue to hold down the Shift key on the keyboard, and click on the sleeves and inside of the T-shirt using the Magic Wand Tool. The marching ants should be active around all three sections of the garment. Note: If the Layer palette is not visible, choose Window: Layers at the bottom of the Layers palette. If the pattern covers the whole file after choosing Pattern, the T-shirt selection was made incorrectly. To correct, click on the Adjustment Layer icon at the bottom of the Layers palette and choose Pattern. The Pattern Fill Adjustment Layer dialog box will appear. Choose the arrow next to the fabric swatch's small picture icon to correct the fill (see Figure 12.14).

7. Choose the Pattern option listed in the New Adjustment Layer at the bottom of the Layers palette. Click a pattern square from the pop-up palette as shown in Figure 12.15. While the Pattern

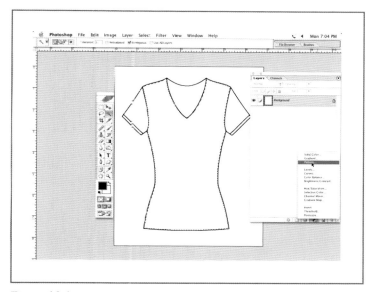

Figure 12.14 Using the Magic Wand Tool inside the T-shirt.

Fill Adjustment Layer dialog box is open, drag the Scale Triangle to the left until it reads 50 percent. The flat will now be filled with the desired fabrication and should appear as shown in Figure 12.16.

Adjusting the Fabric Color

1. To change any particular fabric's color, go to the New Adjustment Layer icon located at the bottom of the Layers palette.
2. Choose the Hue: Saturation option in the pull-down menu under Adjustment. This adds a second adjustment layer, affecting the layer below it (the fabric layer). The Hue: Saturation dialog box will now appear.
3. Click the Colorize button to ensure all original colors will change toward a particular color hue; otherwise, original highlights and shadows will project an undesired colorcast.
4. Drag the Hue: Saturation sliders in the dialog box to view how the fabric color is affected (see Figure 12.17). Experiment with different color options. Photoshop produces a wide range of interesting color effects. To see

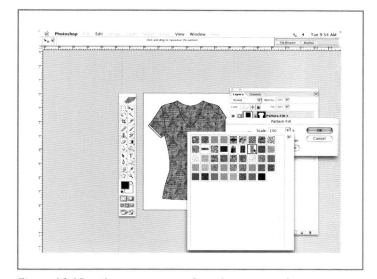

Figure 12.15 Choosing a pattern from the pop-up palette.

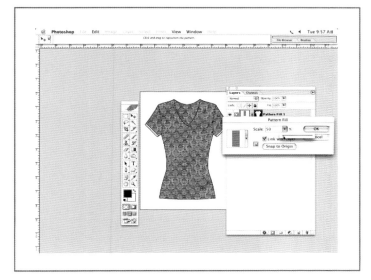

Figure 12.16 The Pattern Fill Adjustment Layer dialog box shown at 50 percent.

the new Hue/Saturation adjustment, select the Background Layer in the Layers palette after changing the color. Choose the Eyedropper Tool from the toolbox and click in the T-shirt. The new color will appear in the Foreground Swatch located at the bottom of the toolbox. Click the swatch box to enable the Color Picker to appear. To locate the Pantone Color equivalent, select the Solid Color option in the New Adjustment Layer dialog box. Click on Custom. The Pantone Color Picker pop-up menu will appear.

Method Three

1. The file fabric for t-shirt.psd should be open. Choose Select: All from the pull-down menu. The marching ants should encircle the fabric. This denotes the fabric selection is active.
2. Choose Edit: Copy from the pull-down menu. This copies the fabric to the clipboard.
3. Open the t-shirt flat.psd file from the Chapter 12 folder on the CD-ROM ⊙.
4. Choose the Magic Wand Tool in the toolbox. Click in the center of the flat. The marching ants will move around the inside of the garment.
5. Choose Edit: Paste Into from the pull-down menu. Note: If the screen is completely covered by the fabric, choose Edit: Paste. An extra layer is automatically added when a Layer Mask is activated. This extra mask on the layer results from earlier selections made with the Magic Wand Tool. Note: A mask created in Photoshop is a selection used to determine the areas of transparency and opacity on a layer. The mask will allow users to rotate fabric.

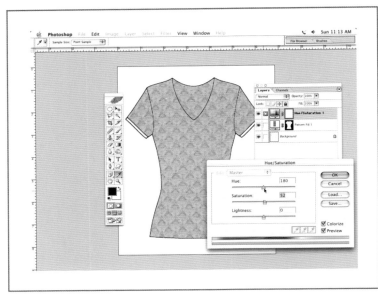

Figure 12.17   Adjusting the hue and saturation.

Filling the Flats with Solid Color

1. Choose the Magic Wand Tool to select a solid color fill area.
2. Choose the Layer Adjustment icon in the Layers palette. Click the Solid Color option from the dialog box (see Figure 12.18). Note: The Solid Color Adjustment Layer appears black because it is the active Foreground Color in the Fill Swatch toolbox.

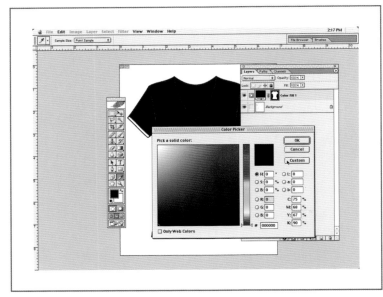

Figure 12.18   Solid Color option.

The Pantone Color System

To view or use an optional Pantone color, select the Custom option in the Color Picker dialog box. Many design studios, graphics companies, textile artists, and costume designers in the United States and Europe use the Pantone Color System primarily because of its accessibility and consistency. Pantone colors are part of a universal spot color matching system. Spot colors are uniform premixed inks. The Toyo Color System is more widely used by design professionals in Japan.

If the Pantone Textile Color Chooser is loaded onto the system, choose this option (see Figure 12.19). Pantone has card swatches, textile books, and CD-ROMs available to view and identify (by Pantone number) the actual colors as they appear on paper, textiles, and the Web.

3. Select a Pantone color from the dialog box, and click on the OK button in the field. The flat is now complete and filled with a solid color as shown in Figure 12.20. To find the CMYK equivalent, click on the Color Picker option in the Color Palette.

Lesson 2: Tracing Flats with the Illustrator Pen Tool, Importing Illustrator Files into Photoshop, and Creating and Saving Pattern Sets

Tracing Flats with the Illustrator Pen Tool

Mastering the Pen Tool is an important aspect of working with Adobe Illustrator. Scanned files can be brought into Illustrator, allowing flat drawings to be traced with the Pen Tool, creating templates. These flats can then be manipulated or filled with various colors or pat-

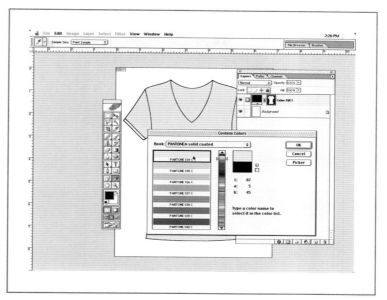

Figure 12.19 The Pantone Textile Color option.

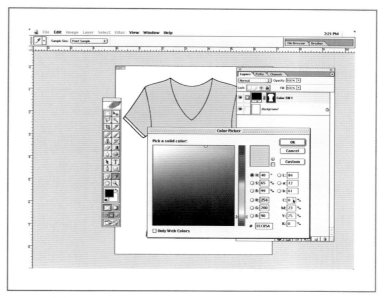

Figure 12.20 The completed flat filled with a solid color.

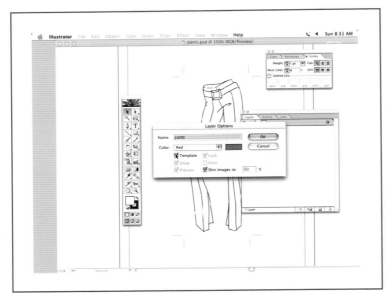

Figure 12.21   The Template box option in the Layer Options window.

1. Launch Illustrator. Choose File: Open and navigate to the Chapter 12 folder on the CD-ROM ⊙. Double-click on the file pants.psd.

2. Double-click on the pants layer in the Layers palette.

3. The Layer Options dialog box should be open. Click the Template box option (see Figure 12.21).

4. To select a Pen Tool outline color in the Layer Options dialog box, simply click on a desired color from the pull-down menu next to Color. Click OK. Note: When working with multiple layers, it is helpful to have each object outlined in a different color. This will avoid inaccurate selections.

5. Adjust the opacity of your template layer by setting the Dim Images option in the Layer Options dialog box to the desired number. By adjusting the opacity level, you get a better view of the lines and anchor points.

6. The template layer is automatically locked when it's activated. To unlock the template layer, click on the arrow icon in the upper right-hand corner of the Layers palette and choose New Layer. A new unlocked layer will appear in the Layers palette. Name the new layer "Art" (see Figure 12.22).

7. Set the Fill box to None. Click on the box with the red line crossed through it at the bottom of the toolbar. This indicates that no color will be applied inside the pants. Set the adjacent Stroke Box in the toolbox to black. A black stroke and a white fill are the default colors and are represented with smaller Fill Box icons in the upper left-hand corner. This is how the actual colors will appear when they

terns. Creating pattern sets is a useful technique you will learn in this lesson.

The advantages of creating a flat in Illustrator are the clean, sharp vector lines it creates, so superior to the sketchy pixilated lines Photoshop creates. Vector files can be scaled as large or small as desired. This is because vector objects are numerical creations—bits and bytes of information—or 0s and 1s. Pixels are painterly dots of digital information, as in a photograph. Illustrator, or any vector-based software application, enables users to create straight lines and curves. These curves are called Bezier curves. They can be manipulated by activating their anchor points and pulling on the handlebars. Lesson 2 guides users through the creation of a pants template. The Illustrator Pen Tool is used to trace around a pencil sketch that was first scanned through Photoshop and imported to Illustrator. The color was added or filled into the flat after the file was copied and pasted into a new Photoshop document.

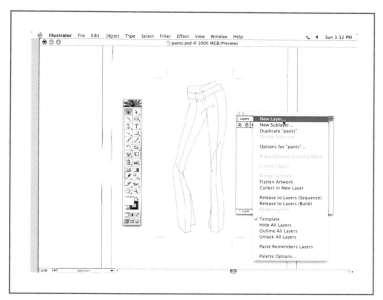

Figure 12.22 Creating a new layer.

are on-screen and in print. The fill and stroke colors should not be confused with the Pen Tool outline colors, which are only utilized to create segments and Bezier curves. The No Fill, as indicated by the red line going across the box, simply means that the object is transparent so that components underneath are visible (see Figure 12.23). This feature is especially important with clothing, as collars, cuffs, and pockets won't be visible if the No Fill is not activated.

Remember that an image cannot be utilized or filled until it is completely outlined with anchor points and segments. The points are then considered a completed vector object that is recognized by the application. A vector object can be filled with color, pattern, texture, or gradients once it is activated with any of the Selection Tools in the Illustrator toolbar or translated into an .eps file.

8. Choose the Pen Tool in the toolbar. The Pen Tool is represented

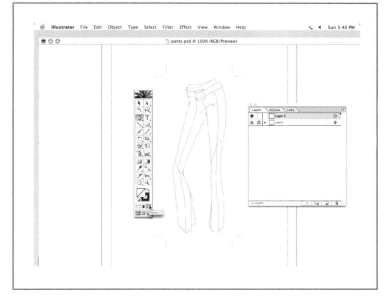

Figure 12.23 A flat with no fill.

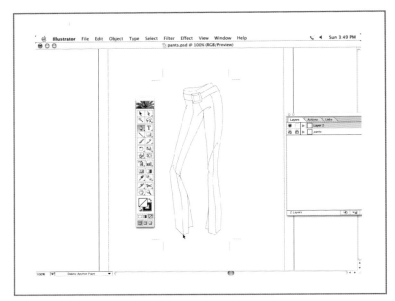

Figure 12.24   Using the Pen Tool.

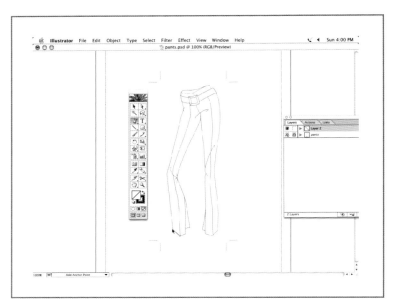

Figure 12.25   The colored outline shows the active Pen Tool lines.

by the icon to the left of the Text Tool (see Figure 12.24). Begin tracing the flat by clicking and releasing the mouse at the bottom left crease of the pants hem. This creates an anchor point. Connect the anchor points to draw the outline of an object.

9. Click again at the next point as shown in Figure 12.25. Then release the mouse. The highlighted colored outline means the Pen Tool lines are active.

10. Continue to click and release to add another anchor point at the knee (see Figure 12.26).

11. Now add another anchor point at the hip as shown in Figure 12.27.

12. Create another anchor point at the waistline. This time click and slightly drag in the direction of the side seam. By slightly pulling the Pen Tool after a click, a Bezier curve is created (see Figure 12.28).

13. Continue to click and drag

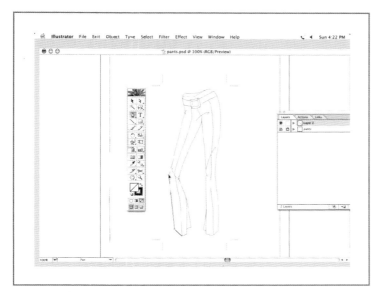

Figure 12.26 Adding an anchor point to the knee.

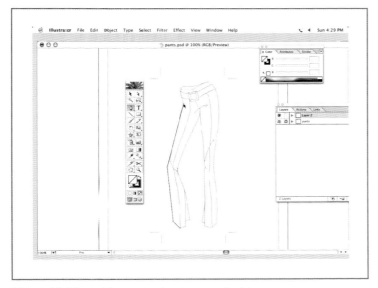

Figure 12.27 Adding an anchor point to the hip.

around the outside of the pants until you get to the first anchor point. There will be a small circle next to the Pen Tool. This indicates that the outline is complete and the shape is closed.

14. Turn off the Visibility on the template layer by clicking the Eye icon in the Layers palette (see Figure 12.29).

15. Click the Eye icon again so the template layer reappears.

16. Zoom in on the belt using the Zoom Tool selected from the

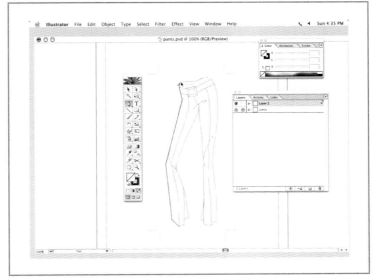

Figure 12.28 Adding an anchor point to the waistline.

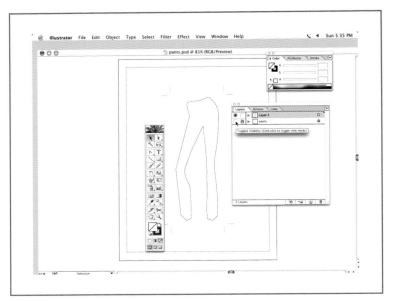

Figure 12.29   Turning off the Visibility on the template.

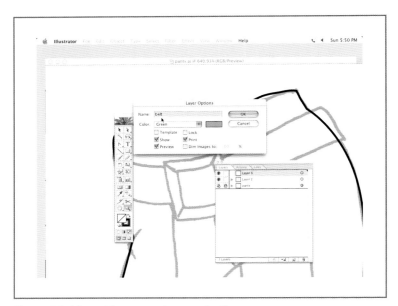

Figure 12.30   Adding a new layer to the flat.

toolbar. This will enlarge the object only on the screen, not in the final printed version.

17. Add a layer by clicking on the New Layer icon at the bottom of the Layers palette. Name the new layer "Belt" in the New Layer dialog box field, and click OK (see Figure 12.30).

18. Select the Pen Tool from the toolbar. Click each one of the outer four belt buckle corners on the active Art layer until it forms a square. To make a straight line for the buckle,

hold down the Shift key while dragging from one point to another.

19. Choose the Selection Tool in the toolbar, and click on the newly created square. The arrow that is solid black activates the entire selection. The empty arrow only activates one anchor point on a segment.

20. Copy and paste to create a duplicate buckle shape.

21. Grab a corner of the active square with the Direct Select (empty arrow) Tool. Holding down the mouse, drag the corner toward the center until it is the approximate size of the middle square (see Figure 12.31).

22. Choose the Pen Tool in the toolbar. Click on any outer corner of the belt buckle. Hold down the Shift key, and click again on the inner square corner.

23. Choose the Full Selection Tool in the toolbar, and click anywhere outside of the pants area. This will deselect the pants and avoid unwanted anchor points from being placed irregularly.

24. Select the Pen Tool again, and click on another corner of the inner belt buckle corners. Repeat this process until it looks like Figure 12.32.

25. Repeat Step 18, and click to connect the endpoints.

26. Choose the Full Selection Tool in the toolbar Choose the Pen Tool and begin the process again.

27. Hold down the Option key for Mac or the ALT key for PC. The status bar changes to Convert Anchor Point. Now users can change the direction of the Pen Tool. Remember that pressing Command and Z on Macs or CTRL and Z on PCs will undo actions and let users go back one step.

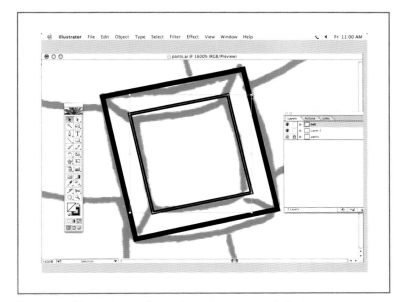

Figure 12.31 Using the Direct Select (empty arrow) Tool.

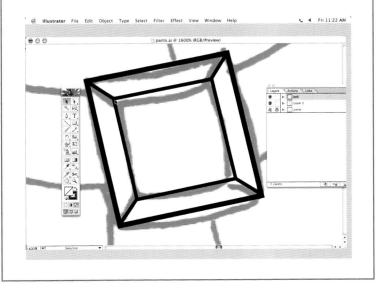

Figure 12.32 Using the Pen Tool to modify the image.

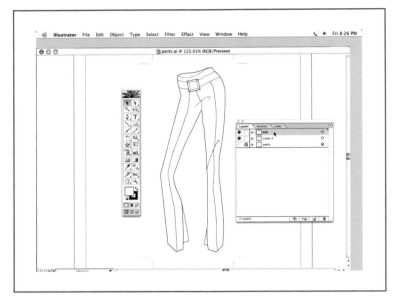

Figure 12.33   The completed pants.

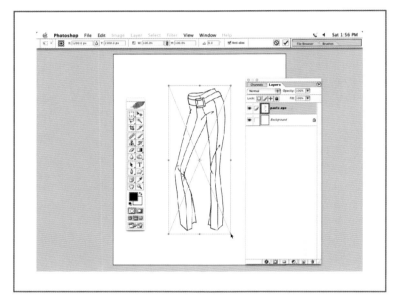

Figure 12.34   Bounding bars around the pants.

28. When the pants are complete, they will look like Figure 12.33. Note: The Pen Tool is difficult to maneuver at first and cannot be mastered in just one lesson. It requires patience and practice. There are garment files in the Chapter 12 folder labeled as garments 1, 2, 3, 4, and 5 on the CD-ROM ⚙ that you can use for exercises or practice assignments. Try tracing around the garments or writing in a word with the Pen Tool.

Incorporating Illustrator Files into Photoshop

After creating a vector outline or object in Illustrator with the Pen Tool, select the object with the Fill Select Tool or Select: All from the pull-down menu. Choose Edit: Copy.

1. Activate the Illustrator pants by dragging the Selection Tool around the object with the mouse button, and keep it held down. Once selected, choose Edit: Copy from the pull-down menu.

2. To create a new file in Photoshop, choose File-New from the pull-down menu. Type the name "Placed Pants" in the file field. The Preset Options field will allow users to size the file. Choose the 8" by 10" format. Note: The resolution becomes 300 dpi. The Illustrator file that was placed will be imported at the same resolution as the Photoshop file.

3. Choose Edit: Paste. When the file opens, it will have bounding bars around the pants, as shown in Figure 12.34. To scale the image, click on the bounding bars' corner point and drag a corner while holding down the Shift key. Press the Return or Enter key to commit the change. The image must be sized before the Return key is pressed. The Illustrator file is still a vector image while the bounding bars are present in the Photoshop file, as shown in Figure 12.34. The visual will not lose any image quality when it is scaled. If the image is committed in Illustrator before it is scaled, the pixel-based image will remain a pixel-based image and lose quality.

Creating and Saving Pattern Sets in Adobe Illustrator

Pattern sets are swatches of scanned fabric that can be saved in the Photoshop Presets Manager palette. This functionality allows designers to record and store prints, patterns, and solid fabrics for use at a later date in a design archival library asset. A fill swatch should be made seamless before it is used to create a textile fill pattern. Refer to Chapter 9 to create a seamless pattern.

1. Choose File: Open from the Illustrator pull-down menu, and navigate to the Chapter 12 folder on the CD-ROM 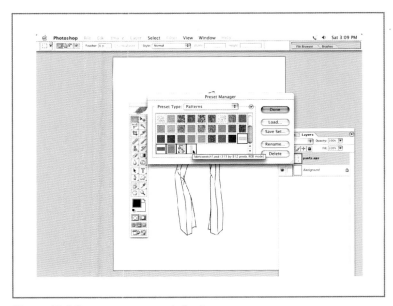 . Open the psd files labeled as fabric swatches 1, 2, 3, 4, and 5.
2. Choose Edit: Define Pattern on the pull-down menu to open each file. This creates a pattern set for each of the five swatches.
3. Choose Edit: Preset Manager in the pull-down menu. Select Pattern as the present option. Scroll until the five patterns defined are located. Move the cursor over the patterns—notice how the names pop up, making them easier to find.

4. Locate the pattern in the Preset Manager dialog box, and hold down the Shift key on the keyboard (see Figure 12.35).
5. Click the Save: Set button in the Preset Manager dialog box and name the set "fabric.pattern" in the untitled field box. One reason for creating a set is so pattern sets can be accessible on other computers. After scanning in a fabric swatch and saving it as a set in the Preset Manager, it can be transported. To load a pattern set or swatch, choose File: Open from the pull-down menu and locate the Photoshop folder marked Preset Manager in the Photoshop application folder. Click on the Load button in the dialog box, then click OK.
6. Locate the saved Illustrator pattern set or open the fabric library located in the Bonus Library folder on the CD-ROM and create a new pattern set (see Figure 12.36).
7. The pattern sets will show up in the Pattern Adjustment Layer for use.

Figure 12.35   Preset Manager dialog box.

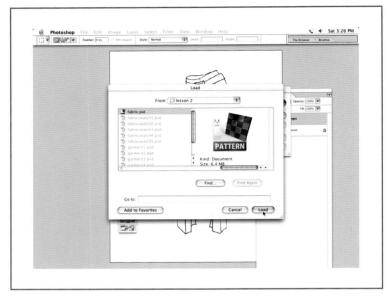

Figure 12.36 Creating a new pattern set.

To access the sets, click on the icon at the bottom of the Pattern Adjustment Layer.

Lesson 3: Adjusting and Replacing Color in Prints and Illustrations

In this lesson you will learn to scan a sketch or illustration and change the color and pattern using Quick Masks, Saved Selections, and Adjustment Layers.

The ability to quickly change colors in an illustration, flat, drawing, or fabric swatch is particularly useful in the design room. Garments, prints, and color combinations can be viewed and changed with the click of a mouse (see Figure 12.37).

Adjusting and Replacing Color in Prints and Illustrations

1. Open the file fashion figure.tif from the Chapter 12 folder on the CD-ROM ◎.

Figure 12.37 Altering the color of prints and illustrations.

2. Choose the Magic Wand Tool from the Photoshop toolbox. Click on the white background area to activate a selection. Hold down the Shift key, and select the inside of the figure's right art. This will add to the background selection (see Figure 12.38).

3. Choose Select: Inverse from the pull-down menu

4. Press Quick Mask on the keyboard. This will switch the mode to Quick Mask mode. The file should look like Figure 12.39. Note: The Quick Mask is a way of improving an existing selection made with one of the selection tools in the toolbox. When the Quick Mask mode is turned on, a ruby overlay is displayed over the areas of the image that are not part of the selection.

5. Choose the Zoom Tool, and click on the figure's face to get a larger view.

6. Choose the Airbrush Tool and press Default on the keyboard to activate the default foreground and background colors of black and white. With black as the

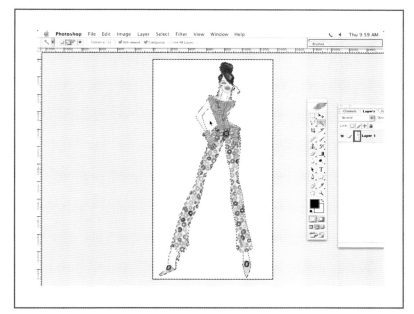

Figure 12.38   Using the Magic Wand Tool and activating a selection.

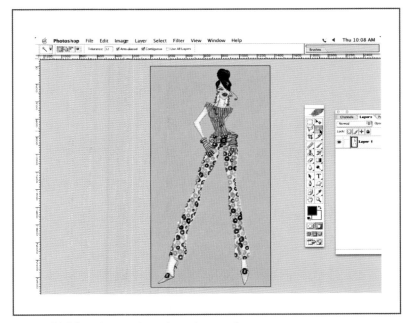

Figure 12.39   The Quick Mask Mode turned on.

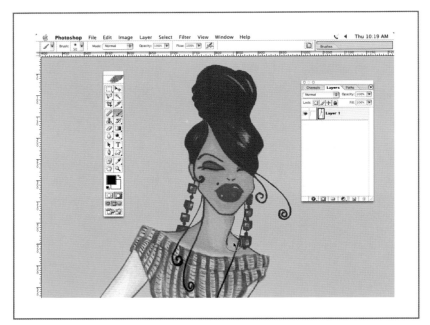

Figure 12.40   The illustration painted with the Airbrush Tool.

foreground color, begin painting over her face and skin until it looks like Figure 12.40.

7. Continue to paint over the entire skin area. This important process allows for the user to refine the edges on an illustration or drawing. An illustration can be seamlessly placed in a photograph by using this technique. Note: If an area of her garment is accidentally painted, press the X key on the keyboard. This will toggle to the white Fill Box or the default foreground Swatch Box in the toolbox. When painting with the white Fill Box activated, the user is eliminating the mask. When painting with the black Fill Box activated, the user is adding a mask. Therefore, toggling will further refine the selection.

8. Completely cover the skin area with the mask. Press Quick Mask on the keyboard to check the selection. Press Quick Mask on the keyboard again to return to the Quick Mask mode to continually check the selection.

9. Once the selection is complete, choose Select: Save Selection in

the pull-down menu. Name the completed selection in the untitled field box (see Figure 12.41). A good habit to develop is to always save difficult selections. This will create an Alpha Channel. Always choose Select: Load Selection from the pull-down menu to retrieve the selection. If the final selection is not active, choose Select: Load Selection from the pull-down menu.

10. Choose the Adjustment Layer icon from the bottom of the open Layers palette. Choose the Hue: Saturation option under Adjustment from the pull-down menu.

11. The dialog box will appear. Activate the Colorize option by clicking in the box next to it. A check mark should appear in the box indicating that the illustration can now be colorized.

12. Move the Hue and Saturation sliders around until you get a desirable color, as shown in Figure 12.42.

13. Once the new color appears, press the Return key on the keyboard to commit the color change. To preview the new Hue: Saturation color, select the Background Layer in the Layers palette. Choose the Eyedropper Tool, and click on the Background Layer in the Layers palette. Click in the T-shirt with the Eyedropper Tool. The color will appear in the Foreground Swatch box. Double click on the Foreground Swatch box to activate the Color Picker dialog box. To find the Pantone equivalent, click on the Custom option in the Color Picker. The Pantone Color Swatch Palette will appear. Save the file; the completed lesson should look like Figure 12.42.

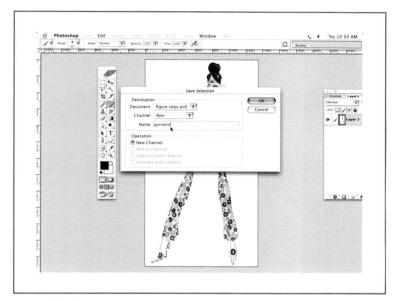

Figure 12.41   Save Selection.

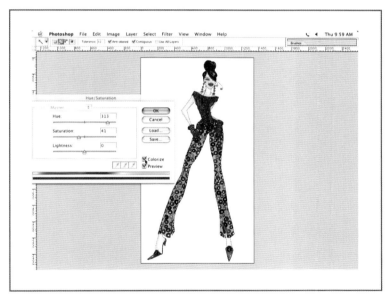

Figure 12.42   Changing the Hue and Saturation to create a new color.

Review Questions

1. How does a user toggle between Mask modes?

2. What is an adjustment layer, and what are its advantages?

3. Why is a mask used?

4. How do you create a template in Illustrator?

5. How do you reduce a color in Photoshop?

Suggested Practice Project

To be proficient with the Pen Tool, practice is essential. Scan any piece of art or photograph into Photoshop. Import the art into Illustrator. After the image has been locked in a Template Layer, trace around the image with the Pen Tool.

Key Terms

Adjustment Layer

Bounding Bars

Hue/Saturation

Mask

Pattern Set

Preset Manager

Selection

13

Advanced Illustrator and Photoshop Techniques

What You Will Learn in Chapter 13

Chapter 13 will teach you advanced techniques for Illustrator and Photoshop. Advanced Illustrator techniques such as clipping masks, gradient mesh shadows, and seamless textile patterns will enhance and vary your design options. The advanced Photoshop techniques can be utilized with the advanced Illustrator techniques to add depth, dimension, and creative alternatives.

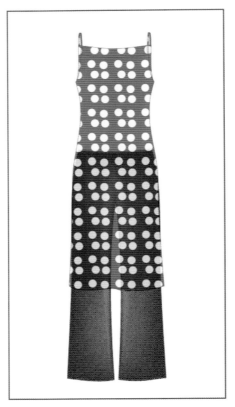

Figure 13.1   Flat filled with print.

Working with Illustrator CS

Illustrator CS offers many upgrades for the fashion and/or textile designer, one of which is the ability to take any of their many preset patterns and alter the color or design of the chosen pattern. Pulling a pattern swatch from the pattern palette onto the document and selecting any aspect of the pattern with the Direct Select Tool can alter the color and/or design. Illustrator also allows the user to import textiles created in Photoshop (such as the piece of denim to be used in the following lesson) to be dragged directly into the pattern swatch palette so that the user can create a pattern (previous versions of Illustrator do not allow this).

Also, the document resolution can be changed using the Print dialog box, which also displays document information and warnings, such as color mode and transparency flat-

tening. Transparencies in Illustrator often have to be flattened for them to print correctly. Choose Advanced from the Print options to specify low, medium, or high-resolution output.

Working with Photoshop CS

Photoshop CS offers many advanced features for fashion and textile designers, including precise color management and replacement, a filter gallery for textile design, as well as PDF presentation and a Web photo gallery for portfolio presentation. Photo draping is another common advanced usage in Photoshop. Photo draping is the process of making a textile appear as though it is actually on an object in a photograph. This process can be applied to garments, interiors, or almost any object. Photoshop offers many tools that allow for photo draping, including Blend Mode, adjustment layers, layer masks, and various selection tools that will be covered in this chapter.

Photoshop and Illustrator work well together by combining the best of both vector (Illustrator) and raster (Photoshop) imagery. Fabric can be scanned in Photoshop, made seamless, and color managed, then brought into Illustrator so that the print can fill a flat (see Figure 13.1). The following lessons are advanced techniques and should be attempted only after learning the basics of both Photoshop and Illustrator.

Advanced Illustrator Techniques

The following lesson is an advanced-level Illustrator tutorial that will involve: transparent fabrics, seamless patterns, clipping masks, and gradient meshes. Once these lessons have been mastered, these techniques can be applied to other fabrics and design concepts.

1. A pair of jeans is required for this lesson. (Refer to Chapter 11, "Mastering the Pen Tool" to create the pants or open the file dress and pants.ai on the CD-ROM ○ in the Chapter 13 folder). The pants should look like Figure 13.2.

2. Copy the jeans by selecting the Move Tool, holding down the Option key on the keyboard, and dragging the mouse. Fill them with any dark blue from the Color Swatch palette, and click on the blue color swatch (see Figure 13.3).

3. Choose File: Place from the pull-down menu. The Chapter 13 folder on the CD-ROM ○ contains a denim swatch created using the techniques described in Chapter 9.

4. Drag the denim swatch labeled denim.psd from the Chapter 13 folder on the CD-ROM ○ into the Swatches palette to create a pattern. The denim was made seamless using techniques described in Chapter 9, "Working with Photoshop to Create Textile Pattern Designs." To fill the jeans with the denim pattern, choose the jeans with the Select Tool and click on the denim pattern swatch.

Clipping Mask

5. If your version of Illustrator is an earlier version, create a clipping mask. Start by moving the denim swatch behind one of the jeans (see Figure 13.4).

6. Choose the full selection tool in the toolbox (the black arrow) and drag around while holding your finger on the mouse button to select both the denim swatch and the jeans. Choose Object:

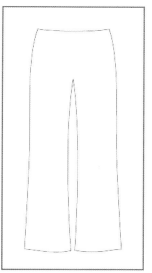
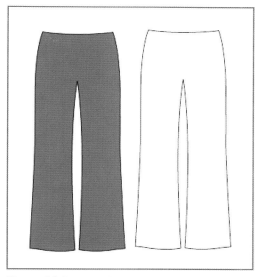

Figure 13.2   Pants without print or fill.

Figure 13.3   Pants filled with a blue color swatch.

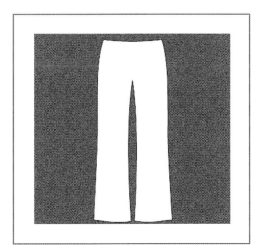

Figure 13.4   Moving the denim swatch behind one of the jeans.

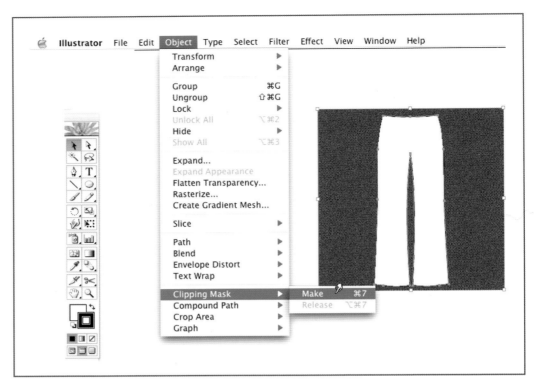

Figure 13.5   Creating a clipping mask.

Figure 13.6   Pants filled with
                 denim fabric.

Clipping Mask: Make from the pull-down menu (see Figure 13.5).

7. The denim fabric should now be inside the jeans and look like Figure 13.6.

If the fabric texture did not fill the flat, the most common mistakes are the following:

- The jeans were not on top of the denim swatch when the selection was made. To correct this, click on the jeans with the Full Select Tool (black arrow) and choose Object: Arrange: Bring to Front from the pull-down menu.
- Both objects were not selected. To correct this, drag the Full Select Tool (black arrow) around both objects.
- The flat is not joined. To correct this, use the Pathfinder as described in Chapter 11.

Continue the lesson after the texture has been properly applied.

8. Select the jeans copy and fill with blue (see Figure 13.7).

Gradient Mesh

9. Select the jeans with the Selection Tool by clicking on any area of the pants, and choose Object Create Gradient Mesh from the pull-down menu. Make sure the Preview box is checked in the Gradient Mesh dialog box, and choose four rows and four columns. The appearance field should be set to center and 100 percent for the highlight (see Figure 13.8).

10. Place the jeans with the gradient mesh on top of the jeans with the denim clipping mask, and choose Window: Transparency from the pull-down menu. Drop the opacity to 60 percent to complete the denim wash effect (see Figure 13.9).

The objects should be layered in the following order: jeans, gradient mesh, and denim clipping mask. When these three items are aligned one on top of another, choose Window: Transparency from the pull-down menu.

A dialog box will appear. Drop the opacity in the dialog box to 60 percent using the slider. This will complete the denim wash effect (see Figure 13.9).

How to Create Transparent Fabrics

11. Drag the Selection Tool around both flats, all of them are active and choose Object: Group from the pull-down menu. After saving the file, set the jeans aside for now. Next you will need to create a dress to use an overlay or transparent fabric, such as chiffon, lace, etc. To create a dress, follow the methods described in Chapter 11, or

Figure 13.7   Copy of jeans selected.

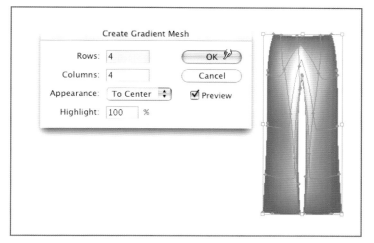

Figure 13.8   Gradient Mesh Dialog Box.

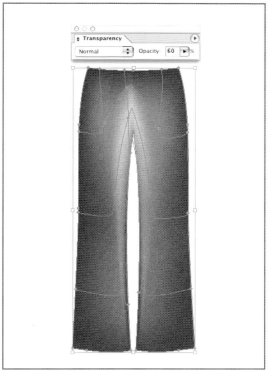

Figure 13.9   Transparency opacity set to 60 percent.

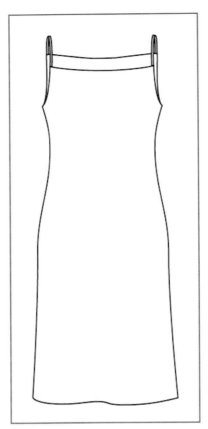

Figure 13.10   A dress flat to be used as an overlay.

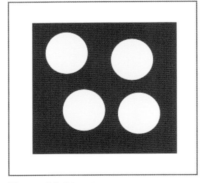

Figure 13.11   Creating a pattern design.

draw a silhouette, and use any styling details from the Bonus Library on the CD-ROM ⊙. For silhouette ideas, refer to Chapter 5. It should look similar to Figure 13.10.

12. Create a pattern design similar to Figure 13.11 by choosing the Ellipse Tool. Create a circle and click on a yellow color swatch from the Swatches palette, then choose the Selection Tool (black arrow) and hold the Option key while dragging with the mouse to create copies of the circle. Next choose the Rectangle Tool from the toolbox; create a square with a red fill and select None for the color of the stroke. Select the Rectangle Tool by clicking the rectangle with the Selection Tool (black arrow), and choose Object: Arrange: Send to Back.

13. Choose Window: Swatches from the pull-down menu to show the Swatches palette. Select all the elements in the pattern swatch and drag the swatch into the Swatches palette; this will create a seamless pattern (see Figure 13.12). The swatch will appear in the palette and can be saved to be used at a later date.

14. Make sure the foreground is in front of the stroke in the toolbar. Select the dress and click

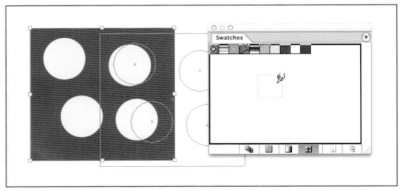

Figure 13.12   Dragging the new pattern design into the Swatches Palette.

Figure 13.13   The dress flat filled with the new pattern swatch.

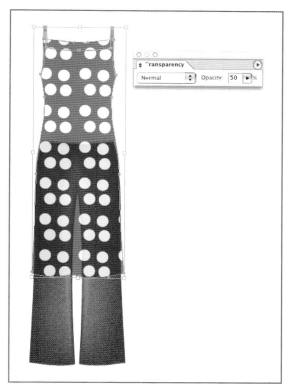

Figure 13.14   The dress and jeans pattern combined.

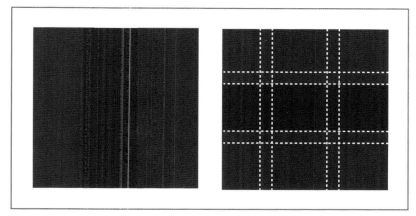

Figure 13.15   Creating a seamless pattern using the Rectangle Tool.

on the pattern swatch just created (see Figure 13.13).

Transparent Fabrics

15. Select the dress and place it on top of the jeans. Change the opacity to 13 percent (see Figure 13.14).

Seamless Patterns

1. Choose the Rectangle Tool with a solid color and no stroke. Create three stripes, then copy the three stripes and rotate them 90 percent. Add dashed lines (see Figure 13.15).

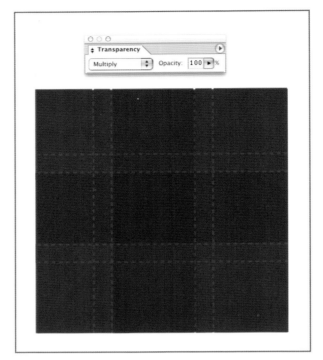

Figure 13.16   Blend mode set to multiply.

Figure 13.17   The dress flat filled with the striped pattern.

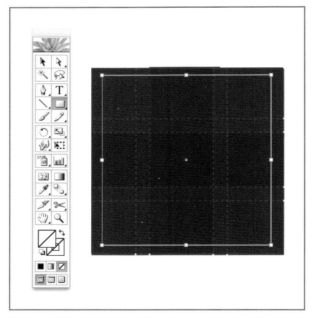

Figure 13.18   The area is defined to create a seamless swatch.

2. Select the swatch that has the dashed lines on it and group it. Move the swatch over the first striped swatch and change the Blend Mode to Multiply. Make sure the swatch with the dashed lines is in front of the other swatch (see Figure 13.16).

3. Select both swatches and group them.

4. Drag the grouped swatch into the Swatches palette.

5. Make a copy of the dress from the previous lesson. Select the dress and click on the swatch that was just created; notice the white gaps separating the tiles (see Figure 13.17).

6. Choose the Rectangle Tool from the toolbar. Select none for both the foreground and the stroke. Drag a rectangle in the grouped swatch and choose Object: Arrange: Send to Back to send the empty rectangle to the back. This is how Illustrator defines the area to create a seamless tile (see Figure 13.18).

7. Drag the Selection Tool around the swatch and the empty rectangle and choose Object: Group.

Figure 13.19 The dress flat filled with the new seamless swatch.

Figure 13.20 An example of photo draping on a three-dimensional body.

8. Drag this grouped swatch into the Swatches palette. Then select the dress and click on the new seamless swatch (see Figure 13.19).

Advanced Photoshop Techniques

Photo draping is taking a flat textile pattern and applying it to a three-dimensional body using Photoshop tools and techniques to represent shadow, depth, and dimension (see Figure 13.20).

Paths

1. Open the white dress.psd file in the Chapter 13 folder on the CD-ROM.
2. Click on the Pen Tool in the toolbar and choose paths from the option bar (see Figure 13.21).
3. Choose Window: Paths from the menu.

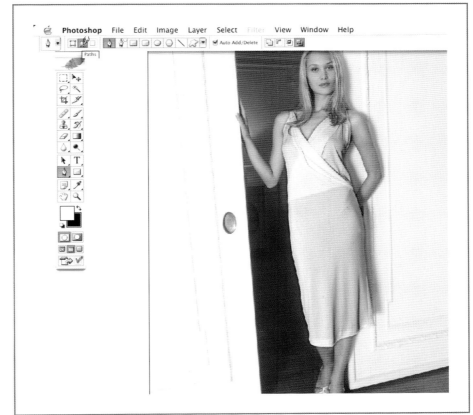

Figure 13.21 Using the Pen Tool for an advanced Photoshop technique.

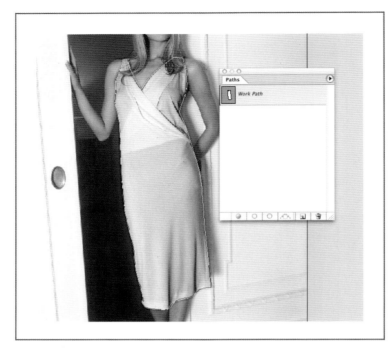

Figure 13.22 A Work Path.

Figure 13.23 Adjusting the pattern fill of the dress.

4. Click and drag the Pen Tool around the dress while ignoring her hair. Note that a work path has been created (see Figure 13.22).

5. Once the path is complete, click the Load Path as a selection icon at the bottom of the Paths palette. This will turn the path into a selection.
6. Choose Select: Feather and two pixels to soften the transition between the pattern and the dress.
7. While the selection is active, choose Window: Layers.
8. Click on the Adjustment Layer icon at the bottom of the Layers palette and choose Pattern. While the Pattern Fill palette is open, the pattern can be adjusted by moving the mouse over the dress (see Figure 13.23). (The seamless flower pattern was created from the Chapter 9 textile tutorial. There is also a seamless flower file labeled as seamless flower.psd in Chapter 13 on the CD-ROM ◎ .) Choose Edit: Define Pattern to turn it into a pattern.
9. Click OK to commit the pattern.
10. Choose Select: Deselect.

Blend Modes

11. Blend modes will reveal different aspects of the layer that is below the layer with the blend-mode change. Change the Blend Mode of the adjustment layer to Multiply. Note that the folds become visible (see Figure 13.24).
12. Zoom in to the area where the pattern covers her hair.

Layer Masks

13. Choose the Brush Tool and black as the foreground color.

(Note that the Pattern Adjustment layer comes with a mask, which is a saved selection. The white part of the mask represents the selection

Figure 13.24   Changing the blend mode of the adjustment layer to multiply.

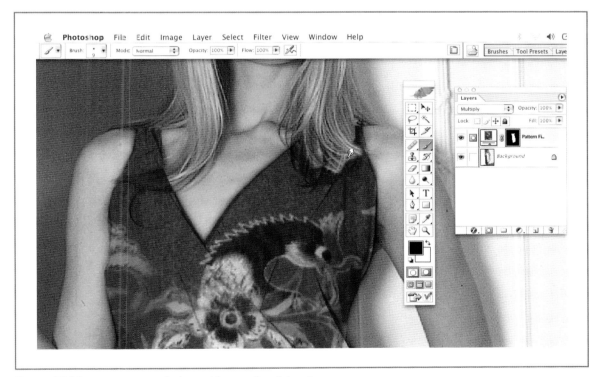

Figure 13.25   Painting over the hair with a small, soft brush.

that was created earlier with the Pen Tool. A layer mask can be modified. By painting with black, the layer below is revealed; using white, the pattern will be painted back in. This is how the selection mask can be improved.)

14. Begin painting over the hair with a small, soft brush (see Figure 13.25).

15. Switch between black and white by pressing X on the keyboard. Continue to paint on the mask until the hair and any other

Figure 13.26 Adjusting the Layer Mask and paint brush size.

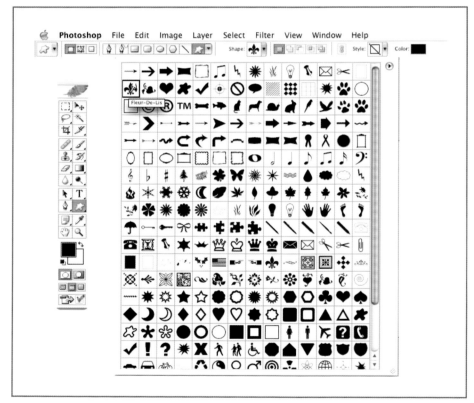

Figure 13.27 Selecting a vector shape.

part of the selection is adjusted. Brush size can be adjusted by pressing the bracket keys next to the P on the keyboard (see Figure 13.26).

Combining Illustrator and Photoshop

Creating textiles in Photoshop and exporting them to Illustrator can often prove to be more efficient than trying to create the same effects from scratch in Illustrator. Photoshop features many preset shapes that can be exported into Illustrator and edited there. Shapes can also be downloaded off the Internet and changed in Illustrator. The following lesson discusses the advantages of working with Photoshop and Illustrator at the same time.

Creating and Exporting Vector Shapes in Photoshop

1. Open Photoshop and create a new file that is 5" × 5" at 72 pixels/inch. The resolution does not matter because the shape created is going to be exported to Illustrator.

2. Select the Custom Shape Tool; make sure the Shape Layer Option is selected in the Options palette. To show all the shapes, select the arrow and choose all. Select a shape (see Figure 13.27).

3. Click and drag this shape into the document window and choose Edit: Copy (see Figure 13.28).

4. Open Adobe Illustrator and create a new letter-size file.

5. Choose Edit: Paste. The shape will paste as an empty path (see Figure 13.29).

6. To fill the path with a color, choose Window: Swatches to show the color swatches. Click on a color swatch to fill the path (see Figure 13.30).

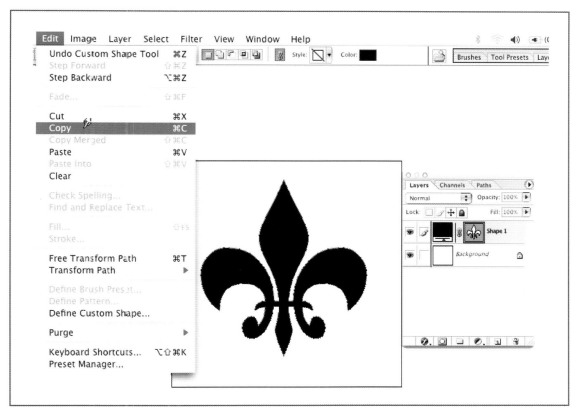

Figure 13.28 Copying the fleur de lis shape.

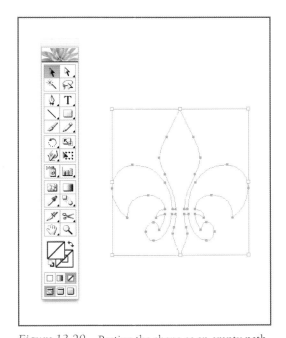

Figure 13.29 Pasting the shape as an empty path.

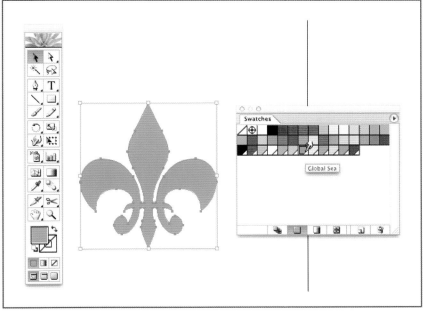

Figure 13.30 Selecting a color swatch to fill the path.

Creating a Half-Drop Repeat Pattern

7. To create a half-drop, select the shape and hold the Option key while dragging the shape to make a copy.

8. Place the copy down and to the right of the original.

9. Select both shapes by dragging the Selection Tool around both shapes and drag the shapes into the Swatches palette. To name

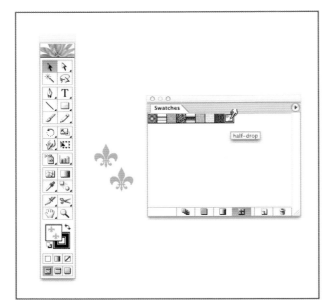

Figure 13.31 Dragging the shapes into the Swatches Palette.

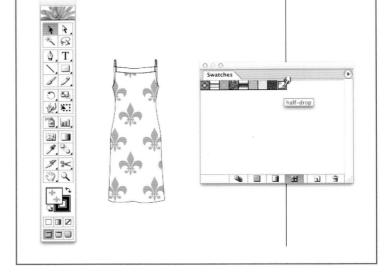

Figure 13.32 Half-drop pattern swatch.

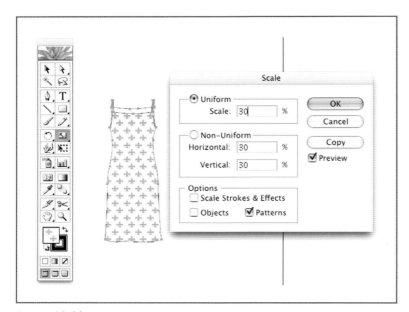

Figure 13.33 Scaling patterns within a flat.

the new pattern, double click on the pattern swatch (see Figure 13.31).

10. Open the dress and pant.ai file from the Chapter 13 folder on the CD-ROM ⊙. Select the dress by dragging the Selection Rool around the dress and choose Edit: Copy. Go back to the half-drop document and choose Edit: Paste.

11. Select the dress and click on the half-drop pattern swatch (see Figure 13.32).

Rotating and Scaling Patterns Within a Flat in Illustrator

12. To scale a pattern once it is inside a flat, select the flat and choose the Scale Tool.

13. Double click on the Scale Tool and choose Uniform. Select the Patterns option and make sure the Objects and Scale Strokes and Effects options have been deselected/unchecked. Type in a percentage and click on the Preview box (see Figure 13.33).

14. To rotate a pattern inside a flat, select the flat and double click on the Rotate Tool.

15. Choose an angle for the rotation. Select Patterns and deselect Objects. Check the Preview box to see the results (see Figure 13.34).

Previewing Color for a Pattern

16. Select the dress with the pattern and choose Edit: Copy, Edit: Paste in Back. This will paste a copy of the dress behind the original.
17. With the dress in the background still selected, click on different color swatches to see how the pattern will look against different solid colors (see Figure 13.35).

Using a Fabric Scan as a Template

Often there are advantages to creating a vector version of fabric that has been scanned in. Following are a few of the advantages:

- Vector versions are clearer and not pixilated.
- Color can be changed quickly in different elements of the textile.
- It can be scaled up or down and still retain its detail.

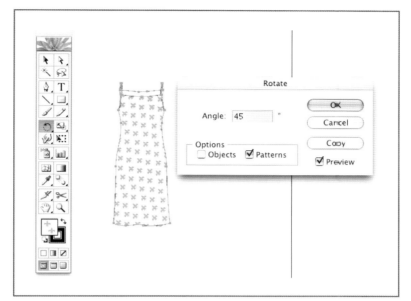

Figure 13.34   Rotating a pattern within a flat.

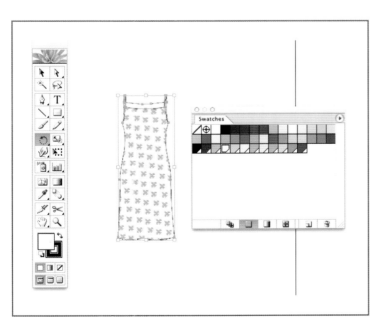

Figure 13.35   Previewing color for a pattern.

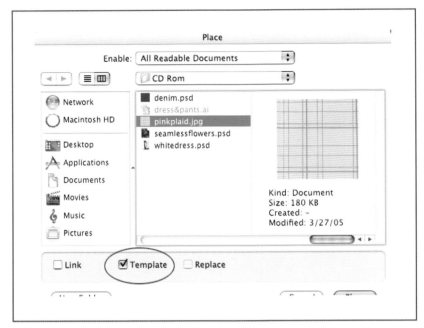

Figure 13.36 Place Dialog Box and Template option.

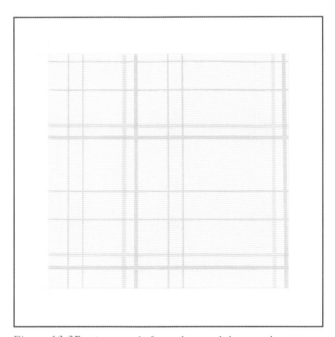

Figure 13.37 A rectangle formed around the swatch, using the horizontal and vertical rulers.

Altering a Fabric Swatch

1. Open Adobe Illustrator and choose File: New, and create a new letter-size file. Go to the Chapter 13 folder on the CD-ROM ⊙ and choose the pink plaid.jpg swatch. Check the template option and click on place (see Figure 13.36).

2. Choose View: Rulers: Show Rulers. Pull guides from the horizontal and vertical rulers to form a rectangle around the swatch (see Figure 13.37).

3. Within the toolbar, click on the fill and choose None for the fill. Click on the stroke and choose black. Choose the Line Segment Tool from the toolbar and create all the horizontal lines by clicking and dragging while holding the Shift key to create straight lines. To change the thickness of the line strokes, choose Window: Stroke and change the thin lines to one point and the thicker ones to two points (see Figure 13.38).

4. To change the color of the lines, select the line with the Selection Tool (black arrow) by clicking on it and click on a color swatch. For this lesson, Global Pink, Global Mocha, and Global Rust were used.

5. Create the vertical lines the same way as the horizontal and color them the same way as described in Step 4 (see Figure 13.39).

6. Choose the Rectangle Tool and choose Global Pink for the fill (the fill swatch should be in front of the stroke in the toolbar) to fill the rectangle with pink. Make sure all the line segments are covered with the pink.

7. With the rectangle still selected, choose Object: Arrange: Send to Back.

8. Choose View: Hide Guides. Illustrator will not make patterns

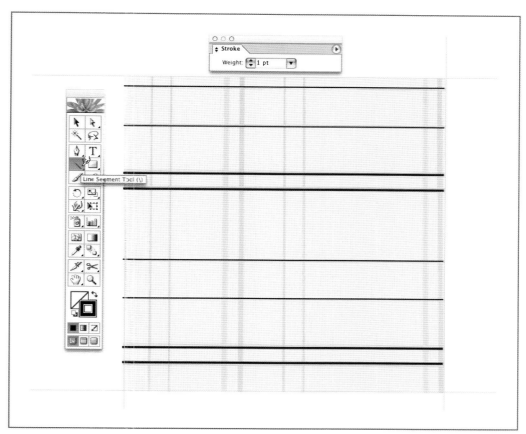

Figure 13.38 Changing the thickness of the horizontal lines in the rectangle.

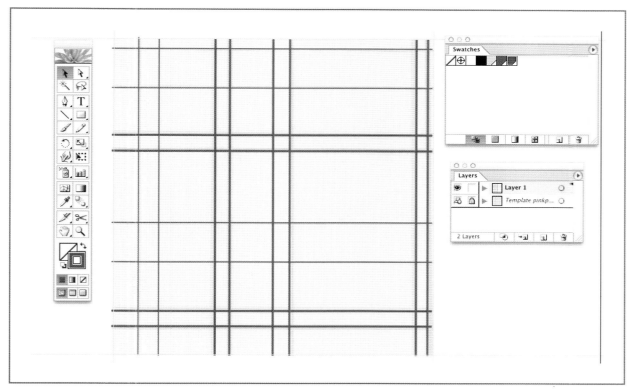

Figure 13.39 Changing the appearance of the vertical lines in the rectangle.

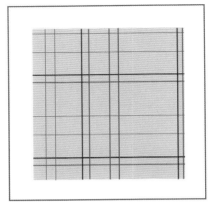

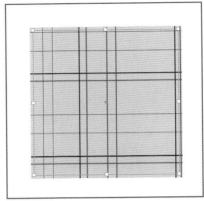

Figure 13.40   Rectangle with the
            guides hidden.

Figure 13.41   Rectangle placed inside
            the plaid swatch.

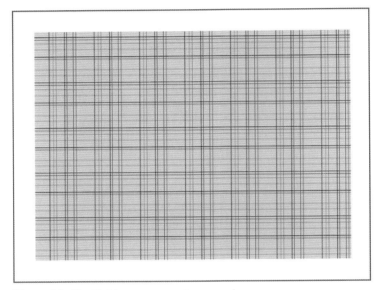

Figure 13.42   Plaid pattern swatch repeated.

from anything that contains
guides (see Figure 13.40).

9. Create another rectangle with
no fill and no stroke (the fill
and stroke should have a red
diagonal line through them).
Drag the rectangle so it is just
inside the plaid swatch. Choose
Object: Arrange: Send to Back
(see Figure 13.41).

10. Choose Select: All and drag the
swatch into the Swatches
palette to create a pattern
swatch.

11. To see what the swatch will
look like in repeat, create
another rectangle and click on
the new plaid pattern swatch. It
should repeat without any
breaks (see Figure 13.42).

Review Questions

1. What is a clipping mask?

2. Describe a way a gradient mesh can be created.

3. Describe how to make a fabric transparent.

4. What are the advantages to creating a vector version of a scanned fabric swatch?

5. Describe how to create a repeat pattern without any breaks (in Illustrator).

Suggested Practice Project

Scan in a fabric swatch and create a vector version of it in Illustrator.

Key Terms

Clipping mask

Gradient mesh

Opacity

Vector

14

Presentation Is Everything: Successful Resumes, Interviews, and Portfolios

What You Will Learn in Chapter 14

This chapter gives an overview of the basic presentation tools necessary for people to communicate their creative skills while seeking work in the fashion industry. The step-by-step analysis of the job market, research preparation for the resume and company interview, and formation of a stylishly successful portfolio clearly help to match a candidate's creativity to the needs of a company. The previous chapters have focused on how to digitally build and present work. However, this chapter focuses on creating a personal ad campaign that summarizes the value of education, past experience, and creative activities, which will lead to an artistically fulfilling position.

Introduction

The basic tools you will use to effectively communicate your skills to large corporations, small companies, or sole designers are the resume, cover letter, portfolio, and your personality. Each tool relies on the others to sell the complete package—you! Applicants who have a beautifully set up resume and cover letter and an impressive portfolio but weak personalities or personal styles will weaken the entire package.

The fashion business is one of those tremendously large industries that also feels tremendously small. In other words, everyone seems to know someone in the industry, be it retail, wholesale, design, or marketing. It is almost a stylish "six degrees of separation." This makes networking all the more important. It is important to create bonds with everyone involved directly and indirectly with the fashion world, preferably from the time you are still in school (be it with professors, fellow students, guest speakers, and internship sponsors) and continually afterward. This building of relationships is a major tool in networking.

Employees in many other industries are unhappy with their jobs due to the rut or boredom that inevitably exists in uncreative or repetitive-task fields. The world of fashion is anything but dull or repetitive. Happiness is doing what you enjoy and getting paid for it. Some of the most prolific fashion editors, photographers, creative directors, stylists, and designers are in their sixties, seventies, and eighties, and still going strong. The greats—Erté, Coco Chanel, Roger Vivier, Tony Duquette, Richard Avedon, and Horst—directly or indirectly worked in the fashion world for a really long time. They definitely were not in a rut.

The Resume—Your Personal Advertisement

When creating your resume, analyze aspects of your current position. Do not simply list your job description. In today's workplace, often every one person does two or more jobs. Tasks we take for granted can become part of a long list of marketable skills, including the ability to multitask!

This is a time for self-analysis. We often underestimate the skills we have. Now is the time to enumerate the following:

- Scholarships, awards, grants, and fellowships
- Professional organizations
- Certificates of training or proficiency
- Civic and community involvement
- Volunteer work
- Fluency in foreign languages
- Typing, operation of business machines, computer skills (including Internet and various software programs)
- Internships
- Study abroad programs or specific study tours
- Outside personal hobbies or interests related to the design field

Transcripts from your college or university may be required. It may take several weeks to get your transcripts, so it is wise to order them as soon as possible; consider ordering four or five official sets of transcripts to have in reserve.

Resume Formats

The two resume formats that are commonly used are the chronological resume and the functional resume. The chronological resume begins with educational information, then details employment history, beginning with the most current (see Figure 14.1a). Figure 14.1b is a chronological resume worksheet to help you create your resume. The functional resume lists information about employment history but by function; there is no time frame followed (see Figure 14.2a). Figure 14.2b is a functional resume worksheet to help you create your resume. The fashion industry tends to prefer the chronological resume.

Be consistent in how you organize your information and the amount of information you give. Also important is grammar (i.e., use present tense for current jobs and past tense for former jobs). As with quality design, the key to creating a quality resume is to make it visually appealing. Liken the singular page of a resume to the three-second rule of first impressions. As superficial as it may sound, people make snap judgments of others very quickly. The first glance at a resume or the first impression a candidate makes at an interview may determine the likelihood of getting the job (see Common Sense Don'ts and Do's in Interviewing later in this chapter).

Quality fashion design equals quality resume design. Quality grooming, clothes, shoes, and accessories on a first interview equal quality paper, pleasing font layout, spacing, and the proper balance, proportion, and harmony of the overall resume page.

Too much jewelry or accessories, too much makeup, and/or too many layers equals too many long sentences or excessive and repetitive terminology. Poor-quality knockoffs or counterfeit logos equals exaggeration or overly boastful content. Chipped nail polish and bad shoes equal too many (or any!) misused or misspelled words (see Common Sense Don'ts and Do's in Interviewing later in this chapter). As with clothing design, your resume and appearance on your interviews should be crisp, clean, and sharp. Remember the elements of clothing design (see Chapter 3) and apply them to your resume. They are as follows:

Silhouette—this refers to the overall outline of the resume. Visual weight on the page should have a visible boundary or ratio of white space to typeface.

Color—paper should be white, ivory, or light gray. Don't try to express creativity by using bold paper colors; what's in the resume should express creativity.

Texture—weight of paper, envelope, CD jacket, and other such items should all be of high quality

Details—less is more in resume formation. There should be no clip art or overbearing borders. Subtly using a bold or italic font against the standard is enough to set content apart.

The following principles of design apply as well:

Balance—keep the visual weight balanced throughout the resume.

Emphasis—key titles, including employment history, education, references, and so on should be set in bold or italic type and properly spaced before and after each category.

Ellen Clair
111 Any Street
Los Angeles, CA 00000
310-111-0000
name@email.com

Objective	Seeking a freelance position at a growing knitwear design company where I can utilize my sketching, illustration, and computer skills.
Educational Background	**Cleveland Institute of Design** December 1996 Bachelor of Fine Arts: Fashion design Graphic arts minor
Employment History	**Johanna Knits** Los Angeles, CA 2001 to Present Chief Designer [Helen Savi, VP] • Women's Bridge Collection
	LisaLisa Couture Pittsburgh, PA 1998 to 2001 Freelance Illustrator [Lisa Mark, owner] • Preliminary sketches, technical flats, and presentation board illustrations
	Margaret Christina Pittsburgh, PA 1997 to 1998 Assistant Activewear Designer [Ed Frank, VP] • Fabric sourcing • Inspiration board development
Special Skills	Fluent in French, working knowledge of German Mac literate: Photoshop, Illustrator PC literate: Microsoft Office Suite Highly skilled in figure drawing
Memberships	Fashion Group International (Los Angeles) California Fashion Association (CFA) Textile Association of Los Angeles (TALA) International Textile and Apparel Association (ITAA)
References	Available upon request

Figure 14.1a   Chronological resume.

Name
Address
City, State, Zip
Phone/Cell Phone
E-mail Address

Objective	(optional)

Educational Background   **Current university/college** Graduation date
Degree/major/field of study   (or dates attending)

Employment History

Current Company	Location	Date to Present
Position Title	[Contact Name]	
Duties:		

Previous Company	Location	Date to date
Position Title	[Contact Name]	
Duties:		

Previous Company	Location	Date to date
Position Title	[Contact Name]	
Duties:		

Special Skills
Fluent/conversational language?
Computer literacy in Mac/PC?
Software competency lists?
Organizational/team skills?

Memberships
Professional organizations?
Conferences attended?
Activities pertinent to position?

References
Available upon request

Figure 14.1b   Chronological resume worksheet.

Robin Palmer
1956 Any Street
Wayne, New Jersey 00088
888-999-0000
name@email.com

Objective	To obtain a Summer 2006 internship
Skills Summary	**Design Technology and Construction**
	• Computer expertise in Photoshop/Illustrator
	• Proficiency in computer-generated flats presentations
	• Inspiration and trend board for client presentations
	• Freelance swimwear/boardsport sketch artist/ illustrator
	• Proficiency in pattern drafting/draping
Education	**American Fashion University** (New York, NY)
	Bachelor of Arts: Fashion Design 2005
Professional Memberships	Fashion Group International (FGI) New York Chapter
Honors	Rosenberg Scholarship: Outstanding in Design, 2004
	Textile Association, first place, 2003
	Fashion Journalism Award, 2001/2002
Employment History	**Lakeland Design Group** Erie, NY 2003 to Present
	Design Room Computer Tech [Director: Mary Ann Warren]
	• Scan fabrics, trims, rough sketches for review
	• Create digital inspiration and trend boards
	• Oversee computer lab for in-house designers
	George of the Jungle Surf Carmel, NJ 2001 to 2003
	Freelance designer [Owner: George Palmer]
	• Young men's and junior girls' line surf separates
	• Inspiration boards for advertising collateral
	• Logo-development for private labels
References	Available upon request

Figure 14.2a   Functional resume.

Name
Address
City, State, Zip
Phone/Cell Phone
E-mail Address

Objective   (optional)

Education   **College/university**
                            Degree achieved   Date
                            Major

Skills Summary   **Skill sets**
                            Bullet-point detail of skill
                            Bullet-point detail of skill
                            Bullet-point detail of skill

Professional   **Group Affiliation**
Memberships   **Group Affiliation**

Honors   **Scholarship**
                            Award
                            Award

Employment   **Current Company**   Location   Date to Present
History   Position title   [Contact Name]
                            Duties:

                            Previous Company Location   Date to date
                            Position title   [Contact Name]
                            Duties:

References   Available upon request

Figure 14.2b   Functional resume worksheet.

Harmony—boldface and nonbold standard fonts work well with the spacing of categories throughout the page.

Proportion—focus on the lead heading, where your name goes, and the body, where your employment and educational history go.

Radiation—the energy or focus of the resume should stem from the heading (your name and contact info) to each category in order of importance (see resume formats on page 358).

Repetition—be consistent with title formats and sections and the amount and type of information listed.

The resume reviewers, interviewers, and employers all agree with the following:

> If you can't get ONE sheet of paper about YOURSELF spelled correctly, ONE sheet clean, with proper layout, etc. . . . or if you cannot spend a little more time to appear well-groomed head to toe for ONE appointment, what are the chances you will be an asset to our firm not only for ONE day, but also EVERY day?

The resume should be an introduction to *who* the applicant is, *what* the applicant's skills and career objectives are, *when* the knowledge and experience was developed, *where* the applicant has worked and gone to school, and *why* the applicant would be an asset to the company.

Who Should Receive the Resume

There are three sources that lead to job referrals.

- People you know
- People who are recommended as potential employers by those you know
- People who make the actual job offers

The often-used phrase "it's who you know" is used for good reason. Each person who you interact with, from people you meet while you're still at school through people you meet at work, provides an instrument for enlarging the pool of career resources.

Types of Resumes

Resumes bring designers' talents to the forefront. Think of skill sets as facets of a multifaceted diamond. Each may be of different size and reflective strength, but all are valuable. The same is true of the intent of the applicant. The resume is worded differently depending on intent. Is the applicant looking for an **internship** position, an **entry-level** position, a career change with **new skills**, a **proposed** position, or a **freelance** position?

The basic types of resumes and their definitions are as follows:

Intern: focuses on the direction of education, then lists employment history.

Entry-level: focuses on education completed, which is then validated by employment and intern experience.

New skills: focuses on the current skills necessary for new positions in the industry, with other achievements reinforcing credibility and experience.

Proposed position: focuses on blending current skills, prior work experience, knowledge of consumer needs, and filling the niche without being critical of the assumed lack of this position.

Freelance: focuses on varied client base and creative niche fulfilled for each.

The Reference Sheet

References are never printed on the primary resume, but assembled on one sheet with the corresponding contact information. Under the "References" section of the resume, it is standard to type "Available upon request" (see Figure 14.1a). Remember that a resume may be circulated to hundreds of establishments via the Internet, and no one offering to be a reference wants their personal information circulated. On a separate sheet that has your name, address, city, state, zip, phone numbers, and e-mail address centered as the heading, list your references beneath the title heading "References." Each reference name should include the person's title, address, phone, and e-mail information (see Figures 14.3a and b).

List three solid references from various aspects of your educational, professional, and personal life. A mentor during college, an employment supervisor, and a personal reference from any volunteer group or membership makes for a well-rounded list. If a personal reference is not available (and don't substitute with a family member!), include another employment supervisor or educator. Remember to contact each person for permission, as well as to retrieve the most direct method of contact. An employer will question references listed with ineffective contact information and delay the processing of hiring.

Common Sense Don'ts and Do's in Developing the Resume

- *Don't bring or send out a resume with typos or grammatical errors!* Check, recheck, then have two others read for content and errors.
- *Don't use unreadable fonts or too many fonts.* Clarity in the content and readability are crucial. Use one font and vary with bold or italics to emphasize headings or other points. Many nontraditional fonts cannot be read when sent by electronic methods.
- *Don't use paragraphs—use bullet points.* People review resumes quickly. Blocks of information will get passed over.
- *Don't forget dates or company information.* Omitting facts only draws attention to the lack of information.
- *Don't vary the depth of information for each category.* Be consistent throughout. Giving too much information in one section and not enough in the others lowers overall effectiveness.

The Cover, Application, Prospecting, and Networking Letters

Written communication may be the first impression a prospective employer has in the entire interview selection process. It may make or break the chances of future face-to-face communication. The letter must convey enough of your personality to stand out among a sea of hopeful applicants. As with face-to-face communication, what is conveyed should be clear, pleasant, and understandable.

Lauren Scott
930 Any Street
Malibu, California 90265
310-210-5111
name@email.com

REFERENCES

Reference name	**Troy Crumley**
Title	Creative Director
Company name	MoKat Activewear
Address	123 LaGrange
City, state, zip	Los Angeles, California 90000
Phone	310-991-0000
E-mail	Tbenjamin@fashionfocus.com

Reference name	**E. Marie Haffner, Ph.D.**
Title	Fashion Department Chair
Company name	Skahan University
Address	1222 Vine Street
City, state, zip	Eastlake, California 90000
Phone	213-111-2222
E-mail	Haffner_EM@youruniv.edu

Reference name	**Bailey Brandt**
Title	Owner and Designer
Company name	Chopper Couture
Address	10 Montana Avenue
City, state, zip	Santa Monica, CA 90000
Phone	310-999-9999
E-mail	baileychopper@choppercouture.com

Figure 14.3a   Reference list.

Name
Address
City, State, Zip
Phone/Cell Phone
E-mail Address

REFERENCES

Reference name
Title
Company name
Address
City, state, zip
Phone
E-mail

Reference name
Title
Company name
Address
City, state, zip
Phone
E-mail

Reference name
Title
Company name
Address
City, state, zip
Phone
E-mail

Figure 14.3b   Reference list worksheet.

Cover Letter

Each letter sends a specific message that hopefully propels a positive relationship with each employer, be it a job match or a respectful resignation. As important as first impressions are, it is interesting to note that a well-written letter creates quite an impression of its own in an interviewer's mind. There are seven letters that can be used alternatively through the job search process. The first three are sent before the actual interview, and the last four may be sent after the interview. The preinterview letters include the application cover letter, the prospecting cover letter, and the networking cover letter.

Application Cover Letter

The goal of the application cover letter is to get the attached resume read and to generate interest in setting up an interview with the appropriate personnel. This letter is sent in direct response to a specific job advertisement. The letter must match the applicant's qualifications with the posted job requirements (see Figure 14.4).

Prospecting Cover Letter

The goal of the prospecting cover letter is to get the attached resume read and to generate interest in setting up an interview as well, but with this letter, applicants apply for possible vacancies in a company that hasn't posted an available opening. The content focuses on the applicant's capabilities and adaptable skills in hopes of matching them with a possible vacancy (see Figure 14.5).

Networking Letter

This letter is designed to generate an informational conversation rather than a job interview. Meetings generated with individuals who can give specific facts about the industry are a viable way to conduct job market research, refine career goals, and discover vacancy information (see Figure 14.6).

Tailoring the Cover Letter

Tailor the resume's cover letter to follow the three steps below; each should be in paragraph form as follows:

A—Introduce yourself and identify the position for which you are applying.
B—Reiterate how you will be a great asset to the company.
C—Thank them for taking the time to review your resume and for considering scheduling an interview.

The cover letter, whether it's application or prospecting, should reflect the intent of the resume (internship, entry-level, new skills, position proposal, or freelance).

Who: Research the Company

Knowledge is power. Knowing everything about the company before sitting for an interview allows for utmost preparedness, be it in the resume, cover letter, interview phase, or in the content of the portfolio presentation. You should tailor your resumes to present skills that are especially attractive to particular companies and cover letters to do so more specifically. Avoid awkward interview silence by being ready to discuss the company's history or latest acquisition. This lets the interviewer know that you've done your homework.

The importance of knowing *who* you are interviewing with is vital to the content of your portfolio. If the company's image and product is targeted to the teen to mid-twenties female (Hot Topic), teen to thirties female (Gap), or 40-plus-year-old baby boomers (Chico's), present design ideas appropriate for those consumer groups. Researching a company's current and future plans may warrant including a plus-size young woman's line for Hot Topic (Torrid), or designing for the 35-plus age group at The Gap. Keeping these target markets and size ranges in mind when presenting your portfolio clarifies what you can do for the company (see Chapter 3 for target groups and sizing).

Step-by-Step Overview to Company Research

The best strategy to gather information on a company is to begin by "playing the consumer." The clothing company or retailer may run print consumer advertisements with a toll-free number to call or a Web site to visit. E-mail the company, requesting any background history if there is no information on the Web site.

The Internet search engines, including google.com, yahoo.com, askjeeves.com, lycos.com, or altavista.com, sometimes provide additional information on companies, but many sites may not be reliable since authors can editorialize the facts accordingly. Knowing who wrote the page, who can be contacted, who published the document, when was it produced and updated with links, and how objective the information is becomes invaluable to ensure viability. Librarians use www.lii.org (Librarians' Index to the Internet) to view valid organized sites.

Visit the public or college/university libraries to utilize databases including Hoovers.com, EbscoHost

MasterFile Premiere, FIS Online, and other proprietary databases available to search for company information. These databases retrieve the most current updates.

Reference directories provide another source for ownership information and detailed facts possibly not covered in fashion trades. These include the following:

- *Brands and Their Companies* (Gale Group Research Co.)
- *Hoover's Handbook of American Businesses* (Hoover's Inc.)
- *Directory of Corporate Affiliations* (National Register Publishing Co.)
- *Directory of Leading Private Companies* (National Register Publishing Co.)
- *Million Dollar Directory* (Dun's Marketing Services)
- *Reference Book of Corporate Management* (Dun's Marketing Service)
- *Standard & Poor's Register of Corporations, Directors, and Executives* (Standard & Poor's Corp.)
- *Thomas Register* (Thomas Register)
- *Ward's Business Directory* (Gale Research Inc.)
- *Who's Who in Finance and Industry*

Keep up on the current trade publications for the industry, such as clothing (*Women's Wear Daily, DNR, The Apparel News*) and interior design/lifestyle merchandising (*HFN*), especially several weeks before the interview for up-to-the-minute knowledge of what is happening. This, along with knowing the company's own history, allows you to gain confidence in the interview. It also provides an overview of the company's competition.

1448 East Harland
Timberlake, NY 22111

July 20, 2006

Joan Robinson
Director of Personnel
B & B Trend Inc.
222 Avenue H
New York, NY 22000

Dear Ms. Robinson:

I am responding to your recent advertisement for the assistant visual coordinator in the July 19 issue of *Women's Wear Daily*. The position seems to fit very well with my education, experience, and career interests.

Your position requires skills in various types of visual presentation, including flat sketching, Photoshop, and Illustrator. I have extensive experience in all, as well as After Effects and Dreamweaver. My experience as a freelance design consultant has given me exposure to both PC and Mac platforms. Additionally, I have worked as a summer intern for B&P Associates Buying Office. My enclosed resume provides more details of my qualifications.

My background and career goals seem to match your job requirements, and I am genuinely interested in the position and in working for B & B Trend Inc. Your company has an excellent reputation and comes highly recommended to me.

I would very much like the opportunity to interview with you so we can further discuss my qualifications and so I can learn more about this opportunity.

Thank you in advance for your consideration. I look forward to meeting with you.

Sincerely,

Lisa S. Malacky

Figure 14.4   Application cover letter.

55 Any Street
Pacific Palisades, CA 90000

April 13, 2006

Ms. Michelle Scott
Director of Fashion PR
MalibuMainLine Corp.
444 Pacific Coast Highway
Malibu, CA 90001

Dear Ms. Scott:

I read *Pacific Style*'s article highlighting your company in the April 2005 issue and would like to inquire about either part-time or full-time employment opportunities in your Malibu office.

I shall receive my B.A. in fashion design this May. My interest is fashion started in high school and developed further through a variety of retail and visual merchandising positions during college. My internship with Marks & Co. convinced me to pursue a career in fashion advertising and visual merchandising. My classes in Photoshop, Illustrator, and Virtual Store Design has made me very comfortable with working with marketing collateral.

My resume is enclosed for your consideration. My education and experience match the qualifications that would hopefully make me a very necessary addition to your office.

I know how busy you must be during this time of year, but I would appreciate a few minutes of your time. I will call your office the first week in May to discuss employment possibilities. If you need to contact me beforehand, I can be reached at 310-333-3333. My e-mail address is blublack@mindspring.com.

Thank you so much for considering my request. I look forward to talking with you soon.

Sincerely,

Ana D. Kirk

Figure 14.5   Prospecting cover letter.

130 Any Street #H
New York, NY 20002

October 24, 2005

Mr. Hugh Gregg
Surfworld Apparel Group
3311 Bob Lane
New York, NY 20000

Dear Mr. Gregg:

Bob Fields, controller for Wave Inc., suggested that I contact you. He thought that you would be very helpful in coordinating an interview with the chief designer, Ned Hareld, and design room manager Joanne Brian.

I am a freelance designer specializing in surfwear for men, women, and kids. I am able to come in and address any needs in the design room and work either on- or off-site. Mr. Fields mentioned that someone with my qualifications and flexibility would definitely be an asset to your company's impending growth. Bubba & Sweet Pea Surfwear's design director, Chris Addy, also suggested we join forces.

I shall call you next week to see if we can arrange a brief meeting at your convenience. Thank you for considering my request.

Sincerely,

Ramona Katt

Figure 14.6 Networking letter.

Once enough information has been accrued, organize the facts into the following basics:

- How old the company is
- Whether it is privately or publicly owned
- What their company reputation is
- What they create
- Who their target markets are
- Who their competitors are
- Their locations
- Their future plans

Many people do not realize that The Gap, Inc. owns Old Navy and Banana Republic as well or that The Limited Corporation owns Victoria's Secret and Bath & Body Works. When interviewing for a fashion position, you are not solely a member of the shopping public but also a fashion specialist who has overall knowledge of prestigious, moderate, and promotional priced brands and/or retailers, all in the scope of competition.

Salary

After reviewing a company's background (both structurally and financially), questions about its future and salary may arise. Web sites that include www.Monster-Board.com and www.CareerBuilder.com have salary calculators for job titles. They include other valuable information as well. Reviewing these categories may open up new possibilities as well as broaden negotiation skills.

The question of how to indicate salary history and/or requirements often appears since many companies do request salary history. A practical way to communicate this private information, if it is requested, is in the cover letter. Ranges of salary, stated annually, are the most effective, such as "previous and current positions ranged from $38,000 to $44,000."

The Portfolio

The portfolio is a visual summation of your creative, design, and organizational skills and should be arranged as creatively as its contents. It can be presented as a story of your career or a categorization or series of skills. Versatility needs to be clearly shown to succeed in an industry where new merchandising concepts and consumer targets are added to the already fast-paced seasonal lines. The amount of creative freedom in the world of fashion allows for an amazing network of career options (designing, styling, wardrobing, visual merchandising, public relations, event planners, Web design, and more) and lateral promotions. A designer may end up working in any of these positions.

This flexibility should be reflected in the designer's portfolio. If your specialty is junior or contemporary sportswear, make sure to showcase that, but also include experience with missy, plus-size, and petite. This shows versatility and capacity to be an all-around addition to a company.

"Lifestyle merchandising" has been the buzz phrase of the nineties and has grown in popularity ever since. The millennium has proven that many major fashion companies have successfully merged interiors with lifestyle product development possibilities. Setting illustrations with time periods or themes that can be encapsulated with a visual image in the background setting—a mid-century modern wallpaper

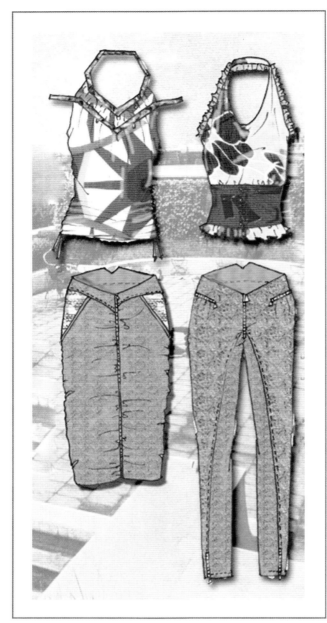

Figure 14.7   Junior sportswear group of flats.

with separates and perhaps partner a female or child in the mix. Applicants should "wow" potential employers with their creative abilities while not leaving the impression that these skills cannot be translated into other product areas. The following inventory lists the basic contents of a fashion designer's portfolio.

Inventory

Include two full-color figure renderings/illustrations of the following designs:

- designer sportswear
- junior dresses
- cocktail/after-five
- menswear

Include samples of any two or more specialty areas that are not detailed as strongly in your resume as follows:

- your senior collection (how John Galliano and Stella McCartney were discovered)
- costume design (theatrical or cinematic showcasing)
- bridal (wedding, bridal party, mother-of-the-bride)
- accessories (shoes, handbags, jewelry suites)
- children's wear
- formal evening
- plus-size
- maternity
- pet couture

It is vital that you show design groups to reinforce your skills in design and line-building as well. The key to successful design is the ability to merchandise jackets, pants, tops, skirts, and so on for multiple sales. The skills of presenting these in Photoshop and Illustrator further market your value (see Figure 14.7).

print or lamp—suggests awareness of the interplay among interior design, graphic design, and the fashion industry.

Portfolio Contents: What to Include

A designer, as a creative professional, is a multifaceted individual. The trick is to show every facet without blurring the importance of each. Samplings of personal strengths/skills—be it in product development, a specialty area of clothing design, illustration, or textile design—should clearly stand as viable skills that the interviewer can translate into company benefits. The key is to effectively promote your design and illustration skills in effective ways, perhaps as mock-up ads for specialty stores or boutiques. Show a style or two as a promotional piece for a special event, trunk show, or charity function.

If your specialization is menswear, include activewear, formalwear,

Figure 14.8 Computer-generated flats.

Design groups detailed in technical flat presentation form clearly show a designer's steady hand and attention to detail. Other groups shown in computer-generated flats in alternative categories present a designer's skills in textile colorways and print variations, scanned photo background interest, as well as the obvious mastering of the computer's capacity (see Figure 14.8).

Figure 14.9a   Roberto Cavalli eveningwear.

Figure 14.9b   Roberto Cavalli eveningwear.

The display of computer mastery is vital, but it must be remembered that the computer is merely a tool. Do not forsake the cultivated skills and painterly techniques created with marker, pen-and-ink, and charcoal (see Figure 14.9a and b).

Digital Portfolio

The digital portfolio is the newest way to present your design work, as well as highlighting that you have entered the twenty-first century in technology. The convenient CD size is easy to duplicate and transport, and you can leave the CD with the interviewers for further review. The introductory page of the digital portfolio is similar to the splash

Figure 14.10   Promotional splash page using Adobe Photoshop for self-promotional digital portfolio Web site.

page—the introductory page of a Web site (see Figure 14.10).

The CD jacket, possibly customized with your name and favored design illustration, may also lend itself to reinforcing skills in branding and packaging. It can be the splash page design as well. The CD label is yet another place to showcase your knowledge of the importance of branding and continuity of design communication (see Figure 14.11).

Figure 14.11   Personalized self-promotional CD-ROM label.

The digital portfolio may include pieces of work that can't be conveniently included in a portfolio due to various size ranges, weight, or the wear-and-tear that would generate an ungainly presentation. The same rules of quality control still exist as with the physical portfolio: Quality is the rule, not quantity. The digital portfolio does indeed afford a bit more quantity, if desired, but more important, it demonstrates the technological skills of scanning artwork and burning compact discs. These two new verbs are now added to the traditional vocabulary of the fashion designer!

e-Portfolio: The PDF File

The latest permutation of presenting your design work with the least amount of technical breakdown is the e-Portfolio. The PDF file can be e-mailed immediately, printed out as a booklet, or printed out in a larger format for the actual interview appointment. One important benefit of the e-Portfolio over the CD portfolio is the assurance that all receivers can actually open the portfolio. Some companies may not be able to open a CD-ROM or may have trouble navigating through it. The initial reviewer may not have the latest Mac or PC.

This e-Portfolio can be scaled to two or three teaser PDF pages that are attached to the resume. This speeds the process immensely and places your resume/PDF sample at the top of the list. Time is on your side. The time it takes for an interviewer to open a link to a URL is avoided. There is just the simple click of opening another attachment while having just read—and been impressed by— the resume.

This time-saving tactic is especially effective when dealing with freelance needs. When a design company requires a freelancer, they usually need that person immediately. If your portfolio book is being reviewed by another firm, you can e-mail your e-Portfolio in its place. The company can see your work immediately and, even if it doesn't exactly fit its current requirements, the company representatives can keep the first two pages or so for future reference.

Think of the cover of an e-Portfolio as a personal collage—as if you are being introduced to the inteviewer. It should reflect your style, whether bohemian, corporate, hip-hop or postmodern. The title page, and the twelve to fifteen pages thereafter, are the $11" \times 8\frac{1}{2}"$ horizontal screen shots that highlight your talents. Each page should flow into the next. Each click should lead the viewer to see and appreciate your versatility, so avoid disjointed images of work, as this only leads to confusion and lack of consistency.

If the real estate world's mantra is "location, location, location," the professional opinion of portfolio reviewers is "editing, editing, editing." The industry looks not at the size of the portfolio but the scope of creativity. Here is where the "less is more" concept prevails; each piece should speak for itself.

The Personal Web Site

What better way to express your well-rounded embracing of current technology than a personal Web site? Potential employers will realize the full scope of your developed skills if they can check your work on your own Web site. This step is an important self-promotional tool for designers who are seeking freelance jobs as well. A step-by-step guide to creating a personal Web site (splash page and home page), as well as signing up and uploading with a Web host, is included at the end of this chapter.

PowerPoint Presentation

The benefits and versatility of Microsoft PowerPoint are endless. The program has made the task of lugging pounds of sketches or carousels of slides unnecessary and archaic. Every visual sample can be scanned into a PowerPoint presentation with the added organizational element of titling and categorizing sections of work. If a candidate is a bit tense (as is understandable in any interview situation), it is easy to forget some aspect of a presentation. PowerPoint provides an ethical cheat sheet of cues to help recall what is important in each piece of artwork, design project, and so on. The smooth transitions constantly draw attention to all of a candidate's talents. The simple pressing of a button advances a presentation smoothly. The capacity of setting the length of the presentation allows for everything to fit in on schedule, avoiding a slow start with a rushed end.

Everything from a photograph (or collage of photographs) to actual artwork can be scanned into a PowerPoint presentation. Inspiration boards accompanying design groups present a complete story from concept to completion. If it can be scanned into the computer, it can be included (see Figure 14.12). This is a wonderful tool that completely explains the elements of inspiration when presenting design group categories or trend forecast messages to the interview committee.

PowerPoint presentations may also include candid site location photographs of the applicant in the design room, at the drafting table, at the computer, or draping on a dress form at previous firms. This technique personalizes the collection of visuals and validates the hands-on experience.

Figure 14.12   Inspiration board by Sarah Kim, AIU fashion student.

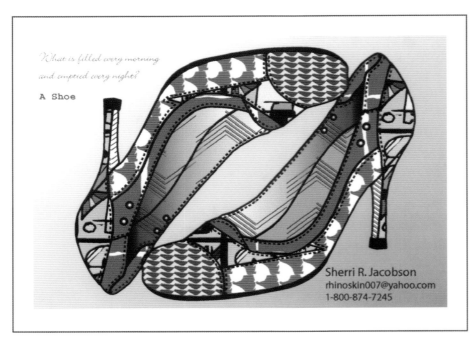

What is filled every morning
and emptied every night?

A Shoe

Sherri R. Jacobson
rhinoskin007@yahoo.com
1-800-874-7245

Figure 14.13   The leave-behind shoe card created in Adobe Illustrator by Sherri Jacobsen.

The Leave-Behind

The leave-behind is a brochure designed to remind the interviewer of your skills, creativity, and pertinent communication data. It is similar to your personal advertisement that is left behind after the interview—hence the term **leave-behind**. The portfolio, thus far, is the only tangible evidence of education and design skills previously noted only in narrative form on your resume and orally presented in the interview. Unless you have left behind your portfolio, there are no tangible samples of personal work while more and more portfolios are being reviewed. Even though a strong impression is made, remember that many applicants before and after may also be making strong impressions. Names and design styles get shuffled in the employer's memory, so the way to really keep your name and style fresh on everyone's mind is to leave behind a sample of work (see Figure 14.13).

The leave-behind can vary in size from a single-fold postcard size to a two-fold brochure. It should be a scaled-down version of your portfolio. Select one or two choice pieces, mindful to include the scope of your talents. This is a personal advertisement, so your name and contact information should be the headline.

Common Sense Don'ts and Do's in Portfolio Presentations

The process of putting your portfolio together will be much more efficient if certain mistakes are avoided.

- *Do not include everything you have ever designed.*
  This is not a diary of all your creative ventures or a trip down fashion history lane, but a tight, slick array of skills: versatility and current design, illustrating, and editing abilities. Reviewers don't want to review spring 1999 when they are thinking spring 2009.
- *Do not date your work.*
  Dating designs limits their ability to be used in your portfolio for a long time. It also prejudices the reviewer into not thinking future but past.
- *Do not use a well-worn, over-stuffed, or off-scale portfolio case.*
  The phrase "you can't judge a book by its cover" does not apply here. People can and do. The packaging of your skills is the second "first" impression you make after the first interview and resume. The enthusiasm to review the portfolio will be brought down a notch or two if you don't have a clean, well-structured case. A portfolio larger than your arm span is also a no-no.
- *Do not use the portfolio as an exclusive platform for your dream collections.*

Remember that you are interviewing for a position in a design business. Businesses have target consumers who purchase items, bringing profit to that business. The design groups should be geared to actual consumer markets, and the job entails designing specifically for consumer markets—hopefully theirs!

- *Do not mix quality or detail of presentation.*
  Consistency is key. An introductory page turned to four to six major themes that can relate to a whole collection shows that you can edit your work, present cohesive concepts, and show knowledge of fabrication, colorways, and trend awareness.
- *Do not forget one is visually telling a story.*
  The portfolio is not only a visual story of one's skills but also the story of your design concept development. Include a theme or inspiration page, fabrication and colorways, a sample of technical flats, freehand flat sketching, a spec sheet, and full illustrations.
- *Do not mix your fashion sketchbook or design journal in the formal portfolio.*
  The design journal, although an important supplement, is a separate entity when dealing with a portfolio presentation. It can be presented afterward as a reinforcement of across-the-board creativity and the ability to sketch from various sources of inspiration, but distracts the focus if presented within the formal portfolio.
- *Do not lay out work vertically, horizontally, and diagonally.*
  Remember you are presenting work to someone who is either sitting next to or across from the table. As each page is turned, each should be viewable from the same reference point without having to turn the portfolio 180 degrees for every other page.
- *Do not hand-label sections or elements in the portfolio.*
  Unless you are applying as a calligrapher, use computer-generated print or press-on letters.
- *Do not have an entire portfolio filled with rigid, identically formed figures.*
  Vary the format of the figures, with full-figure, three-quarter, overlapping, and interacting body parts and angles, various postures, and figure types.
- *Do not arrange work from weakest to strongest in content.*
  The sequence of the "wow" factor cannot rely on a mild or weak start and still ensure interest all the way to the supposedly strong close. Think dramatic impact first, a strong middle, and the big finish. Or "wow" with a major opener and major closer, also known as "get them comin' and goin'."
- *Do not forget to have others review your portfolio for clarity and consistency.*
  Use the same criteria as you do for your resume. Have other people lend their fresh eyes in evaluating the overall quality of the presentation. You may not see your own mistakes or editing problems.

The Interview

The company research is done, the resume is set, the cover letter is perfect, and the portfolio is zipped and ready for show. Now you are ready for the interview! Much of the following list may seem like common sense, but a quick review will prove that there may be one or two things overlooked before or during the interview. Better to be safe than sorry.

Common Sense Don'ts and Do's in Interviewing

- *Do not be late!*
  If you are, they will suspect you will continue to do the same if you get the job. Plan ahead and figure out the route by car or public transportation to ensure you arrive fifteen minutes early.
- *Do not chew gum or mints!*
  It is distracting and unprofessional. Eat beforehand to avoid stomach growls but don't leave any hints of what you ate on your teeth.
- *Do not smoke beforehand.*
  Breath and smell of smoke on clothing is a turnoff. Feel free to pop a mint in to freshen your breath, but remove it before the interview.
- *Do not have a hairstyle that invites fiddling, rearranging, or shaking!*
  Think stylish yet comfortable. Rock star hair doesn't spell professional unless you are applying for a rock star position.
- *Do not have dirty or unsightly fingernails or hands!*
  Nothing is more off-putting than chipped polish or dirt under the nails. Invest in a manicure. It may be the best few dollars you ever spent.
- *Do not be unaware of your personal conditions!*
  If you have dandruff or a tendency to shed, wear textures that camouflage, or brush off your shoulders before the interview! If you have allergies that act up in air-conditioned areas, have a tissue for your drippy nose. Women who have to go on an interview while they are menstruating should wear dark skirts or pants. This is no time to break out the white trousers as part of the interview outfit.
- *Do not dress to overimpress!*
  Excessive jewelry and distracting accessories only spell poor taste and a lack of fashion awareness.
- *Do not wear clothing that does not sit, stand, or bend well!*
  Your uncomfortable writhing will be noticed during the interview, and an unkempt appearance shows poor choice in wardrobe.
- *Do not wear clothing that spells disaster if a bathroom visit is needed!*
  Having to safety pin your skirt, or having to deal with intricate reknotting, refluffing, or rewrapping spells disaster.
- *Do not carry multiple or oversize bags, briefcases, or portfolios!*
  Travel light with a practical portfolio case and resume file/briefcase-style bag if possible. You are not moving in.
- *Have a friend perform the three-second once-over!*
  The quick head-to-toe wardrobe review is mandatory. Remove whatever is distracting. Check the quality of what you have on. Although the idea of looking at a person's shoes and accessories to judge their professionalism and aesthetic design choices may sound elitist to some, it is a reality. Quality, freshness, clean lines, and appropriateness are what you want to strive toward. Fashion is a creative industry as well as a business. Business attire with creative touches shows respect for the interview process while sending out a stylish message.
- *Do not forget the basics: three copies of resume, Social Security card, pen, a sample application with correct addresses and phone numbers of previous employers, and a list of references with contact numbers.*

Having these items at your disposal will create a stress-free encounter and allow all forms to be filled out correctly.

- *Do not speak in a low or mumbled voice!*
  Speak distinctly. Your responses are not a secret.
- *Do not give grim "yes" or "no" answers as if you were on trial!*
  Show confidence. The interview is a tool to gain insight into your personality, competency level, and professional demeanor.
- *Do not brag!*
  The resume, portfolio, and personality should speak for themselves.
- *Do not be overly self-deprecating, joking, or sarcastic for attention!*
  Natural wit is welcome in the dialogue, but there is no need for a stand-up comic routine.
- *Do not check your watch during the interview!*
  Be calm and collected. Got somewhere else to be? Counting the harrowing minutes does not instill confidence.
- *Do not run the show!*
  Remember that you are the one being interviewed. Hogging the conversation will only alienate the interviewer
- *Do not interrupt the interviewer!*
  Pace yourself in the conversation. Dialogue means two people are communicating. Everyone will get a turn to speak.
- *Do not denigrate or bad-mouth the last (or current) employer!*
  There are two sides to every story. The interview is about how you will be an asset to the company.
- *Don't mention salary until the interviewer brings up the subject!*
  It is impolite and rushes the flow of the interview process.
- *Don't ask immediately if you will get the job!*

Again, it won't be a secret. The interviewer may not be the actual person who makes the offer. Be patient.
- *Don't lie.*
  Not on the resume, not during the interview, not ever!

Interview questions

Interview questions vary according to the type of company, prior relationship (if any) with the interviewer, and time frame allotted to fill the position. As reviewed in the previous types of job sourcing—prospecting a position, answering a job ad, or proposing a position—the conversation may lean in various directions. The following questions are generally asked in the interview conversation:

- *Tell me about yourself.*
  This is a bit of an icebreaker. This question involves a topic you should be familiar with . . . yourself!
- *Why do you want to work with us?*
  This is the time to be thankful that you researched the company. You should and will be able to include specifics regarding what you like about the company's structure, designs, and retail strategy.
- *What are you looking forward to accomplishing in this position?*
  This is the chance to talk of your talents and how you would be an asset to the company, without bragging but in a confident way.
- *Are you a good manager? Team player? Do you work well alone?*
  This question allows the interviewer to assess your attitude in regards to working alone and with others, as well as whatever long-range positions may be in line in the company structure.

- *Tell me of some of your accomplishments at your former positions.*
  The interviewer is perhaps scanning through your resume and desires to get some feedback on the various positions you've held. This may be a time to elaborate on skills that are not so clearly explained in the resume.
- *What important trends do you see coming in our industry?*
  The interviewer wants to see your grasp of the big picture and what direction you see this company going toward future growth and success.
- *How would you define an ideal working environment?*
  This broad question lends a view into personality type, how you like to interact with others, and so on. It also allows the interviewer to measure your hopes or presumptions against the actualities of the available position.
- *Why are you leaving your present job? Why did you leave your past job?*
  This is a way for the interviewer to gain insight into how you ethically make a transition from one position to another.
- *What were some of your accomplishments most recently in your present (or past) position?*
  This gives you a chance to narrate some accomplishments that were personally fulfilling and perhaps not so clearly defined in the resume.
- *Can you work under pressure and meet deadlines, or does this affect your creativity?*
  It is best to be honest. Creativity is organic, but discipline is also a part of a professional designer's work plan.
- *What are your long-range goals?*
  Use common sense with this question. If your goal is to open your own design firm, do not state this at the interview. They are not in the business of training their competition.
- *How would you define success?*
  The answer to this question will say a lot about you—things that perhaps were missed in other interview questions.

Don'ts and Do's of Asking Questions During the Interview

The interview is a dialogue. Two people will be communicating. It surrounds the visual presentation of your design skills. While the portfolio should visually "wow" potential employers, the interview gives them insight into your ability to mold those visual skills into their work culture. Avoiding the following questions will allow for positive interaction and feedback. Not avoiding them ensures that the interview will be the last conversation you will have with someone at the company.

- *What exactly does your company do?*
  This will be your last question at that company! It shows disrespect of the interviewer's time, among too many negative messages to mention.
  Do ask:
  Is the company considering entering new markets in the future?
- *Can you guarantee that I will have this job a year from now?*
  You aren't even hired so you can't expect guarantees that no one already working there even has!
  Do ask:
  What are the opportunities for advancement? or What are the plans for future growth and expansion with the company?

- *Does this job really entail weekend work, as mentioned in the ad?*
  If it was mentioned in the ad, it is a part of the work conditions. Questioning the topic makes it seem that you want to avoid it.
  Do ask:
  What is the typical day or assignment like in this position?
- *How stringent are the coming in late and leaving early rules?*
  This is another question that dooms the interview from the beginning.
  Do ask:
  What are the office hours in this department?
- *Can you go over the medical benefits and retirement plan?*
  It is not the best first impression to make to ask about the benefits before you have proven worthy to be a part of the company.
  Do ask:
  How would you describe the company's cultural and work environment?
- *Will you pay for my education?*
  Again, asking for what they can do for you before you show them what you can do for them is never acceptable.
  Do ask:
  Does your company encourage its employees to pursue additional education?

What Interviewers Cannot Ask

It is important to know the boundaries in an interview dialogue. Due to the stress naturally associated with an interview, it may be difficult to qualify each question, but the following are no-no's. They include the following:

- *Are you married or single?*
- *Do you have any children?*
- *What is your sexual preference?*
- *How old are you?*

- *What is your religion?*
- *What is your nationality or race?*
- *How is your health?*
- *What is your political affiliation?*
- *Do you have any disabilities?*

If a question makes you uncomfortable, it is wise to ask for clarification. Let the burden of clarification be on the interviewer's part.

Post-interview Communications

The actual interview is over. Close the conversation graciously by presenting the leave-behind (see Figure 14.13). This piece of collateral is the last visual link to those you met during the interview. The next step is up to the interviewer. A follow-up interview may be scheduled, the company may call back in a prescribed length of time, or the job may be offered on the spot. Whatever the outcome, it is up to you to keep the lines of communication open. The first thing on your list is to write the thank-you letter.

Thank-you Letter

There are two schools of thought regarding writing the follow-up thank-you letter. Some require the thank-you letter to be typed, following the setup of the other professional materials provided in the interview (see Figure 14.14).

The other school of thought sends the opposite message: This is where you can be a bit more personal and creative. You may select a fashionably artistic card (or create one yourself. Perhaps it can be a stylish illustration of something you sensed the interviewer would like to keep at their desk. The leave-behind is given immediately at the end of the interview, but a version of this could serve the purpose of a

1111 Any Street
Hilger, New York 55455

September 1, 2006

Therese Marie, Director
Therese B Design Group
233 North Washington Street
New York, NY 23607

Dear Ms. Marie:
I want to thank you very much for interviewing me yesterday for the assistant design position. I enjoyed meeting you and learning more about your great company.

My enthusiasm for the position and my interest in working for Therese B Design Group were strengthened as a result of the interview. I think my education and experience in the activewear market fits nicely with the job requirements, and I am sure that I could make a significant contribution.

I want to reiterate my strong interest in the position and in working with you and your design team. You provide the kind of opportunity I seek. Please feel free to contact me at 222-333-4444 or at PRuffleRossi@hotmail.com if you need me to provide you with any additional information.

Again, thank you for the interview and your consideration.

Sincerely,

Phyllis Ruffle

Figure 14.14   Thank-you letter.

stylish thank-you card. Again, as in advertising, think of what the receiver would want to read and keep, rather than toss.

No matter which choice is made (the standard or creative) the content of the letter remains the same. The opening paragraph expresses sincere appreciation. The second paragraph reinforces mutually beneficial assets. The closing paragraph thanks the interviewer for his or her time and interesting conversation. This letter creates goodwill and is often overlooked in the rush and stress of a job search. It may be the most important letter you write since it cements your feelings of appreciation for the interviewer's time and consideration. This letter should be sent within twenty-four hours so it creates a positive feeling and a prompt call for the second interview.

Success! You've Got the Job!

The hard work, research, planning, resume construction, portfolio building, Web site creation, and interview preparation have all paid off. But this is not the time to let it all unravel. The creative and professional package created is now going to be utilized at a company where both shall benefit. A formal acceptance letter keeps this professionalism on track.

Acceptance Letter

This letter accepts the job offer, usually after you've been offered the position via telephone conversation. It confirms details of the employment procedure, including starting date, salary, and other points covered in prior conversations. It also acts as a positive reinforcement of the employer's decision (see Figure 14.15).

The job search process is now completed, but along the way many interviews may have taken place. The old adage of "never burn bridges" holds true in situations where you may have been offered a job at another firm as well. This means you need to send an offer rejection letter as a professional message of thanks, but clearly stating your inability to accept the position.

Offer Rejection Letter

This letter is sent to decline an employment offer graciously. The first paragraph acknowledges the offer. The second paragraph communicates the sincere consideration of the position. The closing paragraph expresses appreciation of the offer to become part of the company (see Figure 14.16).

Withdrawal Letter

Other job interviews may not lead to a quick decision. The proper procedure is to submit a withdrawal letter to communicate your inability to accept the position if it was offered and the request to withdraw your name from the candidate list. This letter should be sent as a professional courtesy. The opening paragraph provides an explanation for the withdrawal decision while the last paragraph expresses appreciation for the employer's time, courtesy, and consideration of your application (see Figure 14.17).

To maintain success, you must maintain the high standards set that led you to this point. The following checklist, developed as an outline for success, effectively summarizes how to get ahead (see box 14.1 on page 391 "Ahead of the Game").

2001 Any Street
Cleveland, Ohio 00000

June 20, 2006

Mr. Joe Conte, Design Director
FashionArt Inc.
130 Lake Shore Boulevard
Cleveland, Ohio 40000

Dear Mr. Conte:

I am writing to confirm my acceptance of your employment offer on June 18 and to tell you how delighted I am to be joining FashionArt Inc. The position is exactly what I have prepared to take on, both educationally and professionally. I feel confident that I will make a significant contribution to your firm, and I am grateful for the opportunity you have given me.

As we discussed, I will report to work at 9:00 AM for the orientation on July 1 and will have completed all the personnel, medical, and insurance forms by the start date.

I look forward to working with you and your design team.

Sincerely,

Dylan Connor

Figure 14.15   Acceptance letter in full-block format.

443 Any Street
Santa Cinzia, CA 95555

July 20, 2006

Ms. Jan Duff
Duff Designs
Bond Bridal Division
222 Avenue J
New York, NY 20000

Dear Ms. Duff:

Thank you very much for offering me the position of chief design director. I appreciate that you discussed the details of the position with me and gave me time to consider your offer and relocation allotment to move back to the East Coast.

You have a fine organization, and there are many aspects of the position that are very appealing to me. However, I believe it is in our mutual best interests that I decline your kind offer. This has been a difficult decision for me, but I believe it is the appropriate one at this time.

I want to thank you for the consideration and courtesy given to me. It was a pleasure meeting you and your staff.

Sincerely,

Delilah Onyx

Figure 14.16   Offer rejection letter in modified block format.

42 Any Street
Santa Monica, CA 90000

March 30, 2006

Haven D. Kirk
Design Director
LinHaven Graphic Group
222 Eagle Avenue
Los Angeles, CA 90000

Dear Ms. Kirk:

I am writing to inform you that I am withdrawing my application for the program coordinator position with your organization. As I indicated in my interview with you, I have been exploring several employment possibilities. This week I was offered a design position with a small manufacturing firm and, after careful consideration, I decided to accept it. The position provides a good match for my skills at this point in my career. My strengths in licensing and logo design for special events needed by your firm are not as strong as my skills in activewear design.

I want to thank you very much for interviewing and considering me for your position. I enjoyed meeting you and learning about the innovative community programs you are planning with the art, graphic, and fashion design industries. You have a fine company, and I wish you and your staff well.

Sincerely,

Jaime H. O'Kitte

Figure 14.17   Withdrawal letter.

Charlotte Jenkins, a freelance trend specialist and former vice president of a Los Angeles buying office, has hired, fired, and coordinated freelance work, interns, and seasoned professionals. She also has served on advisory boards of fashion colleges and universities. She has developed a guide titled "Successful Graduates Are Always AHEAD of the Game."

Successful graduates/employees are always

AHEAD OF THE GAME

(you are in charge of your own destiny)

Dress for Success . . . Know what is appropriate. And if you don't know, ask! Be smart . . . dare to ask what the dress code is on any particular day: when clients are visiting; when working on a special project, attending a meeting or seminar, doing a presentation, attending a business dinner, or going on a business trip. No matter what the business occasion, *fashionably appropriate* goes a long way . . . up the corporate ladder! Employers are impressed when you have the drive, desire, and initiative to want to represent their company by making a great "first impression."

Dress for the Interview . . . How you look is the first (and possibly last) impression. Too casual may convey you don't take the interview seriously. If you are unsure of the dress code, err on the side of professionalism. Avoid wearing clothes that are too tight, too sexy, too revealing, or too trendy. Look clean and neat. Shoes should be clean and polished. Nails trimmed and well manicured.

Show Sincere Enthusiasm for Your Job . . . No matter how menial, there is always something to learn in any work-related situation. While your employer looks for what benefits you bring to their company, they also will focus on what you take from each experience you are exposed to (and how you grow from it). Sometimes, the greatest work ethics and lessons learned are derived from the most minute and menial tasks.

Stay Focused . . . Never lose sight of the ultimate goals of your client, your employer, and your peers. Set personal goals as well. Do your job and do it well, regardless of the task. Stay true to yourself and your employer by getting the job done well.

Become Those You Encounter . . . Treat ALL as if they were your "biggest" client. Look at every business associate as special (from your employer and supervisor to your peers, your consumers, and the janitor). At any given time, you must be willing to greet and treat others with the utmost respect, courtesy, and patience. There are no minor players in the business world, only a network of people who can appear on any rung of the corporate ladder at any given point in your career.

Keep Your "Bridges" Operable . . . Don't burn them. It is a very small world. Maintain your contacts and keep your relationships and reputation positive. You never know who you might meet again (and under what circumstances) or need a reference from or someone to put in a good word on your behalf.

Be Confident . . . But not too confident. Speak clearly and make eye contact.

Phone Etiquette Is Key . . . Good phone manners are essential to your success. Good phone manners are based on common sense. You should respond on the phone in a way you would like others to respond to you. Your attitude matters. Courtesy counts for more than you can imagine, and the tone in your voice will make or break your "connection" with the other side.

Learn to be a Good Listener . . . Truly pay attention to your employer and peers. Sounds simple, but it can be a number one faux pas in business. Train yourself to listen better. This is a basic communication skill often unused. Give your undivided attention to those who seek it.

Integrity . . . It represents who you are. Take responsibility. Keep your word. Be faithful, honest, and stand your ground for what is right. Be morally upright . . . never blame others. Integrity is not something you pretend to have . . . you either have it, or you don't. If you have it, do not trade it for anything. Integrity has value that goes a long way. So, try to do the right thing because it is the right thing to do.

Lead Well and Follow with Compassion . . . Never pass up an opportunity to be a role model or mentor, and . . . never pass up an opportunity to learn from the best.

Box 14.1   "Ahead of the Game," by Charlotte Jenkins, former vice president of logistics for Bregman and Associates, Los Angeles, California.

Creating a Promotional Web Site

The following lesson is a step-by-step guide to create a self-promotional Web site consisting of a splash page (introduction page) and a home page (navigational links). Once you master these two pages, the following Web pages can be created using the same techniques. The lesson will also include the steps involved to sign up with a Web host and to upload the Web site to the host.

1. Open the application Photoshop. In the pull-down menu click on File: New. A dialog box will appear. Set the file perameters at 800 × 600 pixels and 72 dpi resolution.
2. Select any original art, images, or new designs that best represent your portfolio for the splash page (see Figure 14.18).
3. Create a rollover first. A rollover is an effect applied when the mouse rolls over an area of the Web page. To create a rollover, copy the word "Enter" by dragging the "Enter" text layer to the New Layer icon at the bottom of the Layers palette.

4. Apply an Outer Glow to the "Enter" text layer by selecting Layer: Layer Styles: Outer Glow in the pull-down menu. This will be the rollover effect (see Figure 14.18).
5. Save this page as "Splash Page."
6. Open ImageReady by clicking on the ImageReady icon at the bottom of the toolbar.
7. Choose the Slice Tool from the toolbox (it looks like a knife), and drag a square around the "Enter" button. Drag another square around the fabric and girl, using the slice tool. Then drag another square around the "My Portfolio" text.
8. Choose the Slice Select Tool in the toolbox (O on the keyword). Click on the "Enter" slice. Then choose Window: Slice from the pull-down menu.
9. In the URL (uniform resource locator) option in the Slice palette, type in home.html. This will create a link to the home page (see Figure 14.19).

Creating the Rollover Animation

10. Choose Window: Web Content in the pull-down menu, and click on the arrow. Select New

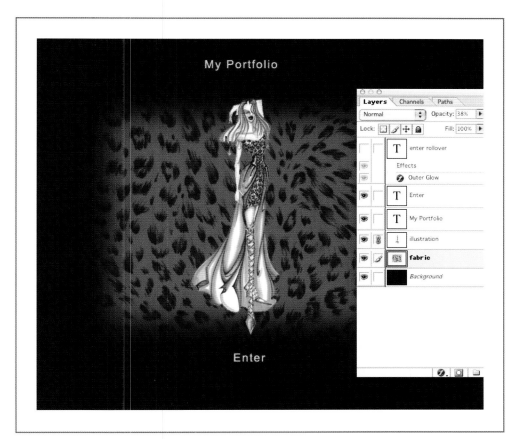

Figure 14.18   Self-Promotional Web Site.

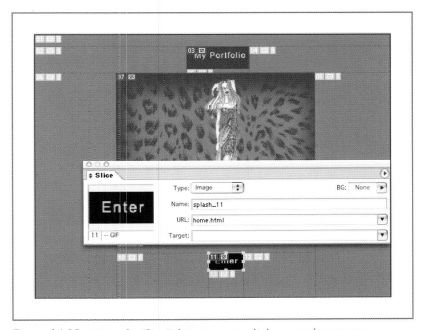

Figure 14.19   Using the Slice Palette to create a link to your home page.

Rollover State (see Figure 14.20).

11. Choose Window: Layers in the pull-down menu and activate the eye in the Layers palette for the "Enter" layer with the outer glow (see Figure 14.21).

12. If the images used contain photographs or gradations of color, select the slice with the Slice

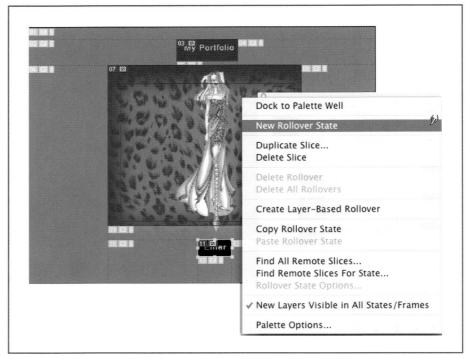

Figure 14.20   New Rollover State option.

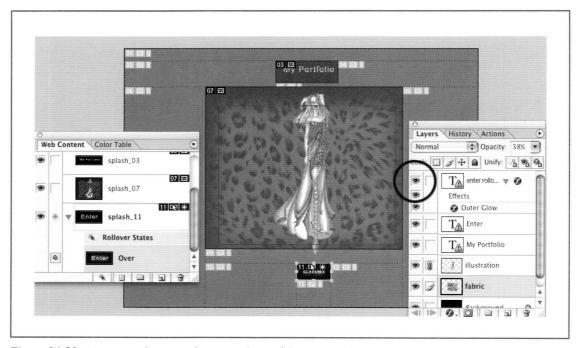

Figure 14.21   Activating the eye in the "Enter" layer of the Layers Palette.

Select Tool in the toolbox and choose Window: Optimize. Then choose the JPEG option in the dialog box. If you are utilizing a flat color (i.e., text) choose the GIF option in the dialog box.

13. To fill the screen with a background color (the default is white), choose File: Output Settings: Background in the pull-down menu. Go to BG Color and choose a color in the Color Palette that appears.

14. For an online preview, choose File: Preview in the pull-down menu and select and open a browser application.

Saving Files for the Internet

15. Choose File: Save Optimized As in the pull-down menu. Make sure "html" and "images" are selected.

16. Create a new folder and name it "mywebsite." Name the file "index.html." The splash page, or the first page the user sees, will always be named index.html in the files.

17. ImageReady is a separate program within Photoshop. It will automatically create a folder called "images." All the slices (GIF and JPEG files) will be located there. Do not place any .psd (Photoshop) or .ai (Illustrator) files in the "mywebsite" folder.

Creating the Home Page

18. Go to the pull-down menu in Photoshop and select File: New. Select 800 by 600 pixels with 72 dpi resolution in the dialog box.

19. To internally navigate the site (jump from page to page), navigation links need to be structured. The content of the portfolio utilized on the Web site will dictate the navigation links. This tutorial includes "Moodboards," "Flats," and "Contact" as portfolio content. Personalized portfolios may have "Illustrations," "Shoe Designs," or any specific content desired. Follow the same steps as the splash page to create personal links (URL) and rollovers.

20. For the tutorial mood board page, name the URL "moodboard.html" and for flats name the page "flats.html" (see Figure 14.22).

21. For the contact slice, type "mailto:youremailhere @aol.com" in the URL option in the Slice palette.

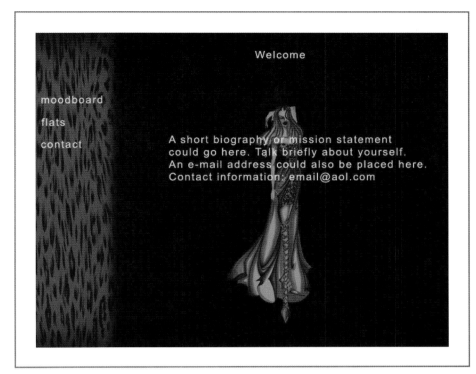

Figure 14.22   Mood board page.

22. To save this page for the Internet, choose File: Save Optimized As in the pull-down menu. Name the file "home.html." Make sure to name the files exactly as they are named in the URL options; otherwise, the links will be broken. Everything has to be the same: lowercase, spelling, and so on.

23. Save this file in the same folder as the index.html file (splash page file "mywebsite").

Signing Up with Tripod for Free Hosting

Tripod offers free hosting, but the domain name will include tripod in it (http://myportfolio.tripod.com). Tripod also offers domain name registration for a yearly fee where the site would read www.myportfolio.com. The free site comes with ad banners. There is an upgrade fee to eliminate the banners.

Figure 14.23   Home page for Tripod.

Network Membership
Step 1: Membership

Choose Your Lycos Member Name and Password

Your member name will become part of your
Tripod site name.

Member Name: [   ]

You will use your
member name &
password to access
Lycos Network sites.
**Please use only
letters, numbers
and hyphens.**

(Examples: hey-joe, or janeysmith2)

Password: [   ]

Repeat Password: [   ]

Figure 14.24   Network Membership screen.

1. Go to the Web site www.tripod.lycos.com.
2. Click on the New Users option (see Figure 14.23).
3. Click on the Tripod Free option.
4. Next to Member Name on the screen, type in the Web site name (see Figure 14.24). Typing in "myportfolio" results in the site address as http://myportfolio.tripod.com. Do not have any spaces in the member name, and do not type in ".com."
5. For the password, pick something easy to remember, and write it down! It will be necessary for uploading the site. Continue filling in the balance of information.

Uploading the Web site with Dreamweaver MX

The following lesson shows how to upload a Web site using Dreamweaver MX. There are free upload

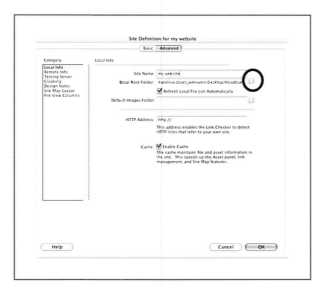

Figure 14.25   Choosing advanced option.

Figure 14.26   Local Root Folder for site "my website."

programs available on the Internet at FTPplanet.com: *WS_FTP* for Windows or *Fetch and Captain FTP* for Macs. The only necessary information is the member name and password for all FTP (File Transfer Protocol) programs.

1. Make sure the folder with the Web site (all the html files plus the image folder) is on the desktop.
2. Open Dreamweaver MX in the Applications folder.
3. A prompt will appear asking for a Root Folder. If the prompt does not appear, choose Site: New from the pull-down menu.
4. Choose Advanced (see Figure 14.25).
5. Click on Local Info. Under Site Name, type in the name of the site.
6. Next to Local Root Folder, click on the folder that is circled, as in Figure 14.25.
7. Select "mywebsite" folder. Notice only "html" files and the "images" folder are in the "mywebsite" folder. Click on Open (see Figure 14.26).
8. Click on Remote Info listing in the Category side box (see Figure 14.27 for corresponding Steps 9 through 16).

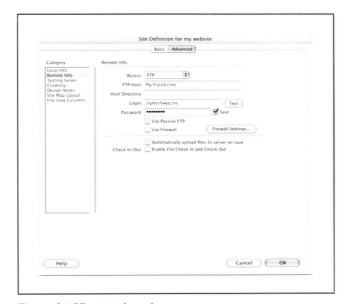

Figure 14.27   FTP drop-down menu.

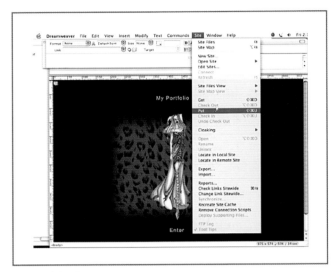

Figure 14.28   Dreamweaver screen.

9. For Access options, choose FTP in the drop-down menu.
10. At FTP Host, type in "ftp.tripod.com."
11. Leave Host Directory blank.
12. For Login, type in the name of the Web site (same as the member name for Tripod).
13. For Password, type in the same password as the one for Tripod.
14. Next click on Test. This will test the connection to the host (Tripod).
15. Click OK.
16. Click Done.
17. Choose Site: Put to upload the site. The finished site should look like Figure 14.28.

Review Questions

1. What are the two formats of resumes? Define them.

2. What is a cover letter?

3. What are the information contents of a reference list?

4. What are the benefits of an e-Portfolio over a CD-ROM?

5. What are three useful points to remember when presenting a portfolio during an interview?

Suggested Practice Project

Select your seven best pieces of work. Then review the Do's and Don'ts (see page 380). Edit down to four pieces.

Key Terms

Application cover letter

Chronological resume

Colorways

Entry-level resume

e-Portfolio

Flats

Freelance resume

Functional resume

Home page

Intern resume

Line

Line sheet

Networking letter

New skills resume

Proposed position resume

Prospecting cover letter

Resume

Splash page

Upload

Useful Web Sites

www.ResumeDoctor.com
www.Mediabistro.com
www.6FigureJobs.com

Internships/Job Sites:

The Apparel News, www.apparelnews.net
Apparel Search, www.apparelsearch.com/
    employment.htm
Apparel Search Agencies, www.apparelsearch.com/
    employment_agencies.htm
Black Entertainment Television, www.bet.com
Brilliant Sales Jobs, www.BrilliantsalesJobs.com
Career Builder, www.CareerBuilder.com
Career Threads, www.CareerThreads.com
Jobs for college grads, www.collegegrad.com
Computer jobs, www.computerwork.com
Cool Works, www.coolworks.com/showme
www.cweb.com Career Web
www.FashionCareer.com
www.fashion-career.com
www.fashioncareercenter.com
www.Stylecareers.com
Fashion Group International, www.fgi.org
www.flipdog.com
www.gazzettes.com
Gotta Job, www.gottajob.com
Head Hunter, www.headhunter.com
Career Mosaic, www.headhunter.net
Hispanic Business, www.HispanicBusiness.com
Hot Jobs, www.HotJobs.com

Interweb, www.interweb.com
Internship Programs, www.internshipprograms.com
America's Job Bank (AJB), www.itjobsearch.org
www.ivillage.com
www.job.com
Job Direct, www.JobDirect.com
Job Find, www.jobfind.com
Jobs in Fashion, www.jobsinfashion.com
Job Track, www.jobtrack.com
Job Web, www.jobweb.com
Los Angeles Times, www.latimes.com
NationJob Network, www.nationjob.com
The *New York Times* (or choose your city paper),
    www.nytimes.com
Monster, www.monster.com
Paul Marks – Hire Resources Corporate Recruiters,
    www.paulamarks.com
Plus Jobs, www.plusjobs.org
Power Students, www.powerstudents.com
www.register.com
Vault, www.vault.com
Wet Feet, www.wetfeet.com
www.women.com
Women's Wear Daily, www.wwd.com

International Job Searches:

Asia Job Search, www.Asiajobsearch.org
www.eurojobs.com

Job Web, www.Jobweb.com
www.Taps.com

Entertainment:
www.mandy.com
Show Biz Jobs, www.showbizjobs.com

Costume Design Sites:
The Costumer's Guild, www.cgia.org
Debbie's Book, www.debbiesbook.com
Theatre Jobs, www.theatrejobs.com

Jobs and Salary Info
www.joboption.com
www.jobstar.org
www.salary.com
www.salarysource.com
craigslist.org
AmericasJobbank.com

Transferable skills:
www.careerstorm.com/tools/skills/skills02.asp

Career Quiz
www.review.com/career/careerquizhome/cfm?menuID=0&careers.6

Psychological Personality Profile
http://dir.yahoo.com/social_science/psychology/branches/personality/online_tests/

Fashion Business Information
www.interfashion.net
www.fashion.about.com
www.fashion.net.com
www.retailology.com

www.hcdonline.com
Who Wears It, www.whowearsit.com

Verizon SuperPages, www.SuperPages.com
www.interbiznet.com/hunt
www.quintcareers.com/career_books.html
Weddle's, www.weddles.com/associations/index.htm
www.rileyguide.com

Fashion Company Database, www.infomat.com
Hoover's, www.hoovers.com
www.lgi.org

Suggested Readings

There are many fashion industry texts that provide an overview of the business's growth and development in apparel and accessories. This type of information is so necessary for successful entry or reentry into the fash- ion business. The following list provides the best resources for learning about the fashion business, leading to a confident interview and a successful portfolio:

Abling, Bina. *Fashion Sketching, 4th edition.* New York: Fairchild, 2004.

Brannon, Evelyn L. *Fashion Forecasting, 2nd edition.* New York: Fairchild, 2005.

Burns, Leslie Davis and Nancy O. Bryant. *The Business of Fashion: Designing, Manufacturing, and Marketing, 2nd edition.* New York: Fairchild, 2002.

Diamond, Jay and Ellen Diamond. *The World of Fashion, 3rd edition.* New York: Fairchild, 2002.

Stall-Meadows, Celia. *Know Your Fashion Accessories.* New York: Fairchild, 2004.

Stone, Elaine. *Dynamics of Fashion, 2nd edition.* New York: Fairchild, 2004.

Tain, Linda. *Portfolio Presentation for Fashion Designers, 2nd edition.* New York: Fairchild, 2004.

Glossary

activewear: sector of sportswear including casual attire for sports such as running and tennis. Also know as active sportswear.

Adobe Illustrator: A vector-based drawing program.

Adobe Photoshop: A raster-based image-editing program.

alpha channel: Location of information regarding the transparency of a pixel; a separate channel from the RGB and CMYK channels in image files.

anti-aliasing: The process of blending the color of adjacent pixels to eliminate the "jaggies" or stair-stepping associated with pixel-based images.

apparel: Term for clothing.

application: A computer program.

application cover letter: Sent in direct response to a specific job advertisement, matching qualifications with the posted position requirements.

anime: Japanese term for animation.

avant-garde: A new or experimental concept that is ahead of its time.

Backup: Creating a copy of your work.

bit: Abbreviation for binary digit; smallest piece of info used by computer.

bitmap: Refers to an image made up of pixels, each having a specific size, expressed in terms of resolution.

balance: An aesthetically pleasing integration of elements.

blog: A Web site that is used to post thoughts, share links to Web sites, and interact with people online; journalists often use this medium for posting commentary or breaking news.

blogger: One who submits written opinions on a blog.

BMP: Bitmap images store pixels or grid of dots in Windows format, using color codes.

bridge fashion: A price zone that bridges the gap between designer and better prices.

burn tool: Used in Photoshop, this tool darkens the pixels in an image.

chronological resume: Outlines education and employment history in a sequence of most recent listed first.

classic: A style or design that satisfies a basic need and remains in general fashion acceptance for an extended period of time.

clipping paths: A bèzier outline defining which areas of an image should be "clipped"; vector-based selection masks that can be imbedded into an EPS image for silhouetting bitmap images with resolution-independent masks in external programs such as Illustrator or Quark Xpress.

CMYK: The four process colors in printing: cyan, magenta, yellow, K represented as black.

color: Light waves perceived according to the visible hue spectrum, divided into hue, value, and intensity and classified as warm, cool, or neutral; the most prominent design element of consumer response.

color depth: Number of colors available to each pixel, with information stored in bits; the greater the number of bits, the greater selection of color. For example, 8-bit = 256 colors; 24-bit = 16.8 million colors.

color palette: Usually eight to ten colors that provide inspiration to create a collection.

color reduction: Lessening the number of colors in an image.

collection: A term used in the United States and Europe for an expensive line that is assigned for a specific season.

colorway: Color choices for items or groups of designs that complement one another: variations of color sets available in a textile print.

compression: Rearranging data so it occupies less space on disk and transfers faster between devices or communication lines; defined as lossless (no data lost) or lossy (some data lost) during the process.

concept boards: Array of color chips, magazine clippings, found objects, fabric swatches, and other items arranged on a cardboard poster board; used to show concepts visually in product development.

contemporary: Term for clothing category that is "updated" and "young."

contone: Image containing infinite continuous shades, unlike a line illustration of only one shade.

contrast: Juxtaposition of dissimilar elements (as color, tone, or emotion) in a work of art.

couturier: Male designer of a French couture house (e.g., Christian LaCroix).

couturiere: Female designer of a French couture house (e.g., Coco Chanel).

croquis: Working sketch or line drawing to illustrate a garment; actual painted design sample for a printed fabric.

cross-platform: Program can be used on a Mac or IBM-compatible PC (personal computer).

definition: Overall quality or clarity of an image, determined by graininess or resolution in a digital image.

demographics: The study of vital statistics of a population (e.g., births, deaths, marital status, education).

diffusion line: Clothing lower in price and a secondary version of a designer collection.

dodge tool: Used inPhotoshop, this tool lightens the pixels in an image.

DPI: Dots per inch; measurement unit used to represent resolution of printers and imagesetters (72DPI for a monitor; 300DPI for LaserWriter; 2,450DPI for an imagesetter).

emphasis: Dominance created by a focal point or center of attention.

entry-level resume: Strong focus on education earned; employment and intern experience validates the direction of your entry into the field.

e-portfolio: Electronic portfolio; the recommended file format is PDF.

EPS: Encapsulated postscript; standard graphics file format for storing object-oriented or vector graphics files; usually has two, taking up more space than a TIFF file.

exposure: Refers to the amount of light a photograph is exposed to in a darkroom.

extension: Three-character code to identify a saved file format, as in "collar.psd."

fabric simulation: Computer-generated rendering of a textile design or weave type.

fabrication: Content of material used for a garment.

fad: Short-lived fashion with distinct identity.

fashion cycle: The rise, widespread popularity, and then decline in acceptance of a style.
> Rise: The acceptance of either a newly introduced design or its adaptations by an increasing number of consumers.
> Culmination: That period when a fashion is at the height of its popularity and use. The fashion then is in such demand that it can be mass-produced, mass-distributed, and sold at prices within the reach of most consumers.
> Decline: The decrease in consumer demand because of boredom resulting from widespread use of a fashion.
> Obsolescence: When disinterest occurs and a style can no longer be sold at any price.

fashion illustration: A completed, rendered drawing of a garment.

file: Collection of data itemized and stored on a disk as a document, folder, application, or resource.

file extension: Abbreviated suffix of a filename, separated by a period, describing its type or origin (e.g., gif., jpg., tiff).

file format: How a program arranges data to be stored or displayed on a computer.

flats: Two-dimensional line drawings of garments showing how they appear when laid out on a flat surface.

frame grabbers: Capturing a single frame from a video sequence.

freelance resume: Focus is on varied client base and creative niches.

functional resume: Strongest skill sets listed first, followed with work history listed chronologically.

fuzziness: In the color range dialog box, it is the same as tolerance. It refers to the number of pixels in a color that is selected: the higher the fuzziness, the more pixels are selected.

GIF: Graphics interchange format; a bitmapped graphics format suitable for line images and text, using the lossless compression technique.

group: Part of a line or collection with common style, color, or fabrication.

half-drop: A type of pattern repeat in which the design is offset by half.

hanger appeal: The attraction rate of a garment presented on a hanger rather than on a 3-D form.

harmony: Consistency created by a pleasing combination of different things used in combination.

haute couture (pronounced "oat-koo-TOUR"): The French term literally meaning "fine sewing" but actually having much the same sense as our own term "high fashion."

high culture: Fashion and lifestyle trends derived from the fine and performing arts.

home page: Web site page with navigational links to enter the site.

hyperdesigning: Design philosophy eliminating the traditional boundaries or rules of what should or should not be done in construction or creative choices.

image degradation: Decrease in the quality of the visual.

intensity: The relative brightness (strength) or paleness (weakness) of a color.

intern resume: Strong focus on the direction of your education first, then employment history.

jaggies: Stair-stepping caused by pixels on the edge of the elements in an image.

JPEG: Joint Photographic Image Experts Group; compressed file.

knock-off: A trade term referring to the copying, at a lower price, of an item that has had good acceptance at higher prices.

label: Tag identifying designer, manufacturer, content and care instructions; used as interchangeable term with brand, designer.

layers: A component of object-based raster imaging, where a set of pixels or vector shapes can be separately addressed from the rest of the pixels or vector shapes in the image.

lifestyle merchandising: The merging of the interior and fashion design industry in product development (e.g., coordinating bedding, window, wall, and light treatments with the seasonal design directions of clothing designers/manufacturers).

line: Effect made by the edge of an object or image; also an assortment of apparel items offered seasonally.

line-for-line copy: These are exactly like the original designs except that they have been mass-produced in less expensive fabrics to standard size measurements.

line sheet: A designer's line illustrated or scanned onto a sheet of paper with color and size annotations to view pieces in relation to one another.

logo: Brand name or trademarked symbol of a designer or design company.

lossless: Methods of file compression where no data is lost, such as GIF and LZW formats.

lossy: Methods of file compression where some data is lost during compression, such as JPEG.

low culture: Fashion and lifestyle trends derived from subcultures and groups that are not considered mainstream.

Mac: Abbreviated name for a Macintosh computer.

magalog: Magazines with shopping information (similar to a catalog) as core content rather than subject editorials.

manga: Japanese comic books.

mask: An area used to protect a portion of an image while exposing another for manipulation.

mass dissemination: Fashions from all sources (high and low culture) to achieve popularity with the mass-market consumer.

midtones: The tonal range of an image that can be seen in the Levels Dialog box. Midtones can be adjusted with the middle slider, which is between the shadow and the highlight slider.

mood board: Combination of composite images juxtaposed to create a statement or seasonal inspiration for design direction.

mosaic: A type of pattern repeat that produces a mirror effect.

MS-DOS: Microsoft Disc Operating System used on PCs.

Native file format: File format used exclusively by an application in which the files were created; some applications can read files in another's native format.

networking letter: Designed to generate an informational conversation rather than a job interview; a viable way to research the job market, to refine career goals, and uncover vacancy information.

neutrals: Pleasing, nondistracting colors that have become fashion basics, including black, white, beige, brown, and tan.

new skills resume: Focus on the current skills necessary for new positions in the industry; the other achievements follow to reinforce credibility and experience.

object-oriented software: Technology using mathematical points (objects) based on vectors to define lines and shapes; data for each shape is stored in these points, which then passes information on how paths

should be described, whether in straight lines, bèzier curves, or arcs.

output resolution: The resolution of a monitor screen or printer, usually measured in DPI (dots per inch); monitor resolution typically is 72 to 90DPI; laser printer is 600dpi.

path: A vector-based bèzier curve made with the pen tool that can be edited at any time; used to make masks and clipping paths requiring very little storage space.

pattern: Arrangement of lines, spaces, and images on fabric.

PC: Abbreviation for personal computer, compatible with IBM.

PDF: An acronym for portable document format; a cross-platform format that has the ability to handle the creation of complex documents, retaining text and picture formatting when viewed or printed.

PDS: A CAD system used to create and manipulate patterns.

PICT: An acronym for picture, a file format for storing bitmapped and object-oriented images on a MAC.

pixels: An acronym for picture element; the smallest subdivision of a digital image formed as dots.

pop culture: Sourcing inspiration for design from trends derived from popular entertainment and media; often popularized by celebrities.

predictive service: Trend reporting service or company that puts out comprehensive design reports or trends and directions for a fee.

PPI: Pixels per inch.

prêt-à-porter (pronounced "preht-ah-por-TAY"): A French term meaning "ready-to-wear."

private label: Designs manufactured to the specifications of a retailer for exclusive merchandising.

proportion: Relationship between one aspect of design to another.

product type: Specific apparel category produced by a company.

progressive jpeg: The digital image format used to display JPEG images on the Web; also known as projpeg.

prospecting cover letter: Content focuses on one's capabilities and adaptable skills in hopes of matching with a possible vacancy.

proposed position resume: Focus on blending current skills, prior work experience, knowledge of consumer needs, and filling the niche without being critical of the assumed "lack" of the position.

proprietary: A system or software designed by a private company.

PSD: Native Photoshop format.

psychographics: The study of personal characteristics including lifestyles, interests, values and social standing.

radiation: Feeling of movements steadily bursting outward in all directions from the central point.

raster-based image: Line and shape defined by individual pixels.

raster-based software: Creates raster or bitmaps based on pixels.

rasterization: The method of creating images and display on computer monitors where the screen image is comprised of several hundred parallel lines "raking" the screen (at the speed of one-sixtieth of a second) from top to bottom; derived from the Latin word "rastrum" or rake.

rasterize: The process of converting vector information to bitmap or raster-based.

ready-to-wear (RTW): Apparel mass-produced using standardized sizing; also called "off the rack."

repetition: Use of same image more than once.

resolution: Size of pixels or dots, expressed as pixels-per-inch (PPI) or dots-per- inch (DPI); degree of clarity in which an image is displayed (i.e., the higher the resolution, the finer the detail).

resolution independent: An image that can be scaled up or down and

manipulated while retaining its sharp edges.

resume: Summary of qualifications (education, employment history, activities, etc.) used to market yourself to prospective employers.

RGB: The standard color coordinate system for most images files; a combination of red, green, and blue used to create all other colors when direct or transmitted light is used.

roughs: Preliminary sketches documenting designer's ideas for further development.

saturation: The amount of color intensity that is reflected back to the eye. A highly saturated color will have the brightest or highest degree of color value.

scale: To size an image up or down; comparative relationship of size.

scanner: Electronic device using a sequentially moving light beam to convert artwork or photographs into digital form for manipulation by a computer.

screen shot/screen grab/screen capture: A snapshot of all or part of a monitor display.

selection: A part of an image that has been segregated from the rest to change or duplicate.

shape: Outline or contour of an object in two dimensions (2-D).

SIGGRAPH: Special Interest Group Graphics; mission of the organization is to promote the generation and dissemination of information about computer graphics and interactive techniques.

silhouette: The outline or shape of a garment, often described by a basic geometric shape (rounded, rectangular, triangular, etc.).

smudge tool: Used in Photoshop, this tool blends pixels together.

space: 2-D or 3-D area to be organized by filling or clearing.

splash page: Introductory page of Web site.

storyboards: Presentation of design collection via mood inspiration (mood boards), coordinated fabrics and trim, final illustrations, visual explanation of theme, color selections, and target market.

stylist/designer: Person who adapts the designs of others appropriately for their target market, as opposed to "stylist" who creates a look with already-designed garments and accessories for presentation purposes.

styling direction: Product line concepts with a consistent theme of silhouette, color, texture, and details.

subcultures: Groups that differentiate themselves, through dress and activities, from other subcultures and mainstream populations.

swatch: A small piece of fabric used as a sample.

target customer: Description of the common demographic, psychographic, and geographic profiles of a group.

technical flats: Original concept sketches drawn in a detailed format.

texture: Visible/tactile quality of the surface.

TIFF: An acronym for tagged image file format; used for scanned, high-resolution, bitmapped images as well as color separations; black and white = 1 bit, gray = 8 bit; RGB color = 24 bit; CMYK color = 32 bit.

tint: White added to a color.

tolerance: The amount of pixels in a color that is selected; the higher the tolerance, the more pixels are selected.

tone: Gray added to a color.

toss and repeat: A type of pattern repeat that looks random.

transition: Smooth-flowing passage from one condition and position to another.

trend: The path and direction of a particular style (e.g., garment, activity, or any element of popular culture) tracked by its popularity and acceptance; predicting trends is part science, part intuition.

trend board: Specific influences and ideas to give design direction for color, fabric, key items, silhouettes, and details.

trickle-up theory (also known as upward flow): Street style popularized through media exposure and appropriated into a designer's collection.

trickle-down theory (also known as downward flow): High-end designer looks appropriated by lower-income consumers via actual purchase at reduced prices, lesser-priced knock-offs, or copyright infringement knock-offs.

trimmings: Items that embellish and finish the garment, such as beading, buckles, lace, fringe, zippers.

unity: A combination or ordering of parts in a literary or artistic production that constitutes a whole or promotes an undivided, total effect; sense of cohesion.

upload: The process of sending data from one computer to another computer (e.g., a server).

value: Variation of the lightness and darkness of a color.

vector-based software: A tiny database that gives information of magnitude and direction of a line or shape.

vector images: Basic geometric shapes created with a bezier tool; these images cannot be broken down into pixels. *See also* object-oriented software.

Photo Credits

Figure 1.1 Anais (19th c.) Reprinted with permission of the Fine Art Photographic Library, London/Art Resource, NY.

Figure 1.2 Original artwork by Helen Dryden. Copyright © 1922. Condé Nast Publications Inc. Reprinted with permission. All Rights Reserved.

Figure 1.6a Original artwork by Eduardo Garcia Benito. Copyright © 1925. Condé Nast Publications Inc. Reprinted with permission. All Rights Reserved.

Figure 1.6b Original artwork by Eduardo Garcia Benito. Copyright © 1926. Condé Nast Publications Inc. Reprinted with permission. All Rights Reserved.

Figure 1.8 Original artwork by Marcel Vertes. Copyright © 1936. Condé Nast Publications Inc. Reprinted with permission. All Rights Reserved.

Figure 1.9 Original artwork by Carl Erickson. Copyright © 1948. Condé Nast Publications Inc. Reprinted with permission. All Rights Reserved.

Figure 1.10 Original artwork by Rene R. Bouche. Copyright © 1947. Condé Nast Publications Inc. Reprinted with permission. All Rights Reserved.

Figure 1.11 Original artwork by René Gruau. Copyright © 1949. Condé Nast Publications Inc. Reprinted with permission. All rights reserved.

Figure 1.14 Copyright © Thierry Perez, www.thierryperez.com.

Figure 1.15 Courtesy, Nordstrom, Inc.

Figure 2.1 Courtesy, Sarah Singh.

Figure 2.3 Copyright © Izak Zenou.

Figure 2.6 Copyright © Graham Rounthwaite/Graham Rounthwaite Studio.

Figure 2.8 Copyright © Thierry Perez, www.thierryperez.com.

Figure 2.9 Copyright © Ed Tsuwaki.

Figures 3.1 and 3.2 Copyright © CBS/Landov.

Figure 3.3 and 3.4 Copyright © Corbis.

Figure 3.5 Copyright © Steve Sands/New York Newswire/Corbis.

Figure 14.12 Courtesy, Sarah Kim, AIU fashion student.

Figures 14.23–14.28 Copyright © 2006 Lycos, Inc. Lycos ® is a registered trademark of Lycos, Inc. All rights reserved.

Index